SELECTED PLAYS
BRIAN FRIEL

IRISH DRAMA SELECTIONS

Published in Great Britain by Colin Smythe, Ltd.,
Gerrards Cross, Buckinghamshire

SELECTED PLAYS

BRIAN FRIEL

Introduction by Seamus Deane

IRISH DRAMA SELECTIONS 6

Colin Smythe
Gerrards Cross, Bucks.

The Catholic University of America Press
Washington, D.C.

This collection first published in 1984
by Faber and Faber Limited
3 Queen Square London WC1N 3AU

Philadelphia, Here I Come © Brian Friel, 1965
The Freedom of the City © Brian Friel, 1974
Living Quarters © Brian Friel, 1978
Aristocrats © Brian Friel, 1980
Faith Healer © Brian Friel, 1980
Translations © Brian Friel, 1981
Introduction © Seamus Deane, 1984

Published in North America in 1986 by
The Catholic University of America Press,
Washington, D.C., 20064

Printed in the United States of America
Paperbound edition reprinted
with new title page and cover 1988

LIBRARY OF CONGRESS CATALOGING-IN-
PUBLICATION DATA
Friel, Brian
  Selected plays.

  (Irish drama selections; 6)
  Bibliography: p.
  Contents: Introduction/by Seamus Deane—Philadelphia,
  here I come!—The freedom of the city—[etc.]
  I. Title. II. Series.
PR6056.R5A6 1986   822'.914   85-31340
ISBN 0-8132-0626-X
ISBN 0-8132-0627-8 (pbk.)

CONTENTS

ACKNOWLEDGEMENTS

The publishers acknowledge with thanks the financial assistance of the Arts Council of Northern Ireland in the publication of this volume.

In *The Freedom of the City*, the song quotations 'Lily of Laguna', 'Man who broke the bank', 'Where did you get that hat?', reproduced by permission of Francis Day & Hunter Ltd.

In *Aristocrats*, lines quoted from the poem 'My Father Dying' from *Weathering* by Alastair Reid, Canongate, Edinburgh. 'Sweet Alice' by J. Kneass © 1933, Amsco Music Sales Co., New York City.

In *Faith Healer*, the song 'The Way You Look Tonight' from the film *Swingtime* with music by Jerome Kern, words by Dorothy Fields © 1936 T. B. Harms Co., British publishers Chappell Music Ltd. Reproduced by kind permission.

INTRODUCTION

Brian Friel was born into, and grew up in, the depressed and
depressing atmosphere of the minority Catholic community in
Northern Ireland. Derry, or, to give it its official name,
Londonderry, had been, since the inception of the new Northern
state as part of the United Kingdom in 1922, an economically
depressed area. Male unemployment never sank below eighteen
per cent, even during the artificial boom induced by the Second
World War. Among the Catholic population, which was in the
majority in the local electoral area, the rate was much higher. A
corrupt electoral system also ensured that this local majority was
deprived of power even within the limited field of borough
politics. As a result, political tension remained high in the city
during the decades of the 1930s, 1940s and 1950s, even though it
was paradoxically combined with a strange apathy which arose
out of bad social conditions and a general feeling of desolation.
These factors have profoundly impressed themselves on Friel's
writing in which the same blend of disappointment and unyield-
ing pressure is found time and again to characterize the
experience of his protagonists. There is another leavening
element, however, which also takes its origin from the social and
political circumstances of the place where he grew up. Derry is no
more than a few miles from the political border which separates it
from its natural hinterland, the county of Donegal, part of the
Irish Free State, as it was then called. Friel spent his childhood
and boyhood holidays in Donegal, where his family had
originated. Famous for the beauty of its scenery, although no
more fortunate in its economic condition, Donegal has remained
for him as a powerful image of possibility, an almost pastoral

place in which the principle of hope can find a source. The town of Ballybeg, which occurs so often in his plays as a standard setting, has fused within it the socially depressed and politically dislocated world of Derry and the haunting attraction of the lonely landscapes and traditional mores of rural Donegal.

Yet it would be wrong to emphasize these factors to the point of describing Friel's work as being wholly political in its motivations and obsessions. Politics is an ever-present force, but Friel, conscious of the recurrent failures of the political imagination in Ireland, is concerned to discover some consolatory or counterbalancing agency which will offer an alternative. The discovery is never made. But the search for the alternative to and the reasons for failure brings Friel, finally, to the recognition of the peculiar role and function of art, especially the theatrical art, in a broken society. The moods of his plays and stories can change very rapidly from the farcical to the satirical to the sentimental to the tragic and at times the transition from one to another is disturbingly abrupt. The reason for this is that Friel has always found it necessary to struggle with the problem of temperament, an enhanced feature of people who are bedevilled by failure and compensate for it by making out of their own instability a mode of behaviour in which volatility becomes a virtue. Out of volatility, one can make a style; style can give off the effect of brilliance; but the brightness of the effect is very often in inverse ratio to the emptiness for which it is the consolation. This is not to say that Friel rehearses in his plays the conventional 'Celtic' temperament. But he does touch upon that convention, does even exploit it at times, but with the purpose of analysing the forces which produce it. Brilliance in the theatre has, for Irish dramatists, been linguistic. Formally, the Irish theatrical tradition has not been highly experimental. It depends almost exclusively on talk, on language left to itself to run through the whole spectrum of a series of personalities, often adapted by the same individual. Friel is unique, though, in his recognition that Irish temperament and Irish talk has a deep relationship to Irish desolation and the sense of failure. It is not surprising that his drama evolves, with increasing sureness, towards an analysis of the behaviour of language itself and, particularly, by the ways in which that behaviour, so ostensibly in the power of the individual, is fundamentally dictated by historical circumstances. His art, therefore, remains political to the degree that it becomes an art ensnared by, fascinated by its own linguistic medium. This is not obliquely political theatre. This is profoundly political, precisely because it is so totally committed to the major theatrical medium of words.

It is natural, given this, that Friel should make use of a conventional situation from the Irish theatrical tradition – that comic situation in which the dominant (but not necessarily heroic) figure on the stage is a social outsider or outcast who is nevertheless gifted with eloquence. The plight of such a figure always runs the risk of being sentimentalized, for it is an historical and political convention too, based on the experience of exile. From the beginning, in early plays like *This Doubtful Paradise* (1959) and *The Enemy Within* (1962), up to and including *Philadelphia, Here I Come!*, Friel has played a number of variations on the theme of exile. The central figures in these plays find themselves torn by the necessity of abandoning the Ireland which they love, even though, or perhaps because, they realize that they must bow to this necessity for the sake of their own integrity as individuals rather than as a consequence of economic or political pressures. Although the different kinds of pressure forcing them to leave their homeland are interconnected, their ultimate perception is that fidelity to the native place is a lethal form of nostalgia, an emotion which must be overcome if they are, quite simply, to grow up. So Friel, in this first phase of his career, depicts a struggle already well known in other European literatures – the conflict between emotional loyalties to the backward and provincial area and obligations to the sense of self which seeks freedom in a more metropolitan, if shallower, world. The movement of historical forces has set against his provincial Donegal world and it has therefore become anachronistic. In feeling itself to be so, it also becomes susceptible to sentimentality, self-pity, and, in the last stages, to a grotesque caricaturing of what it had once been. For all that, it exercises a charm, a potent spell which the desire for freedom and for the future has tragic difficulty in breaking. In

13

Philadelphia, Gar O'Donnell recites on several occasions the opening lines of Edmund Burke's famous apostrophe to the *ancien régime* of France, written in 1790 by an Irishman who had made the preservation of ancestral feeling the basis for a counter-revolutionary politics and for a hostility to the shallow cosmopolitanism of the modern world. 'It is now sixteen or seventeen years since I saw the Queen of France, then the Dauphiness, at Versailles; and surely never lighted on this orb, which she hardly seemed to touch, a more delightful vision . . .' Friel uses Burke here, at some risk, to display the fact that the Ballybeg which Gar O'Donnell is trying to leave is indeed the remnant of a past civilization and that the new world, however vulgar it may seem, is that of Philadelphia and the Irish Americans. Although Gar is aware of the actual squalor of village life and of the coarseness of modern city life, his intelligence is of little consolation to him. To know the score is not a form of happiness. The most intolerable suspicion, however, is that, in leaving Ballybeg, he is forsaking the capacity to feel deeply. So he plays a game, cast in the form of a dialogue between his two selves, generating out of his own internal split a wonderful, comic and histrionic virtuosity which is nevertheless tinged throughout by grief. For this is a man who has been theatricalized by society, a man who must play the fool with his own feelings, thereby becoming the possessor of a temperament only because he has had no opportunity to stabilize into that achievement of a moral position which we call character. Gar O'Donnell is, in many ways, a recognizably modern case of alienation. He has all the narcissism that goes with the condition of being driven back in upon the resources of the self. But Friel is so specific in his evocation of the conditions of Irish life, so insistent in the deep-rooted sense of inherited failure, that the play has the freshness of a revelation rather than the routine characteristics of a well-known situation. Since the beginning of this century, Irish drama has been heavily populated by people for whom vagrancy and exile have become inescapable conditions about which they can do nothing but talk, endlessly and eloquently and usually to themselves. The tramps of Yeats and Synge and Beckett, the stationless slum dwellers of O'Casey or

14

Behan, bear a striking family resemblance to Friel's exiles.

After 1965, for six years, Friel's career seemed to hesitate. Although his popularity with the Irish audience actually grew, and although that audience gratefully accepted plays like *The Loves of Cass McGuire* (1967), *Lovers* (1968), *Crystal and Fox* (1970), and the rather crude political satire, *The Mundy Scheme* (1970), there does seem, in retrospect, to have been an uncertainty in his writing which might account for its increasing sentimentality. Cass McGuire is an exile who returns home to harbour the illusion that the old people's home she finds herself in is the real thing, rather than a junk yard for derelicts like herself. Although the play is brutal enough in its way, it hovers uneasily between satire and tragedy before finally settling for sentiment. In a similar manner, Fox Melarkey, the chief character in *Crystal and Fox*, destroys his masquerade of a showman's life out of a frustration which we can sympathize with but which is offered to our understandings only as a glorified grumpiness that the world is not, after all, the Utopia he would like it to be. But in *The Gentle Island* (produced 1971, published 1973), Friel turned on all the illusions of pastoralism, ancestral feeling, and local piety that had been implicit in his dramatization of the world of Ballybeg. It is a savage play, ironically titled, executed in a destructive, even melodramatic spirit. The lives of the Sweeney family in the island of Inishkeen, off the west coast of County Donegal, are shown to be brutal, squalid, beset by sexual frustration and violence. A visitor is maimed, a whole tissue of illusions is swept aside, and a son finally escapes into the comparative freedom of the life of the Irish labourer in the Glasgow slums. The delicate tensions which had been so finely balanced in *Philadelphia* are now surrendered in an almost vengeful spirit. Lost illusions, and the sweetness of sexual love, are denied even a residual consolation. After this play, Friel had effectively cut himself off from his early work. He was seeking a new kind of drama, one in which the emotions of utter repudiation would replace the half-lights of exiled longing. *The Mundy Scheme* was a momentary attempt to turn towards political satire. But it was little more than a caricature play (although not, on that account, distant from the truth about the corruption of Irish political life). In a sense, up to 1971, Friel's plays had been drawing a great deal of their power from the tenderness with which he had portrayed the decaying provincial world of Donegal – Derry in his short stories. Although he had early abandoned that form, he had not abandoned the attitudes which it had embodied. The plays gave more successful, subtler expression to those attitudes. But now, with the new, deeply angry sense of repudiation and disgust dominating his work, Friel moved on to the next phase of his writing career. From this point forward, his plays are more frankly ambitious, their form more flexible, their tone more resonantly that of drama which had reached a pitch of decisive intensity. All of Friel's major work dates from the mid-1970s. Before that, he had been an immensely skilful writer who had found himself being silently exploited by the ease with which he could satisfy the taste for Irishness which institutions like the *New Yorker* and the Irish Theatre had become so expert in establishing. Although *Philadelphia* was a remarkable play, prefiguring some of the later work in its preoccupations, it was a virtuoso performance of the kind of Irish eloquence which had come to be expected from Irish playwrights in particular. It was 'fine writing'. The horrifyingly stupefied condition of the Irish social and political world which it also revealed was treated almost as a foil to that brilliant chat of Gar O'Donnell. Friel had the courage to deprive himself of that ready-made appeal, that fixed audience, that commercial success, and to set out to write all over again the stories and plays of his immediate past.

He was stimulated to do so by the fact that the society he had known all his life began to break down, publicly and bloodily, in 1968. From the first marches of that year, in the summer and late autumn, to the murder of fourteen civilian marchers by British paratroopers in Derry in early 1972, Northern Ireland entered on the first phase of its long, slow disintegration. It was what everyone who knew the place had always expected; yet it was shocking when it came. Police and army, guerrillas and assassins, bombers and torturers became so prominent in a suddenly militarized society that the notion of its ever having been a decent unpolluted place seemed utterly absurd. The

16

collapse of institutions and codes, the aridity of myths and slogans, all of which had seemed serenely potent only months before, had and still has profound repercussions for the people of that society. Friel had been there, imaginatively, before it happened. But the forces released by the breakdown inevitably had a transforming effect on him. Those first years of the 'troubles' saw him reject his own writing past; in those years he also began to confront what would dominate his writing in the future – the sense of a whole history of failure concentrated into a crisis over a doomed community or group.

Friel's next four plays were produced in the Abbey Theatre before beginning their runs abroad in London and New York. After that, the pattern was broken and, although the Abbey will continue to produce his plays, it no longer has an assumed right to the first production. The plays, with dates of first perform-ance, were *The Freedom of the City* (1973), *Volunteers* (1975), *Living Quarters* (1977) and *Aristocrats* (1979). In the first two of these, the political atmosphere is highly charged. The three central characters in *Freedom* are civil rights marchers trapped by the British Army in the mayor's parlour of a city's Guildhall. As they and others talk of their plight, it becomes clear that they will emerge only to be shot as terrorists. In *Volunteers*, the victimized group is a squad of IRA prisoners who have volunteered, against the orders of their own organization, to take temporary release from prison in order to help with an archaeological excavation. They know that, on their return to prison at the end of the dig, they will be murdered. *Living Quarters* and *Aristocrats* are studies in the breakdown of a family and its illusory social and cultural authority in the small-town setting of Ballybeg. All of these plays have in common an interest in the disintegration of traditional authority and in the exposure of the violence upon which it had rested. Despite the bleakness of the general situation, Friel manages to make his central victims appealing even in their futility and in their frequent bouts of self-pity. He still adheres to his fascination with the human capacity for producing consoling fictions to make life more tolerable. Although he destroys these fictions he does not, with that, destroy the motives that produced them motives which are rooted in the human being's wish for dignity as well as in his tendency to avoid reality.

In addition, these plays are full of what we may call displaced voices. American sociologists, English judges, and voice-overs from the past play their part in the dialogue in set speeches, tape-recordings, through loudspeakers. The discourse they produce is obviously bogus. Yet its official jargon represents something more and something worse than moral obtuseness. It also represents power, the one element lacking in the world of the victims where the language is so much more vivid and spontaneous. Once again, in divorcing power from eloquence, Friel is indicating a traditional feature of the Irish condition. The voice of power tells one kind of fiction – the lie. It has the purpose of preserving its own interests. The voice of powerlessness tells another kind of fiction – the illusion. It has the purpose of pretending that its own interests have been preserved. The contrast between the two becomes unavoidable at moments of crisis. Each of these plays presents us with such a moment, when both sets of voices are pitted against one another in a struggle which leads to a common ruin. Yet within the group of the victims there is another opposition which is perhaps more crucial and is certainly even more tense. It takes the form of a contrast too, between the fast-talking, utterly sceptical outsider and the silent, almost aphasic insider. At first, it seems to be a comic confrontation between a witty intelligence and a dumb stupidity. But it becomes tragic in the end and we are left to reflect that intelligence may be a gift, eloquence may be an attraction but that neither is necessarily a virtue and that the combination of both, in circumstances like these, may be disastrous. These outsiders are, dramatically speaking, dominating and memorable presences. Skinner in *The Freedom of the City*, Keeney in *Volunteers*, Ben in *Living Quarters*, Eamon in *Aristocrats*, are all men who make talk a compensation for their dislocation from family or society. They see clearly but, on that account, can do nothing. Against them, in the same plays, are ranged, respectively, Lily, Smiler, Ben in his second role of stammering nervousness and Casimir. Surrounding them are the voices of control – fathers, judges, narrators, expert analysts.

18

Friel found in these plays a way to quarantine his central cast, with its tension between eloquence and silence, within a zone of official discourse with its ready-made jargon of inauthenticity. As a result, the plays are even more fiercely *spoken* plays. Language, in a variety of modes and presented in a number of recorded ways, dominates to the exclusion of almost everything else. The Babel of educated and uneducated voices, of speech flowing and speech blocked, the atmosphere of permanent crisis and of unshakable apathy, is as much a feature of Friel's as it is of Beckett's or of O'Casey's plays.

Although *The Freedom of the City* and *Volunteers* were evidently related, in however oblique a manner, to the troubles in Northern Ireland, it was still surprising to see the ferocity and the blindness with which critics, especially in London and New York, reacted to them. During those years (1973–6), the IRA campaign against the British presence in the North was at its height and the propaganda war was, as a consequence, intensified to an almost unprecedented degree. Friel was accused by some rather hysterical English and American reviewers of defending the IRA by his attacks upon the British Army and the whole system of authority which that army was there to defend. Wisely, he ignored this hack reviewing, although it cost him dear financially, especially in New York. Instead, Friel kept his attention fixed on the evolving form of his own work and in 1979, at the Longacre Theatre in New York, with José Quintero as director and James Mason in the leading part, he presented one of his most important, if also one of his most unexpected ✳ plays – *Faith Healer*.

Faith Healer has no political background. It is the story of Frank Hardy, the faith healer, his wife Grace, and his manager Teddy. The play is composed of four monologues, the first and last spoken by Frank, the second and third spoken by Grace and Teddy in turn. A ramshackle caravan, patrolling the remote villages of England, Scotland and Wales, offering to the chronically ill the prospect of a miracle cure at the hands of the faith healer; within that, another story, of a drastic event, the death of Frank's and Grace's child, or of Frank's mother, or of something which both of these are emblems of; and beyond that,

the final return to Donegal and Ballybeg, where Frank's
treacherous gift will finally betray him into the brutal death he
has begun to long for and expect. We have here a complex
metaphor of the artist who is possessed by a gift over which he
has no control. A travelling showman, putting on his little
theatrical production night after night, waiting for the miracle to
happen, for the moment at which the audience will be cured,
energized by a miracle, he is also, very clearly, the artist as
playwright. However, the return to home and death out of exile,
often inspected by Friel before (as in *The Loves of Cass McGuire*)
reinstitutes the social and political dimension which had been
otherwise so subdued. Home is the place of the deformed in
spirit. The violent men who kill the faith healer are intimate
with him, for their savage violence and his miraculous gift are no
more than obverse versions of one another. Once again, Friel is
intimating to his audience that there is an inescapable link
between art and politics, the Irish version of which is the
closeness between eloquence and violence. The mediating
agency is, as always, disappointment, but it is a disappointment
all the more profound because it is haunted by the possibility of
miracle and of Utopia. *Faith Healer* is the parable which gives
coherence to the preceding four plays. With them, it marks the
completion of another passage in Friel's career. It is his most
triumphant rewriting of his early work and stands in a peculiarly
ironic, almost parodic relationship to *Philadelphia*, of which it is
both the subversion and the fulfilment.

With the new decade of the 1980s, Field Day was born. It is a
theatre company, founded by Friel and Stephen Rea, the Irish
actor, and it is a cultural group embracing three poets, Seamus
Heaney, Tom Paulin and the present writer as well as the
broadcaster and musician, David Hammond. It was founded to
put on plays outside the confines of the established theatre and,
through that, to begin to effect a change in the apathetic
atmosphere of the North. Although Field Day will not be an
exclusively theatrical venture, that aspect of its activities is the
only one pertinent here. Derry was chosen as the centre of its
operations. All the plays have their world première there. The
first of these was *Translations*, widely acclaimed both in Ireland

and abroad as Friel's masterpiece. It was first produced in Derry, in the Guildhall, on 23 September 1980. Since then, it has had long runs in London and New York. However, the play is best seen in relation to the third Field Day production (the second was Friel's translation of Chekhov's *Three Sisters* in 1981), *The Communication Cord* (produced 1982, published 1983). For this most recent play is an antidote to *Translations*, a farce which undermines the pieties sponsored by the earlier play, a defensive measure against any possible sentimentality in its predecessor. *Translations* is not, in fact, sentimental, but it treats of a theme which is powerfully emotive in the Irish context and one which has been subjected to a great deal of vulgarization and hypocrisy. That theme is the death of the Irish language. Friel locates the moment of its final decline in the Donegal of the 1830s, the years in which the British Army Engineer Corps carried out its famous ordnance survey of Ireland, mapping and renaming the whole country to accord with its recent (1800) integration into the United Kingdom of Great Britain and Ireland. The crisis of the language is expressed in terms of the crisis in a family. Owen, the son of a hedge-school master, who teaches Latin and Greek through Irish, arrives home from Dublin with the British Army corps to help them in the mapping and renaming of his native territory. He is the recognizable Frielian outsider who has the intimacy of an insider, the man who is betraying his ancestral and anachronistic community into the modern, Anglicized world. The subsequent events demonstrate once more the salience of the connection between language (its loss and its mastery) and politics (its violence and its authority). It states with unprecedented clarity and force much that had been implicit in Friel's work since the beginning. The crisis he is concerned with is a crisis both of language and of civilization and it is experienced directly by people who are trapped within the confines of a place and an attitude of mind from which there is no escape. It is, thus, a tragic play. Military and cultural imperialism, provincial rebellion and cultural fantasy collide with such force that the worst aspects of each are precipitated into a permanent and deadly confrontation. It is a play about the tragedy of English

21

imperialism as well as of Irish nationalism. Most of all, it is a play about the final incoherence that has always characterized the relationship between the two countries, the incoherence that comes from sharing a common language which is based upon different presuppositions. The failure of language to accommodate experience, the failure of a name to fully indicate a place, the failure of lovers to find the opportunity to express their feeling whether in words or deed, are all products of this political confrontation. In *Translations*, Friel has found a sequence of events in history which are transformed by his writing into a parable of events in the present day. Paradoxically, although his theme is failure, linguistic and political, the fact that the play has been written is itself an indication of the success of the imagination in dealing with everything that seems opposed to its survival. What is most characteristically tragic about the play is the sense of exhilaration which it transmits to the audience. Language lost in this fashion is also language rediscovered in such a way that the sense of loss has been overcome. In that strange, contradictory triumph, Brian Friel has reached a culmination in his dramatic career. No Irish writer since the early days of this century has so sternly and courageously asserted the role of art in the public world without either yielding to that world's pressures or retreating into art's narcissistic alternatives. In the balance he has achieved between these forces he has become an exemplary figure.

SEAMUS DEANE
January 1984

▲▲▲▲▲▲▲▲▲▲▲▲▲▲▲▲▲▲▲▲▲▲▲▲▲▲▲▲▲▲▲▲▲▲▲▲▲▲▲

PHILADELPHIA,
HERE I COME!

▲▲▲▲▲▲▲▲▲▲▲▲▲▲▲▲▲▲▲▲▲▲▲▲▲▲▲▲▲▲▲▲▲▲▲▲▲▲▲

for my father and mother

CHARACTERS

MADGE	Housekeeper
GAR O'DONNELL (PUBLIC) ⎱	Son of the house
GAR O'DONNELL (PRIVATE) ⎰	
S. B. O'DONNELL	Gar's father
KATE DOOGAN/MRS KING	Daughter of Senator Doogan
SENATOR DOOGAN	
MASTER BOYLE	Local teacher
LIZZY SWEENEY	Gar's aunt
CON SWEENEY	Lizzy's husband
BEN BURTON	Friend of the Sweeneys
NED ⎫	
TOM ⎬	The boys
JOE ⎭	
CANON MICK O'BYRNE	The parish priest

The first performance of *Philadelphia, Here I Come!* was given at the Gaiety Theatre, Dublin, on 28 September 1964 by Edwards-MacLiammoir: Dublin Gate Theatre Productions Ltd in association with the Dublin Theatre Festival and Oscar Lewenstein Ltd. The cast was as follows:

MADGE		Maureen O'Sullivan
GARETH O'DONNELL	in Public	Patrick Bedford
	in Private	Donal Donnelly
S. B. O'DONNELL		Éamonn Kelly
KATE DOOGAN		Máire Hastings
SENATOR DOOGAN		Cecil Barror
MASTER BOYLE		Dominic Roche
LIZZY SWEENEY		Ruby Head
CON SWEENEY		Tom Irwin
BEN BURTON		Michael Mara
NED		Éamon Morrissey
TOM		Brendan O'Sullivan
JOE		Emmet Bergin
CANON MICK O'BYRNE		Alex McDonald
Direction		Hilton Edwards
Setting		Alpho O'Reilly

Set

When the curtain rises the only part of the stage that is lit is the kitchen, i.e. the portion on the left from the point of view of the audience. It is sparsely and comfortlessly furnished – a bachelor's kitchen. There are two doors; one left which leads to the shop, and one upstage leading to the scullery (off). Beside the shop door is a large deal table, now set for tea without cloth and with rough cups and saucers. Beside the scullery door is an old-fashioned dresser. On the scullery wall is a large school-type clock.

Stage right, now in darkness, is Gar's bedroom. Both bedroom and kitchen should be moved upstage, leaving a generous apron. Gar's bedroom is furnished with a single bed, a wash-hand basin (crockery jug and bowl), a table with a record-player and records, and a small chest of drawers.

These two areas – kitchen and Gar's bedroom – occupy more than two-thirds of the stage. The remaining portion is fluid: in Episode I for example, it represents a room in Senator Doogan's home.

The two Gars, PUBLIC GAR and PRIVATE GAR, are two views of the one man. PUBLIC GAR is the Gar that people see, talk to, talk about. PRIVATE GAR is the unseen man, the man within, the conscience, the *alter ego*, the secret thoughts, the id. PRIVATE GAR, the spirit, is invisible to everybody, always. Nobody except PUBLIC GAR hears him talk. But even PUBLIC GAR, although he talks to PRIVATE GAR occasionally, never sees him and *never looks at him*. One cannot look at one's *alter ego*.

Time: the present in the small village of Ballybeg in County Donegal, Ireland. The action takes place on the night before, and on the morning of Gar's departure for Philadelphia.

Music
Mendelssohn's Violin Concerto in E Minor, Op. 64
Ceilidh music
'All Round My Hat' – first verse
'She Moved through the Fair' – second verse
'California, Here I Come!'
'Give the Woman in the Bed more Porter'

EPISODE ONE

Kitchen in the home of County Councillor, S. B. O'DONNELL, *who owns a general shop. As the curtain rises* MADGE, *the housekeeper, enters from the scullery with a tray in her hands and finishes setting the table. She is a woman in her sixties. She walks as if her feet were precious. She pauses on her way past the shop door.*

MADGE: Gar! Your tea!

PUBLIC: (*Off*) Right!

    (*She finishes setting the table and is about to go to the scullery door when* PUBLIC GAR *marches on stage. He is ecstatic with joy and excitement: tomorrow morning he leaves for Philadelphia.*)

PUBLIC: (*Singing*) 'Philadelphia, here I come, right back where I started from . . .' (*Breaks off and catches Madge.*) Come on, Madge! What about an old time waltz!

MADGE: Agh, will you leave me alone.

    (*He holds on to her and forces her to do a few steps as he sings in waltz time.*)

PUBLIC: 'Where bowers of flowers bloom in the spring' –

MADGE: (*Struggling*) Stop it! Stop it! You brat you!

PUBLIC: Madge, you dance like an angel. (*Suddenly lets her go and springs away from her.*) Oh, but you'd give a fella bad thoughts very quick!

MADGE: And the smell of fish of you, you dirty thing!

    (*He grabs her again and puts his face up to hers, very confidentially.*)

PUBLIC: Will you miss me?

MADGE: Let me on with my work!

PUBLIC: The truth!

MADGE: Agh, will you quit it, will you?

PUBLIC: I'll tickle you till you squeal for mercy.

MADGE: Please, Gar . . .

PUBLIC: (*Tickling her*) Will you miss me, I said?

MADGE: I will – I will – I will – I –

PUBLIC: That's better. Now tell me: what time is it?

MADGE: Agh, Gar –

PUBLIC: What time is it?

MADGE: (*Looking at clock*) Ten past seven.

PUBLIC: And what time do I knock off at?

MADGE: At seven.

PUBLIC: Which means that on my last day with him he got ten
minutes overtime out of my hide. (*He releases Madge.*)
Instead of saying to me: (*Grandly*) 'Gar, my son, since
you are leaving me forever, you may have the entire day
free,' what does he do? Lines up five packs of flour and
says: (*In flat dreary tones*) 'Make them up into two-pound
pokes.'

MADGE: He's losing a treasure, indeed!

PUBLIC: So d'you know what I said to him? I just drew myself
up and looked him straight in the eye and said to him:
'Two-pound pokes it will be' – just like that.

MADGE: That flattened him.
(*She goes off to the scullery. He stands at the door and talks in
to her.*)

PUBLIC: And that wasn't it all. At six o'clock he remembered
about the bloody pollock, and him in the middle of the
Angelus. (*Stands in imitation of the Father: head bowed,
hands on chest. In flat tones –*) 'Behold-the-handmaid-of-
the-Lord-Gut-and-salt-them-fish.' So by God I lashed so
much salt on those bloody fish that any poor bugger that
eats them will die of thirst. But when the corpses are strewn
all over Ballybeg, where will I be? In the little old USA!
Yip-eeeeee! (*He swings away from the scullery door and does a
few exuberant steps as he sings –*) 'Philadelphia, here I come,
rightah backah where Ah started from –' (*He goes into his
bedroom, flings himself down on his bed, rests his head on his*

30

hands, and looks at the ceiling. Sings alternate lines of
'Philadelphia' – first half – with PRIVATE *(off)*).

PUBLIC: It's all over.

PRIVATE: (*Off, in echo-chamber voice*) And it's all about to
begin. It's all over.

PUBLIC: And it's all about to begin.

PRIVATE: (*Now on.*) Just think, Gar.

PUBLIC: Think . . .

PRIVATE: Think . . . Up in that big bugger of a jet, with its
snout pointing straight for the States, and its tail belching
smoke over Ireland; and you sitting up at the front (PUBLIC
acts this) with your competent fingers poised over the
controls; and then away down below in the Atlantic you see
a bloody bugger of an Irish boat out fishing for bloody
pollock and –
(PUBLIC *nose-dives, engines screaming, machine guns
stuttering.*)

PUBLIC: Rat-tat-tat-tat-tat-tat-tat-tat-tat-tat.

PRIVATE: Abandon ship! Make for the life-boats! Send for
Canon Mick O'Byrne!
(PUBLIC *gains altitude and nose-dives again.*)

PUBLIC: Rat-tat-tat-tat-tat-tat-tat-tat-tat.

PRIVATE: To hell with women and children! Say an Act of
Contrition!

PUBLIC: Yip-eeeee!
(*He finishes taking off the shop coat, rolls it into a bundle, and
places it carefully on the floor.*)

PRIVATE: It looks as if – I can't see very well from the
distance – but it looks as if – yes! – yes! – the free is being
taken by dashing Gar O'Donnell (PUBLIC *gets back from the
coat, poises himself to kick it*), pride of the Ballybeg team. (*In
commentator's hushed voice*) O'Donnell is now moving back,
taking a slow, calculating look at the goal, I've never seen
this boy in the brilliant form he's in today – absolute magic
in his feet. He's now in position, running up, and –
(PUBLIC *kicks the shop coat into the air.*)

PUBLIC: Ya-hoooo! (*Sings and gyrates at same time.*)
'Philah-delph-yah, heah Ah come, rightah backah weah Ah

31

stahted from, boom-boom-boom-boom–'
(*He breaks off suddenly when* PRIVATE *addresses him in sombre tones of a judge.*)

PRIVATE: Gareth Mary O'Donnell.
(PUBLIC *springs to attention, salutes, and holds this absurd military stance. He is immediately inside his bedroom door, facing it.*)

PUBLIC: Sir.

PRIVATE: You are fully conscious of all the consequences of your decision?

PUBLIC: Yessir.

PRIVATE: Of leaving the country of your birth, the land of the curlew and the snipe, the Aran sweater and the Irish Sweepstakes?

PUBLIC: (*With fitting hesitation*) I-I-I-I have considered all these, Sir.

PRIVATE: Of going to a profane, irreligious, pagan country of gross materialism?

PUBLIC: I am fully sensitive to this, Sir.

PRIVATE: Where the devil himself holds sway, and lust– abhorrent lust–is everywhere indulged in shamelessly?
(PUBLIC *winks extravagantly and nudges an imaginary man beside him.*)

PUBLIC: Who are you tellin'? (*Poker-stiff again.*) Shamelessly, Sir, shamelessly.
(MADGE *has entered from the scullery, carrying an old suitcase and a bundle of clothes.*)

PRIVATE: And yet you persist in exposing yourself to these frightful dangers?

PUBLIC: I would submit, Sir, that these stories are slightly exaggerated, Sir. For every door that opens–
(MADGE *opens the bedroom door.*)

MADGE: Oh! You put the heart across me there! Get out of my road, will you, and quit eejiting about!

PUBLIC: Madge, you're an aul duck.

MADGE: Aye, so. There's the case. And there's a piece of rope for I see the clasp's all rusted. And there's your shirts and your winter vests and your heavy socks. and you'll need to

32

air them shirts before you – Don't put them smelly hands on them!

PUBLIC: Sorry!

MADGE: See that they're well aired before you put them on. He's said nothing since, I suppose?

PUBLIC: Not a word.

PRIVATE: The bugger.

MADGE: But he hasn't paid you your week's wages?

PUBLIC: £3 15s – that'll carry me far.

MADGE: He'll have something to say then, you'll see. And maybe he'll slip you a couple of extra pounds.

PUBLIC: Whether he says good-bye to me or not, or whether he slips me a few miserable quid or not, it's a matter of total indifference to me, Madge.

MADGE: Aye, so. Your tea's on the table – but that's a matter of total indifference to me.

PUBLIC: Give me time to wash, will you?

MADGE: And another thing: just because he doesn't say much doesn't mean that he hasn't feelings like the rest of us.

Eloquent vs. Silence [handwritten]

PUBLIC: Say much? He's said nothing!

MADGE: He said nothing either when your mother died. It must have been near daybreak when he got to sleep last night. I could hear his bed creaking.

Father is coping with the inevitable in a different way. [handwritten]

PUBLIC: Well to hell with him –

MADGE: (*Leaving*) Don't come into your tea smelling like a lobster-pot.

PUBLIC: If he wants to speak to me he knows where to find me! But I'm damned if I'm going to speak to him first!
(MADGE *goes off to the scullery.*)
(*Calling after her*) And you can tell him I said that if you like!

PRIVATE: What the hell do you care about him. Screwballs! Skinflint! Skittery Face! You're free of him and his stinking bloody shop. And tomorrow morning, boy, when that little ole plane gets up into the skies, you'll stick your head out the window (PUBLIC *acts this*) and spit down on the lot of them!
(S.B. *appears at the shop door. He is in his late sixties. Wears a*

33

hat, a good dark suit, collar and tie, black apron. S. B.
O'DONNELL *is a responsible, respectable citizen.*)

S.B.: Gar!

(PUBLIC *reacts instinctively.* PRIVATE *keeps calm.*)

PRIVATE: Let the bugger call.

S.B.: (*Louder*) Gar!

(*Instinct is stronger than reason:* PUBLIC *rushes to his door
and opens it. But as soon as he opens it and looks out at his
father he assumes in speech and gesture a surly, taciturn
gruffness. He always behaves in this way when he is in his
father's company.*)

PUBLIC: Aye?

S.B.: How many coils of barbed-wire came in on the mail-van
this evening?

PUBLIC: Two. Or was it three?

S.B.: That's what I'm asking you. It was you that carried them
into the yard.

PUBLIC: There were two – no, no, no, three – yes, three – or
maybe it was . . . was it two?

S.B.: Agh!

(S.B. *retires to the shop.* PUBLIC *and* PRIVATE *come back into
the bedroom.*)

PRIVATE: What sort of a stupid bugger are you? Think, man!
You went out and stood yarning to Joe the Post; then you
carried one coil into the yard and came out with the sack of
spuds for the parochial; then you carried in the second
coil . . . and put it in the corner . . . and came out again to
the van . . . and . . .

(PUBLIC *skips into the air.*)

Ah, what the hell odds! That's his headache, old
Nicodemus! After tomorrow a bloody roll of barbed-wire
will be a mere bagatelle to you. (*In cowboy accent*) Yeah,
man. You see tham thar plains stretchin' 's far th'eye can
see, man? Well, tham thar plains belongs to Garry the Kid.
An' Garry the Kid he don't go in for none of your fancy
fencin'. No siree. (*His eye lights on the fresh laundry* MADGE
brought in.) And what'll you wear on the plane tomorrow,
old rooster, eh?

34

(PUBLIC *picks up a clean shirt, holds it to his chest, and surveys himself in the small mirror above his wash-handbasin.*)
Pretty smart, eh?

PUBLIC: Pretty smart.

PRIVATE: Pretty sharp?

PUBLIC: Pretty sharp.

PRIVATE: Pretty oo-là-là?

PUBLIC: Mais oui.

PRIVATE: And not a bad looker, if I may say so.

PUBLIC: You may. You may.

PRIVATE: (*In heavy US accent*) I'm Patrick Palinakis, president of the biggest chain of biggest hotels in the world. We're glad to have you, Mr O'Donnell.

PUBLIC: (*Sweet, demure*) And I'm glad to be here, Sir.

PRIVATE: Handsomely said, young man. I hope you'll be happy with us and work hard and one day maybe you'll be president of the biggest chain of biggest hotels in the world.

PUBLIC: That's my ambition, Sir.

PRIVATE: You are twenty-five years of age, Mr O'Donnell?

PUBLIC: Correct.

PRIVATE: And you spent one year at University College Dublin?

PUBLIC: Yes, Sir.

PRIVATE: Would you care to tell me why you abandoned your academic career, Mr O'Donnell?

PUBLIC: (*With disarming simplicity*) Well, just before I sat my First Arts exam, Sir, I did an old Irish turas, or pilgrimage, where I spent several nights in devout prayer, Sir.

PRIVATE: St Patrick's Pilgrimage – on Lough – ?

PUBLIC: St Harold's Cross, Sir. And it was there that I came to realize that a life of scholarship was not for me. So I returned to my father's business.

PRIVATE: Yeah. You mentioned that your father was a businessman. What's his line?

PUBLIC: Well, Sir, he has – what you would call – his finger in many pies – retail mostly – general dry goods – assorted patent drugs – hardware – ah – ah – dehydrated fish – men's

35

king-size hose – snuffs from the exotic East . . . of
Donegal – a confection for gourmets, known as Peggy's
Leg – weedkiller – (*Suddenly breaking off: in his normal
accent: rolling on the bed –*) Yahoooooo! It is now sixteen or
seventeen years since I saw the Queen of France, then the
Dauphiness, at Versailles –

PRIVATE: Let's git packin', boy. Let's git that li'l ole saddle bag
opened and let's git packin'. But first let's have a li'l ole
music on the li'l ole phonograph. Yeah man. You bet. Ah
reckon. Yessir.

(PUBLIC *puts a record on the player: First Movement,
Mendelssohn's Violin Concerto.* PUBLIC *is preening himself
before his performance, and while he is flexing his fingers and
adjusting his bow-tie,* PRIVATE *announces in the reverential
tones of a radio announcer:*)

The main item in tonight's concert is the First Movement
of the Violin Concerto in E minor, Opus 64, by Jacob
Ludwig Felix Mendelssohn. The orchestra is conducted by
Gareth O'Donnell and the soloist is the Ballybeg half-back,
Gareth O'Donnell. Music critics throughout the world
claim that O'Donnell's simultaneous wielding of baton and
bow is the greatest thing since Leather Ass died.
Mendelssohn's Violin Concerto, First Movement.

(PRIVATE *sits demurely on the chair.* PUBLIC *clears his throat.
Now* PUBLIC *plays the violin, conducts, plays the violin,
conducts, etc. etc. This keeps up for some time. Then* PRIVATE
rises from his chair.)

Agh, come on, come on, come on! Less aul foolin'. To
work, old rooster, to work.

(PUBLIC *stops. Turns player down low and changes from the
First to the Second Movement. Takes a look at the case Madge
brought in.*)

Ah, hell, how can any bloody bugger head into a jet plane
with aul' cardboard rubbish like that!

(PUBLIC *examines the surface.*)

Dammit, maybe you could give it a lick of paint! Or wash
it!

(PUBLIC *spits on the lid and rubs it with his finger.*)

36

God, you'll rub a hole in the damn thing if you're not careful!
Maybe aul Screwballs'll slip you a fiver tonight and you can
get a new one in Dublin.

PUBLIC: What a hope!

(PUBLIC *opens the case and sniffs the inside.*)

PRIVATE: Oh! Stinks of cat's pee!

(PUBLIC *lifts out a sheet of faded newspaper.*)

PUBLIC: (*Reads*) The *Clarion* – 1st January 1937.

PRIVATE: Precious medieval manuscript . . . my God, was
it? . . . By God it was – the day they were married – and it
(*the case*) hasn't been opened since their honeymoon . . . she
and old Screwballs off on a side-car to Bundoran for three
days . . .

PUBLIC: O God, the Creator and Redeemer of all the faithful,
give to the soul of Maire, my mother, the remission of all her
sins, that she may obtain . . .

PRIVATE: She was small, Madge says, and wild, and young,
Madge says, from a place called Bailtefree beyond the
mountains; and her eyes were bright, and her hair was loose,
and she carried her shoes under her arm until she came to the
edge of the village, Madge says, and then she put them on . . .

PUBLIC: Eternal rest grant unto her, O Lord, and let perpetual
light shine . . .

PRIVATE: She was nineteen and he was forty, and he owned a
shop, and he wore a soft hat, and she thought he was the
grandest gentleman that ever lived, Madge says; and he – he
couldn't take his eyes off her, Madge says . . .

PUBLIC: O God, O God the Creator and Redeemer . . .

PRIVATE: And sometimes in that first year, when she was
pregnant with you, laddybuck, the other young girls from
Bailtefree would call in here to dress up on their way to a
dance, Madge says, and her face would light up too, Madge
says . . .

(PUBLIC *puts the newspaper carefully inside the folds of a shirt.*)
. . . And he must have known, old Screwballs, he must have
known, Madge says, for many a night he must have heard her
crying herself to sleep . . . and maybe it was good of God to
take her away three days after you were born . . . (*Suddenly*

37

boisterous.) Damn you, anyhow, for a bloody stupid
bastard! It is now sixteen or seventeen years since I saw the
Queen of France, then the Dauphiness, at Versailles! And
to hell with that bloody mushy fiddler!
(PUBLIC *goes quickly to the record-player and sings boisterously
as he goes.*)

PUBLIC: 'Philadelphia, here I come –'

PRIVATE: Watch yourself, nut-head. If you let yourself slip that
way, you might find that –

PUBLIC: ' – right back where I started from.'
(PUBLIC *has taken off the Mendelssohn and is now searching
for another.*)

PRIVATE: Something lively! Something bloody animal! A bit of
aul thumpety-thump!
(PUBLIC *puts on the record.*)
An' you jist keep atalkin' to you'self all the time, Mistah,
'cos once you stop atalkin' to you'self ah reckon then you
jist begin to think kinda crazy things – (*The record
begins – Any lively piece of Ceilidhe Band music.*) Ahhhhh!

PUBLIC: Yipeeeeeeeee!
(PUBLIC *dances up and down the length of his bedroom.
Occasionally he leaps high into the air or does a neat bit of
foot-work. Occasionally he lilts. Occasionally he talks to
different people he meets on the dance floor.*)
Righ-too-del-loo-del-oo-del-oo-del-oo-del-oo-del-ah,
Rum-ta-del-ah-del-ah-del-agh-del-ah-del-ah-del-agh.
Hell of a crowd here the night, eh? Yah-ho! Man, you're
looking powerful! Great!
(PRIVATE *sits on the chair and watches. When he speaks his
voice is soft.* PUBLIC *pretends not to hear him.*)

PRIVATE: Remember – that was Katie's tune. You needn't
pretend you have forgotten. And it reminds you of the
night the two of you made all the plans, and you thought
your heart would burst with happiness.

PUBLIC: (*Louder*) Tigh-righ-tigh-righ-scal-del-de-da-del-ah,
Come on! A dirty big swing! Yaaaaaaaaaaah!

PRIVATE: (*Quietly, rapidly insisting*) Are you going to take her
photograph to the States with you? When are you going to

38

say good-bye to her? Will you write to her? Will you send
her cards and photographs? You loved her once, old
rooster; you wanted so much to marry her that it was a
bloody sickness. Tell me, randy boy; tell me the truth: have
you got over that sickness? Do you still love her? Do you
still lust after her? Well, do you? Do you? Do you?

PUBLIC: Bugger!

(PUBLIC *suddenly stops dancing, switches – almost knocks – off
the record-player, pulls a wallet out of his hip pocket and
produces a snap. He sits and looks at it.*)

PRIVATE: Shhhhhhhhhhhhh . . .

PUBLIC: (*Softly*) Kate . . . sweet Katie Doogan . . . my darling
Kathy Doogan . . .

PRIVATE: (*In same soft tone*) Aul bitch. (*Loudly*) Rotten aul snobby
bitch! Just like her stinking rotten father and mother – a
bugger and a buggeress – a buggeroo and a buggerette!

PUBLIC: No, no; my fault – all my fault –

PRIVATE: (*Remembering and recalling tauntingly*) By God, that
was a night, boy, eh? By God, you made a right bloody
cow's ass of yourself.

(PUBLIC *goes off right.*)

Remember – when was it? – ten months ago? – you had just
come back from a walk out the Mill Road, and the pair of you
had the whole thing planned: engaged at Christmas, married
at Easter, and fourteen of a family – seven boys and seven
girls. Cripes, you make me laugh! You bloody-well make me
die laughing. You were going to 'develop' the hardware lines
and she was going to take charge of the 'drapery'! The
drapery! The fishy socks and the shoebox of cotton spools and
rusted needles! And you – you were to ask Screwballs for a rise
in pay – 'in view of your increased responsibilities'! And you
were so far gone that night, Laddybuck, –

(PUBLIC *and* KATE *enter from the left and walk very slowly
across the front of the stage. They stop and kiss. Then they move
on again.*)

– so bloody well astray in the head with 'love' that you went
and blabbed about your secret egg deals that nobody knew
anything about – not even Madge! Stupid bloody get! O my

39

God, how you stick yourself I'll never know!

PUBLIC: Kate – Kathy – I'm mad about you: I'll never last till Easter! I'll – I'll – I'll bloody-well burst!

(*He catches her again and kisses her.*)

PRIVATE: Steady, boy, steady. You know what the Canon says: long passionate kisses in lonely places . . .

PUBLIC: Our daughters'll all be gentle and frail and silly, like you; and our sons – they'll be thick bloody louts, sexy goats, like me, and by God I'll beat the tar out of them!

KATE: But £3 15s, Gar! We could never live on that.

PUBLIC: (*Kissing her hair*) Mmmm.

KATE: Gar! Listen! Be sensible.

PUBLIC: Mmm?

KATE: How will we *live*?

PRIVATE: (*Imitating*) 'How will we *live*?'

PUBLIC: Like lords – free house, free light, free fuel, free groceries! And every night at seven when we close – except Saturday; he stays open till damn near midnight on Saturdays, making out bloody bills; and sure God and the world knows that sending out bills here is as hopeless as peeing against the wind –

KATE: Gar! No matter what you say we just couldn't live on that much money. It – it's not possible. We'll need to have more security than that.

PUBLIC: Maybe he'll die – tonight – of galloping consumption!

KATE: Gar . . .

PUBLIC: What's troubling you?

(*He tries to kiss her again and she avoids him.*)

KATE: Please. This is serious.

PRIVATE: 'Please. This is serious.'

PUBLIC: (*Irritably*) What is it?

KATE: You'll have to see about getting more money.

PUBLIC: Of course I'll see about getting more money! Haven't I told you I'm going to ask for a rise?

KATE: But will he – ?

PUBLIC: I'll get it; don't you worry; I'll get it. Besides, (*With dignity*) I have a – a-a source of income that he knows nothing about – that nobody knows nothing about – knows anything about.

KATE: (*With joy*) Investments? Like Daddy?

PUBLIC: Well . . . sort of . . . (*Quickly*) You know when I go
round the country every Tuesday and Thursday in the lorry?

KATE: Yes?

PUBLIC: Well, I buy eggs direct from the farms and sell them
privately to McLaughlin's Hotel – (*Winks*) – for a handsome
profit – (*Quickly*) – but he knows nothing about it.

KATE: And how much do you make?

PUBLIC: It varies – depending on the time of year.

KATE: Roughly.

PUBLIC: Oh, anything from 12s 6d to £1.

KATE: Every Tuesday and Thursday?

PUBLIC: Every month. (*Grabs her again.*) God, Kate, I can't
even wait till Christmas!

KATE: Shhhh.

PUBLIC: But I can't. We'll have to get married sooner – next
month – next week –

PRIVATE: Steady, steady. . . .

PUBLIC: Kate . . . my sweet Katie . . . my darling Kathy . . .
(*They kiss. Suddenly* KATE *breaks off. Her voice is urgent.*)

KATE: We'll go now, rightaway, and tell them.

PUBLIC: Who?

KATE: Mammy and Daddy. They're at home tonight.
(*She catches his arm and pulls him towards the left.*)
Come on. Quickly. Now, Gar, now.

PUBLIC: (*Adjusting his tie*) God, Kathy, I'm in no – look at the
shoes – the trousers –

KATE: What matter. It must be now, Gar, now!

PUBLIC: What – what – what'll I say?

KATE: That you want their permission to marry me next week.

PUBLIC: God, they'll wipe the bloody floor with me!

KATE: Gar!
(*She kisses him passionately, quickly, then breaks off and goes.*)
(*Stage right, now lit. A room in Doogan's house.*)

PUBLIC: God, my legs are trembling! Kathy . . .

KATE: Anybody at home? Mammy! Daddy!
(PUBLIC *hesitates before entering* DOOGAN's *house.* PRIVATE
is at his elbow, prompting him desperately.)

41

PRIVATE: Mr Doogan – Senator Doogan – I want to ask
your permission . . . O my God! . . .

KATE: Yo-ho!

PRIVATE: Mrs Doogan, Kate and I have to get married
rightaway – Cripes, no! –

KATE: Where is everybody! Yo-ho-yo-ho!

PRIVATE: If the boys could see you now!

(KATE *comes back to him, gives him a quick kiss on the cheek.*)

KATE: Don't look so miserable. Here . . . (*Fixes his tie*).

PUBLIC: Kathy, maybe we should wait until – until – until next
Sunday –

KATE: (*Earnestly*) Remember, it's up to you, entirely up to you.

DOOGAN: (*Off*) That you, Kate?

KATE: (*Rapidly*) You have £20 a week and £5,000 in the bank
and your father's about to retire. (*Turning and smiling at*
DOOGAN *who has now entered.*) Just Gar and I, Daddy.

(DOOGAN, *Lawyer, Senator, middle forties.*)

DOOGAN: Hello, Gareth. You're a stranger.

PRIVATE: Speak, you dummy you!

KATE: (*Filling in*) Where's Mammy?

DOOGAN: She's watching TV. (*To* GAR.) And how are things
with you, Gareth?

PUBLIC: Mr Doogan, I want –

PRIVATE: Go on.

PUBLIC: I won't be staying long.

DOOGAN: (*To* KATE) Francis arrived when you were out. Took a
few days off and decided to come north.

PRIVATE: Cripes!

KATE: He – he's – he's here – now?

DOOGAN: Inside with your mother. Ask them to join us, will you?

(KATE *gives* PUBLIC *a last significant look.*)

KATE: You talk to Daddy, Gar.

PRIVATE: God, I will, I will.

(KATE *goes off right.*)

DOOGAN: You've met Francis King, haven't you, Gareth?

PUBLIC: Yes – yes –

PRIVATE: King of the bloody fairies!

DOOGAN: We don't want to raise Kate's hopes unduly, but

42

strictly between ourselves there's a good chance that he'll get the new dispensary job here.

PUBLIC: Kate's hopes?

DOOGAN: Didn't she tell you? No, I can see she didn't. Of course there's nothing official yet; not even what you might call an understanding. But if this post does fall into his lap, well, her mother and I . . . let's say we're living in hope. A fine boy, Francis; and we've known the Kings, oh, since away back. As a matter of fact his father and I were class-fellows at school . . .

(DOOGAN *goes on and on. We catch an occasional word. Meantime* PRIVATE *has moved up to* PUBLIC's *elbow.*)

PRIVATE: Cripes, man!

DOOGAN: . . . and then later at university when he did medicine and I did law, we knocked about quite a bit . . .

PRIVATE: O God, the aul bitch! Cripes, you look a right fool standing there – the father of fourteen children! Get out, you eejit you! Get out! Get out quick before the others come in and die laughing at you! And all the time she must have known – the aul bitch! And you promised to give her breakfast in bed every morning! And you told her about the egg money!

Did she know?

DOOGAN: . . . your father, Gareth?

PRIVATE: He's talking to you, thick-skull.

PUBLIC: What – what – what's that?

DOOGAN: Your father – how is he?

PUBLIC: Oh he – he – he's grand, thanks.

PRIVATE: Get out! Get out!

PUBLIC: Look, Mr Doogan, if you'll excuse me, I think I'd better move on –

DOOGAN: Aren't you waiting for supper? The others will be along in a moment for –

PUBLIC: No, I must run. I've got to make up half-a-hundredweight of sugar bags.

PRIVATE: Brilliant!

PUBLIC: Say good-bye to –

DOOGAN: Certainly – certainly. Oh, Gareth –

(PUBLIC *pauses.*)

43

(*Awkwardly, with sincerity*) Kate is our only child, Gareth,
and her happiness is all that is important to us –

PRIVATE: (*Sings*) 'Give the woman in the bed more porter – '

DOOGAN: What I'm trying to say is that any decision she makes
will be her own –

PRIVATE: ' – Give the man beside her water, Give the woman in
the bed more porter, – '

DOOGAN: Just in case you should think that her mother or I
were . . . in case you might have the idea . . .

PUBLIC: (*Rapidly*) Good night, Mr Doogan.

(PUBLIC *rushes off.*)

DOOGAN: Good-bye . . . Gareth.

(DOOGAN *stands lighting his pipe.*)

KATE: (*Enters down right of* DOOGAN *and sees that* GAR *is no
longer there*) Where's Gar?

DOOGAN: He didn't seem anxious to stay.

KATE: But didn't he – did he – ?

DOOGAN: No, he didn't.

(*He crosses* KATE *to exit down right as light fades to black out.*)
(*Black out Doogan's room.* PUBLIC *and* PRIVATE *move back
to the bedroom where* PUBLIC *is putting away the photograph
and begins washing.*)

PRIVATE: (*Wearily*) Mrs Doctor Francis King. September 8th.
In harvest sunshine. Red carpet and white lilies and Sean
Horgan singing 'Bless This House' – and him whipped off
to Sligo jail two days later for stealing turf. Honeymoon in
Mallorca and you couldn't have afforded to take her to
Malahide. By God, Gar, aul sod, it was a sore hoke on the
aul prestige, eh? Between ourselves, aul son, in the privacy
of the bedroom, between you and me and the wall, as the
fella says, has it left a deep scar on the aul skitter of a soul,
eh? What I mean to say like, you took it sort of bad,
between you and me and the wall, as the fella says –

PUBLIC: (*Sings*) 'Philadelphia, here I come, right back – '

PRIVATE: But then there's more fish in the sea, as the fella says,
and they're all the same when they're upside down; and
between you and me and the wall, the first thing you would
have had to do would have been to give the boot to Daddy

44

Senator. And I'm thinking, Gar, aul rooster, that wouldn't have made you his pet son-in-law, Mister Fair-play Lawyer Senator Doogan – 'her happiness is all that is important to us'! You know, of course, that he carries one of those wee black cards in the inside pocket of his jacket, privately printed for him: 'I am a Catholic. In case of accident send for a bishop.' And you know, too, that in his spare time he travels for maternity corsets; and that he's a double spy for the Knights and the Masons; and that he takes pornographic photographs of Mrs D. and sends them anonymously to reverend mothers. And when you think of a bugger like that, you want to get down on your knees and thank God for aul Screwballs. (*Imitating his father's slow speech.*) So you're going to America in the morning, son? (PUBLIC *carries on with his washing and dressing and at the same time does this dialogue.*)

PUBLIC: Yes, Father.

PRIVATE: Nothing like it to broaden the mind. Man, how I'd love to travel. But there's some it doesn't agree with – like me, there.

PUBLIC: In what way, Father?

PRIVATE: The bowels, son. Let me move an inch from the house here – and they stall.

PUBLIC: No!

PRIVATE: Like the time I went to Lough Derg, away back in '35. Not a budge. The bare feet were nothing to the agonies I went through. I was bound up for two full weeks afterwards.

PUBLIC: It taught you a lesson.

PRIVATE: Didn't it just? Now I wouldn't even think of travelling.

PUBLIC: Anchored by the ass.

PRIVATE: Bound by the bowels.

PUBLIC: Tethered by the toilet. Tragic.
(PUBLIC *has now finished dressing. He surveys himself in the mirror.*)

PRIVATE: Not bad. Not bad at all. And well preserved for a father of fourteen children.

PUBLIC: (*In absurd Hollywood style*) Hi, gorgeous! You live in my block?

PRIVATE: (*Matching the accent*) Yeah, big handsome boy. Sure do.

PUBLIC: Mind if I walk you past the incinerator, to the elevator?

PRIVATE: You're welcome, slick operator.

(PUBLIC *is facing the door of his bedroom.* MADGE *enters the kitchen from the scullery.*)

PUBLIC: What'ya say, li'l chick, you and me – you know – I'll spell it out for ya ifya like.

(*Winks, and clicks his tongue.*)

PRIVATE: You say the cutest things, big handsome boy!

PUBLIC: A malted milk at the corner drug-store?

PRIVATE: Wow!

PUBLIC: A movie at the downtown drive-in?

PRIVATE: Wow-wow!

PUBLIC: Two hamburgers, two cokes, two slices of blueberry pie?

PRIVATE: Wow-wow-wow.

PUBLIC: And then afterwards in my apartment –

(MADGE *enters the bedroom.*)

MADGE: Gee, Mary, and Jay! Will you quit them antics!

PUBLIC: Well, you should knock anyway before you enter a man's room!

MADGE: Man! I bathed you every Saturday night till you were a big lout of fourteen! Your tea's cold waiting.

(*She makes towards door. She goes into the kitchen.* PUBLIC *and* PRIVATE *follow her.*)

PUBLIC: How was I to know that?

MADGE: Amn't I hoarse calling you? Dear, but you're in for a cooling when you go across! (*As she passes through the shop door on way to scullery.*) Boss!

PRIVATE: (*In imitation*) 'Boss!'

(*She pauses at the scullery door.*)

MADGE: (*With shy delight*) I forgot to tell you. Nelly had a wee baby this morning.

PUBLIC: Go on!

46

MADGE: A wee girl – 7 lb 4 oz.

PUBLIC: How many's that you have now?

MADGE: Four grandnieces and three grandnephews.
(*Pause.*) And they're going to call this one Madge – at least
so she *says*.

PUBLIC: I'll send it a – a – a – an elephant out of my first wages!
An elephant for wee Madge!

MADGE: I had a feeling it would be a wee girl this time. Maybe
I'll take a run over on Sunday and square the place up for
her. She could do with some help, with seven of them.

PUBLIC: You're a brick, Madge.

MADGE: Aye, so. (*As she goes to scullery.*) Wee Madge,
maybe . . .
(PUBLIC *sits at the table.* PRIVATE *leans against the wall
beside him.*)

PRIVATE: And now what are you sad about? Just because she
lives for those Mulhern children, and gives them whatever
few half-pence she has? Madge, Madge, I think I love you
more than any of them. Give me a piece of your courage,
Madge.
(S.B. *enters from the shop and goes through his nightly routine.
He hangs up the shop keys. He looks at his pocket watch and
checks its time with the clock on the wall. He takes off his
apron, folds it carefully, and leaves it on the back of his chair.
Then he sits down to eat. During all these ponderous jobs*
PRIVATE *keeps up the following chatter:*)
And here comes your pleasure, your little ray of sunshine.
Ladies and Gentlemen, I give you – the one and only – the
inimitable – the irrepressible – the irresistible – County
Councillor – S – B – O'Donnell! (*Trumpet – hummed – fanfare.
Continues in the smooth, unctuous tones of the commentator at a
mannequin parade.*) And this time Marie Celeste is wearing a
cheeky little head-dress by Pamela of Park Avenue,
eminently suitable for cocktail parties, morning coffee, or
just casual shopping. It is of brown Viennese felt, and
contrasts boldly with the attractive beach ensemble, created
by Simon. The pert little apron is detachable – (S.B. *removes
apron*) – thank you, Marie Celeste – and underneath we have

47

the tapered Italian-line slacks in ocelot. I would draw your
attention to the large collar stud which is highly decorative
and can be purchased separately at our boutique. We call
this seductive outfit 'Indiscretion'. It can be worn six days a
week, in or out of bed. (*In polite tone*) Have a seat,
Screwballs.

(S.B. *sits down at the table.*)

Thank you. Remove the hat.

(S.B. *takes off the hat to say grace. He blesses himself.*)

On again. (*Hat on.*) Perfectly trained; the most obedient
father I ever had. And now for our nightly lesson in the
English language. Repeat slowly after me: another day
over.

S.B.: Another day over.

PRIVATE: Good. Next phrase: I suppose we can't complain.

S.B.: I suppose we can't complain.

PRIVATE: Not bad. Now for a little free conversation. But no
obscenities, Father dear; the child is only twenty-five.
(S.B. *eats in silence. Pause.*)
Well, come on, come on! Where's that old rapier wit of
yours, the toast of the Ballybeg coffee houses?

S.B.: Did you set the rat-trap in the store?

PUBLIC: Aye.

PRIVATE: (*Hysterically*) Isn't he a riot! Oh my God, that father
of yours just kills me! But wait – wait – shhh-shhh –

S.B.: I didn't find as many about the year.

PRIVATE: Oooooh God! Priceless! Beautiful! Delightful! 'I
didn't find as many about the year!' Did you ever hear the
beat of that? Wonderful! But isn't he in form tonight? But
isn't he? You know, it's not every night that jewels like
that, pearls of wisdom on rodent reproduction, drop from
those lips! But hold it – hold it – !
(S.B. *takes out a handkerchief, removes his teeth, wraps them in
the handkerchief, and puts them in his pocket.* PRIVATE
exhales with satisfaction.)

PRIVATE: Ah! That's what we were waiting for; complete
informality; total relaxation between intimates. Now we can
carry on. Screwballs. (*Pause.*) I'm addressing you,

48

Screwballs.
(S.B. *clears his throat.*)
Thank you.
(*As the following speech goes on all trace of humour fades from*
PRIVATE'*s voice. He becomes more and more intense and it is*
with an effort that he keeps his voice under control.)
Screwballs, we've eaten together like this for the past
twenty-odd years, and never once in all that time have you
made as much as one unpredictable remark. Now, even
though you refuse to acknowledge the fact, Screwballs, I'm
leaving you forever. I'm going to Philadelphia, to work in
an hotel. And you know why I'm going, Screwballs, don't
you? Because I'm twenty-five, and you treat me as if I were
five – I can't order even a dozen loaves without getting your
permission. Because you pay me less than you pay Madge.
But worse, far worse than that, Screwballs, because *we*
embarrass one another. If one of us were to say, 'You're
looking tired' or 'That's a bad cough you have', the other
would fall over backways with embarrassment. So tonight
d'you know what I want you to do? I want you to make one
unpredictable remark, and even though I'll still be on that
plane tomorrow morning, I'll have doubts: maybe I should
have stuck it out; maybe the old codger did have feelings;
maybe I have maligned the old bastard. So now,
Screwballs, say . . . (*Thinks*) . . . 'Once upon a time a
rainbow ended in our garden' . . . say, 'I like to walk across
the White Strand when there's a misty rain falling' . . . say,
'Gar, son –' say, 'Gar, you bugger you, why don't you stick
it out here with me for it's not such a bad aul bugger of a
place.' Go on. Say it! Say it! Say it!

S.B.: True enough . . .
PUBLIC: (*Almost inaudibly*) Aye?
S.B.: I didn't find as many about the year.
PUBLIC: (*Roars*) Madge! Madge!
S.B.: No need to roar like that.
PUBLIC: The – the – the – bread's done. We need more bread.
S.B.: You know where it's kept, don't you?
  (MADGE *at scullery door.*)

49

PUBLIC: Can we have more bread, Madge . . . please? . . .

MADGE: Huh! Pity you lost the power of your legs.

PUBLIC: I'll—I'll get it myself—it doesn't matter . . .

(*Madge comes over to the table and takes the plate from*
PUBLIC. *She gives* S.B. *a hard look.*)

MADGE: (*Irony*) The chatting in this place would deafen a body.
Won't the house be quiet soon enough—long enough?
(*She shuffles off with the plate.*)

PRIVATE: Tick-tock-tick-tock-tick-tock. It is now sixteen or
seventeen years since I saw the Queen of France, then the
Dauphiness, at Versailles . . . Go on! What's the next line?
(S.B. *produces a roll of money from his pocket and puts it on the
table.*)

S.B.: I suppose you'll be looking for your pay.

PUBLIC: I earned it.

S.B.: I'm not saying you didn't. It's all there—you needn't count
it.

PUBLIC: I didn't say I was going to count it, did I?

PRIVATE: Tick-tock-tick-tock-tick-tock—

PUBLIC: More tea?

S.B.: Sure you know I never take a second cup.

PRIVATE: (*Imitating*) 'Sure you know I never take a second
cup.' (*Brittle and bright again.*) Okay, okay, okay, it's better
this way, Screwballs, isn't it? You can't teach new tricks to
two old dogs like us. In the meantime there's a little matter
I'd like to discuss with you, Screwballs . . . (*With
exaggerated embarrassment*) it's—it's nothing really . . . it's
just something I'm rather hesitant to bring up, but I'm
advised by the very best Church authorities that you'll be
only too glad to discuss it with your son. Admittedly we're
both a bit late in attacking the issue now, but—ha—you
see—

(MADGE *enters with a plate of bread.* PRIVATE *makes a very
obvious show of changing the subject.*)

Oh marvellous weather—truly wonderful for the time of
year—a real heat wave—all things considered—

MADGE: A body couldn't get a word in edgeways with you two!

PRIVATE: Madge has such a keen sense of humour, don't you

agree? I love people with a sense of humour, don't you? It's
the first thing I look for in a person. I seize them by the
throat and say to them, 'Have you a sense of humour?' And
then, if they have, I feel – I feel _at home_ with them
immediately . . . But where was I? Oh, yes – our little
talk – I'm beginning to wonder, Screwballs – I suspect – I'm
afraid – (_In a rush, ashamed_) – I think I'm a sex maniac!
(_Throws his hands up._) Please, please don't cry, Screwballs;
please don't say anything; and above all please don't stop
eating. Just – just let me talk a bit more – let me
communicate with someone – that's what they all
advise – communicate – pour out your pent-up feelings into
a sympathetic ear. So all I ask for the moment is that you
listen – just listen to me. As I said, I suspect that I'm an
s.m. (_Rapidly, in self-defence_) But I'm not the only one,
Screwballs; oh indeed I am not; all the boys around – some
of them are far worse than I am. (_As if he had been asked the
question._) Why? Why do I think we're all s.ms.? Well,
because none of us is married. Because we're never done
boasting about the number of hot courts we know – and the
point is we're all virgins. Because –
(_Voices off._)
Shhhh! Someone's coming. Not a word to anybody. This is
our secret. Scouts' honour.
(_Enter_ MASTER BOYLE _from the scullery. He is around sixty,
white-haired, handsome, defiant. He is shabbily dressed; his
eyes, head, hands, arms are constantly moving – he sits for a
moment and rises again – he puts his hands in his pockets and
takes them out again – his eyes roam around the room but see
nothing._ S.B. _is barely courteous to him._)

S.B.: Oh, good night, Master Boyle. How are you doing?

PUBLIC: Master.

BOYLE: Sean. Gar. No, no, don't stir. I only dropped in for a
second.

PUBLIC: Sit over and join us.

BOYLE: No. I'm not stopping.

S.B.: Here's a seat for you. I was about to go out to the shop
anyway to square up a bit.

BOYLE: Don't let me hold you back.

S.B.: I'll be in again before you leave, Master.

BOYLE: If you have work to do . . .

PRIVATE: (*To* S.B.) Ignorant bastard! (*Looking at* BOYLE.) On his way to the pub! God, but he's a sorry wreck too, arrogant and pathetic. And yet whatever it is about you . . .

BOYLE: Tomorrow morning, isn't it?

PUBLIC: Quarter past seven. I'm getting the mail van the length of Strabane.

BOYLE: You're doing the right thing, of course. You'll never regret it. I gather it's a vast restless place that doesn't give a curse about the past; and that's the way things should be. Impermanence and anonymity – it offers great attractions. You've heard about the latest to-do?

PUBLIC: Another row with the Canon? I really hadn't heard –

BOYLE: But the point is he can't sack me! The organization's behind me and he can't budge me. Still, it's a . . . a bitter victory to hold on to a job when your manager wants rid of you.

PUBLIC: Sure everybody knows the kind of the Canon, Master.

BOYLE: I didn't tell you, did I, that I may be going out there myself?

PRIVATE: Poor bastard.

BOYLE: I've been offered a big post in Boston, head of education in a reputable university there. They've given me three months to think it over. What are you going to do?

PUBLIC: Work in an hotel.

BOYLE: You have a job waiting for you?

PUBLIC: In Philadelphia.

BOYLE: You'll do all right. You're young and strong and of average intelligence.

PRIVATE: Good old Boyle. Get the dig in.

BOYLE: Yes, it was as ugly and as squalid as all the other to-dos – before the whole school – the priest and the teacher – dedicated moulders of the mind. You're going to stay with friends?

PUBLIC: With Aunt Lizzy.

BOYLE: Of course.

52

PRIVATE: Go on. Try him.

PUBLIC: You knew her, didn't you, Master?

BOYLE: Yes, I knew all the Gallagher girls: Lizzy, Una, Rose, Agnes . . .

PRIVATE: And Maire, my mother, did you love her?

BOYLE: A long, long time ago . . . in the past . . . He comes in to see your father every night, doesn't he?

PUBLIC: The Canon? Oh, it's usually much later than this –

BOYLE: I think so much about him that – ha – I feel a peculiar attachment for him. Funny, isn't it? Do you remember the Christmas you sent me the packet of cigarettes? And the day you brought me a pot of jam to the digs? It was you, wasn't it?

PRIVATE: Poor Boyle –

BOYLE: All children are born with generosity. Three months they gave me to make up my mind.

PUBLIC: I remember very well –

BOYLE: By the way – (*Producing a small book*) a little something to remind you of your old teacher – my poems –

PUBLIC: Thank you very much.

BOYLE: I had them printed privately last month. Some of them are a bit mawkish but you'll not notice any distinction.

PUBLIC: I'm very grateful, Master.

BOYLE: I'm not going to give you advice, Gar. Is that clock right? Not that you would heed it even if I did; you were always obstinate –

PRIVATE: Tch, tch.

BOYLE: But I would suggest that you strike out on your own as soon as you find your feet out there. Don't keep looking back over your shoulder. Be one hundred per cent American.

PUBLIC: I'll do that.

BOYLE: There's an inscription on the fly-leaf. By the way, Gar, you couldn't lend me 10s until – ha – I was going to say until next week but you'll be gone by then.

PUBLIC: Surely, surely.

BOYLE: I seem to have come out without my wallet . . .

PRIVATE: Give him the quid.

53

(PUBLIC *gives over a note.* BOYLE *does not look at it.*)

BOYLE: Fine. I'll move on now. Yes, I knew all the Gallagher girls from Bailtefree, long, long ago. Maire and Una and Rose and Lizzy and Agnes and Maire, your mother . . .

PRIVATE: You might have been my father.

BOYLE: Oh, another thing I meant to ask you: should you come across any newspapers or magazines over there that might be interested in an occasional poem, perhaps you would send me some addresses –

PUBLIC: I'll keep an eye out.

BOYLE: Not that I write as much as I should. You know how you get caught up in things. But you have your packing to do, and I'm talking too much as usual.
(*He holds out his hand and they shake hands. He does not release* PUBLIC's *hand.*)
Good luck, Gareth.

PUBLIC: Thanks, Master.

BOYLE: Forget Ballybeg and Ireland.

PUBLIC: It's easier said.

BOYLE: Perhaps you'll write me.

PUBLIC: I will indeed.

BOYLE: Yes, the first year. Maybe the second. I'll – I'll miss you, Gar.

PRIVATE: For God's sake get a grip on yourself.

PUBLIC: Thanks for the book and for –
(BOYLE *embraces* PUBLIC *briefly.*)

PRIVATE: Stop it! Stop it! Stop it!
(BOYLE *breaks away and goes quickly off through the scullery. He bumps into* MADGE *who is entering.*)

MADGE: Lord, the speed of him! His tongue out for a drink!

PRIVATE: Quick! Into your room!

MADGE: God knows I don't blame the Canon for wanting rid of that –
(PUBLIC *rushes to the bedroom.* PRIVATE *follows.*)
Well! The manners about this place!
(*She gathers up the tea things.* PUBLIC *stands inside the bedroom door, his hands up to his face.* PRIVATE *stands at his elbow, speaking urgently into his ear.*)

PRIVATE: Remember – you're going! At 7.15. You're still going! He's nothing but a drunken aul schoolmaster – a conceited, arrogant wash-out! ✓

PUBLIC: O God, the Creator and Redeemer of all the faithful –

PRIVATE: Get a grip on yourself! Don't be a damned sentimental fool! (*Sings*) 'Philadelphia, here I come –'

PUBLIC: Maire and Una and Rose and Agnes and Lizzy and Maire –

PRIVATE: Yessir, you're going to cut a bit of a dash in them thar States! Great big sexy dames and night clubs and high living and films and dances and –

PUBLIC: Kathy, my own darling Kathy –

PRIVATE: (*Sings*) 'Where bowers of flowers bloom in the spring'

PUBLIC: I don't – I can't –

PRIVATE: (*Sings*) 'Each morning at dawning, everything is bright and gay/A sun-kissed miss says Don't be late –' Sing up, man!

PUBLIC: I – I – I –

PRIVATE: (*Sings*) 'That's why I can hardly wait.'

PUBLIC: (*Sings limply*) 'Philadelphia, here I come.'   *Scars on his soul:*

PRIVATE: That's it, laddybuck!

TOGETHER: 'Philadelphia, here I come.'   *Gor – Grew up motherless*
– Dropped out of U.
– Not "respectable enough" for Kathy Doogan

Curtain

Responses to soul's pain: 1) Prayerful ejaculations 2) Song (incl. Philadelphia) 3) Drunken Friend

EPISODE TWO

A short time later. PUBLIC *is lying on the bed, his hands behind his head.* PRIVATE *is slumped in the chair, almost as if he were dozing.* PUBLIC *sings absently.*

PUBLIC: (*Sings*)
Last night she came to me, she came softly in,
So softly she came that her feet made no din,
And she laid her hand on me, and this she did say,
'It will not be long love till our wedding day'.

(*When the singing stops there is a moment of silence. Then, suddenly,* PRIVATE *springs to his feet.*)

PRIVATE: What the bloody hell are you at, O'Donnell? Snap out of it, man! Get up and keep active! The devil makes work for idle hands! It is now sixteen or seventeen years since I saw the Queen of France, then the Dauphiness, at Versailles.

(PUBLIC *goes off the bed and begins taking clothes from the chest of drawers and putting them into his case.*)

PRIVATE: (*Lilting to a mad air of his own making*)
Ta-ra-del-oo-del-ah-dol-de-dol-de-dol-del-ah – (*Continuing as rapidly as he can speak*) – Tell me this and tell me no more: Why does a hen cross the road?

PUBLIC: Why?

PRIVATE: To get to the other side. Ha-ha! Why does a hen lay an egg?

PUBLIC: Why?

PRIVATE: Because it can't lay a brick. Yo-ho. Why does a sailor wear a round hat?

PUBLIC: Why?

PRIVATE: To cover his head. Hee-hee-hee. Nought out of three; very bad for a man of average intelligence. That's the style. Keep working; keep the mind active and well stretched by knowing the best that is thought and written in the world, and you wouldn't call Daddy Senator your father-in-law. (*Sings.*)

    Give the woman in the bed more porter
    Give the man beside her water
    Give the woman in the bed more porter
    More porter for the woman in the bed.

(*Confidentially*) D'you know what I think, laddie, I mean, just looking at you there.

PUBLIC: What?

PRIVATE: You'd make a hell of a fine President of the United States.

(PUBLIC *straightens up and for a second surveys the room with the keen eye of a politician. Relaxes again.*)

PUBLIC: Agh!

56

PRIVATE: But you would!

PUBLIC: You need to be born an American citizen.

PRIVATE: True for you. What about Chairman of General Motors?

(PUBLIC *shrugs indifferently*.)

Boss of the Teamsters' Union?

(PUBLIC *shrugs his indifference*.)

PRIVATE: Hollywood – what about Hollywood?

PUBLIC: Not what it was.

PRIVATE: Dammit but you're hard to please too. Still, there must be something great in store for you. (*Cracks his fingers at his brainwave*.) The US Senate! Senator Gareth O'Donnell, Chairman of the Foreign Aid Committee! (*He interviews* PUBLIC *who continues packing his clothes busily*.)

Is there something you would like to say, Senator, before you publish the findings of your committee?

PUBLIC: Nothing to say.

PRIVATE: Just a few words.

PUBLIC: No comment.

PRIVATE: Isn't it a fact that suspicion has fallen on Senator Doogan?

PUBLIC: Nothing further to add.

PRIVATE: Did your investigators not discover that Senator Doogan is the grandfather of fourteen unborn illegitimate children? That he sold his daughter to the king of the fairies for a crock of gold? That a Chinese spy known to the FBI as Screwballs –

PUBLIC: Screwballs?

PRIVATE: Screwballs.

PUBLIC: Describe him.

PRIVATE: Tall, blond, athletic-looking –

PUBLIC: Military moustache?

PRIVATE: – very handsome; uses a diamond-studded cigarette-holder.

PUBLIC: Usually accompanied by a dark seductive woman in a low-cut evening gown?

PRIVATE: – wears a monocle, fluent command of languages –

PUBLIC: But seldom speaks? A man of few words?

PRIVATE: – drives a cream convertible, villas in Istanbul, Cairo and Budapest –

PUBLIC: (*Declaims*) Merchant Prince, licensed to deal in tobacco –

PRIVATE: An' sowl! That's me man! To a T! The point is – what'll we do with him?

PUBLIC: Sell him to a harem?

PRIVATE: Hide his cascara sagrada?

(MADGE *comes into the kitchen to lift the tablecloth.*)

PUBLIC: (*Serious*) Shhh!

PRIVATE: The boys? Is it the boys? To say good-bye?

PUBLIC: Shhhh!

PRIVATE: It's Madge – aul fluke-feet Madge.

(*They both stand listening to the sound of* MADGE *flapping across the kitchen and out to the scullery.*)

PUBLIC: (*Calls softly*) Madge.

(PRIVATE *drops into the armchair.* PUBLIC *stands listening until the sound has died away.*)

PRIVATE: (*Wearily*) Off again! You know what you're doing, don't you, laddybuck? Collecting memories and images and impressions that are going to make you bloody miserable; and in a way that's what you want, isn't it?

PUBLIC: Bugger!

(PRIVATE *springs to his feet again. With forced animation.*)

PRIVATE: Bugger's right! Bugger's absolutely correct! Back to the job! Keep occupied. Be methodical.
Eanie-meanie-minie-mow
Catch-the-baby-by-the-toe.
Will all passengers holding immigration visas please come this way.

(PUBLIC *produces documents from a drawer. He checks them.*)

PRIVATE: Passport?

PUBLIC: Passport.

PRIVATE: Visa?

PUBLIC: Visa.

PRIVATE: Vaccination cert.?

PUBLIC: Vaccination cert.

PRIVATE: Currency?

PUBLIC: Eighty dollars.

PRIVATE: Sponsorship papers?

PUBLIC: Signed by Mr Conal Sweeney.

PRIVATE: Uncle Con and Aunt Lizzy. Who made the whole thing possible. Read her letter again – strictly for belly-laughs.

PUBLIC: (*Reads*) Dear Nephew Gar, Just a line to let you know that your Uncle Con and me have finalized all the plans –

PRIVATE: Uncle Con and I.

PUBLIC: – and we will meet you at the airport and welcome you and bring you to our apartment which you will see is located in a pretty nice locality and you will have the spare room which has TV and air-conditioning and window meshes and your own bathroom with a shower –

PRIVATE: Adjacent to RC church. No children. Other help kept.

PUBLIC: You will begin at the Emperor Hotel on Monday 23rd which is only about twenty minutes away.

PRIVATE: Monsieur, madam.

PUBLIC: Con says it is a fine place for to work in and the owner is Mr Patrick Palinakis who is half-Irish –

PRIVATE: Patrick.

PUBLIC: – and half-Greek.

PRIVATE: Palinakis.

PUBLIC: His grandfather came from County Mayo,

PRIVATE: By the hokey! The Greek from Belmullet!

PUBLIC: We know you will like it here and work hard.

PRIVATE: (*Rapidly*) Monsieur-madam-monsieur-madam-monsieur-madam –

PUBLIC: We remember our short trip to Ireland last September with happy thoughts and look forward to seeing you again. Sorry we missed your father that day. We had Ben Burton in to dinner last evening. He sends his regards.

PRIVATE: Right sort, Ben.

PUBLIC: Until we see you at the airport, all love, Elise.

PRIVATE: 'Elise'! Dammit, Lizzy Gallagher, but you came up in the world.

59

PUBLIC: PS About paying back the passage money which you mentioned in your last letter – desist! – no one's crying about it.

PRIVATE: Aye, Ben Burton was a right skin.

PUBLIC: (*Remembering*) September 8th.

PRIVATE: By God Lizzy was in right talking form that day –

PUBLIC: 'You are invited to attend the wedding of Miss Kathleen Doogan of Gortmore House –'

PRIVATE: (*Snaps*) Shut up, O'Donnell! You've got to quit this moody drivelling! (*Coaxing*) They arrived in the afternoon; remember? A beautiful quiet harvest day, the sun shining, not a breath of wind; and you were on your best behaviour. And Madge – remember? Madge was as huffy as hell with the carry-on of them, and you couldn't take your eyes off Aunt Lizzy, your mother's sister – so this was your mother's sister – remember?

(*Three people have moved into the kitchen:* CON SWEENEY, LIZZY SWEENEY, *and* BEN BURTON. *All three are in the fifty-five to sixty region.* BURTON *is American, the* SWEENEYS *Irish-American.* CON SWEENEY *sits at the kitchen table with* BEN BURTON. LIZZY *moves around in the centre of the kitchen.* PUBLIC *stands at the door of his bedroom.* PRIVATE *hovers around close to* PUBLIC. *The three guests have glasses in their hands. None of them is drunk, but* LIZZY *is more than usually garrulous. She is a small energetic woman, heavily made-up, impulsive.* CON, *her husband, is a quiet, patient man.* BURTON, *their friend, sits smiling at his glass most of the time. As she talks* LIZZY *moves from one to the other, and she has the habit of putting her arm around, or catching the elbow of, the person she is addressing. This constant physical touching is new and disquieting to* PUBLIC. *A long laugh from* LIZZY:)

LIZZY: Anyhow, there we are, all sitting like stuffed ducks in the front seat – Una and Agnes and Rose and Mother and me – you know – and mother dickied up in her good black shawl and everything – and up at the altar rails there's Maire all by herself and her shoulders are sorta working – you know – and you couldn't tell whether she was crying or giggling – she was a helluva one for giggling – but maybe she

60

was crying that morning – I don't know –

CON: Get on with the story, honey.

LIZZY: (*With dignity*) Would you please desist from bustin' in
on me?

(CON *spreads his hands in resignation.*)

LIZZY: But listen to this – this'll kill you – Mother's here, see?
And Agnes is here and I'm here. And Agnes leans across
Mother to me – you know – and she says in this helluva loud
voice – she says – (*Laughs*) – this really does kill me – she
says – in this whisper of hers – and you know the size of
Bailtefree chapel; couldn't swing a cat in that
place – (*Suddenly anxious.*) That chapel's still there, isn't it?
It hasn't fell down or nothing, has it?

CON: (*Dryly*) Unless it fell down within the last couple of hours.
We drove up there this morning. Remember?

LIZZY: (*Relieved*) Yeah. So we did. Fine place. Made me feel
kinda – you know – what the hell was I talking about?

BEN: Agnes leaned over to you and said –

(LIZZY *puts her arm around him and kisses the crown of his
head.*)

LIZZY: Thanks, Ben. A great friend with a great memory! I'll
tell you, Gar, Ben Burton's one hundred per cent. The first
and best friend we made when we went out. (*To* CON.)
Right, honey?

CON: Right.

LIZZY: Way back in '37.

CON: '38.

LIZZY: (*Loudly*) October 23rd, 19 and 37 we sailed for the
United States of America. (CON *spreads his hands.*) Nothing
in our pockets. No job to go to. And what does Ben do?

CON: A guy in a million.

LIZZY: He gives us this apartment. He gives us dough. He gives
us three meals a day – until Bonzo (CON) finally gets himself
this job. Looks after us like we were his own skin and bone.
Right, honey?

CON: Right.

LIZZY: So don't let nobody say nothing against Ben Burton.
Then when he (CON) gets this job in this downtown store –

61

CON: First job was with the construction company.

LIZZY: Would you please desist? (CON *spreads hands.*) His first job was with Young and Pecks, hauling out them packing cases and things; and then he moved to the construction company, and *then* we got a place of our own.

PUBLIC: You were telling us about that morning.

LIZZY: What's he talking about?

PUBLIC: The day my father and mother got married.

LIZZY: That day! Wasn't that something? With the wind howling and the rain slashing about! And Mother, poor Mother, may God be good to her, she thought that just because Maire got this guy with a big store we should all of got guys with big stores. And poor Maire – we were so alike in every way, Maire and me. But he was good to her. I'll say that for S. B. O'Donnell – real good to her. Where the hell is he anyhow? Why will S. B. O'Donnell, my brother-in-law, not meet me?

CON: He (PUBLIC) told you – he's away at a wedding.

LIZZY: What wedding?

CON: Some local girl and some Dublin doc.

LIZZY: What local girl? You think I'm a stranger here or something?

CON: (*To* PUBLIC) What local girl?

PUBLIC: Senator Doogan's daughter.

PRIVATE: Kathy.

LIZZY: Never heard of him. Some Johnny-hop-up. When did they start having senators about this place for Gawd's sakes?

BEN: (*To* PUBLIC) You have a senate in Dublin, just like our Senate, don't you?

LIZZY: Don't you start telling me nothing about my own country, Ben. You got your own problems to look after. Just you leave me to manage this place, okay?

BEN: Sorry, Elise.

LIZZY: Ben! (*She kisses the top of his head.*) Only that I'm a good Irish-American Catholic – (*To* PUBLIC) and believe me, they don't come much better than that – and only that I'm stuck with Rudolph Valentino (CON) I'd take a chance with Ben Burton any day (*Kisses him again.*) black Lutheran and all that he is.

(MADGE *appears at the door of the shop. She refuses to look at the visitors. Her face is tight with disapproval. Her accent is very precise.*)

MADGE: Are there any *Clarions* to spare or are they all ordered?

PUBLIC: They're all ordered, Madge.

LIZZY: Doing big deals out there, honey, huh?

MADGE: Thank you, Gareth.

(MADGE *withdraws.*)

LIZZY: 'Thank you, Gareth!'

(*She giggles to herself.*)

CON: Honey! (*To* PUBLIC) You'll think about what we were discussing?

PUBLIC: I will, Uncle Con.

CON: The job's as good as you'll get and we'd be proud to have you.

LIZZY: Don't force him.

CON: I'm not forcing him. I'm only telling him.

LIZZY: Well now you've told him – a dozen times. So now desist, will you?

(CON *spreads his hands.*)

PUBLIC: I will think about it. Really.

LIZZY: Sure! Sure! Typical Irish! He will think about it! And while he's thinking about it the store falls in about his head! What age are you? Twenty-four? Twenty-five? What are you waiting for? For S.B. to run away to sea? Until the weather gets better?

CON: Honey!

LIZZY: I'm talking straight to the kid! He's Maire's boy and I've got an interest in him – the only nephew I have. (*To* BEN.) Am I right or am I wrong?

BEN: I'm still up in Bailtefree chapel.

LIZZY: Where? (*Confidentially to* CON) Give him no more to drink. (*Patiently to* BEN) You're sitting in the home of S. B. O'Donnell and my deceased sister, Maire, Ben.

CON: You were telling us a story about the morning they got married, honey, in Bailtefree chapel.

LIZZY: Yeah, I know, I know, but you keep busting in on me.

PUBLIC: You were about to tell us what Agnes whispered to you.

LIZZY: (*Crying*) Poor Aggie – dead. Maire – dead. Rose,
Una, Lizzy – dead – all gone – all dead and gone . . .

CON: Honey, you're Lizzy.

LIZZY: So what?

CON: Honey, you're not dead.

LIZZY: (*Regarding* CON *cautiously*) You gone senile all of a
sudden? (*Confidentially to* BEN) Give him no more to drink.
(*To* CON) For Gawd's sakes who says I'm dead?

BEN: You're very much alive, Elise.
(*She goes to him and gives him another kiss.*)

LIZZY: Thank you, Ben. A great friend with a great intellect.
Only one thing wrong with Ben Burton: he's a black
Baptist.

BEN: Just for the record, Gar, I'm Episcopalian.

LIZZY: Episcopalian – Lutheran – Baptist – what's the
difference? As our pastor, Father O'Flaherty, says – 'My
dear brethren,' he says, 'Let the whole cart-load of them,
and the whole zoo of them, be to thee as the Pharisee and
the publican.'

CON: Honey!

LIZZY: But he's still the best friend we have. And we
have many good, dear, kind friends in the US.
Right, honey?

CON: Right.

LIZZY: But when it comes to holding a candle to Ben
Burton – look – comparisons are – he's not in the halfpenny
place with them!

BEN: (*Laughing*) Bang on, Elise!

LIZZY: Am I right or am I wrong?

CON: Honey!

LIZZY: (*To* PUBLIC) And that's why I say to you: America's
Gawd's own country. Ben?

BEN: Don't ask me. I was born there.

LIZZY: What d'ya mean – 'Don't ask me?' I am asking you. He
should come out or he should not – which is it?

BEN: It's just another place to live, Elise: Ireland – America –
what's the difference?

LIZZY: You tell him, honey. You tell him the set-up we have.

64

(*Now with growing urgency, to* PUBLIC.) We have this
ground-floor apartment, see, and a car that's
air-conditioned, and colour TV, and this big collection of
all the Irish records you ever heard, and fifteen thousand
bucks in Federal Bonds –

CON: Honey.

LIZZY: – and a deep freezer and – and – and a back yard with
this great big cherry tree, and squirrels and night-owls and
the smell of lavender in the spring and long summer
evenings and snow at Christmas and a Christmas tree in the
parlour and – and – and –

CON: Elise . . .

LIZZY: And it's all so Gawd-awful because we have no one to
share it with us . . .
(*She begins to sob.*)

CON: (*Softly*) It's okay, honey, okay . .

LIZZY: He's my sister's boy – the only child of five girls of us –

BEN: I'll get the car round the front.
(BEN *goes off through the scullery.*)

LIZZY: – and we spent a fortune on doctors, didn't we, Connie,
but it was no good, and then I says to him (CON), 'We'll go
home to Ireland,' I says, 'and Maire's boy, we'll offer him
everything we have –'

PRIVATE: (*Terrified*) No. No.

LIZZY: '– everything, and maybe we could coax him – you
know –' maybe it was sorta bribery – I dunno – but he
would have everything we ever gathered –

PRIVATE: Keep it! Keep it!

LIZZY: – and all the love we had in us –

PRIVATE: No! No!

CON: Honey, we've a long drive back to the hotel.

LIZZY: (*Trying to control herself*) That was always the kind of us
Gallagher girls, wasn't it . . . either laughing or crying . . .
you know, sorta silly and impetuous, shooting our big
mouths off, talking too much, not like the O'Donnells – you
know – kinda cold –

PRIVATE: Don't man, don't.

CON: Your gloves, honey. It's been a heavy day.

65

LIZZY: (*To* PUBLIC, *with uncertain dignity*) Tell your father that
we regret we did not have the opportunity for to make his
acquaintance again after all these –
PUBLIC: (*Impetuously*) I want to go to America – if you'll have me –
PRIVATE: Laddy!
CON: Sure. You think about it, son. You think about it.
PUBLIC: Now – as soon as I can, Aunt Lizzy – I mean it –
LIZZY: Gar? (*To* CON, *as if for confirmation*) Honey?
CON: Look son –
LIZZY: To us, Gar? To come to us? To our home?
CON: Ben's waiting, Elise.
PUBLIC: If you'll have me . . .
LIZZY: If we'll have him, he says; he says if we'll have him!
That's why I'm here! That's why I'm half-shot-up!
(*She opens her arms and approaches him.*)
Oh Gar, my son –
PRIVATE: Not yet! Don't touch me yet!
(LIZZY *throws her arms around him and cries happily.*)
LIZZY: My son, Gar, Gar, Gar . . .
PRIVATE: (*Softly, with happy anguish*) God . . . my God . . .
Oh, my God . . .

(*Black-out*)

(*When the bedroom light goes up* PUBLIC *and* PRIVATE *are there.
The kitchen is empty.* PUBLIC *bangs the lid of his case shut and*
PRIVATE *stands beside him, jeering at him. While this taunting
goes on* PUBLIC *tries to escape by fussing about the room.*)
PRIVATE: September 8th, the sun shining, not a breath of
wind – and this was your mother's sister – remember? And
that's how you were got! Right, honey? Silly and impetuous
like a Gallagher! Regrets?
PUBLIC: None.
PRIVATE: Uncertainties?
PUBLIC: None.
PRIVATE: Little tiny niggling reservations?
PUBLIC: None.
PRIVATE: Her grammar?

66

PUBLIC: Shut up!

PRIVATE: But, honey, wasn't it something?

PUBLIC: Go to hell.

PRIVATE: Her vulgarity?

PUBLIC: Bugger off.

PRIVATE: She'll tuck you into your air-conditioned cot every night.

(PUBLIC, *so that he won't hear, begins to whistle* 'Philadelphia, Here I Come!')

PRIVATE: And croon, 'Sleep well, my li'l honey child.'

(PUBLIC *whistles determinedly.*)

She got you soft on account of the day it was, didn't she?

(PUBLIC *whistles louder.*)

And because she said you were an O'Donnell – 'cold like'.

PUBLIC: It is now sixteen or seventeen years since I saw the Queen of France –

PRIVATE: But of course when she threw her arms around you – well, well, well!

PUBLIC: – then the Dauphiness, at Versailles –

PRIVATE: Poor little orphan boy!

PUBLIC: Shut up! Shut up!

PRIVATE: (*In child's voice*) Ma-ma . . . Ma-ma.

(PUBLIC *flings open the bedroom door and dashes into the kitchen.* PRIVATE *follows behind.*)

PUBLIC: Madge!

PRIVATE: (*Quietly, deliberately*) You don't want to go, laddybuck. Admit it. You don't want to go.

(MADGE *enters from the scullery.*)

PUBLIC: (*Searching for an excuse*) I can't find my coat. I left it in my room.

(MADGE *gives him a long, patient look, goes to the nail below the school clock, lifts down the coat, and hands it to him. He takes it from her and goes towards the scullery door.*)

PUBLIC: If you would only learn to leave things where you find them you wouldn't be such a bad aul nuisance.

(PUBLIC *and* PRIVATE *go off.*)

MADGE: (Calls) Don't you dare come home drunk!

(PUBLIC's *head appears round the door.*)

PUBLIC: (*Softly*) I'm going to say good-bye to the boys over a quiet drink or two. And how I spend my nights is a matter entirely for myself.

MADGE: 'The Boys!' Couldn't even come here to say good-bye to you on your last night.

PRIVATE: Straight to the bone!

PUBLIC: Just you mind your business and I'll mind mine.

MADGE: How many of them are getting the pension now?

PUBLIC: And in case you're in bed when I get back I want a call at half-six.

MADGE: The clock'll be set. If you hear it well and good.

(PUBLIC *disappears.* MADGE *fusses about the kitchen until* S.B. *enters from the shop. He has a newspaper in his hand and sits at the top of the table. She watches him as he reads. She adjusts a few things. She looks back at him, then suddenly, on the point of tears, she accuses him.*)

MADGE: You sit there, night after night, year after year, reading that aul paper, and not a tooth in your head! If you had any decency in you at all, you would keep them plates in while there's a lady in your presence!

S.B.: (*Puzzled*) Eh?

MADGE: I mean it. It – it – it – it just drives me mad, the sight of you! (*The tears begin to come.*) And I have that much work to do: the stairs have to be washed down, and the store's to be swept, and your room has to be done out – and – and – I'm telling you I'll be that busy for the next couple of weeks that I won't have time to lift my head!

(*She dashes off.* S.B. *stares after her, then out at the audience. Then, very slowly, he looks down at the paper again – it has been upside down – and turns it right side up. But he can't read. He looks across at* GAR's *bedroom, sighs, rises, and exits very slowly to the shop. Silence for a second after* S.B. *leaves. The silence is suddenly shattered by the boisterous arrival of the boys and* GAR. *We hear their exaggerated laughter and talk outside before they burst in. When they enter they take over the kitchen, sprawling on chairs, hunting for tumblers for the stout they produce from their pockets, taking long, deep pulls on their cigarettes, giving the impression that they are busy, purposeful,*

68

*randy gents about to embark on some exciting adventure. But
their bluster is not altogether convincing. There is something
false about it. Tranquillity is their enemy: they fight it valiantly.
At the beginning of this scene* GAR *is flattered that the boys have
come to him. When they consistently refuse to acknowledge his
leaving – or perhaps because he is already spiritually gone from
them – his good humour deserts him. He becomes apart from the
others.* NED *is the leader of the group.* TOM *is his feed-man,
subserviently watching for every cue.* JOE, *the youngest of the
trio, and not yet fully committed to the boys' way of life, is torn
between fealty to* NED *and* TOM *and a spontaneous and simple
loneliness over* GAR'S *departure. Nothing would suit him better
than a grand loud send-off party. But he cannot manage this,
and his loyalty is divided. He is patently gauche, innocent,
obvious.*)

NED: There's only one way to put the fear of God up them
   bastards – (*Points to his boot.*) – every time – you know
   where.

JOE: Who's the ref, Ned?

TOM: Jimmy Pat Barney from Bunmornan. (*Guardedly to*
   PUBLIC) Where's the aul fella?

PUBLIC: Haven't a bloody clue. Probably in the shop. Relax,
   man.

NED: That (*the boot*) or the knee – it's the only game them gets
   can play; and we can play it too.

TOM: (*Relaxing*) They've a hell of a forward line all the same,
   Ned.

NED: They'll be in crutches this day week. By God, I can hardly
   wait to get the studs planted in wee Bagser Doran's face!
   (*He crashes his fist into the palm of his hand.*)

TOM: All the same, Jimmy Pat Barney's the get would put you
   off very quick.

NED: He won't say a word to me. He knows his match when he
   meets it.
   (TOM *laughs appreciatively.* MADGE *appears at the scullery
   door.*)

MADGE: (*Coldly*) Just thought I heard somebody whispering. So
   youse finally made it.

JOE: (*Holding up glass.*) True to our word, Madge, that's us!

PUBLIC: (*Happily*) They were on their way here when I ran into them.

MADGE: Aye, so. (NED *belches.*) Mister Sweeney, too; gentlemanly as ever.

NED: (*Slapping his knee*) Come on away over here and I'll take some of the starch out of you, Madge Mulhern. How long is it since a fella gripped your knee? Haaaaaaaaaaaa!

MADGE: None of your smutty talk here, Mister Sweeney. And if the boss comes in and finds them bottles –

PUBLIC: I'll keep them in order, Madge.

MADGE: 'Boys'! How are you!

(*She goes out.*)

TOM: (*Calling*) You're jealous because you're past it – that's what's wrong with you. Right, Ned?

PUBLIC: (*Raising glass*) Well, boys, when you're lining out on the pitch, you can think of me, because I'll be thinking of you.

JOE: (*Earnestly*) Lucky bloody man, Gar. God, I wish I was in your –

NED: (*Quickly*) By the way, lads, who's the blondie thing I seen at the last Mass on Sunday?

TOM: A big red-head?

NED: Are you bloody well deaf! A blondie! She wouldn't be Maggie Hanna's niece, would she?

TOM: There was two of them, sitting over near the box?

NED: I seen one.

TOM: 'Cos they're English. Staying at the hotel. But the big red thing – she's one of Neil McFadden's girls.

NED: Annie? Is Annie home?

JOE: Aye, she is. So I heard the mammy saying.

NED: Bloody great! That's me fixed up for the next two weeks! Were any of youse ever on that job?

JOE: No, I wasn't, Ned.

TOM: For God's sake, she wouldn't spit on you!

NED: Game as they're going, big Annie. But you need the constitution of a horse. I had her for the fortnight she was home last year and she damned near killed me.

70

PUBLIC: Big Annie from up beyond the quarry?

JOE: You know, Gar – the one with the squint.

NED: (*With dignity*) Annie McFadden has no squint.

PUBLIC: Away and take a running race to yourself, Ned.

NED: (*With quiet threat*) What do you mean?

PUBLIC: You were never out with Big Annie McFadden in your
puff, man.

NED: Are you calling me a liar?

PRIVATE: (*Wearily*) What's the point.

TOM: (*Quickly*) Oh, by God, Ned was there, Gar, many's and
many's the time. Weren't you, Ned?

PUBLIC: Have it your own way.

JOE: (*Nervously*) And maybe she got the squint straightened out
since I saw her last. All the women get the squints
straightened out nowadays. Dammit, you could walk
from here to Cork nowadays and you wouldn't see a woman
with a –

NED: I just don't like fellas getting snottery with me, that's all.
(*There follows an uneasy silence during which* PRIVATE *surveys
the group.*)

PRIVATE: The boys . . . They weren't always like this, were
they? There was a hell of a lot of crack, wasn't there? There
was a hell of a lot of laughing, wasn't there?

TOM: (*Briskly*) Bit of life about the place next week, lads – the
Carnival. Too bad you'll miss it, Gar. By God it was a holy
fright last year, night after night. (*To* NED) Remember?

NED: (*Sulkily*) Bloody cows, the whole bloody lot of them!

TOM: Mind the night with the two wee Greenock pieces?

NED: (*Thawing*) Aw, stop, stop!

TOM: Talk about hot things!

NED: Liveliest wee tramps I ever laid!

TOM: And the fat one from Dublin you picked up at the dance
that night – the one that hauled you down into the ditch!

NED: I was never the same since.

TOM: (*To* PUBLIC) Whatever it is about him (NED), if there's a
fast woman in the country, she'll go for Ned first thing.
Lucky bugger! (*Pause.*) Aye, lucky bugger!
(*Another brief silence. These silences occur like regular cadences.*

71

To defeat them someone always introduces a fresh theme.)

PUBLIC: I'm for off tomorrow, boys.

NED: (*Indifferently*) Aye, so, so . . .

TOM: Brooklyn, isn't it?

PUBLIC: Philadelphia.

TOM: Philadelphia. That's where Jimmy Crerand went to, isn't it? Philadelphia . . .

NED: (*Quickly*) Mind the night Jimmy and us went down to the caves with them Dublin skivvies that was working up at the Lodge? (*To* PUBLIC) Were you? – No, you weren't with us that night.

JOE: Was I there, Ned?

NED: You mind the size of Jimmy? – five foot nothing and scared of his shadow.

PUBLIC: Best goalie we ever had.

NED: One of the women was Gladys and the other was Emmy or something –

TOM: Dammit, I mind now! Gladys and Emmy – that was it, Ned!

NED: Anyhow the rest of us went in for a swim –

TOM: In the bloody pelt!

NED: – and your man Jimmy was left in the cave with the women; and what the hell do they do but whip the trousers off him!

JOE: No, I wasn't there that night.

NED: And the next thing we see is wee Jimmy coming shouting across the White Strand and the two Dublin cows haring after him.

TOM: Not a stab on him!

NED: – and him squealing at the top of his voice, 'Save me, boys, save me!'

TOM: Never drew breath till he reached home!

NED: You (GAR) missed that night.

TOM: 'Save me, boys, save me!'

NED: I don't think we went to bed that night at all.

TOM: You may be sure we didn't.

NED: Powerful.

(*Another silence descends. After a few seconds* PRIVATE *speaks.*)

72

PRIVATE: We were all there that night, Ned. And the girls' names were Gladys and Susan. And they sat on the the rocks dangling their feet in the water. And we sat in the cave, peeping out at them. And then Jimmy Crerand suggested that we go in for a swim; and we all ran to the far end of the shore; and we splashed about like schoolboys. Then we came back to the cave, and wrestled with one another. And then out of sheer boredom, Tom, you suggested that we take the trousers off Crerand – just to prove how manly we all were. But when Ned started towards Jimmy – five foot nothing, remember? – wee Jimmy squared up and defied not only the brave Ned but the whole lot of us. So we straggled back home, one behind the other, and left the girls dangling their feet in the water. And that was that night.

PUBLIC: If the ground's not too hard, you'll do well on Sunday.

NED: Hard or soft – (*Examining his boot.*) – I've a couple of aul scores to settle.

PUBLIC: You'll never get as good a half-back as the one you're losing.

NED: (*Quickly, with pretended interest*) D'you know what I'm thinking? We'd better see about transport.

TOM: Dammit, you're right. I'll get the aul fella's van easy enough. Can you get your Charlie's lorry?

NED: Just maybe. I'd better try him the night.

JOE: What about a song from Gar, boys, before we break up?

NED: What time is it?

JOE: It's early in the night yet.

TOM: Twenty past nine.

NED: We'd better move then; Charlie was talking about going to a dance in Ardmore.

TOM: Dammit, that's an idea!

JOE: We'll all go – a big last night for Gar!

NED: Ardmore? Are you mad? Bloody women in that place don't know what they're for!

TOM: True for you. Scream their heads off if you laid a hand on them.

NED: But I'll tell you what we'll do – call in home first to see
Charlie and then go on to the hotel for a dirty big booze-up.
JOE: I don't like drinking in that place.
NED: Them two English bits – what's their name?
TOM: Them strangers? Agh you wouldn't have a chance there.
They do nothing but walk and look at weeds and stuff –
NED: Who wouldn't have a chance?
TOM: I know, Ned. But them two – they're sort of
stiff-looking – like – like they worked in a post-office or
something.
NED: They're women, aren't they?
TOM: Dammit, we might! . . . Still I don't know . . . They knit
a lot . . . (*To* PUBLIC) What d'you think?
JOE: I vote we stay here.
PUBLIC: And you can count me out. I've an early start.
NED: £10 to a shilling I click with one or other of them!
PUBLIC: I won't be here to collect my winnings.
NED: Come on! Any takers? Never clapped eyes on them and
I'm offering ten notes to a bob!
TOM: Cripes, I know that look in his eyes!
NED: Wise bloody men! The blood's up, lads! Off to the
front! Any volunteers for a big booze-up and a couple of
women?
TOM: Did he say women? Sign me on!
JOE: I don't think I'm in form the night, boys –
NED: We'll show them a weed or two, eh?
TOM: Out to the sandbanks! Get them in the bloody bent!
NED: We're away – Wait! Wait! – How much money have you?
(*They both produce their money – a fistful of small coins.*)
TOM: 2s 6d . . . 2s 11d . . . 3s 3d . . . 3s 5½d.
NED: And I have 6s 2d. It'll have to do. Say a prayer they're fast
and thrifty.
TOM: Dirty aul brute! Lead the way, Bull!
NED: I'm telling you – the blood's up!
TOM: Coming, lads?
PUBLIC: I'm getting up at half six.
NED: (*Casually from the door*) So long, Gar. You know the aul
rule – if you can't be good . . .

74

TOM: Send us a pack of them playing cards – the ones with the dirty pictures on the back!

NED: And if the women are as easy as the money out there, we might think of joining you. (*To* TOM) Right, old cock?

TOM: Bull on regardless! Yaaaaaaaaaaah!

(*They open the door.* NED *hesitates and begins taking off the broad leather belt with the huge brass buckle that supports his trousers.*)

NED: (*Shyly, awkwardly*) By the way, Gar, since I'll not see you again before you go –

TOM: Hi! What are you at? At least wait till you're sure of the women!

NED: (*Impatiently to* TOM) Agh, shut up! (*To* PUBLIC) If any of them Yankee scuts try to beat you up some dark night, you can . . . (*Now he is very confused and flings the belt across the room to* PUBLIC) . . . you know . . . there's a bloody big buckle on it . . . many's a get I scutched with it . . . *Ned is embarassed & gives him his belt!*

TOM: Safe enough, lads: he has braces on as well!

NED: I meant to buy you something good, but the aul fella didn't sell the calf to the jobbers last Friday . . . and he could have, the stupid bastard, such a bloody stupid bastard of an aul fella!

PUBLIC: (*Moved*) Thanks, Ned . . . thanks . . .

JOE: Dammit, I have nothing for you, Gar.

TOM: (*Quickly*) Are we for the sandbanks or are we not?

NED: You'll make out all right over there . . . have a . . .

TOM: I know that look in his eyes!

(NED *wheels rapidly on* TOM, *gives him a more than playful punch, and says savagely:*)

NED: Christ, if there's one get I hate, it's you!

(*He goes off quickly.* TOM *looks uncertainly after him, looks back at* PUBLIC, *and says with dying conviction:*)

TOM: The blood's up . . . Oh, by God, when he goes on like that, the . . . the blood's up all right . . .

(TOM *looks after* NED, *then back to* JOE *and* GAR, *as if he can't decide which to join, then impetuously he dashes off after* NED, *calling:*)

Hi! Ned, Ned, wait for me . . .

(*There is a silence.* PUBLIC *is looking at the belt.* JOE *begins to fidget. Now* PUBLIC *becomes aware of him.*)

PUBLIC: What the hell are you waiting for?

JOE: Dammit, man, like it's your last night and all, and I thought –

PUBLIC: Get to hell and run after them.

JOE: Sure you know yourself they'll hang about the gable of the hotel and chat and do nothing.

PUBLIC: For God's sake, man, those English women will be swept off their feet!

JOE: (*Uncertainly*) You're taking a hand at me now.

PUBLIC: I'm telling you, you're missing the chance of a lifetime.

JOE: Maybe – eh? – what d'you think?

PUBLIC: Go on! Go on!

JOE: God, maybe you're right. You never know what'll happen, eh? You finish that (*drink*) for me! God, maybe we'll click the night! Say a wee prayer we do! Cripes, my blood's up too! Where's my cap?
(*He grabs the cap, dashes to the door, remembers he won't see* GAR *again.*)

JOE: Send us a card, Gar, sometimes, eh?

PUBLIC: Surely, Joe.

JOE: Lucky bloody man. I wish I was you.

PUBLIC: There's nothing stopping you, is there?

JOE: Only that the mammy planted sycamore trees last year, and she says I can't go till they're tall enough to shelter the house.

PUBLIC: You're stuck for another couple of days, then. Away off with you, man.

JOE: Good luck, Gar. And tell Madge that the next time she asks us up for tea we'd bloody well better get it.

PUBLIC: She *asked* you?

JOE: That's why I was joking her about us keeping our word. As if we wanted tea, for God's sake! But I'd better catch up with the stirks before they do damage . . . So long, aul cock!
(*He runs off.*)

PUBLIC: Madge . . . Oh God . . .
(PRIVATE *moves over beside him. He speaks quickly, savagely*

76

at first, spitting out the first three lines. Gradually he softens,
until the speech ends almost in a whisper:)

PRIVATE: They're louts, ignorant bloody louts and you've
always known it! And don't pretend you're surprised;
because you're not. And you know what they'll do tonight,
don't you? They'll shuffle around the gable of the hotel and
take an odd furtive peep into the lounge at those English
women who won't even look up from their frigid knitting!
Many a time you did it yourself, bucko! Aye, and but for
Aunt Lizzy and the grace of God, you'd be there tonight,
too, watching the lights go out over the village, and hearing
the front doors being bolted, and seeing the blinds being
raised; and you stamping your feet to keep the numbness
from spreading, not wanting to go home, not yet for
another while, wanting to hold on to the night although
nothing can happen now, nothing at all . . . Joe and Tom
and big, thick, generous Ned . . . No one will ever know or
understand the fun there was; for there *was* fun and there
was laughing – foolish, silly fun and foolish, silly laughing;
but what it was all about you can't remember, can you? Just
the memory of it – that's all you have now – just the
memory; and even now, even so soon, it is being distilled of
all its coarseness; and what's left is going to be precious,
precious gold . . .
(There is a knock at the door. PUBLIC *goes off to answer it.)*

KATE: *(Off)* Hello, Gar.

PRIVATE: Kate!

KATE: *(On)* This isn't a healthy sign, drinking by yourself.

PRIVATE: Talk! Talk!

PUBLIC: What – what are you doing here?

KATE: I hear you're off to America.

PUBLIC: First thing in the morning.

KATE: You wouldn't think of calling to say good-bye to your
friends, I suppose?

PUBLIC: I was going to, but I –

PRIVATE: Careful!

PUBLIC: – it went clean out of my mind. You know how it is,
getting ready . . .

77

KATE: I understand, Gar.

PRIVATE: She's a married woman, you bugger!

KATE: Philadelphia?

PUBLIC: Yes. Take a seat.

KATE: To an aunt, isn't it?

PUBLIC: That's right. A sister of mother's.

KATE: And you're going to work in a hotel.

PUBLIC: You know as much about it as I do.

KATE: You know Baile Beag – Small Town.

PUBLIC: I'll probably go to night-school as well – you know, at night –

PRIVATE: Brilliant.

PUBLIC: – do law or medicine or something –

PRIVATE: Like hell! First Arts stumped you!

KATE: You'll do well, Gar; make a lot of money, and come back here in twenty years' time, and buy the whole village.

PUBLIC: Very likely. That's my plan anyhow.

PRIVATE: Kate . . . Kathy . . .

PUBLIC: How's your father and mother?

KATE: Fine, thanks. And Mr O'Donnell?

PUBLIC: Grand, grand. Is Dr King well?

KATE: I hear no complaints.

PRIVATE: Then the Dauphiness of Versailles. And surely never lighted on this orb, which she hardly seemed to touch, a more delightful vision. I saw her just above the horizon, decorating and cheering the elevated sphere she just began to move in –

PUBLIC: (*A shade louder than necessary*) I'll come home when I make my first million, driving a Cadillac and smoking cigars and taking movie-films.

KATE: I hope you're very happy there and that life will be good to you.

PUBLIC: (*Slightly louder*) I'll make sure life's good to me from now on.

KATE: Your father'll miss you.

PUBLIC: (*Rapidly, aggressively*) That's his look out! D'you know something? If I had to spend another week in Ballybeg, I'd go off my bloody head! This place would drive anybody

78

crazy! Look around you, for God's sake! Look at Master
Boyle! Look at my father! Look at the Canon! Look at the
boys! Asylum cases, the whole bloody lot of them!

PRIVATE: (*Pained*) Shhhhhhh!

PUBLIC: Listen, if someone were to come along to me tonight
and say, 'Ballybeg's yours – lock, stock, and barrel,' it
wouldn't make that (*Cracks his fingers*) much difference to
me. If you're not happy and content in a
place – then – then – then you're not happy and content in a
place! It's as simple as that. I've stuck around this hole far
too long. I'm telling you: it's a bloody quagmire, a
backwater, a dead-end! And everybody in it goes crazy
sooner or later! Everybody!

PRIVATE: Shhhhhhhh . . .

PUBLIC: There's nothing about Ballybeg that I don't know
already. I hate the place, and every stone, and every rock,
and every piece of heather around it! Hate it! Hate it! And
the sooner that plane whips me away, the better I'll like it!

KATE: It isn't as bad as that, Gar.

PUBLIC: You're stuck here! What else can you say!

PRIVATE: That'll do!

PUBLIC: And you'll die here! But I'm not stuck! I'm free! Free
as the bloody wind!

KATE: All I meant was –

PUBLIC: Answerable to nobody! All this bloody yap about
father and son and all this sentimental rubbish about
'homeland' and 'birthplace' – yap! Bloody yap!
Impermanence – anonymity – that's what I'm looking for; a
vast restless place that doesn't give a damn about the past.
To hell with Ballybeg, that's what I say!

PRIVATE: Oh, man . . .

KATE: I'd better go. Francis'll be wondering what's keeping me.

PUBLIC: (*Recklessly*) Tell him I was asking for him.

KATE: Good-bye, Gar.

PUBLIC: (*In same tone*) Enjoy yourself, Kate. And if you can't
be good – you know?

(PUBLIC *goes with* KATE.)

(*Off*) Be sure to call the first one after me.

(*She is gone.* PUBLIC *returns and immediately buries his face in his hands.*)

PRIVATE: Kate . . . sweet Katie Doogan . . . my darling Kathy Doogan . . .

(PUBLIC *uncovers his face and with trembling fingers lights a cigarette and takes a drink. As he does:*)

PRIVATE: (*Very softly*) Oh, my God, steady man, steady – it is now sixteen or seventeen years since I saw the Queen of France, then the Dauphiness, at Versailles, and surely never lighted on this orb – Oh, God, Oh, my God, those thoughts are sinful – (*Sings*) 'As beautiful Kitty one morning was tripping with a pitcher of milk – '

(PUBLIC *attempts to whistle his song 'Philadelphia, Here I come!' He whistles the first phrase and the notes die away.* PRIVATE *keeps on talking while* PUBLIC *attempts to whistle.*)

PRIVATE: We'll go now, right away, and tell them – Mammy and Daddy – they're at home tonight – now, Gar, now – it must be now – remember, it's up to you entirely up to you – gut and salt them fish – and they're going to call this one Madge, at least so she *says* –

(PUBLIC *makes another attempt to whistle.*)

– a little something to remind you of your old teacher – don't keep looking back over your shoulder, be one hundred per cent American – a packet of cigarettes and a pot of jam – seven boys and seven girls – and our daughters'll all be gentle and frail and silly like you – and I'll never wait till Christmas – I'll burst, I'll bloody well burst – good-bye, Gar, it isn't as bad as that – Good-bye, Gar, it isn't as bad as that – good-bye, Gar, it isn't as bad as that –

PUBLIC: (*In whispered shout*) Screwballs, say something! Say something, Father!

Quick Curtain

80

EPISODE THREE

PART I

A short time later. The rosary is being said. PUBLIC *is kneeling with his back to the audience.* S.B. *is kneeling facing the audience.* MADGE *is facing the shop door.* PRIVATE *kneels beside* PUBLIC. MADGE *is saying her decade, and the other three—* S.B., PUBLIC *and* PRIVATE—*are answering. The words are barely distinct, a monotonous, somnolent drone. After a few moments* PRIVATE *lowers his body until his rear is resting on the backs of his legs. We cannot see* PUBLIC'S *face. While* PRIVATE *talks, the rosary goes on.*

PRIVATE: (*Relaxing, yawning*) Ah-ho-ho-ho-ho-ho. This time tomorrow night, bucko, you'll be saying the rosary all by yourself—unless Lizzy and Con say it (*Joins in a response in American accent*)—Holy Mairy, Mother of Gawd, pray for us sinners now and at the hour . . . (*He tails off as his mind wanders again.*) No, not this time tomorrow. It's only about half-four in Philadelphia now, and when it's half-nine there it'll be the wee hours of the morning here; and Screwballs'll be curled up and fast asleep in his wee cot—(*To* S.B.)—right, honey? And when he's dreaming, you'll be swaggering down 56th Street on Third at the junction of 29th and Seventh at 81st with this big blonde nuzzling up to you—(*Suddenly kneels erect again and responds in unison with* PUBLIC. *Keeps this up for two or three responses and slowly subsides again.*) You'd need to be careful out there, boy; some of those Yankee women are dynamite. But you'll never marry; never; bachelor's written all over you. Fated to be alone, a man without intimates; something of an enigma. Who is he, this silent one? Where is he from?

81

Where does he go? Every night we see him walking beneath the trees along the bank of the canal, his black cloak swinging behind him, his eyes lost in thought, his servant following him at a respectful distance. (*In reply*) Who is he? I'll tell you who he is: The Bachelor. All the same, laddybuck, there are compensations in being a bachelor. You'll age slowly and graciously, and then, perhaps, when you're quite old – about forty-three – you'll meet this beautiful girl of nineteen, and you'll fall madly in love. Karin – that's her name – no – ah – ah – Tamara – (*Caressing the word*) Tamara – grand-daughter of an exiled Russian prince, and you'll be consumed by a magnificent passion; and this night you'll invite her to dinner in your penthouse, and you'll be dressed in a deep blue velvet jacket, and the candles will discover magic fairy lights in her hair, and you'll say to her, 'Tamara', and she'll incline her face towards you, and close her eyes, and whisper –
(*From a few seconds back the droning prayers have stopped. Now* MADGE *leans over to* PUBLIC *and gives him a rough punch.*)

MADGE: Your decade!

(PRIVATE *and* PUBLIC *jump erect again and in perfect unison give out their decade. Gradually, as the prayers continue, they relax into their slumped position.*)

PRIVATE: When you're curled up in your wee cot, Screwballs, do you dream? Do you ever dream of the past, Screwballs, of that wintry morning in Bailtefree, and the three days in Bundoran? . . .
(PUBLIC *stays as he is.* PRIVATE *gets slowly to his feet and moves over to* S.B. *He stands looking down at him.*)
. . . and of the young, gay girl from beyond the mountains who sometimes cried herself to sleep? (*Softly, nervously, with growing excitement*) God – maybe – Screwballs – behind those dead eyes and that flat face are there memories of precious moments in the past? My God, have I been unfair to you? Is it possible that you have hoarded in the back of that mind of yours – do you remember – it was an afternoon in May – oh, fifteen years ago – I don't remember every

82

detail but some things are as vivid as can be: the boat was
blue and the paint was peeling and there was an empty
cigarette packet floating in the water at the bottom between
two trout and the left rowlock kept slipping and you had
given me your hat and had put your jacket round my
shoulders because there had been a shower of rain. And you
had the rod in your left hand – I can see the cork nibbled
away from the butt of the rod – and maybe we had been
chatting – I don't remember – it doesn't matter – but
between us at that moment there was this great happiness,
this great joy – you must have felt it too – although nothing
was being said – just the two of us fishing on a lake on a
showery day – and young as I was I felt, I knew, that this
was precious, and your hat was soft on the top of my ears – I
can feel it – and I shrank down into your coat – and then,
then for no reason at all except that you were happy too,
you began to sing: (*Sings*)

> All round my hat I'll wear a green coloured ribbono,
> All round my hat for a twelve month and a day.
> And if anybody asks me the reason why I wear it,
> It's all because my true love is far, far away.

(*The rosary is over.* MADGE *and* S.B. *get slowly to their feet.*
PUBLIC *and* PRIVATE *are not aware that the prayers are
finished.* S.B. *does the nightly job of winding the clock.*)

MADGE: Will you take your supper now?
S.B.: Any time suits you.
   (MADGE *goes to* PUBLIC, *still kneeling.*)
MADGE: And what about St Martin de Porres?
PUBLIC: Mm?
   (*He blesses himself hurriedly, in confusion, and gets to his
   feet.*)
MADGE: Supper.
PUBLIC: Yes – yes – please, Madge –
MADGE: (*Going off*) I suppose even the saints must eat now and
   again, too.
   (*Pause.* S.B. *consults his pocket watch.*)
S.B.: What time do you make it?
PUBLIC: Quarter to ten.

83

s.b.: It's that anyhow.

PRIVATE: Go on! Ask him! He must remember!

s.b.: The days are shortening already. Before we know we'll be burning light before closing time.

PRIVATE: Go on! Go on!

PUBLIC: (*In the churlish, off-hand tone he uses to* s.b.) What ever happened to that aul boat on Lough na Cloc Cor.

s.b.: What's that?

PRIVATE: Again!

PUBLIC: That aul boat that used to be up on Lough na Cloc Cor – an aul blue thing – d'you remember it?

s.b.: A boat? Eh? (*Voices off.*) The Canon!

PRIVATE: Bugger the Canon!
(*The* CANON *enters; a lean, white-haired man with alert eyes and a thin mouth. He is talking back to* MADGE *in the scullery.*)

CANON: Hee-hee-hee – you're a terrible woman.

s.b.: Well, Canon!

CANON: That Madge . . . hee-hee-hee.

PUBLIC: Good night, Canon.

CANON: She says I wait till the rosary's over and the kettle's on . . . hee-hee-hee.

s.b.: She's a sharp one, Madge.

CANON: 'You wait,' says she, 'till the rosary's over and the kettle's on!'

PRIVATE: Hee-hee-hee.

s.b.: Pay no heed to Madge, Canon.

PRIVATE: And how's the O'Donnell family tonight?

CANON: And how's the O'Donnell family tonight?
(PUBLIC *sits when the* CANON *sits.*)

s.b.: Living away as usual. Not a thing happening.

PRIVATE: Liar!

CANON: Just so, now, just so.

s.b.: Will we have a game now or will we wait till the supper comes in?

CANON: We may as well commence, Sean. I see no reason why we shouldn't commence.

s.b.: (*Setting the board*) Whatever you say, Canon.

CANON: Hee-hee-hee. 'You wait,' says she, 'till the rosary's over and the kettle's on.'

PRIVATE: She's a sharp one, Madge.

S.B.: She's a sharp one, Madge.

CANON: It'll be getting near your time, Gareth.

PUBLIC: Tomorrow morning, Canon.

CANON: Just so, now. Tomorrow morning.

PRIVATE: Tomorrow morning.

CANON: Tomorrow morning.

S.B.: Here we are.

CANON: Powerful the way time passes, too.

S.B.: Black or white, Canon?

CANON: (*Considering the problem*) Black or white . . .

PRIVATE: Black for the crows and white for the swans.

CANON: Black for the crows and white for the swans.

PRIVATE: Ha-ha! (*He preens himself at his skill in prophecy.*)

S.B.: Have a shot at the black the night.

CANON: Maybe I will then.

PRIVATE: Can't take the money off you every night.

CANON: Can't take the trousers off you every night. Hee-hee-hee.

PRIVATE: (*Shocked*) Canon O'Byrne!

S.B.: You had a great streak of luck last night, I'll grant you that.

CANON: (*A major announcement*) D'you know what?

S.B.: What's that, Canon?

CANON: You'll have rain before morning.

S.B.: D'you think so?

CANON: It's in the bones. The leg's giving me the odd jab.

S.B.: We could do without the rain then.

CANON: Before the morning you'll have it.

S.B.: Tch tch tch. We get our fill of it here.

CANON: The best barometer I know.

S.B.: Aye. No want of rain.

CANON: Before the morning.

S.B.: As if we don't get enough of it.

CANON: The jabs are never wrong.

PRIVATE: (*Wildly excited*) Stop press! News flash! Sensation! We interrupt our programmes to bring you the news that

Canon Mick O'Byrne, of Ballybeg, Ireland, has made the
confident prediction that *you'll* have rain before the
morning! Stand by for further bulletins!

CANON: 'You wait,' says she, 'till the rosary's over and the
kettle's on!'

S.B.: Usual stakes, Canon?

CANON: I see no reason to alter them.

S.B.: What about putting them up – just for the first game?

CANON: The thin end of the wedge, eh, as the Bishop says? No,
Sean, the way I see it, a half-penny a game'll neither make
nor break either of us.

(*Enter* MADGE *with cups of tea and a plate of biscuits.*)

MADGE: Have you begun already?

S.B.: Shh!

MADGE: If it was turkeys or marble clocks they were playing for
they couldn't be more serious!

S.B.: Quiet!

MADGE: Agh!

(*She leaves their tea beside them and brings a cup over to*
PUBLIC. *They talk in undertones.*)

MADGE: Wouldn't you love to throw it round them!

PUBLIC: Scalding hot!

MADGE: And raise blisters on their aul bald pates! – God forgive
me!

PUBLIC: Madge.

MADGE: What?

PUBLIC: Why don't you take a run over to see the new baby?

MADGE: I've more on my mind than that.

PUBLIC: I'll put up the jars and wash up these few things.

MADGE: And this the last night we'll have you to torment us?

PUBLIC: Go on. Go on. We won't start swopping the dirty
stories till we get you out of the road.

S.B.: Shhhhhh!

PUBLIC: Hurry up. Nelly'll be wondering why you didn't show
up.

MADGE: Aye, so.

PUBLIC: Your own namesake, isn't it?

MADGE: So she *says*.

PUBLIC: Get a move on. You'll be back before bedtime.

MADGE: What d'you think?

PUBLIC: Quick!

MADGE: I'm away! (*She takes a few steps away and comes back.*) Don't forget: them shirts isn't right aired. (*Just when she is at the scullery door.*)

PUBLIC: Madge.

MADGE: What is it?

PRIVATE: Don't! Don't!

PUBLIC: Why did my mother marry him (S.B.) instead of Master Boyle?

MADGE: What?

PUBLIC: She went with both of them, didn't she?

MADGE: She married the better man by far.

PUBLIC: But she went with Boyle first, didn't she?

MADGE: I've told you before: she went with a dozen – that was the kind of her – she couldn't help herself.

PUBLIC: But is that what started Boyle drinking?

MADGE: If it was, more fool he. And any other nosing about you want to do, ask the Boss. For you're not going to pump me. (*She goes off.*)

PRIVATE: What the hell had you to go and ask that for! Snap, boy, snap! We want no scenes tonight. Get up and clear out of this because you're liable to get over-excited watching these two dare-devils dicing with death. (PUBLIC *takes his cup and goes towards his bedroom.*) Into your survival shelter and brood, brood, brood. (*As if replying to the draught players – who have not noticed his exit.*) No, no, I'm not leaving. Just going in here to have a wee chat with my Chinese mistress. (PUBLIC *goes into his bedroom, leaving the door open.* PRIVATE *stays in the kitchen.* PUBLIC *in the bedroom mimes the actions of* PRIVATE *in the following sequence.* PRIVATE *stands at the table between* S.B. *and* CANON:)

PRIVATE: Canon battling tooth and nail for another half-penny; Screwballs fighting valiantly to retain his trousers! Gripped in mortal combat! County Councillor versus Canon! Screwballs versus Canonballs! (*Stares intently at them.*) Hi,

87

kids! Having fun, kids? (*Gets to his feet, leans his elbow on the table, and talks confidentially into their faces.*) Any chance of a game, huh? Tell me, boys, strictly between ourselves, will you miss me? You will? You really will? But now I want you both to close your eyes – please, my darlings – don't, don't argue – just do as I say – just close your eyes and think of all the truly wonderful times we've had together. Now! What'll we chat about, eh? Let's – chat – about – what? No, Screwballs, not women; not before you-know-who. (*Looking at the* CANON.) Money? Agh, sure, Canon, what interest have you in money? Sure as long as you get to Tenerife for five weeks every winter what interest have you in money? But I'm wasting my time with you, Canon – Screwballs here is different; there's an affinity between Screwballs and me that no one, literally no one could understand – except you, Canon (*Deadly serious*), because you're warm and kind and soft and sympathetic – all things to all men – because you could translate all this loneliness, this groping, this dreadful bloody buffoonery into Christian terms that will make life bearable for us all. And yet you don't say a word. Why, Canon? Why, arid Canon? Isn't this your job? – to translate? Why don't you speak, then? Prudence, arid Canon? Prudence be damned! Christianity isn't prudent – it's insane! Or maybe this just happens to be one of your bad nights – (*Suddenly bright and brittle again*) – A pound to a shilling I make you laugh! (*Dancing around, singing to the tune of 'Daisy'*:) 'Screwballs, Screwballs, give me your answer do. I'm half crazy all for the love of you. I'm off to Philadelphey, and I'll leave you on the shelfey –'
(S.B. *gives a short dry laugh.*)

PRIVATE: A pound you owe me! Money for aul rope! And you, Canon, what about giving us a bar or two?
CANON: Aye.
PRIVATE: You will? Wonderful! What'll it be? A pop number? An aul Gregorian come-all-ye? A whack of an aul aria?
CANON: I had you cornered.
PRIVATE: 'I had you cornered' – I know it! I know it! I know it! (*Sings in the style of a modern crooner.*) I had you

88

cornered/That night in Casablanca/That night you said you
loved me – all set? Boys and girls, that top, pop recording
star, Kenny O'Byrne and the Ballybeg Buggers in their
latest fabulous release, 'I Had You Cornered'.
(PRIVATE *stands with head lowered, his foot tapping, his
fingers clicking in syncopated rhythm, waiting for the* CANON *to
begin. He keeps this up for a few seconds. Then in time to his
own beat he sings very softly, as he goes to the bedroom –*
    Should aul acquaintance be forgot
    And never brought to min'?
    Should aul acquaintance be forgot
    And days o' lang-syne?
    Yah – ooooo.
(PUBLIC *suddenly sits up in bed.*)
Mendelssohn! That's the bugger'll tear the guts out of you!
(PUBLIC *puts on a recording of the Second Movement of the
Violin Concerto.* PRIVATE, *now almost frenzied, dashes back
to the kitchen.*)
Give us a bar or two, Mendelssohn, aul fella. Come on, lad;
resin the aul bow and spit on your hands and give us an aul
bar!
(*The record begins.* PRIVATE *runs to the table and thrusts his
face between the players.*)
Listen! Listen! Listen! D'you hear it? D'you know what
the music says? (*To* S.B.) It says that once upon a time a
boy and his father sat in a blue boat on a lake on an
afternoon in May, and on that afternoon a great beauty
happened, a beauty that has haunted the boy ever since,
because he wonders now did it really take place or did he
imagine it. There are only the two of us, he says; each of us
is all the other has; and why can we not even look at each
other? Have pity on us, he says; have goddam pity on every
goddam bloody man jack of us. (*He comes away from the
table and walks limply back to the bedroom. When he gets to
the bedroom door he turns, surveys the men.*) To hell with all
strong silent men!
(*He goes into the bedroom, drops into the chair, and sits
motionless.* PUBLIC *sinks back on to the bed again.*)

(*Silence.*)

CANON: What's that noise?

S.B.: What's that, Canon?

CANON: A noise of some sort.

S.B.: Is there?

(*They listen.*)

S.B.: I don't hear –

CANON: Wait.

S.B.: Is it –

CANON: It's music – is it?

S.B.: Music?

CANON: Aye. It's music.

S.B.: That'll be Gar then.

CANON: Oh.

S.B.: Playing them records of his.

CANON: Thought I heard something.

S.B.: All he asks is to sit in there and play them records all day.

CANON: It makes him happy.

S.B.: Terrible man for the records.

CANON: Just so, now. It'll be getting near his time, he tells me.

S.B.: Tomorrow morning.

CANON: Tomorrow morning.

S.B.: Aye, tomorrow morning. Powerful the way time passes, too.

CANON: You wait, says she, till the rosary's over and the kettle's on.

S.B.: A sharp one, Madge.

CANON: Ah-hah. There's hope for you yet.

S.B.: I don't know is there.

CANON: No. You're not too late yet.

S.B.: Maybe . . . maybe . . .

CANON: No, I wouldn't say die yet – not yet I wouldn't.

Slow Curtain

PART II

*The small hours of the morning. The kitchen is dimly lit. In the
kitchen, just outside the bedroom door, are Gar's cases, and lying
across them are his coat, his cap, and a large envelope containing his
X-ray and visa. The bedroom is in darkness: just enough light to see*
PUBLIC *on the bed and* PRIVATE *in the chair.* S.B. *comes in from
the scullery carrying a cup of tea in his hand. He is dressed in long
trousers, a vest, a hat, socks. He moves slowly towards the table, sees
the cases, goes over to them, touches the coat, goes back towards the
table, and sits there, staring at the bedroom door. He coughs.
Immediately* PRIVATE *is awake and* PUBLIC *sits up sleepily in bed.*

PRIVATE: What – what – what's that? (*Relaxing.*) Madge
  probably. Looking to see is the door bolted.
  (PUBLIC *gets out of bed and switches on the light. Looks at his
  watch.*)
  You'll not sleep again tonight, laddo.
PUBLIC: Bugger.
  (PUBLIC *looks at himself in the mirror and then sits on edge of
  bed.*)
PRIVATE: Four more hours. This is the last time you'll lie in
  this bed, the last time you'll look at that pattern on the
  wallpaper, the last time you'll listen to the silence of
  Ballybeg, the last time you'll –
PUBLIC: Agh, shut up!
PRIVATE: It is now sixteen or seventeen years since I saw the
  Queen of France. Go into the shop, man, and get yourself a
  packet of aspirin; that'll do the trick. (*Looking up at ceiling.*)
  Mind if I take a packet of aspirin, Screwballs? Send the bill
  to the USA, okay? Out you go, boy, and get a clatter of
  pills!
  (*They both go into the kitchen.* PUBLIC *stops dead when he sees*
  S.B. *staring at him.*)
PUBLIC: My God! Lady Godiva!
PRIVATE: Is this where you are?

S.B.: Aye – I – I – I – I wasn't sleeping. What has you up?
(PUBLIC *goes to where the key of the shop is hung up*.)
PUBLIC: I – I wasn't sleeping either. I'll get some aspirins inside.
S.B.: It's hard to sleep sometimes . . .
PUBLIC: It is, aye . . . sometimes . . .
S.B.: There's tea in the pot.
PUBLIC: Aye?
S.B.: If it's a headache you have.
PUBLIC: It'll make me no worse anyway.
(PUBLIC *goes into the scullery*. PRIVATE *stands at the door and talks into him*.)
PRIVATE: Now's your time, boy. The small hours of the morning. Put your head on his shoulder and say, 'How's my wee darling Daddy?'
(PUBLIC *puts his head round the door*.)
PUBLIC: You take some?
S.B.: Sure you know I never take a second cup.
PRIVATE: Playing hard to get. Come on, bucko; it's your place to make the move – the younger man. Say – say – say – say, 'Screwballs, with two magnificent legs like that, how is it you were never in show biz?' Say, 'It is now sixteen or seventeen – Say – oh, my God – say – say something.
(PUBLIC *enters with a cup of tea*.)
PUBLIC: You'll need a new tyre for the van.
S.B.: What one's that?
PUBLIC: The back left-hand one. I told you. It's done.
S.B.: Aye. So you did.
PUBLIC: And – and –
PRIVATE: What else?
PUBLIC: – and don't forget the fencing posts for McGuire next Wednesday.
S.B.: Fencing posts.
PUBLIC: Twelve dozen. The milk lorry'll take them. I spoke to Packey.
S.B.: Aye . . . right . . .
PRIVATE: Go on! Keep talking!
PUBLIC: And if you're looking for the pliers, I threw them into

92

the tea chest under the counter.

S.B.: Which tea chest?

PUBLIC: The one near the window.

S.B.: Oh, I see – I see . . .

PRIVATE: You're doing grand. Keep at it. It's the silence that's the enemy.

PUBLIC: You'll be wanting more plug tobacco. The traveller'll be here this week.

S.B.: More plug.

PUBLIC: It's finished. The last of it went up to Curran's wake.

S.B.: I'll – I'll see about that.

PUBLIC: And you'll need to put a new clasp on the lower window – the tinkers are about again.

S.B.: Aye?

PUBLIC: They were in at dinner time. I got some cans off them.

S.B.: I just thought I noticed something shining from the ceiling.

PUBLIC: It's the cans then.

S.B.: Aye.

PUBLIC: That's what it is. I bought six off them.

S.B.: They'll not go to loss.

PUBLIC: They wanted me to take a dozen but I said six would do us.

S.B.: Six is plenty. They don't go as quick as they used to – them cans.

PUBLIC: They've all got cookers and ranges and things.

S.B.: What's that?

PUBLIC: I say they don't buy them now because the open fires are nearly all gone.

S.B.: That's it. All cookers and ranges and things these times.

PUBLIC: That's why I wouldn't take the dozen.

S.B.: You were right, too. Although I mind the time when I got through a couple of dozen a week.

PUBLIC: Aye?

S.B.: All cans it was then. Maybe you'd sell a kettle at turf-cutting or if there'd be a Yank coming home . . .
(*Pause.*)

PUBLIC: Better get these pills and then try to get a couple of hours sleep –

S.B.: You're getting the mail-van to Strabane?
(PUBLIC *gives him a quick, watchful look.*)

PUBLIC: At a quarter past seven.

S.B.: (*Awkwardly*) I was listening to the weather forecast
there . . . moderate westerly winds and occasional showers,
it said.

PUBLIC: Aye?

S.B.: I was thinking it – it – it – it would be a fair enough day for
going up in thon plane.

PUBLIC: It should be, then.

S.B.: Showers – just like the Canon said . . . And I was meaning
to tell you that you should sit at the back . . .

PRIVATE: It is now sixteen or seventeen years – the longest way
round's the shortest way home –

S.B.: So *he* was saying, too . . . you know there – if there was an
accident or anything – it's the front gets it hardest –

PUBLIC: I suppose that's true enough.

S.B.: So *he* was saying . . . not that I would know – just that he
was saying it there . . .

PRIVATE: (*Urgently, rapidly*) Now! Now! He might
remember – he might. But if he does, my God, laddo – what
if he does?

PUBLIC: (*With pretended carelessness*) D'you know what kept
coming into my mind the day?

S.B.: Eh?

PUBLIC: The fishing we used to do on Lough na Cloc Cor.

S.B.: (*Confused, on guard*) Oh, aye, Lough na Cloc
Cor – aye – aye –

PUBLIC: We had a throw on it every Sunday during the
season.

S.B.: That's not the day nor yesterday.

PUBLIC: (*More quickly*) There used to be a blue boat on it –
d'you remember it?

S.B.: Many's the fish we took off that same lake.

PUBLIC: D'you remember the blue boat?

S.B.: A blue one, eh?

PUBLIC: I don't know who owned it. But it was blue. And the
paint was peeling.

S.B.: (*Remembering*) I mind a brown one the doctor brought
from somewhere up in the –

PUBLIC: (*Quickly*) It doesn't matter who owned it. It doesn't
even matter that it was blue. But d'you remember one
afternoon in May – we were up there – the two of us – and it
must have rained because you put your jacket round my
shoulders and gave me your hat –

S.B.: Aye?

PUBLIC: – and it wasn't that we were talking or anything – but
suddenly – suddenly you sang 'All Round My Hat I'll Wear
a Green Coloured Ribbono' –

S.B.: Me?

PUBLIC: – for no reason at all except that we – that you were
happy. D'you remember? D'you remember?
(*There is a pause while* S.B. *tries to recall.*)

S.B.: No . . . no, then, I don't . . .
(PRIVATE *claps his hands in nervous mockery.*)

PRIVATE: (*Quickly*) There! There! There!

S.B.: 'All Round My Hat'? No, I don't think I ever knew that
one. It wasn't 'The Flower of Sweet Strabane', was it? That
was my song.

PUBLIC: It could have been. It doesn't matter.

PRIVATE: So now you know: it never happened!
Ha-ha-ha-ha-ha.

S.B.: 'All Round My Hat'? – that was never one of mine. What
does it go like?

PUBLIC: I couldn't tell you. I don't know it either.

PRIVATE: Ha-ha-ha-ha-ha-ha-ha-ha.

S.B.: And you say the boat was blue?

PUBLIC: It doesn't matter. Forget it.

S.B.: (*Justly, reasonably*) There was a brown one belonging to
the doctor, and before that there was a wee
flat-bottom – but it was green – or was it white? I'll tell you,
you wouldn't be thinking of a punt – it could have been
blue – one that the curate had down at the pier last
summer –
(PRIVATE's *mocking laughter increases.* PUBLIC *rushes quickly
into the shop.* PRIVATE, *still mocking, follows.*)

95

–a fine sturdy wee punt it was, too, and it could well have
been the . . .

(*He sees that he is alone and tails off. Slowly he gets to his feet
and goes towards the scullery door. He meets* MADGE *entering.
She is dressed in outside clothes. She is very weary.*)

MADGE: What has you up?

S.B.: Me? Aw, I took medicine and the cramps wouldn't let me
sleep. I thought you were in bed?

MADGE: I was over at Nelly's. The place was upside down.

S.B.: There's nothing wrong, is there?

MADGE: Not a thing.

S.B.: The baby's strong and healthy?

MADGE: Grand – grand.

S.B.: That's all that matters.

MADGE: They're going to call it Brigid.

S.B.: Brigid – that's a grand name . . . Patrick, Brigid, and
Colmcille . . .

(*She takes off her hat and coat.*)

Madge . . .

MADGE: You'll get a cold padding about in yon rig.

S.B.: Madge, I'll manage rightly, Madge, eh?

MADGE: Surely you will.

S.B.: I'll get one of Charley Bonner's boys to do the van on
Tuesdays and Thursdays and I'll manage rightly?

MADGE: This place is cold. Away off to bed.

S.B.: It's not like in the old days when the whole countryside
did with me; I needed the help then. But it's different now.
I'll manage by myself now. Eh? I'll manage fine, eh?

MADGE: Fine.

S.B.: D'you mind the trouble we had keeping him at school just
after he turned ten. D'you mind nothing would do him but
he'd get behind the counter. And he had this wee sailor suit
on him this morning –

MADGE: A sailor suit? He never had a sailor suit.

S.B.: Oh, he had, Madge. Oh, Madge, he had. I can see him,
with his shoulders back, and the wee head up straight, and
the mouth, aw, man, as set, and says he this morning, I can
hear him saying it, says he, 'I'm not going to school. I'm

96

going into my daddy's business' – you know – all
important – and, d'you mind, you tried to coax him to go to
school, and not a move you could get out of him, and him
as manly looking, and this wee sailor suit as smart looking
on him, and – and – and at the heel of the hunt I had to go
with him myself, the two of us, hand in hand, as happy as
larks – we were that happy, Madge – and him dancing and
chatting beside me – mind? – you couldn't get a word in
edge-ways with all the chatting he used to go through . . .
Maybe, Madge, maybe it's because I could have been his
grandfather, eh?

MADGE: I don't know.

S.B.: I was too old for her, Madge, eh?

MADGE: I don't know. They're a new race – a new world.

S.B.: (*Leaving*) In the wee sailor suit – all the chatting he used to
go through . . . I don't know either . . .

MADGE: (*Looking at case*) Tomorrow'll be sore on him (GAR):
his heart'll break tomorrow, and all next week, and the
week after maybe . . . Brigid – aye, it's all right – (*Trying out
the sound of the name*) Brigid – Biddy – Biddy
Mulhern – Brigid Mulhern – aye – like Madge Mulhern
doesn't sound right – (*Trying it out*) – Madge Mulhern –
Madge Mulhern – I don't know – It's too aul'-fashioned or
something . . . Has he his cap? (*Finds it in the pocket of the
coat. Also finds an apple.*) . . . Aye, he has. And an apple, if
you don't mind – for all his grief. He'll be all right. That
Lizzy one'll look after him well, I suppose, if she can take
time off from blatherin'. Garden front and back, and a TV
in the house of lords – I'll believe them things when I see
them! Never had much time for blatherin' women . . .
(*Remembering*) An envelope . . . (*She takes two notes from
her pocket, goes to the dresser, and finds an envelope. She puts
the money into the envelope, and slips the envelope into the coat
pocket.*) That'll get him a cup of tea on the plane. I had put
them two pounds by me to get my feet done on the fair day.
But I can wait till next month. From what I hear, there's no
big dances between now and then . . . (*She stands looking at
the bedroom door.*) So. I think that's everything . . . (*She

raises her hand in a sort of vague benediction, then shuffles towards the scullery.) When the boss was his (GAR's) age, he was the very same as him: leppin, and eejitin' about and actin' the clown; as like as two peas. And when he's (GAR) the age the boss is now, he'll turn out just the same. And although I won't be here to see it, you'll find that he's learned nothin' in-between times. That's people for you – they'd put you astray in the head if you thought long enough about them.

(PUBLIC *and* PRIVATE *enter from the shop.*)

PUBLIC: You down too? Turning into a night club, this place.

MADGE: I'm only getting back.

PUBLIC: Well, how's the new Madge?

MADGE: Strong and healthy – and that's all that matters. Were you and the boss chatting there?

PUBLIC: When's the christening?

MADGE: Sunday. After last Mass.

PUBLIC: Madge Mulhern. Are you proud?

MADGE: I'm just tired, son. Very tired.

PUBLIC: You're sure there's nothing wrong, Madge?

MADGE: If there was something wrong, wouldn't I tell you?

PRIVATE: Of course she would. Who else has she?

PUBLIC: Did you tell her she's getting an elephant out of my first wages?

MADGE: Aye, so. The jars are up?

PUBLIC: They are.

MADGE: And the dishes washed?

PUBLIC: All done.

MADGE: I'll give you a call at half-six, then.

PUBLIC: Madge – Madge, you'd let me know if – if he got sick or anything?

MADGE: Who else would there be?

PUBLIC: Just in case . . . not that it's likely – he'll outlive the whole of us . . .

MADGE: Good night.

PUBLIC: Sleep well, Madge.

MADGE: Sleep well yourself.

(MADGE *goes off.* PUBLIC *and* PRIVATE *watch her shuffle off.*)

98

THE FREEDOM OF
THE CITY

for Dan Herr

CHARACTERS

PRESS PHOTOGRAPHER
PRIEST
THREE SOLDIERS
JUDGE
POLICE CONSTABLE
DR DODDS   Sociologist
MICHAEL
LILY
SKINNER (Adrian Casimir Fitzgerald)
BALLADEER AND FRIENDS
BRIGADIER JOHNSON-HANSBURY
ARMY PRESS OFFICER
DR WINBOURNE   Forensic Expert
PROFESSOR CUPPLEY   Pathologist
RTE COMMENTATOR

The Freedom of the City was first performed in Dublin at the Abbey Theatre on 20 February 1973. The cast was as follows:

PRIEST	Ronnie Walsh
SOLDIERS	Niall O'Brien
	Dermot Crowley
	Colm Meaney
JUDGE	John Kavanagh
POLICE CONSTABLE	Geoffrey Golden
DR DODDS – Sociologist	Pat Laffan
MICHAEL	Raymond Hardie
LILY	Angela Newman
SKINNER	Eamon Morrissey
BALLADEER	Michael O'hAonghusa
BRIGADIER JOHNSON-HANSBURY	Clive Geraghty
ARMY PRESS OFFICER	Emmet Bergin
DR WINBOURNE – Forensic Expert	Edward Golden
PROFESSOR CUPPLEY – Pathologist	Derek Young
RTE COMMENTATOR	Bob Carlile
ACCORDIONIST	Dinny O'Brien
Direction	Tomas MacAnna
Setting and costumes	Alan Barlow

Set

The Mayor's parlour takes up almost the entire stage, with the exception of the apron and a small area stage left (left and right throughout are from the point of view of the audience).

The parlour is on the first floor of a neo-gothic building. One arched doorway upstage leads to a dressing-room off. Another arched doorway left opens on to a corridor. A stained-glass window right looks out on Guildhall Square.

The doors and walls of the parlour are oak-panelled, and at ceiling height the walls are embattled. The furnishings are solid and dated, the atmosphere heavy and staid. A large conference table with a leather-covered top. A glass display cabinet. An old-fashioned radiogram on top of which sits a vase of artificial flowers. On one side of the door leading into the dressing-room stands a Union Jack flag. On the other side a large portrait of a forgotten civic dignitary. A grand baroque chair for the Mayor; several upright carved chairs for his guests.

MICHAEL is twenty-two. Strong, regular features but not handsome.

SKINNER is twenty-one. Very lean, very tense, very restless. He is described as 'glib' but the adjective is less than just. A quick volatile mind driving a lean body.

LILY is forty-three. She has eleven children and her body has long since settled into its own comfortable contours. But poverty and child-bearing have not completely obliterated the traces of early prettiness.

Time: 1970.
Place: Derry City, Northern Ireland.

ACT ONE

The stage is in darkness except for the apron which is lit in cold blue. we already mean prayin Dead — "knees"
  Three bodies lie grotesquely across the front of the stage –
SKINNER *on the left,* LILY *in the middle,* MICHAEL *on the right.*
  *After a silence has been established we hear in the very far
distance the wail of an ambulance siren.*
  A PHOTOGRAPHER, *crouching for fear of being shot, runs on
from the right and very hastily and very nervously photographs the
corpses, taking three or four pictures of each. His flash-bulb eerily
lights up the stage each time.*
  When he gets the length of SKINNER, *a* PRIEST *enters right,
crouching like the* PHOTOGRAPHER *and holding a white
handkerchief above his head. He gets down on his knees beside*
MICHAEL, *hastily blesses him and mumbles prayers into his ear. He
then moves on to* LILY *and to* SKINNER *and goes through the same
ritual with each.*
  While the PRIEST *crouches beside* MICHAEL, *a spot picks out the*
JUDGE *high up in the battlements. And at the same moment a*
POLICEMAN *in dark glasses enters from the left, removes his cap
and faces the* JUDGE. *The* POLICEMAN *reads from his notebook; the*
JUDGE *takes notes.*
  The JUDGE *is English, in his early sixties; a quick fussy man with
a testy manner.*

POLICEMAN: Hegarty, my lord.
JUDGE: Speak up, Constable, please.
POLICEMAN: Hegarty, my lord.
JUDGE: Yes.

POLICEMAN: Michael Joseph. Unmarried. Unemployed. Lived with his parents.

JUDGE: Age?

POLICEMAN: Twenty-two years, my lord.

JUDGE: Was the deceased known to you personally, Constable B?

POLICEMAN: No, my lord.

JUDGE: And when you arrived at the body, did you discover any firearms on his person or adjacent to his person?

POLICEMAN: I wasn't the first to get there, my lord.

JUDGE: Would you answer my question?

POLICEMAN: I personally saw no arms, my lord.

JUDGE: Thank you.

(Three SOLDIERS *in full combat uniform run on from right. Two of them grab* MICHAEL *by the feet and drag him off right, while a third, tense and scared, covers them with his rifle. The* PHOTOGRAPHER *runs off left. The* PRIEST *moves to* LILY.)

POLICEMAN: Doherty. Elizabeth. Married. Aged forty-three years.

JUDGE: Occupation?

POLICEMAN: Housewife. Also a cleaning woman. Deceased lived with her family in a condemned property behind the old railway – a warehouse that was converted into eight flats and . . .

JUDGE: We are not conducting a social survey, Constable. Was the deceased known to you?

POLICEMAN: No, my lord.

JUDGE: And did you discover any firearms on her person or adjacent to her person?

POLICEMAN: I wasn't the first on the scene, my lord.

JUDGE: I am aware of that, Constable.

POLICEMAN: I saw no weapons, my lord.

(The PRIEST *moves on to* SKINNER. *The three* SOLDIERS *return and drag* LILY *off.)*

POLICEMAN: Fitzgerald. Adrian Casimir.

JUDGE: Pardon?

POLICEMAN: Fitzgerald . . .

JUDGE: I've got that.

POLICEMAN: Adrian Casimir.

JUDGE: Yes.

POLICEMAN: Aged twenty-one. Single. No fixed address. *Outsider*

JUDGE: You mean he wasn't native to the city?

POLICEMAN: He was, my lord. But he moved about a lot. And we haven't been able to trace any relatives.

JUDGE: Had the deceased a profession or a trade?

POLICEMAN: No, my lord.

JUDGE: Was he bearing any firearms – when you got to him?

POLICEMAN: Not when I got to him, my lord.

JUDGE: And was he known to you personally, Constable B?

POLICEMAN: Yes, my lord.

JUDGE: As a terrorist? ✓

POLICEMAN: He had been in trouble many times, my lord. Petty larceny, disorderly behaviour – that sort of thing.

JUDGE: I see. Thank you, Constable.

(*The* PRIEST *goes off left. The* POLICEMAN *follows him. The three* SOLDIERS *enter right and drag* SKINNER *away as before. A ceremonial hat (the Mayor's) is lying beside* SKINNER's *body. One of the* SOLDIERS *takes it off with him.*)

JUDGE: I should explain that I have permitted soldiers and policemen to give evidence under pseudonym so that they may not expose themselves to the danger of reprisal. And before we adjourn for lunch, may I repeat once more and make abundantly clear once more my words of the first day: that this tribunal of inquiry, appointed by her Majesty's *like the* Government, is in no sense a court of justice. Our only *Narrators* function is to form an objective view of the events which *in* occurred in the City of Londonderry, Northern Ireland, on *hours* the tenth day of February 1970, when after a civil rights meeting British troops opened fire and three civilians lost their lives. It is essentially a fact-finding exercise; and our concern and our only concern is with that period of time when these three people came together, seized possession of a civic building, and openly defied the security forces. The facts we garner over the coming days may indicate that the deceased were callous terrorists who had planned to seize the Guildhall weeks before the events of February 10th; or the facts may indicate that the misguided scheme occurred to them on that very day while they listened to revolutionary speeches. But whatever conclusion may seem to emerge, it must be understood that it is none of our function to make moral judgements, and I would ask the media to bear this in mind. We will resume at 2.30.

(*He leaves. Light up the full set. Offstage: a civil rights meeting is being held in Guildhall Square and is being addressed by a* WOMAN. *The amplification is faulty and we cannot hear what she is saying; but the speech sounds fiery and is punctuated by clapping and cheering. While the meeting is going on offstage,* DR DODDS *enters left and addresses the audience. An elderly American professor with an informal manner.*)

DODDS: Good evening. My name is Philip Alexander Dodds. I'm a sociologist and my field of study is inherited poverty or the culture of poverty or more accurately the subculture of poverty. And since I'll be using these terms off and on, let me explain what I mean by them. I'm talking about those people who are at the very bottom of the socio-economic scale and more specifically about their distinctive way of life – a way of life which is common to ghetto or slum communities all over the Western world and which is transmitted from generation to generation. And the first thing to be said about this culture or way of life is that it has two aspects: it is the way the poor adapt to their marginal position in a society which is capitalistic, stratified into classes, and highly individuated; and it is also their method of reacting against that society. In other words it is the method they have devised to cope with the hopelessness and despair they experience because they know they'll never be successful in terms of the values and goals of the dominant society. And once it comes into existence – this way of life, this culture – it is handed down from parents to children and to their children, and thus its perpetuation is ensured. Because by the time children are six or seven they have usually taken on the basic values and attitudes of their subculture and aren't psychologically geared to take advantage of changing conditions or increased opportunities

110

that may occur in their lifetime.

(*Suddenly all sounds are drowned by the roar of approaching tanks. Their noise is deafening and fills the whole auditorium. They stop. Silence for five seconds. Then the* WOMAN *who is addressing the meeting*:)

WOMAN: Stand your ground! Don't move! Don't panic! This is your city! This is your city!

(*Her voice is drowned by shooting – rubber bullets and CS gas – and immediate pandemonium in the crowd. Panic. Screaming. Shouting. The revving of engines as tanks and water-cannon pursue fleeing groups. More rubber bullets and the quick plop of exploding gas-canisters. Very slowly the noise fades to background. As it does,* DODDS *resumes as calmly as before.*)

DODDS: People with a culture of poverty are provincial and locally orientated and have very little sense of history. They know only their own troubles, their own neighbourhood, their own local conditions, their own way of life; but they don't have the knowledge or the vision or the ideology to see that their problems are also the problems of the poor in the ghettos of New York and London and Paris and Dublin – in fact all over the Western world. To give you some examples: they share a critical attitude to many of the values and institutions of the dominant class; they share a suspicion of government, a detestation of the police, and very often a cynicism to the church. But the very moment they acquire an objective view of their condition, once they become aware that their condition has counterparts elsewhere, from that moment they have broken out of their subculture, even though they may still be desperately poor. And any movement – trade union, religious, civil rights, pacifist, revolutionary – any movement which gives them this objectivity, organizes them, gives them real hope, promotes solidarity, such a movement inevitably smashes the rigid caste that encases their minds and bodies.

(DODDS *goes off left. As he leaves, a quick succession of shots – and* MICHAEL *staggers onstage right. He has been blinded by CS gas, can scarcely breathe, and is retching. Before he gets to*

[handwritten margin note: Workers of the world unite!]

III

*the centre of the stage he collapses on his hands and knees and
his forehead rests on the ground. Just as he drops,* LILY *enters
right. She, too, is affected by gas, but not as badly as*
MICHAEL. *She holds a handkerchief up to her streaming eyes
and her free hand is extended in front of her as if she were
blind. She, too, is gasping for breath. She bumps into*
MICHAEL *on the ground and without a word staggers past him.*
SKINNER *races on from right. He has been caught by a water-
cannon — the upper half of his body is soaked. He is looking
about frantically for somewhere to hide. He races past*
MICHAEL, *then past* LILY, *and runs upstage. He discovers the
door into the parlour and flings it open. He glances inside and
then calls to* LILY.)

SKINNER: Hi! Missus! There's a place up here!

LILY: Where?

SKINNER: Up here! Come on! Quick! Quick!

LILY: Give me a hand, young fella. You'll have to lead me.
(*He runs down to her, grabs her arm, and drags her roughly
upstage.*)

SKINNER: Come on — come on — come on! Move, will you!
Move!

LILY: No need to pull the arm off me.

SKINNER: Did you get a dose of the CS gas?

LILY: D'you think I'm playing blind-man's-bluff? God, you're a
rough young fella, too.

SKINNER: In here. Quick. Watch the step.

LILY: My good coat! Mother of God, will you watch my good
coat!

SKINNER: I should have left you to the soldiers.

LILY: They'd be no thicker nor you.

SKINNER: D'you want to go back to them, then?

LILY: Don't be so damned smart.

SKINNER: There's a chair behind you.

LILY: I can manage myself.
(*She drops into a chair and covers her face with both hands.*)

LILY: O my God, that's sore on the eyes. There's someone else
back there.

SKINNER: Where?

LILY: Just outside.

(SKINNER *rushes out of the room.*)

LILY: Where's this, young fella? Whose house is this?

(SKINNER *finds* MICHAEL *on his hands and knees and gets down beside him.*)

SKINNER: Come on! Get up! They're going wild out there!

(MICHAEL *groans.*)

SKINNER: Are you hurt? Did you get a rubber bullet?

MICHAEL: Gas.

SKINNER: You're okay. Come on. You can't lie here. Can you walk?

MICHAEL: Leave me.

(*Sudden burst of rubber bullets, followed by screaming and the revving of armoured vehicles.* SKINNER *lies flat on his face until the burst is over. Then he suddenly grabs* MICHAEL *by the back of his jacket and drags him, face down and limp, up to the door and into the parlour. He drops him in the middle of the room, runs back to the door, locks it. As they enter,* LILY *uncovers her eyes momentarily.*)

LILY: I just thought it was a young fella. Is he hurted bad?

(*After locking the door,* SKINNER *moves around the room, examining it with quick, lithe efficiency.*)

SKINNER: No.

LILY: (*To* MICHAEL) Did you get a thump of a baton, young fella?

SKINNER: Gas.

LILY: Maybe he got a rubber bullet in the stomach.

SKINNER: Only gas.

LILY: He might be bleeding internal.

SKINNER: Gas! Are you deaf?

LILY: I like to see the blood. As long as you can see the blood there's always hope.

SKINNER: He'll come round.

LILY: I seen a polisman split a young fella with a baton one Saturday evening on Shipquay Street. His head opened like an orange and the blood spurted straight up – you know like them pictures you see of whales, only it was red. And at twelve Mass the next day who was sitting in the seat in front of me but your man, fresh as a bap, and the neatest

wee plaster from here to here, and him as proud of his-self.
(MICHAEL *gets himself into a sitting position on the floor.*)

MICHAEL: Aaaaagh.

LILY: Are you all right, young fella?

MICHAEL: I think so.

LILY: (*To* SKINNER) I was afeard by the way he was twisting,
the kidneys was lacerated.

MICHAEL: That's desperate stuff.

LILY: It's a help if you cross your legs and breathe shalla.

MICHAEL: God – that's awful.

LILY: Did you walk into it or what?

MICHAEL: A canister burst right at my feet.

LILY: You should have threw your jacket over it. They come on
us very sudden, didn't they?

MICHAEL: I don't know what happened.

LILY: What got into them anyway?

SKINNER: Did no one tell you the march was banned?

LILY: I knew the march was banned.

SKINNER: Did you expect them to give you tea at the end of it?

LILY: I didn't expect them to drive their tanks through us and
shoot gas and rubber bullets into us, young fella. It's a
mercy to God if no one's hurted. (*To* MICHAEL) Where
were you standing?

MICHAEL: Beside the platform. Just below the speakers.

LILY: I was at the back of the crowd, beside wee Johnny
Duffy – you know – the window-cleaner – Johnny the
Tumbler – and I'm telling him what the speakers is saying
'cos he hears hardly anything now since he fell off the
ladder the last time. And I'm just after telling him 'The
streets is ours and nobody's going to move us' when I turn
round and Jesus, Mary and Joseph there's this big Saracen
right behind me. Of course I took to my heels. And when I
look back there's Johnny the Tumbler standing there with
his fists in the air and him shouting, 'The streets is ours and
nobody's going to move us!' And you could hardly see him
below the Saracen. Lord, the chairman'll enjoy that.

(MICHAEL *gets to his feet and sits in the chair.*)

LILY: Are you better?

114

MICHAEL: I'm all right.

LILY: Maybe you concussed yourself when you fell. If you feel
yourself getting drowsy, shout 'Help! Help!'

MICHAEL: I'm fine.

LILY: D'you know what they say? That that CS gas is a sure
cure for stuttering. Would you believe that, young fella?
That's why Celia Cunningham across from us drags her wee
Colm Damien into the thick of every riot from here to
Strabane and him not seven till next May.

(MICHAEL *coughs again. She offers him a handkerchief.*)

LILY: Here.

MICHAEL: Thanks.

LILY: Cough hard.

MICHAEL: I'm fine.

LILY: If you don't get it up, it seeps down through the lungs
and into the corpuscles.

MICHAEL: I'm over the worst of it.

LILY: Every civil rights march Minnie McLaughlin goes
on – she's the floor above me – she wears a miraculous medal
pinned on her vest. Swears to God it's better nor a gas-
mask.

(MICHAEL *chokes again, almost retches.*)

LILY: Good on you, young fella. Keep it rising. Anyways, last
Wednesday week Minnie got hit on the leg with a rubber
bullet and now she pretends she has a limp and the young
fellas call her Che Guevara. If God hasn't said it, she'll be
looking for a pension from the Dublin crowd.

(SKINNER's *inspection is now complete – and he realizes where
he is. He bursts into sudden laughter – a mixture of delight and
excitement and malice.*)

SKINNER: Haaaaaaaaah!

(*Still laughing, he races right round the room, pounds on the
door with his fists, runs downstage and does a somersault across
the table.*)

LILY: Jesus, Mary and Joseph!

SKINNER: Haaaaaaah!

LILY: The young fella's a patent lunatic!

SKINNER: Haaaaaaah!

LILY: Keep away from me, young fella!

(SKINNER *stops suddenly beside her and puts his face up to hers.*)

SKINNER: Do you know where you are, Missus?

LILY: Just you lay one finger on me!

SKINNER: Do you know where you're sitting?

LILY: I'm warning you!

SKINNER: Look around – look around – look around.

(*To* MICHAEL) Where are you? Where do you find yourself this Saturday afternoon? (*To both*) Guess – come on – guess – guess – guess. Ten-to-one you'll never hit it. Fifty-to-one. A hundred-to-one.

MICHAEL: Where?

SKINNER: Where, Missus, where?

LILY: How would I know?

SKINNER: I'll tell you where you are.

MICHAEL: Where?

SKINNER: You. Are. Inside. The Guildhall.

LILY: We are not!

SKINNER: In fact you're in the Mayor's parlour.

LILY: You're a liar!

SKINNER: The holy of holies itself!

LILY: Have a bit of sense, young fella. What would we be doing in – ?

SKINNER: Look around! Look around!

MICHAEL: How did we get in?

SKINNER: By the side door.

MICHAEL: It's always guarded.

SKINNER: The soldiers must have moved into the Square to break up the meeting. (*To* LILY) When the trouble started you must have run down Guildhall Street.

LILY: How would I know where I run. I followed the crowd. ⊀

SKINNER: (*To* MICHAEL) You did the same.

MICHAEL: After the canister burst I don't know what happened.

LILY: So we just walked in?

SKINNER: By the side door and along the corridor and in here. Into the private parlour of His Worship, the Lord Mayor of

Derry. (*He flings a cushion at the wall.*) Yipeeeeeeeee!
(LILY *stands up.* MICHAEL *stands up. They stare in awe at their surroundings. As they gaze: A* SOLDIER *crouches at the very edge of stage right and speaks into his portable radio. His message is received by a* SOLDIER *at the very edge of stage left.*)

SOLDIER 1: Blue Star to Eagle. Blue Star to Eagle.

SOLDIER 2: Eagle receiving. Come in, Blue Star.

SOLDIER 1: The fucking yobbos are inside the fucking Guildhall!

SOLDIER 2: Jesus!

SOLDIER 1: What the fuck am I supposed to do?

SOLDIER 2: How did they get in?

SOLDIER 1: On fucking roller skates – how would I know!

SOLDIER 2: How many of them?

SOLDIER 1: No idea. The side door's wide open.

SOLDIER 2: What's your position, Blue Star?

SOLDIER 1: Guildhall Street. At the junction of the quay. What am I to do?

SOLDIER 2: Hold that position.

SOLDIER 1: Fucking great! For how long?

SOLDIER 2: Until you're reinforced.

SOLDIER 1: Thanks, mate!

SOLDIER 2: Do not attempt to enter or engage.

SOLDIER 1: Okay.

SOLDIER 2: I'll get back to you in a few minutes.

(*They go off. A television newsman,* LIAM O'KELLY, *appears on one of the battlements. Into a microphone:*)

O'KELLY: I am standing on the walls overlooking Guildhall Square in Derry where only a short time ago a civil rights meeting, estimated at about three thousand strong, was broken up by a large contingent of police and troops. There are no reports of serious casualties but unconfirmed reports are coming in that a group of about fifty armed gunmen have taken possession of the Guildhall here below me and have barricaded themselves in. If the reports are accurate, and if the Guildhall, regarded by the minority as a symbol of Unionist domination, has fallen into the hands of the terrorists, both the security forces and the Stormont government will be acutely embarrassed. Brigadier Johnson-Hansbury who was in charge of today's elaborate security operation has, so far, refused to confirm or deny the report. No comment either from the Chief Superintendent of Derry's Royal Ulster Constabulary. But usually reliable spokesmen from the Bogside insist that the story is accurate, and already small groups are gathering at street corners within the ghetto area to celebrate, as one of them put it to me, 'the fall of the Bastille'. This is Liam O'Kelly returning you to our studios in Dublin.

(As he finishes, a man enters left – the BALLADEER. *A glass in one hand, a bottle in the other. He is unsteady on his feet but his aggressive jubilance makes him articulate. Dressed in shirt and trousers; the shirt dirty and hanging over the trousers. As he swaggers across the stage he is followed by an* ACCORDIONIST *and a group of dancing* CHILDREN. *He sings, to the air of 'John Brown's Body'.)*

BALLADEER: A hundred Irish heroes one February day
Took over Derry's Guildhall, beside old Derry's quay.
They defied the British army, they defied the RUC.
They showed the crumbling empire what good Irishmen
could be.

(The CHILDREN *join in the chorus:)*

CHILDREN: Three cheers and then three cheers again for
Ireland one and free,
For civil rights and unity, Tone, Pearce and Connolly.
The Mayor of Derry City is an Irishman once more.
So let's celebrate our victory and let Irish whiskey pour.

BALLADEER: The British Army leader was a gentle English lad;
If he beat those dirty Paddys they might make him a lord.
So he whispered to his Tommies: 'Fix them, chaps; I'll see
you right!'
But the lads inside the Guildhall shouted back 'Come on
and fight!'

TOGETHER: Three cheers and then three cheers again for
Ireland one and free,
For civil rights and unity, Tone, Pearce and Connolly.
The Mayor of Derry City is an Irishman once more.

So let's celebrate our victory and let Irish whiskey pour.
(*They go off right.* MICHAEL *begins to move around the parlour, silently, deferentially.* LILY *stands very still; only her eyes move.* SKINNER *watches her closely. Pause.*)

MICHAEL: Christ Almighty – the Mayor's parlour!
(*Silence.*)

MICHAEL: I was here once before. I don't mean in here – in his public office – the one down the corridor. Three years ago – that bad winter – they were taking on extra men to clear away the snow, and my father said maybe if I went straight to the top and asked himself . . . That public office, it's nice enough. But my God this . . .
(*Silence.*)

LILY: We shouldn't be here.

MICHAEL: God, it's very impressive.

LILY: No place for us.

MICHAEL: God, it's beautiful, isn't it?

SKINNER: (*To* LILY) Isn't it beautiful?
(LILY *still has not moved. She points.*)

LILY: What's that?

SKINNER: Record player and radio.

LILY: And that?

SKINNER: Cocktail cabinet. What'll you have, Missus?

LILY: What's in that yoke?
(SKINNER *tries to open the top of the display cabinet.*)

SKINNER: Locked. But we'll soon fix that.
(*He produces a penknife and deftly forces the lock.*)

MICHAEL: Feel the walls. And the doorhandles. Real oak. And brass. The very best of stuff.
(SKINNER *takes out a ceremonial sword and an ancient musket, each with a descriptive label attached.*)

SKINNER: This is a 'Fourteenth-century ceremonial sword with jewelled handle and silver tip'. How are you off for swords, Missus?

MICHAEL: Feel the carpet. Like a mattress.

SKINNER: And this is a 'Musket used by Williamite garrison besieged by Jacobite army. 1691'.

LILY: Who's that?

119

SKINNER: (*Reads*) Sir Joshua Hetherington MBE, VMH, SHIT. Is he a mate of yours?

LILY: I was thinking it wasn't the Sacred Heart.

(MICHAEL *reverently examines the desk set on the table.*)

MICHAEL: Feel the weight of that – pure silver. And look – look – real leather – run your hand over it (*desk top*).

SKINNER: We'll have to sign the Distinguished Visitors' Book, Missus. Are you distinguished?

LILY: What's in there?

(MICHAEL *opens the dressing-room door and looks in.*)

MICHAEL: Wardrobes – toilet – wash-hand basin – shower. Pink and black tiles all round. And the taps are gold and made like fishes' heads. (*Closes door.*) God, it's very impressive. Isn't it impressive, Missus?

SKINNER: Isn't it, Missus?

LILY: It's all right.

SKINNER: Two pounds deposit against breakages and it's yours for ten bob a week. Or maybe you don't like the locality, Missus?

LILY: Mrs Doherty's the name, young fella, Mrs Lily Doherty.

SKINNER: Are you not impressed, Lily?

(MICHAEL *reads the inscription below the stained-glass window.*)

MICHAEL: 'Presented to the citizens of Londonderry by the Hon. The Irish Society to commemorate the visit of King Edward VII July 1903.'

SKINNER: That's our window, Lily. How would it look in your parlour?

MICHAEL: I read about the Hon. The Irish Society. They're big London businessmen and big bankers and they own most of the ground in the city.

LILY: This room's bigger than my whole place.

SKINNER: Have you no gold taps and tiled walls?

LILY: There's one tap and one toilet below in the yard – and they're for eight families.

SKINNER: By God, you'll sign no Distinguished Visitors' Book, Lily.

LILY: And I'll tell you something, glib boy: if this place was

 Contrast

mine, I'd soon cover them ugly bare boards (*the oak walls*)
with nice pink gloss paint that you could wash the dirt off,
and I'd put decent glass you could see through into them
gloomy windows, and I'd shift Joe Stalin there (*Sir Joshua*),
and I'd put a nice flight of them brass ducks up along that
wall.

(SKINNER *and* MICHAEL *both laugh.*)

SKINNER: You're a woman of taste, Lily Doherty.

LILY: And since this is my first time here and since you
(SKINNER) seem to be the caretaker, the least you might do
is offer a drink to a ratepayer.

(*She sits – taking possession.* MICHAEL *laughs.*)

MICHAEL: The Mayor's parlour – God Almighty!

LILY: (*To* MICHAEL) And will you quit creeping about on your
toes, young fella, as if you were doing the Stations of the
Cross.

MICHAEL: I never thought I'd be in here.

LILY: Well now you are. Sit down and stop trembling like
Gavigan's greyhound.

SKINNER: What'll you have, Lily?

LILY: What have you got?

SKINNER: Whiskey – gin – rum – sherry – brandy – vodka –

MICHAEL: Ah now, hold on.

SKINNER: What?

MICHAEL: Do you think you should?

SKINNER: What?

MICHAEL: Touch any of that stuff.

SKINNER: Why not?

MICHAEL: Well I mean to say, it's not ours and we weren't
invited here and –

LILY: Lookat, young fella: since it was the British troops driv
me off my own streets and deprived me of my sight and
vision for a good quarter of an hour, the least the
corporation can do is placate me with one wee drink.
(*Grandly to* SKINNER) I think I favour a little port wine,
young fella, if you insist.

MICHAEL: Honest to God, this is mad, really mad – sitting in
the Mayor's parlour on a Saturday afternoon – bloody mad!

(*He giggles.*)

LILY: What do they call you, young fella?

MICHAEL: Michael.

LILY: Michael what?

MICHAEL: Michael Hegarty.

LILY: What Hegarty are you?

MICHAEL: I'm from the Brandywell.

LILY: Jack Hegarty's son?

MICHAEL: Tommy. My father used to be in the slaughter house – before it closed down.

LILY: Are you working?

MICHAEL: I was a clerk with a building contractor but he went bust six months ago. And before that I was an assistant-storeman in the distillery but then they were taken over. And now my father's trying to get me into the gas-works. My father and the foreman's mates. And in the meantime I'm going to the tech. four nights a week – you know – to improve myself. I'm doing economics and business administration and computer science.

LILY: You must be smart, young fella.

MICHAEL: I don't know about that. But I'm a lot luckier than my father was. And since that North Sea discovery there's a big future in gas. They can't even guess how big the industry's going to grow.

SKINNER: But you'll be ready to meet the challenge; wise man. Are *you* smart, Lily?

LILY: Me? I never could do nothing right at school except carry round the roll books. And when the inspector would come they used to lock me in the cloakroom with the Mad Mulligans. Lucky for my wanes the chairman's got the brains.

SKINNER: Mr Hegarty?

MICHAEL: What?

SKINNER: A drink.

MICHAEL: I don't think I should. I think –

SKINNER: Suit yourself.

LILY: (*To* MICHAEL) Are you a victim?

MICHAEL: What?

LILY: To the drink.

MICHAEL: No, no, no. It's just that there's no one here and it's not ours and –

LILY: Will you take one drink and don't be such an aul woman! (*To* SKINNER) Give him a drink, young fella.

MICHAEL: A very small whiskey, then.

LILY: Michael's a nice name. I have a Michael. He's seven. Next to Gloria. She's six. And then Timothy – he's three. And then the baby – he's eleven months – Mark Antony. Every one of them sound of mind and limb, thanks be to God. And that includes our Declan – he's nine – though he's not as forward as the others – you know – not much for mixing; a wee bit quiet – you know – nothing more nor shyness and sure he'll soon grow out of that, won't he? They all say Declan's the pet. And praise be to Almighty God, not one of them has the chairman's chest. D'you see his chest, young fella? Ask him to carry the water or the coal up the three flights from the yard and you'd think Hurricane Debbie was coming at you. And give him just wan whiff of the stuff we got the day and before you'd blink he'd be life everlasting.

MICHAEL: Five children?

LILY: Five? God look to your wit! Eleven, young fella. Eight boys and three girls. And they come like a pattern on wallpaper: two boys, a girl, two boys, a girl, two boys, a girl, two boys. If I had have made the dozen, it would have been a wee girl, wouldn't it?

MICHAEL: I – I – it –

LILY: And I would have called her Jasmine – that's a gorgeous yalla' flower – I seen it once in a wreath up in the cemetery the day they buried Andy Boyle's wife. But after Mark Antony the chairman hadn't a puff left in him.

(SKINNER *hands round the drinks.*)

SKINNER: Compliments of the city.

LILY: Hi! What happened to you?

SKINNER: Me?

LILY: Your hair – your shirt – you're soaked!

SKINNER: The water-cannon got me.

123

LILY: Will you take that off you, young fella, before you die of
    internal pneumonia.
SKINNER: I'm dry now.
LILY: Take off that shirt.
SKINNER: I'm telling you – I'm dried out.
LILY: Come here to me.
SKINNER: I'm dry enough.
LILY: I said come here!
    (*She unbuttons his shirt and takes it off – he is wearing nothing
    underneath – and dries his hair with it.*)
LILY: 'Wet feet or a wet chemise/The sure way to an early
    demise.' Lord, there's not a pick on him.
SKINNER: Leave me alone. I'm okay.
LILY: And you've been running about like that for the past
    half-hour! What way's your shoes? Are them gutties dry?
SKINNER: I'm telling you – I'm all right.
LILY: Take them off. Take them off.
    (*He takes off the canvas shoes. He is not wearing socks.*)
LILY: Give them to me.
    (*She hangs the shirt across a chair and puts the shoes on their
    sides.*)
LILY: D'you see our Kevin? He's like him (SKINNER). <u>Eats like
    a bishop and nothing to show for it.</u> I be affronted when he
    goes with his class to the swimming pool. *Respectability*
MICHAEL: Well. To civil rights.
LILY: Good luck, young fella.
SKINNER: Good luck.
MICHAEL: To another great turn-out today.
LILY: Great.
MICHAEL: Good luck.
    (*A PRIEST in a surplice appears on the battlements. He
    addresses a congregation in the parlour.*)
PRIEST: At eleven o'clock tomorrow morning solemn requiem
    Mass will be celebrated in this church for the repose of the
    souls of the three people whose death has plunged this
    parish into a deep and numbing grief. As you are probably
    aware, I had the privilege of administering the last rites to
    them and the knowledge that they didn't go unfortified

before their Maker is a consolation to all of us. But it is
natural that we should mourn. Blessed are they that mourn,
says our Divine Lord. But it is also right and fitting that
this tragic happening should make us sit back and take
stock and ask ourselves the very pertinent question: Why
did they die?
I believe the answer to that question is this. They died for
their beliefs. They died for their fellow citizens. They died
because they could endure no longer the injuries and
injustices and indignities that have been their lot for too
many years. They sacrificed their lives so that you and I and
thousands like us might be rid of that iniquitous yoke and
might inherit a decent way of life. And if that is not heroic
virtue, then the word sanctity has no meaning.
No sacrifice is ever in vain. But its value can be diminished
if it doesn't fire our imagination, stiffen our resolution, and
make us even more determined to see that the dream they
dreamed is realized. May we be worthy of that dream, of
their trust. May we have the courage to implement their
noble hopes. May we have God's strength to carry on where
they left off.
In the name of the Father, Son, and Holy Spirit.
(*When the* PRIEST *finishes he goes off; and immediately we
hear* VOICES *from behind the battlements call to one another in
shocked, awed tones.*)
VOICE 1: There's at least a dozen dead.
VOICE 2: Where?
VOICE 1: Inside the Guildhall.
VOICE 3: I heard fifteen or sixteen.
VOICE 1: Maybe twenty.
VOICE 3: And a baby in a pram.
VOICE 1: And an old man. They blew his head off.
VOICE 2: O my God.
VOICE 3: They just broken the windows and lobbed in
    hand-grenades.
VOICE 2: O my God.
VOICE 1: Blew most of them to smithereens.
VOICE 2: Fuck them anyway! Fuck them! Fuck them!

Fuck them!

(*An* ARMY PRESS OFFICER *appears on the battlements and reads a press release to a few reporters (*O'KELLY, *the* PHOTOGRAPHER *of opening sequence, etc.) below.*)

OFFICER: At approximately 15.20 hours today a band of terrorists took possession of a portion of the Guildhall. They gained access during a civil disturbance by forcing a side-door in Guildhall Street. It is estimated that up to forty persons are involved. In the disturbance two soldiers were hit by stones and one by a bottle. There are no reports of civilian injuries. The area is now quiet and the security forces have the situation in hand. No further statement will be issued.

(*The* PRESSMEN *ask their questions with great rapidity*:)

O'KELLY: What portion of the Guildhall is occupied?

OFFICER: The entire first floor.

PRESSMAN 1: Is it true that there are women in there, too?

OFFICER: Our information is that women are involved.

PRESSMAN 2: Are they armed?

OFFICER: Our information is that they have access to arms.

PRESSMAN 2: They brought the arms with them or the arms are in there?

OFFICER: We understand that arms are accessible to them.

O'KELLY: What troops and equipment have you brought up?

OFFICER: I cannot answer that.

PRESSMAN 1: Have you been in touch with them?

OFFICER: No.

PRESSMAN 2: Are you going to get in touch with them?

OFFICER: Perhaps.

O'KELLY: Are you going to negotiate with them or are you going to go in after them?

OFFICER: Sorry. That's all I can say.

O'KELLY: When are you going in after them?

PRESSMAN 1: Is it a police or an army operation?

OFFICER: Sorry.

PRESSMAN 2: Why wasn't the Guildhall guarded?

O'KELLY: Who's in charge of ground forces?

PRESSMAN 1: Do you expect a reaction from the Bogside?

OFFICER: Sorry, gentlemen.
(*He disappears. The* PRESSMEN *hurry off.* MICHAEL *gets to his feet.*)
MICHAEL: It was a big turn-out, wasn't it?
LILY: Terrible big.
MICHAEL: And the speeches were good, too.
LILY: I don't care much for speeches. Isn't that a shocking thing to say? I can't concentrate – you know?
MICHAEL: They'll never learn, you know; never. All they had to do was sit back nice and quiet; let the speeches be made; let the crowd go home. There wouldn't be no trouble of any kind. But they have to bull in. And d'you know what they're doing? As a matter of fact they're doing two things: they're bringing more and more people out on the streets – that's fine; but they're also giving the hooligan element an excuse to retaliate – and that's where the danger lies.
LILY: (*To* SKINNER) It's a hot whiskey you should be drinking.
MICHAEL: I've been on every civil rights march from the very beginning – right from October 5th. And I can tell you there wasn't the thousands then that there was the day. I've even went on civil rights marches that I was far from satisfied about the people that was running them; for as you know as well as me there's a lot of strange characters knuckled in on the act that didn't give a shite about real civil rights – if you'll excuse me, Missus.
LILY: Port wine's gorgeous.
MICHAEL: But as I say to Norah, the main thing is to keep a united front. The ultimate objectives we're all striving for is more important than the personalities or the politics of the individuals concerned.
SKINNER: At this point in time.
MICHAEL: What's that?
SKINNER: And taking full cognizance of all relative facts.
MICHAEL: What d'you mean?
LILY: Who's Norah, young fella?
MICHAEL: The girl I'm engaged to.
LILY: (*To* SKINNER) Ah! He's engaged.
(SKINNER *raises his glass.*)

127

LILY: Congratulations.

MICHAEL: Thanks.

LILY: I wish you health, wealth and every happiness, young fella, and may no burden come your way that you're not fit to carry.

MICHAEL: Thank you.

LILY: When are you getting married?

MICHAEL: Easter.

LILY: (*To* SKINNER) Easter! I was married at Easter – April 3rd – my seventeenth birthday. And we spent our honeymoon with the chairman's Auntie Maggie and Uncle Ned in Preston, Lancashire, England, and we seen the docks and everything.

MICHAEL: We're getting married on Easter Tuesday.

LILY: And where will you live?

MICHAEL: We'll live with my people till we get a place of our own.

LILY: (*To* SKINNER) A place of their own!

SKINNER: Leely, the language I speak a leetle too – yes?

LILY: Norah's a nice name. If the chairman had have had his way, we'd have had a Norah. But I always favoured a Noelle. She's fourteen now. Between Tom and the twins. Born on a roasting August bank holiday Monday at 3.20 in the afternoon but I called her Noelle all the same.

MICHAEL: (*To* SKINNER) How many would you say was there today?

SKINNER: No idea.

MICHAEL: Six thousand? More?

(SKINNER *shrugs indifferently. Rises and goes to the window where he looks out.* LILY *takes off her shoes.*)

MICHAEL: I'm getting pretty accurate at assessing a crowd and my estimate would be between six and six and a half. When the ones at the front were down at the Brandywell, the last of them were leaving the Creggan. I could see both ways 'cos I was in the middle. And the hooligan element kept well out of the way. It was a good, disciplined, responsible march. And that's what we must show them – that we're responsible and respectable; and they'll come to respect

128

what we're campaigning for.

LILY: D'you see them shoes? Five pounds in Woolworth's and never a day's content since I got them.

MICHAEL: Do you go on all the marches, Lily?

LILY: Most of them. It's the only exercise I get.

MICHAEL: Do you have the feeling they're not as – I don't know – as dignified as they used to be? Like, d'you remember in the early days, they wouldn't let you carry a placard – wouldn't even let you talk, for God's sake. And that was really impressive – all those people marching along in silence, rich and poor, high and low, doctors, accountants, plumbers, teachers, bricklayers – all shoulder to shoulder – knowing that what they wanted was their rights and knowing that because it was their rights nothing in the world was going to stop them getting them.

SKINNER: Shite – if you'll excuse me, Missus. Who's for more municipal booze?

(*He refills his own glass and* LILY'*s.*)

MICHAEL: What do you mean?

LILY: That's enough. Easy – easy.

SKINNER: It's coming off a fine broad back. Another whiskey, Mr Hegarty?

MICHAEL: Are you for civil rights at all?

SKINNER: Course I am. I'm crazy about them. A little drop?

MICHAEL: Not for me.

SKINNER: Just a nip?

MICHAEL: I'm finished.

SKINNER: Have a cigar.

MICHAEL: No.

SKINNER: A cigarette, then.

MICHAEL: No.

SKINNER: Or what about a shower under the golden fish?

(LILY *gives a great whoop of laughter.*)

LILY: Haaaaa! A shower! God but you're a comic, young fella.

(SKINNER *lights a cigar and carries his glass to the phone.*)

MICHAEL: I see nothing funny in that.

129

LILY: D'you see if it was a Sunday I'd take a shower myself. Sunday's my day. We all have our days for bathing over at the granny's – that's the chairman's mother. She has us all up on a time-table on the kitchen wall, and if you miss your night you lose your turn.

SKINNER: (*Phone*) Hello? Could you tell me what won the 3.30?

LILY: (*To* MICHAEL) D'you see the granny, young fella? Seventy-seven years of age. Lives alone. Supple as an aul cat. Her own teeth, her own eyes. And she still does twenty houses a week – you know – cleaning them down; and me that could be her daughter, I can never manage more nor fifteen.

(SKINNER *hangs up.*)

SKINNER: Bingo Mistress at eights. Which leaves me slightly ahead of the millionaire bookie.

LILY: I'd know by the look of you.

(SKINNER *dials again.* LILY *continues to* MICHAEL.)

LILY: Most of them she's been doing for years, and they think the world of her; you know – dentists and solicitors and doctors and all. Very swanky. And the wanes in them houses – they visit her and all – they have a sort of pet name on her – they call her Auntie Dodie. Wouldn't it make you puke? I'll tell you something, young fella: them class of people's a very poor judge of character.

SKINNER: (*Phone*) Jackie? Yes, it's me. No, as a matter of fact I'm stripped to the waist and drinking brandy in the Mayor's parlour. (*To* LILY *and* MICHAEL) He's killing himself laughing! (*Into phone*) Look, Jack, would you put half-a-note on Bunny Rabbit in the 4.30? Decent man. See you tonight. Bye.

LILY: I'm glad you've a nice cushy career.

SKINNER: It's not all sunshine, Lily.

LILY: D'you bet heavy?

SKINNER: When I have it.

LILY: That'll be often. What do they call you, young fella?

SKINNER: Skinner.

LILY: Mr Skinner or Skinner what?

SKINNER: Just Skinner.

130

LILY: Would you be anything to Paddy Skinner that used to keep the goats behind the Mormon chapel?

SKINNER: Both my parents died when I was a baby. I was reared by an aunt. Next question?

Shove – in B.I.

LILY: Lord, I'm sorry, son. (*To* MICHAEL) Both his parents! Shocking. 'Life is not a bed of roses. Sorrow is our daily lot.' (*Suddenly bright*) But I'll bet you're musical like all the others.

SKINNER: Who?

LILY: Sure it's well known that all wee orphans is always musical. Orphans can play instruments before they can talk. There was the poor wee Mulherns opposite us – the father and mother both submitted to TB within three days of other – and when you'd pass that house at night – the music coming out of it – honest to God you'd think it was the Palais de Danse. And sure look at the Nazareth House Ceilidhe Band – thumping away at concerts all over the world – trained armies couldn't stop them. Sure the poor nuns can't get quiet to say their prayers.

music from orphans!

(SKINNER *turns on the radio.*)

SKINNER: I can play the radio, Lily.

(*Waltz music on the radio.*)

LILY: What's that?

SKINNER: Four ways – loud and soft and off and on. Can you?

LILY: Oh, you're great.

SKINNER: And I play the horses and the dogs.

LILY: You're brilliant.

SKINNER: Thanks.

LILY: Are you working?

SKINNER: No.

LILY: Did you ever work?

SKINNER: For a while when I was at grammar school – before they kicked me out.

LILY: What did you ever do since?

SKINNER: Three years ago I did some potato picking.

LILY: (*To* MICHAEL) He has a long memory.

SKINNER: And last August I was a conductor on the buses.

LILY: But travel didn't agree with you.

131

SKINNER: Listen, Lily – isn't that the BBC Orphans' Orchestra?
LILY: I'll tell you something – you never had to study glibness.
Oh, nothing sharpens the wits like idleness. (*To* MICHAEL.)
You stick to your books, son. That's what I say to our boys.
SKINNER: I'll bet you the chairman's glib, Lily.
LILY: The chairman never worked on account of his health.
(SKINNER *sings with the radio and does a parody-waltz off
and into the dressing-room.*)
SKINNER: 1–2–3; 1–2–3; 1–2–3; 1–2–3.
LILY: (*Calls*) And he has more brains than you and a dozen like
you put together! Brat! Put that thing out!
(MICHAEL *switches radio off.*)
LILY: Cheeky young brat, that Skinner! Easy seen he never had
no mother to tan his backside.
MICHAEL: Was he on the march at all?
LILY: Who?
MICHAEL: Skinner.
LILY: How would I know?
MICHAEL: My suspicion is he just turned up for the meeting.
LILY: The chairman worked for a full year after we married. In
Thompson's foundry. But the fumes destroyed the tissues
of his lungs. D'you think he likes sitting at the fire all day,
reading the wanes' comics?
MICHAEL: That Skinner's a trouble-maker.
LILY: But for all he got no education he's a damn-sight smarter
nor that buck.
MICHAEL: That's what I was talking about earlier, Lily.
Characters like that need watching.
LILY: Who?
MICHAEL: Him.
LILY: What about him?
MICHAEL: I have a feeling about him. I wouldn't be surprised if
he was a revolutionary.
LILY: What do they call you again, young fella?
MICHAEL: Michael.
LILY: Michael's a nice name. I have a Michael. He'll be eight
next October. You stick to your books, son.
MICHAEL: We'll watch him, Lily. I'm uneasy about that fella.

(DODDS *enters.*)

DODDS: If you are born into the subculture of poverty, what do you inherit? Well, you inherit an economic condition, and you inherit a social and psychological condition. The economic characteristics include wretched housing, a constant struggle for survival, a chronic shortage of cash, persistent unemployment and very often real hunger or at least malnutrition. And of course the economic environment conditions the psychological and social man so that he constantly feels inferior, marginal, helpless, dependent. Another inheritance is his inability to control impulse: he is present-time orientated and seldom defers gratification, never plans for the future, and endures his here and now with resignation and frustration. The reason for this sense of defeat is the existence of a set of values in the dominant class which stresses the accumulation of wealth and property, the desirability of 'improvement' and explains the low economic status of the poor as a result of their personal shiftlessness and inadequacy.

(*The* JUDGE *appears in the battlements and* BRIGADIER JOHNSON-HANSBURY *enters right.* DODDS *does not move.*)

JUDGE: Brigadier Johnson-Hansbury, you were in charge of security on that day.

BRIGADIER: That is correct, my lord.

JUDGE: Could you tell us what strength was at your disposal?

BRIGADIER: The 8th Infantry Brigade, 1st Battalion Parachute Regiment, 1st Battalion King's Own Border Regiment, two companies of the 3rd Battalion Royal Regiment of Fusiliers.

JUDGE: And equipment?

BRIGADIER: Twelve Saracens, ten Saladins, two dozen Ferrets and four water-cannons, and a modicum of air-cover.

JUDGE: And the Royal Ulster Constabulary and the Ulster Defence Regiment?

BRIGADIER: They were present, my lord.

JUDGE: Under your command?

BRIGADIER: As a civilian authority.

JUDGE: Under your command?

BRIGADIER: Under my command.

133

JUDGE: I'm an old army man myself, Brigadier, and it does seem a rather formidable array to line up against three terrorists, however well armed they could have been.

BRIGADIER: At that point we had no idea how many gunmen were inside the Guildhall. Our first reports indicated forty.

JUDGE: But those reports were inaccurate.

BRIGADIER: They were, my lord. But I would like to point out that we were in an exposed position between the terrorists inside the Guildhall and the no-go Bogside areas at our flank and back.

JUDGE: I see. And you, personally, gave the command over the loudhailer to the terrorists inside to surrender?

BRIGADIER: I did, my lord. On two occasions.

JUDGE: And approximately ten minutes after the second occasion, they emerged?

BRIGADIER: That is correct.

JUDGE: Brigadier, a persistent suggestion keeps cropping up in the various reports about the events of that day and indeed it was voiced strenuously by counsel for the deceased within these very walls, and I would like to have your reaction to it. The suggestion is that no attempt was made to arrest these people as they emerged, but that they were dealt with 'punitively', as it has been phrased, 'to teach the ghettos a lesson'.

BRIGADIER: My lord, they emerged firing from the Guildhall. There was no possibility whatever of effecting an arrest operation. And at that point we understood they were the advance group of a much larger force.

JUDGE: So you dismiss the suggestion?

BRIGADIER: Completely, my lord.

JUDGE: And an arrest was not attempted?

BRIGADIER: Because it wasn't possible in the circumstances.

JUDGE: And had you known, as you learned later, Brigadier, that there were only three terrorists involved, would you have acted differently?

BRIGADIER: My orders would have been the same, my lord.

JUDGE: Thank you, Brigadier.

(*The* JUDGE *disappears.* BRIGADIER JOHNSON-HANSBURY

goes off right.)

DODDS: Middle-class people – with deference, people like you
and me – we tend to concentrate on the negative aspects of
the culture of poverty. We tend to associate negative values
to such traits as present-time orientation, and concrete
versus abstract orientation. Now, I don't want to idealize or
romanticize the culture of poverty; as someone has said,
'It's easier to praise poverty than to live in it.' But there are
some positive aspects which we cannot overlook completely.
Present-orientated living, for example, may sharpen one's
attitude for spontaneity and for excitement, for the
appreciation of the sensual, for the indulgence of impulse;
and these aptitudes are often blunted or muted in people
like us who are middle-class and future-orientated. So that
to live in the culture of poverty is, in a sense, to live with
the reality of the moment – in other words to practise a sort
of existentialism. The result is that people with a culture of
poverty suffer much less from repression than we of the
middle-class suffer and indeed, if I may make the
suggestion with due qualification, they often have a hell of a
lot more fun than we have.

(DODDS *goes off left. The dressing-room door is flung open.*
SKINNER *is dressed in splendid mayoral robe and chain and
wears an enormous ceremonial hat jauntily on his head. At the
door:*)

SKINNER: 'You're much deceived; in nothing am I changed/But
in my garments!' *(what's this from?)*
(*He comes into the parlour carrying robes and head-gear for the
other two.* LILY *gives one of her whoops.*)

LILY: O Jesus, Mary and Joseph!

SKINNER: 'Through tattered clothes small vices do appear;
Robes and furred gowns hide all.'

LILY: Mother of God, would you look at him! And the hat!
What's the rig, Skinner?
(SKINNER *distributes the gowns.*)

SKINNER: Mayor's robes, alderman's robes, councillor's robes.
Put them on and I'll give you both the freedom of the city.

LILY: Skinner, you're an eejit!

135

SKINNER: The ceremony begins in five minutes. The world's press and television are already gathering outside. 'Social upheaval in Derry. Three gutties become freemen.' Apologies, Mr Hegarty! 'Two gutties.' What happened to the Orphans' Orchestra?
(*He switches on the radio. A military band. They have to shout to be heard above it.*)
MICHAEL: Catch yourself on, Skinner.
LILY: Lord, the weight of them! They'd cover my settee just lovely. (*To* MICHAEL) Put it on for the laugh, young fella.
SKINNER: Don the robes, ladies and gentlemen, and taste real power.
(LILY *puts on her robe and head-dress.* MICHAEL *reluctantly puts on the robe only.* SKINNER *has the Union Jack in one hand and the ceremonial sword in the other.*)
LILY: Lookat-lookat-lookat me, would you! (*She dances around the parlour.*) Di-do-do-da-di-doo-da-da.
(*Sings*) 'She is the Lily of Laguna; she is my Lily and my –'. Mother of God, if the wanes could see me now!
SKINNER: Or the chairman.
LILY: Ooooops!
SKINNER: Lily, this day I confer on you the freedom of the City of Derry. God bless you, my child. And now, Mr Hegarty, I think we'll make you a life peer. Arise Lord Michael – of Gas.
LILY: They make you feel great all the same. You feel you could – you could give benediction!
SKINNER: Make way – make way for the Lord and Lady Mayor of Derry Colmcille!
LILY: My shoes – my shoes! I can't appear without my shoes!
(MICHAEL *takes off his robe and sits down.* LILY *joins* SKINNER *in a ceremonial parade before imaginary people. They both affect very grand accents. Very fast.*)
SKINNER: How are you? Delighted you could come.
LILY: How do do.
SKINNER: My wife – Lady Elizabeth.
LILY: (*Blows kiss*) Wonderful people.
SKINNER: Nice of you to turn up.

LILY: My husband and I.

SKINNER: Carry on with the good work.

LILY: Thank you. Thank you.

SKINNER: Splendid job you're doing.

LILY: We're really enjoying ourselves.

(SKINNER *lifts the flowers and hands them to* LILY.)

SKINNER: From the residents of Tintown.

LILY: Oh, my! How sweet! (*Stoops down to kiss a child.*)
Thank you, darling.

(SKINNER *pauses below Sir Joshua. He is now the stern,
practical man of affairs. The accent is dropped.*)

SKINNER: This is the case I was telling you about, Sir Joshua.
Eleven children in a two-roomed flat. No toilet, no running
water.

LILY: Except what's running down the walls. Haaaaa!

SKINNER: She believes she has a reasonable case for a
corporation house.

LILY: It's two houses I need!

SKINNER: Two?

LILY: Isn't there thirteen of us? How do you fit thirteen into
one house?

SKINNER: (*To portrait*) I know. I know. They can't be satisfied.

LILY: Listen! Listen! I know that one! Do you know it,
Skinner?

SKINNER: Elizabeth, please.

LILY: It's a military two-step. The chairman was powerful at it.
Give us your hand! Come on!

SKINNER: I think you're concussed.

(*She drags him into the middle of the parlour and sings as she
dances.* SKINNER *sings with her.*)

LILY: As I walk along the Bois de Boulogne with an
independent air,
You can hear the girls declare, 'He must be a millionaire'
You can hear them sigh and hope to die and can see them
wink the other eye
At the man who broke the bank at Monte Carlo.

(LILY *drops exhausted into a chair.*)

O my God, I'm punctured!

SKINNER: Lovely, Lily. Lovely.

LILY: I wasn't a bad dancer once.

SKINNER: And now Lord Michael will oblige with a recitation – *If* – by the inimitable Rudyard Kipling. 'If you can keep your head when all about you/Are losing theirs and blaming it on you . . .' Ladies and gentlemen, a poem to fit the place and the occasion – Lord Michael of Gas!

(SKINNER *switches off the radio and lights a cigar.*)

MICHAEL: I don't know what you think you're up to. I don't know what sort of a game you think this is. But I happen to be serious about this campaign. I marched three miles today and I attended a peaceful meeting today because every man's entitled to justice and fair play and that's what I'm campaigning for. But this – this – this fooling around, this swaggering about as if you owned the place, this isn't my idea of dignified, peaceful protest.

SKINNER: (*To* LILY) I think he deserves to sign the Distinguished Visitors' Book. Doesn't he?

MICHAEL: You know what you're campaigning for, Missus. You want a decent home. And you want a better life for your children than the life you had. But I don't know what his game is. I don't know what he wants.

SKINNER: Bunny Rabbit to romp home at twenties.

MICHAEL: Oh, as you say, he's glib all right. But if you ask me he's more at home with the hooligans, out throwing stones and burning shops!

(SKINNER *pours himself a drink and sings quietly. Then very deliberately he stubs out his cigar on the leather-top desk.*)

SKINNER: (*Sings*) Will you come into my parlour, said the spider to the fly.

'Tis the prettiest little parlour that ever you did spy.

MICHAEL: Look, Lily, look! I told you! I told you!

SKINNER: The way into my parlour is up a winding stair And I have many curious things to show you when you're there.

MICHAEL: He's a vandal! He's a bloody vandal!

(SKINNER *pours a drink for* LILY.)

SKINNER: Lily?

LILY: You'll have me on my ear – God bless you. (*To* MICHAEL)
Try that port wine, young fella. It's gorgeous.

SKINNER: It's sherry. Mr Hegarty?

(MICHAEL *turns away and prepares to leave.*)

SKINNER: Just the two of us, then, Lily. To . . . dignity.

MICHAEL: I'm going.

LILY: It's time we were all leaving. They'll be waiting for me to
make the tea.

(SKINNER *sits down and puts his feet up on the table.*)

SKINNER: Would anyone object if I had another cigar?

(*He lights one.*)

LILY: What time is it anyway?

MICHAEL: Coming on to five.

LILY: D'you see my wanes? If I'm not there, not one of them
would lift a finger. Three years ago last May the chairman
won the five pound note in the Slate Club raffle and myself
and Declan went on a bus run to Bundoran – I took him
with me 'cos he doesn't play about on the street with the
others, you know – and when we come home at midnight,
there they all were, with faces this length, sitting round the
bare table, waiting since six o'clock for their tea to appear!

MICHAEL: I'm away, Lily. Good luck.

LILY: Good-bye, young fella. And keep at them books.

MICHAEL: (*To* SKINNER) Thanks for pulling me in.

SKINNER: My pleasure. And any time you're this way, don't
pass the door.

LILY: And good luck on Easter Tuesday.

MICHAEL: Thanks. Thanks.

(*Before* MICHAEL *reaches the door:*)

SKINNER: Before you go, take a look out the window.

(MICHAEL *stops, looks at* SKINNER, *then crosses to the window.*)

SKINNER: Are they still there?

LILY: Is who still there?

SKINNER: The army. (*To* MICHAEL) Have they gone yet?

MICHAEL: The place is crawling with them. And there's police
there, too.

LILY: The army's bad enough, but God forgive me I can't stand
them polis.

SKINNER: If I were you I'd wait till they move.

MICHAEL: Why should I?

SKINNER: Go ahead then.

MICHAEL: Why shouldn't I?

SKINNER: Go ahead then.

MICHAEL: I've done nothing wrong.

SKINNER: How do you talk to a boy scout like that?

MICHAEL: I've done nothing I'm ashamed of.

SKINNER: You drank municipal whiskey. You masqueraded as a councillor. Theft and deception.

MICHAEL: All right, smart alec. (*He tosses coins on the table.*) That's for the drink – there – there – there. Now give me one good reason why I can't walk straight out of here and across that Square. One good reason – go on – go on.

SKINNER: Because you presumed, boy. Because this is theirs, boy, and your very presence here is a sacrilege.

MICHAEL: They don't know we're here.

SKINNER: They'll see you coming out, won't they?

MICHAEL: So they'll see me coming out and they'll arrest me for trespassing.

SKINNER: Have a brandy on me. They'll soon shift.

MICHAEL: I certainly don't want to be arrested. But if they want to arrest me for protesting peacefully – that's all right – I'm prepared to be arrested.

SKINNER: They could do terrible things to you – break your arms, burn you with cigarettes, give you injections.

MICHAEL: Gandhi showed that violence done against peaceful protest helps your cause.

SKINNER: Or shoot you.

LILY: God forgive you, Skinner. There's no luck in talk like that.

MICHAEL: As long as we don't react violently, as long as we don't allow ourselves to be provoked, ultimately we must win.

SKINNER: Do you understand Mr Hegarty's theory, Lily?

LILY: Youse are both away above me.

MICHAEL: I told you my name's Michael.

SKINNER: Mr Hegarty is of the belief that if five thousand of us are demonstrating peacefully and they come along and shoot us down, then automatically we . . . we . . . (*To* MICHAEL) Sorry, what's the theory again?

MICHAEL: You know damn well the point I'm making and you know damn well it's true.

SKINNER: It's not, you know. But we'll discuss it some other time. And as I said, if you're passing this way, don't let them entertain you in the outer office.

(MICHAEL *goes back to the window and looks out.* LILY *giggles.*)

LILY: D'you see our place? At this minute Mickey Teague, the milkman, is shouting up from the road, 'I know you're there, Lily Doherty. Come down and pay me for the six weeks you owe me.' And the chairman's sitting at the fire like a wee thin saint with his finger in his mouth and the comics up to his nose and hoping to God I'll remember to bring him home five fags. And below us Celia Cunningham's about half-full now and crying about the sweepstake ticket she bought and lost when she was fifteen. And above us Dickie Devine's groping under the bed for his trombone and he doesn't know yet that Annie pawned it on Wednesday for the wanes' bus fares and he's going to beat the tar out of her when she tells him. And down the passage aul Andy Boyle's lying in bed because he has no coat. And I'm here in the Mayor's parlour, dressed up like the Duchess of Kent and drinking port wine. I'll tell you something, Skinner: it's a very unfair world.

(*The* JUDGE *appears on the battlements.*)

JUDGE: One of the most serious issues for our consideration is the conflict between the testimony of the civilian witnesses and the testimony of the security forces on the vital question – Who fired first? Or to rephrase it – did the security forces initiate the shooting or did they merely reply to it? We have heard, for example, the evidence of Father Brosnan who attended the deceased and he insists that none of the three was armed. And I have no doubt that Father Brosnan told us the truth as he knew it. But I must point

out that Father Brosnan was not present when the three
emerged from the building. We have also the evidence of
the photographs taken by Mr Montini, the journalist, and
in none of these very lucid pictures can we see any sign
whatever of weapons either in the hands of the deceased or
adjacent to their person. But Mr Montini tells us he didn't
take the pictures until at least three minutes after the
shooting had stopped. On the other hand we have the
sworn testimony of eight soldiers and four policemen who
claim not only to have seen these civilian firearms but to
have been fired at by them. So at this point I wish to recall
Dr Winbourne of the Army Forensic Department.
(WINBOURNE *enters left. A Scotsman.*)

WINBOURNE: My lord.

JUDGE: Dr Winbourne, in your earlier testimony you
mentioned paraffin tests you carried out on the deceased.
Could you explain in more detail what these tests involved?

WINBOURNE: Certainly, my lord. When a gun is fired, the
propellant gases scatter minute particles of lead in two
directions: through the muzzle and over a distance of thirty
feet in front of the gun; and through the breach. In other
words, if I fire a revolver or an automatic weapon or a bolt-
action rifle (*He illustrates with his own hand.*) these lead
particles will adhere to the back of this hand and between
the thumb and forefinger. And a characteristic of this
contamination is that there is an even-patterned distribution
of these particles over the hand or clothing.

JUDGE: And the presence of this deposit is conclusive evidence
of firing?

WINBOURNE: I'm a scientist, my lord. I don't know what
constitutes conclusive evidence.

JUDGE: What I mean is, if these lead particles are found on a
person, does that mean that that person has fired a gun?

WINBOURNE: He may have, my lord. Or he may have been
contaminated by being within thirty feet of someone who
has fired in his direction. Or he may have been beside
someone who has fired. Or he may have been touched or
handled by someone who has just fired.

JUDGE: I see. And these distinctions are of the utmost importance because on this point we must be scrupulously meticulous. Thank you, Dr Winbourne, for explaining them so succinctly. So that, if we are to decide whether lead on a person's hand or clothing should be attributed to his having fired a weapon, we must be guided by the pattern of deposit. Is that correct?

WINBOURNE: Yes, my lord.

JUDGE: And now, if I may return to your report – your findings on the three deceased.

WINBOURNE: In the case of Fitzgerald – it's on page four, my lord.

JUDGE: I have it, thank you.

WINBOURNE: In the case of Fitzgerald, a smear on the left hand and on the left shirt sleeve. In the case of the woman Doherty, smear marks on the right cheek and shoulder. In the case of Hegarty an even deposit on the back of the left hand and between the thumb and forefinger.

JUDGE: A patterned deposit?

WINBOURNE: An even deposit, my lord.

JUDGE: So Hegarty certainly did fire a weapon?

WINBOURNE: Let me put it this way, my lord: I don't see how he could have had these regular deposits unless he did.

JUDGE: And Fitzgerald and the woman Doherty?

WINBOURNE: They could have been smeared by Hegarty or they could have been contaminated while they were being carried away by the soldiers who shot them.

JUDGE: Or by firing themselves.

WINBOURNE: That's possible.

JUDGE: But you are certain that Hegarty at least fired?

WINBOURNE: That's what the tests indicate.

JUDGE: And you are personally convinced he did?

WINBOURNE: Yes, I think he did, my lord.

JUDGE: Thank you, Dr Winbourne.

(*The* JUDGE *disappears.* WINBOURNE *goes off.*)

MICHAEL: There's three more tanks coming. And they seem to be putting up searchlights or something.

SKINNER: Are you asleep, Lily?

LILY: D'you know what I heard a man saying on the telly one night? D'you see them fellas that go up into outer space? Well, they don't get old up there the way we get old down here. Whatever way the clocks work there, we age ten times as quick as they do.

SKINNER: You're a real mine of information, Lily.

LILY: So that if I went up there and stayed up there long enough and then come down again, God I could end up the same age as Mark Antony!

SKINNER: No matter how long you'd stay up there, your family'd still be waiting for their tea.

LILY: I'd give anything to see the chairman's face if that happened.

SKINNER: Lily.

LILY: What?

SKINNER: Why don't you ring somebody?

LILY: Who?

SKINNER: Anybody.

LILY: That young fella's out of his mind! Why in God's name would I ring somebody?

SKINNER: To wish them a happy Christmas. To use the facilities of the hotel. Just for the hell of it. Anyone in the street got a phone?

LILY: Surely. We all have phones in every room. Haaaa!

SKINNER: Where do you get your groceries?

LILY: Billy Broderick.

SKINNER: Ring him.

LILY: Sure he's across the road from me.

SKINNER: Tell him you're out of tea.

LILY: Have you no head, young fella? He'd think I couldn't face him just because I owe him fifteen pounds.

SKINNER: You must know someone with a phone.

LILY: Dr Sweeney!

SKINNER: No doubt. Anyone working in a shop – a factory?

LILY: No.

SKINNER: A garage – a café – an office – an –

LILY: Beejew Betty.

SKINNER: Who?

LILY: Betty Breen. She's a cousin of the chairman. She's in the cash desk of the Beejew Cinema. We call her Beejew Betty. (SKINNER *looks up the telephone directory.* MICHAEL *turns upstage.*)

LILY: She used to let our wanes into the Saturday matinée for nothing. And then one Saturday our Tom – d'you see our Tom? Sixteen next October 23 and afeard of no man nor beast – he went up to her after the picture and told her it was the most stupidest picture he ever seen. And d'you know what? She took it personal. Niver let them in for free again. A real snob, Betty.

SKINNER: (*Dials*) 7479336.

LILY: What are you at? Sure I seen her last Sunday week at the granny's. (SKINNER *hands her the phone.*)

LILY: What will I say? What in the name of God will I say to – ? (*Her accent and manner become suddenly stilted.*)

LILY: Hello? Is that Miss Betty Breen? This is Mrs Elizabeth Doherty speaking. Yes – yes – Lily. How are you keeping since we last met, Betty? No, no, he's fine, thank you, fine – the chest apart. No, I'm in good health, too, Betty, thank you. It just happened that I chanced to be with some companions near a telephone and your name come up in casual conversation, and I thought I'd say How-do-do. Yes. Yes. Well, Betty, I'll not detain you any longer, Betty. I'm sure you're busy with finance. Good-bye. No, the kiosk's still broken. I'm ringing from the Mayor's parlour. (*She suddenly bangs down the receiver and covers her face with her hands.*)

LILY: Jesus, young fella, I think she passed out! Oooooops!

SKINNER: That's a great start. Who else is there?

LILY: Give us a second to settle myself, will you? I'm not worth tuppence. Look at my hands. (*The bottle stutters against the glass as she pours herself a drink.*) Didn't I tell you?

SKINNER: I love your posh accent, Lily.

LILY: Hold your tongue. Lily's no yokel. Wait till I tell you: one time when the chairman was in the TB hospital I rung him up to tell him that Gloria had fell off the roof – that was

145

eighteen months ago, she was four and a half then – and the
ward sister I spoke to asked the chairman who the swank
was he was married to!

MICHAEL: I want the two of you to know I object to this carry-
on.

LILY: Sure it's only a bit of innocent fun, young fella. Have
you no give in you at all? (*Examines bottle.*) What d'you call
this port wine?

SKINNER: It's sherry.

LILY: I'm going to get a bottle of it next Christmas.

SKINNER: Who else do you know, Lily? Any friends? Relatives?

MICHAEL: You're behaving exactly as they think we behave.

LILY: As who thinks?

SKINNER: Have you any uncles? Any brothers? Any sisters?

LILY: I have one sister – Eileen.

SKINNER: Is she on the phone?

LILY: She is.

SKINNER: Eileen what? What's her second name?

MICHAEL: No wonder they don't trust us. We're not worthy of
trust.

LILY: You'll not get her in that book.

SKINNER: From the operator, then.

LILY: No, I'm not going to ring Eileen. She'd think something
terrible had happened.

MICHAEL: And even if you have no sense of decency, at least
you should know that that's stealing unless you're going to
leave the money.

LILY: Lookat, young fella: I don't need you nor nobody else to
tell me what's right and what's wrong. (*To* SKINNER) Give
me that.

(SKINNER *hands her the phone.*)

LILY: How do you get the operator?

SKINNER: Dial 100 and give your number.

LILY: I didn't say I wasn't going to leave the money, did I? I'm
as well acquainted with my morals as the next. (*Into phone*)
Operator, this is 7643225, Derry City, Northern Ireland. I
wish to make a call to Mrs Eileen O'Donnell, 275 Riverway
Drive . . . She's getting me inquiries. If you don't mind,

I'll take my glass. Thank you. Inquiries? This is 7643225, Derry City, Northern Ireland. I wish to make a call to Mrs Eileen O'Donnell, 275 Riverway Drive – yes – Riverway – Riverway – (*The accent is dropped.*) God, are you deaf, wee girl? Riverway Drive, Brisbane, Australia. (*She hangs up.*) She'll call me back.

(SKINNER *laughs and slaps the table with delight.*)

SKINNER: Lily, you're wonderful! The chairman's married to a queen. Does he deserve you?

(BRIGADIER JOHNSON-HANSBURY *enters right. He speaks through a loudhailer. He is guarded by three armed* SOLDIERS.)

BRIGADIER: Attention, please! Attention!

MICHAEL: Listen!

LILY: And when I get my breath back, I might even give a tinkle to cousin William in the Philippines.

MICHAEL: Shut up! Listen! Listen!

BRIGADIER: This is Brigadier Johnson-Hansbury. We know exactly where you are and we know that you are armed. I advise you to surrender now before there is loss of life. So lay down your arms and proceed to the front entrance with your hands above your head. Repeat – proceed to the front entrance with your hands above your head. The Guildhall is completely surrounded. I urge you to follow this advice before there is loss of life.

(*The* BRIGADIER *goes off. The* SOLDIERS *follow him. Silence.* LILY *gets to her feet.* SKINNER *gets to his feet. Pause.*)

LILY: Arms? What's he blathering about?

SKINNER: His accent's almost as posh as yours, Lily.

(*Pause.*)

MICHAEL: Some bastard must have done something to rattle them – shouted something, thrown a stone, burned something – some bloody hooligan! Someone like you, Skinner! For it's bastards like you, bloody vandals, that's keeping us all on our bloody knees!

ACT TWO

A short time later.

The parlour is almost in darkness.

MICHAEL, LILY *and* SKINNER *stand beside the positions they had at the opening of Act One. They do not move.*

A BALLADEER *stands at stage right; his* ACCORDIONIST *is behind him. As before, he has a glass in his hand. Before, he was aggressive-drunk; this time he is maudlin-drunk. He is dressed in a dark suit and black tie. He sings (to the air of Kevin Barry):*

BALLADEER: In Guildhall Square one sunny evening three
    Derry volunteers were shot.
  Two were but lads and one a mother; the Saxon bullet was
    their lot.
  They took a stand against oppression, they wanted Mother
    Ireland free.
  Their blood now stains the Guildhall pavements; a cross
    stands there for all to see.

  We'll not forget that sunny evening, nor the names of those
    bold three
  Who gave their lives for their ideal – Mother Ireland, one
    and free.
  They join the lines of long-gone heroes, England's victims,
    one and all.
  We have their memory still to guide us; we have their
    courage to recall.

  (*The* BALLADEER *goes off. The* JUDGE *appears in the battlements.*)

JUDGE: The weight of evidence presented over the past few days seems to be directing the current of this inquiry into two distinct areas. The first has to do with what at first sight might appear to be mere speculation, but it could be a very important element, I suggest, in any understanding of the entire canvas of that Saturday – and I refer to the purpose the three had in using the Guildhall, the municipal nerve-centre of Londonderry, as their platform of defiance. And the second area – more sensible to corroboration or rebuttal, one would think – concerns the arms the deceased were alleged to have used against the army. And I suggest, also, that these two areas could well be different aspects of the same question. Why the Guildhall? Counsel for the deceased pleads persuasively that in the melée following the public meeting the three in their terror sought the nearest possible cover and that cover happened to be the Guildhall – a fortuitous choice. This may be. But I find it difficult to accept that of all the buildings adjacent to them they happened to choose the one building which symbolized for them a system of government they opposed and were in fact at that time illegally demonstrating against. And if the choice was fortuitous, why was the building defaced? Why were its furnishings despoiled? Why were its records defiled? Would they have defaced a private house in the same way? I think the answers to these questions point to one conclusion: that the deceased deliberately chose this building; that their purpose and intent was precise and deliberate. In other words that their action was a carefully contrived act of defiance against, and an incitement to others to defy, the legitimate forces of law and order. No other conclusion is consistent with the facts.

(*When* MICHAEL, LILY *and* SKINNER *speak, they speak calmly, without emotion, in neutral accents.*)

MICHAEL: We came out the front door as we had been ordered and stood on the top step with our hands above our heads. They beamed searchlights on our faces but I could see their outlines as they crouched beside their tanks. I even heard the click of their rifle-bolts. But there was no question of their shooting. I knew they weren't going to shoot. Shooting belonged to a totally different order of things. And then the Guildhall Square exploded and I knew a terrible mistake had been made. And I became very agitated, not because I was dying, but that this terrible mistake be recognized and acknowledged. My mouth kept

trying to form the word mistake – mistake – mistake. And
that is how I died – in disbelief, in astonishment, in shock.
It was a foolish way for a man to die.

LILY: The moment we stepped outside the front door I knew I
was going to die, instinctively, the way an animal knows.
Jesus, they're going to murder me. A second of panic – no
more. Because it was succeeded, overtaken, overwhelmed
by a tidal wave of regret, not for myself nor my family, but
that life had somehow eluded me. And now it was finished;
it had all seeped away; and I had never experienced it. And
in the silence before my body disintegrated in a purple
convulsion, I thought I glimpsed a tiny truth: that life had
eluded me because never once in my forty-three years had
an experience, an event, even a small unimportant
happening been isolated, and assessed, and articulated. And
the fact that this, my last experience, was defined by this
perception, this was the culmination of sorrow. In a way I
died of grief.

SKINNER: A short time after I realized we were in the Mayor's
parlour I knew that a price would be exacted. And when
they ordered us a second time to lay down our arms I began
to suspect what that price would be because they leave
nothing to chance and because the poor are always
overcharged. And as we stood on the Guildhall steps, two
thoughts raced through my mind: how seriously they took
us and how unpardonably casual we were about them; and
that to match their seriousness would demand a total
dedication, a solemnity as formal as theirs. And then
everything melted and fused in a great roaring heat. And
my last thought was: if you're going to decide to take them
on, Adrian Casimir, you've got to mend your ways. So I
died, as I lived, in defensive flippancy.

JUDGE: We now come to the second area – were the deceased
armed? Their counsel insists they were not. The security
forces insist they were. If they opened fire at the army, their
counsel asks with good reason, why were there no military
casualties, and even more pertinently, what became of their
weapons? To this the army replies that the guns were taken

away by the mob which had gathered. Counsel for the deceased strongly denies this. They say that no civilians were allowed into the Guildhall Square until one hour after the shooting. The security forces say this is untrue, and point – for example – to the priest and the newsman who were right beside the deceased within five minutes of the shooting. So, in view of this welter of confusion, I wish to recall the pathologist, Professor Cuppley, tomorrow morning.

(*The* JUDGE *disappears.* MICHAEL, LILY *and* SKINNER *step briskly back into the parlour.* MICHAEL *goes straight into the dressing-room.* SKINNER *fills his empty cigarette packet from the silver box on the table.* LILY *moves about the parlour with an air of business – fixing chairs, emptying ashtrays. She switches on the light.*)

LILY: That's better. I'm a great wan for light. The cold I don't mine but I don't like the dark.

(*She takes off her robe and examines it.*)

LILY: I'll tell you something, Skinner: it's a shocking sin having them lovely things lying idle in a wardrobe and them as fresh as the day they were bought. Lookat – not an elbow out of them nor nothing.

SKINNER: It has the shoulders scratched off me.

LILY: What are you wearing it for then? Give it to me, you clown you! Here's your shirt. And them gutties must be dry by now.

(SKINNER *takes off the robe and puts on the dry shirt. He still wears the hat.*)

LILY: D'you know what it would make? A grand warm dressing-gown, wouldn't it? And that's what the chairman needs for when he be's out in the chest hospital.

SKINNER: Take it with you.

LILY: Wouldn't I look a quare sight walking along the street with this on my back! Like the time the polis came on the Boxer Branningan driving off the petrol lorry. D'you know the Boxer?

SKINNER: Th'old one – two – three – one – two – three.

LILY: And says the Boxer to them: 'I was only looking for a refill for my lighter.' Where's the other one (*robe*)?

SKINNER: Behind you.

LILY: That young fella – what do they call him again?

SKINNER: Michael.

LILY: That's it. A grand sensible lad that.

SKINNER: Admirable.

LILY: I have a Michael. Between Declan and Gloria. His master says he's just throbbing with brains. Like the chairman.
(SKINNER *goes to the window and looks out.* LILY *watches him for a few seconds.*)

LILY: Is the aunt alive or dead, Skinner?

SKINNER: Dead. Ten years dead.

LILY: May the Lord have mercy on her good soul. And where do you live?

SKINNER: Anywhere – everywhere. As they say – no fixed address.

LILY: And sure if you've no fixed address you can't claim no dole.

SKINNER: Right.

LILY: And how do you live?

SKINNER: On my wits.

LILY: But if anything was to happen to you –

SKINNER: If I'm sick, the entire wisdom of the health authority is at my service. And should I die, the welfare people would bury me in style. It's only when I'm alive and well that I'm a problem.

LILY: Isn't that peculiar? All the same, to be put down in style, that's nice.

SKINNER: Great.

LILY: And do you just knock about the town all day?

SKINNER: Sometimes I move out. To England. Scotland. The life of Riley.
(LILY *continues folding the robes.*)

LILY: I can't offer you no bed, Skinner, 'cos there's six in one room and seven in the other. But I could give you a bite to eat most days of the week.
(*Pause. Then* SKINNER *suddenly picks up the ceremonial sword.*)

SKINNER: On guard!

(*He fences with an imaginary opponent.*)

LILY: If you're stuck.

SKINNER: Okay.

LILY: And even if I'm out working, the chairman's always there.

SKINNER: Fine.

LILY: You know the old station. That's where we live. It's a converted warehouse. Third floor up.

SKINNER: Do you like my technique?

LILY: What?

SKINNER: My swordsmanship.

LILY: Lovely.

SKINNER: How do you think I'm doing?

LILY: Great.

SKINNER: Thanks, Lily.

LILY: Who are you fighting?

SKINNER: At the moment the British army.

LILY: God help them.

(LILY *goes on with her housekeeping.* SKINNER *continues fencing for a few seconds and then stops.*)

SKINNER: Lily.

LILY: What?

SKINNER: Has it anything at all to do with us?

LILY: What?

SKINNER: This marching – protesting – demonstrating?

LILY: What are you talking about, young fella?

SKINNER: Has it anything to do with you and me and him – if he only knew it?

LILY: What are you ranting about? It's for us it is. Isn't it?

SKINNER: Doctors, plumbers, teachers, accountants, all shoulder to shoulder – is that us?

LILY: Don't ask me nothing, young fella. I've no head. All I do is march. And if you want to know why you should be marching you ask the buck inside.

SKINNER: Why do you march?

LILY: Me?

SKINNER: Why did you march today?

LILY: Sure everybody was marching the day.

153

SKINNER: Why were you out?

LILY: For the same reason as everybody else.

SKINNER: Tell me your reasons.

LILY: My reasons is no different to anybody else.

SKINNER: Tell me yours.

LILY: Wan man – wan vote – that's what I want. You know – wan man – wan vote.

SKINNER: You got that six months ago.

(*Pause.*)

LILY: Sure I know that. Sure I know we got it.

SKINNER: That's not what you're marching for, then.

LILY: Gerrymandering – that's another thing – no more gerrymandering – that's what I want – no more gerrymandering. And civil rights for everybody – that's what I want – you know – civil rights – civil rights – that's why I march.

SKINNER: I don't believe a word of it, Lily.

LILY: I'm a liar then?

SKINNER: And neither do you.

LILY: You're calling me a liar, is that it?

SKINNER: I'll tell you why you march.

LILY: He'll be telling me my name isn't Lily Doherty next.

SKINNER: Because you live with eleven kids and a sick husband in two rooms that aren't fit for animals. Because you exist on a state subsistence that's about enough to keep you alive but too small to fire your guts. Because you know your children are caught in the same morass. Because for the first time in your life you grumbled and someone else grumbled and someone else, and you heard each other, and became aware that there were hundreds, thousands, millions of us all over the world, and in a vague groping way you were outraged. That's what it's all about, Lily. It has nothing to do with doctors and accountants and teachers and dignity and boy scout honour. It's about us – the poor – the majority – stirring in our sleep. And if that's not what it's all about, then it has nothing to do with us.

(LILY *gazes at him. Pause.*)

LILY: I suppose you're right.

154

(*He switches to flippancy.*)

SKINNER: And that's why I appeal to you, when you go into
that polling station, put an X opposite my name and ensure
that your children, too, will enjoy the freedom of the city.
And now I think we'll have one for the road, Lily.
(*He goes to the cabinet.*)

SKINNER: Let's walk into the future with bloodshot eyes and
unsteady step.
(*Pause.*)

LILY: Did you ever hear tell of a mongol child, Skinner?

SKINNER: Where did you hide the brandy?

LILY: I told you a lie about our Declan. That's what Declan is.
He's not just shy, our Declan. He's a mongol. (*She finds the
brandy bottle and hands it to him.*) And it's for him I go on all
the civil rights marches. Isn't that stupid? You and him
(MICHAEL) and everybody else marching and protesting
about sensible things like politics and stuff and me in the
middle of you all, marching for Declan. Isn't that the
stupidest thing you ever heard? Sure I could march and
protest from here to Dublin and sure what good would it do
Declan? Stupid and all as I am I know that much. But I still
march – every Saturday. I still march. Isn't that the
stupidest thing you ever heard?

SKINNER: No.

LILY: That's what the chairman said when I – you know – when
I tried to tell him what I was thinking. He never talks about
him; can't even look at him. And that day that's what he
said, 'You're a bone stupid bitch. No wonder the kid's bone
stupid, too.' The chairman – that's what he said.
(*She stops abruptly, as if she had been interrupted.* SKINNER
goes to her and puts his glass into her hand.)

LILY: O merciful God.
(PRIEST *appears on the battlements.*)

PRIEST: At eleven o'clock tomorrow morning solemn requiem
Mass will be celebrated in this church for the repose of the
souls of the three people whose death has plunged this
parish into a deep and numbing grief. As you are probably
aware I had the privilege of administering the last rites to

them and the knowledge that they didn't go unfortified to their Maker is a consolation to all of us. And it is natural that we should mourn. But it is also right and fitting that this tragic happening should make us sit back and take stock and ask ourselves the very pertinent question: why did they die? That there are certain imperfections in our society, this I do not deny. Nor do I deny that opportunities for gainful employment, for decent housing, for effective voting were in certain instances less than equal. And because of these imperfections, honest men and women, decent men and women came together and formed the nucleus of a peaceful, dignified movement that commanded the respect not only of this city and this country but the respect of the world. But although this movement was initially peaceful and dignified, as you are well aware certain evil elements attached themselves to it and contaminated it and ultimately poisoned it, with the result that it has long ago become an instrument for corruption.

Who are they, these evil people? I will speak and I will speak plainly. They have many titles and they have many banners, but they have one purpose and one purpose only – to deliver this Christian country into the dark dungeons of Godless communism. I don't suggest for one minute that the three people who died yesterday were part of this conspiracy, were even aware that they were victims of this conspiracy. But victims they were. And to those of you who are flirting with the doctrines of revolution, let me quote to you from that most revolutionary of doctrines – the sermon on the mount: 'Blessed are the meek for they shall possess the land.'

In the name of the Father, Son, and Holy Spirit.

(*The* PRIEST *disappears as* MICHAEL *bustles in from the dressing-room.*)

MICHAEL: Okay – are we all set?

SKINNER: How are the nerves now?

MICHAEL: You're not going out in that (*hat*)?

SKINNER: Why not?

MICHAEL: Put that hat away.

SKINNER: Would it lead to a breach of the peace?

MICHAEL: Put it back where it belongs, Skinner.

SKINNER: I'm keeping it. I think it's . . . sympathetic.
(*He adjusts the angle.*) How about that, Lily?
(*He begins to sing; grabs* LILY *round the waist and turns her round a few times.*)

SKINNER: Where did you get that hat, where did you get that tile?
Isn't it a nobby one and just the proper style?
I should like to have one just the same as that . . .

LILY: Oooooops!

SKINNER: Where'er I go they shout 'Hello! Where did you get that hat?'

LILY: You'll have me as silly as yourself, Skinner.

SKINNER: Last round before closing. Come on, gentlemen, please. Last call – last call. What's your pleasure, Mr Hegarty?

LILY: D'you see our Tom? He found an aul saucepan on the railway lines one day last summer and put it on his head for a laugh – just like that (SKINNER). And didn't his head swell up with the heat and as God's my judge he was stuck in it for two days and two nights and had to sleep with the handle down a rat-hole in the floor!

MICHAEL: The thing to remember is that we took part in a peaceful demonstration and if they're going to charge us, they'll have to charge six thousand others.

SKINNER: Small Scotch?

MICHAEL: Nothing. Now, if they want to be officious, supposing they take our names and addresses, that's all they're entitled to ask for and that's all you're expected to give them. That's the law.

SKINNER: (*Toasts*) The law. Personally speaking I'm a great man for the law myself, you know, like, there's nothing like the law.

MICHAEL: Okay, Lily? And if they try to get you to make a statement, you just say you're making no statement unless your solicitor's present.

SKINNER: My solicitor's in Bermuda. Who's yours, Lily?

LILY: Don't mention them fellas to me. They all have the wan

story; you've a great case—you can't be beat. And then
when you're in jail they won't let you rest till you appeal.

SKINNER: Were you ever in jail, Lily?

LILY: No. Were you?

SKINNER: Not yet.

MICHAEL: Will you listen to me!

LILY: What is it, young fella?

MICHAEL: Give them no cheek and they'll give you no trouble.
We made a peaceful protest and they know that. They're
not interested in people like us. It's the troublemakers
they're after.

SKINNER: They think we're armed.

MICHAEL: They know damned well we're not armed.

SKINNER: Why is the place surrounded by tanks and armoured
cars?

MICHAEL: Are you ready, Missus?

SKINNER: And why are the walls lined with soldiers and police?

MICHAEL: We'll do exactly as they ask. We've nothing to hide.
I'll go first.

(LILY *drains her glass.*)

LILY: D'you see that sherry? I'd get very partial to that stuff.

SKINNER: It's brandy.

MICHAEL: And if they ask you a straight question, give them a
straight answer, and I promise you there'll be no trouble.

LILY: I still think them windows'd be nicer in plain glass.

MICHAEL: These (*robes*) were inside, weren't they?

(*He takes them into the dressing-room.* LILY *moves across the
room and suddenly grabs the back of a chair.*)

LILY: I drunk that glass far too quick. God, I come in reeling
and now I'm going out reeling. D'you think would the
equilibrium of my inner ear be inflamed?

(MICHAEL *returns.*)

MICHAEL: Are we ready?

LILY: What time is it, young fella?

MICHAEL: Just after five.

LILY: That's grand.

MICHAEL: (*To* SKINNER) Okay?

LILY: I'll be back in time to make the tea.

158

MICHAEL: We're going, Skinner.
(SKINNER *slowly crosses to the Mayor's seat, sits in it, and spreads himself.*)
SKINNER: I like it here. I think I'll stay.
MICHAEL: For Christ's sake!
SKINNER: You go ahead.
MICHAEL: We're all going out together.
SKINNER: Why?
MICHAEL: Because they'll think it's some sort of a trick if we split up.
SKINNER: Not if you look them clean in the eye and give them straight, honest answers.
MICHAEL: Skinner, are you coming?
(*Pause. Then* SKINNER *suddenly flings open the drawer in the table, pulls out a pile of papers, scatters them around the table. Talking very rapidly all the time.*)
SKINNER: Yes – I'm coming – after we've had a meeting of the corporation – then I'll go. But we can't spend the afternoon drinking civic booze and smoking civic fags and then walk off without attending to pressing civic business – no, no, no, no. That wouldn't be fair. So. Right. Have we a quorum? We have. Councillor – alderman – how are you? Take a seat. We have a short agenda today, if I remember correctly.
(LILY *sits.*)
LILY: (*Apologetically to* MICHAEL) God, I need a seat, young fella. Just for five minutes. Till my head settles.
(SKINNER *continues at great speed.*)
SKINNER: You have before you an account of last week's meeting. I take it to be an accurate account of the proceedings. So may I sign it? Thank you. Thank you. And now to today's agenda. Item 1. Request for annual subscription for the Royal Society for the Prevention of Cruelty to Animals – I suggest we increase our sub to a hundred pounds. Agreed? Agreed. Item 2. Derry and District Floral Society want the use of the main hall for yearly floral display. Granted. Item 3. Tenders for painting all municipal buildings in the city – in pink gloss? – why not? Tenders accepted.

LILY: Pink gloss! Haaaa – that's me!

SKINNER: Item 4. Invitation to us all to attend the first night of the Amateur Opera Society's season and buffet supper afterwards. Of course we will. Love to. Item 5. Municipal grant sought by Derry Rugby Club to purchase extra acre of land adjacent to their present pitch. All in favour? Good. Grant granted. Unanimous. Fine. Item 6 –

MICHAEL: Are you coming or are you not?

SKINNER: Expenses incurred by elected representatives on our recent trip to Calcutta to study arterial developments. I think we all benefited from that visit, didn't we?

MICHAEL: You!

SKINNER: So I propose those expenses be passed. Seconded? Good. Good. Item 7 –

MICHAEL: When you're finished mouthing there!

SKINNER: What's wrong, Mr Hegarty? Aren't you interested? As one of the city's nine thousand unemployed isn't it in your interest that your idleness is pursued in an environment as pleasant as possible with pets and flowers and music and gaily painted buildings? What more can you want, Mr Hegarty?

MICHAEL: Nothing that you would want, Skinner. I can tell you that.

SKINNER: No doubt, Mr Hegarty. But now's your opportunity to speak up, to introduce sweeping legislation, to change the face of the world. Come on, Mr Hegarty. The voice of the fourteen per cent unemployed. Speak up, man, speak up. You may never have a chance like this again.

LILY: I want the chairman to go before me.

SKINNER: In a moment, Lily. Lord Michael has the floor. Well sir?

(MICHAEL *is very angry but controls himself and speaks precisely.*)

MICHAEL: What I want, Skinner, what the vast majority of the people out there want, is something that a bum like you wouldn't understand: a decent job, a decent place to live, a decent town to bring up our children in – that's what we want.

LILY: Good man, young fella.

SKINNER: Go on – go on.

MICHAEL: And we want fair play, too, so that no matter what
our religion is, no matter what our politics is, we have the
same chances and the same opportunities as the next fella.
It's not very much, Skinner, and we'll get it, believe me,
we'll get it, because it's something every man's entitled to
and nothing can stop us getting what we're entitled to.

LILY: Hear-hear.

MICHAEL: And now, Skinner, you tell us what you want.
You're part of the fourteen per cent too. What do you
want?

(*The* BRIGADIER *enters right as before. Guarded by three*
SOLDIERS. *Speaks through the loudhailer.*)

BRIGADIER: Attention, please! Attention!

LILY: Whist! Listen!

BRIGADIER: This is Brigadier Johnson-Hansbury. I will give
you five minutes more to come out. Repeat – five minutes.
You will lay down your arms immediately and proceed to
the front entrance with your hands above your head. The
Guildhall is completely surrounded. I advise you to attempt
nothing foolhardy. This is your last warning. I will wait five
more minutes, commencing now.

(*He goes off.* SKINNER *lifts the ceremonial sword, looks for a*
second at MICHAEL, *goes to the portrait and sticks the sword*
into it. Turns round and smiles at MICHAEL.)

SKINNER: It's only a picture. And a ceremonial sword.

(*The* JUDGE *appears on the battlements;* PROFESSOR
CUPPLEY *enters left.*)

JUDGE: Professor Cuppley, you carried out post-mortem
examinations on the three deceased.

CUPPLEY: Yes, my lord.

JUDGE: And your report states that all three were killed by SLR
rifle-fire.

CUPPLEY: Yes, my lord.

JUDGE: Could you tell us something about this type of weapon?

CUPPLEY: It's a high-velocity rifle, using 7.62 mm ammunition;
and from my point of view it's particularly untidy to work

with because, if the victim has been hit several times in close proximity it's very difficult to identify the individual injuries.

JUDGE: Could you elaborate on that?

CUPPLEY: Well, the 7.62 is a high-velocity bullet which makes a small, clean entry into the body. There's no difficulty there. But once it's inside the body, its effect is similar to a tiny explosion in that it shatters the bone and flesh tissue. And then, as it passes out of the body – at the point of exit – it makes a gaping wound and as it exits it brings particles of bone and tissue with it which make the wound even bigger.

JUDGE: I see. And your report states that the deceased died from a total of thirty-four wounds?

CUPPLEY: Forgive me correcting you, my lord, but what I said was – the second paragraph on page two – I think I pointed out that thirty-four was an approximation.

JUDGE: I see that.

CUPPLEY: Because, as I say, with the SLR it's very difficult to identify individual injuries if they're close together. But in the case of Fitzgerald there were eight distinct bullet wounds; in the case of the woman Doherty – thirteen; and in the case of Hegarty – twelve, thirteen, fourteen; I couldn't be sure.

JUDGE: I understand.

CUPPLEY: Fitzgerald's wounds were in the legs, lower abdomen, the chest and hands. Doherty's were evenly distributed over the whole body – head, back, chest, abdomen and legs. Hegarty was struck in the legs and arms – two wounds in the left leg, one in each arm; but the majority of the injuries were in the head and neck and shoulders, and the serious mutilation in such a concentrated area made precise identification almost . . . guesswork.

JUDGE: I think we have a reasonably clear picture, Professor Cuppley. Thank you.

CUPPLEY: Thank you.

(*The* JUDGE *disappears.* CUPPLEY *goes off left.* DODDS *walks on.*)

DODDS: All over the world the gulf between the rich and the poor is widening; and to give that statement some definition let me present you with two statistics. In Latin America one per cent of the population owns seventy-two per cent of the land and the vast majority of the farm-labourers receive no wages at all but are paid in kind. And in my own country of 'magnificent affluence', the richest country in the history of civilization, twenty per cent of the population live in extreme poverty.

So the question arises: what of the future? What solutions are the economists and politicians cooking up? Well, the answer to that is that there are about as many solutions as there are theorists, ranging from the theory that the poor are responsible for their own condition and should pull themselves up by their own shoe-strings to the theory that the entire free enterprise system should be totally restructured so that all have equal share of the cake whether they help to bake it or not.

And until these differences are resolved, nothing significant is being done for the poor. New alignments of world powers don't affect them. Changes of government don't affect them. They go on as before. They become more numerous. They become more and more estranged from the dominant society. Their position becomes more and more insecure. They have, in fact, no future. They have only today. And if they fail to cope with today, the only certainty they have is death.

(*The three begin tidying up in silence.* SKINNER *puts on his shoes.* LILY *puts the flowers back into the vase and the glasses back into the cabinet.* MICHAEL *arranges the things on the desk (the papers, etc.) and attempts to rub off the cigar-burn on the leather. All the exuberance is gone. They move about as if they were deep in contemplation.* MICHAEL *goes to the portrait and catches the sword.*)

SKINNER: Don't touch that!

(MICHAEL *looks at him, surprised at his intensity; then shrugs and turns away.* SKINNER *smiles.*)

SKINNER: Allow me my gesture.

(*The chairs are back in place; the room is as it was when they first entered.*)

MICHAEL: That's everything. I'm going now.

LILY: We're all going, young fella.

(LILY *looks around.*)

LILY: I never seen a place I went off as quick.

MICHAEL: It looks right again.

LILY: You can have it.

SKINNER: The Distinguished Visitors' Book! We haven't signed it yet! Come on, Lily!

LILY: Will we?

(SKINNER *opens the book.*)

SKINNER: Of course we will. Aren't you as distinguished as (*Reads*) Admiral Howard Ericson, United States Navy?

LILY: Never heard of him. Give us the pen. What do I write?

SKINNER: Just your name. There.

LILY: Get out of my road. I need space to write. 'Elizabeth M. Doherty'.

SKINNER: What's the 'M' for?

LILY: Marigold. What do I put down over here?

SKINNER: Where?

LILY: There. That Sunday we went to Bundoran we all signed the visitors' book in the hotel we got our tea in and we all writ – you know – remarks and things, about the food and the nice friendly waiters and all. For the food, honest to God, Skinner, it was the nicest I ever eat. I mind I writ 'God bless the cook.' Wasn't that good?

MICHAEL: Lily.

LILY: And d'you see all them people that was staying there? We got terrible friendly with them and we all exchanged addresses and all. And then after me boasting to the chairman about all the letters I was going to get – not as much as a Christmas card from one of them! People let you down.

MICHAEL: Lily.

LILY: Coming, young fella, coming. (*To* SKINNER) You're smart. Tell me what I'll put down there. You know – something grand.

164

SKINNER: 'Atmosphere Victorian but cellar excellent.'

LILY: Whatever that means. Sure they'd know that wouldn't be me.

SKINNER: 'Décor could be improved with brass ducks and pink gloss.'

LILY: Haaa. He's not going to let me forget that.

MICHAEL: Lily, please.

LILY: Hold on now – hold on a minute . . . I have it! 'Looking forward to a return visit.' That's it – you know – nice and ladylike.

SKINNER: Perfect. Mr Hegarty?

MICHAEL: They won't wait any longer.

SKINNER: You're really the one should sign.

LILY: There! Not a bad fist now, is it?

SKINNER: Beautiful.

LILY: They'll think I have a quare cheek on me, won't they? What are you putting down?

SKINNER: My name.

LILY: But over at the side?

SKINNER: 'Freeman of the city'.

LILY: Sure that means nothing.

SKINNER: I suppose you're right, Lily.

MICHAEL: Can we go now?

LILY: God, would you give me one second, young fella? I've got to –

(*She dashes into the dressing-room.*)

MICHAEL: Will you for God's sake – !

LILY: (*Off*) One second, young fella. One second.

MICHAEL: He said five minutes. What's the point in crossing them?

SKINNER: Do you trust them?

MICHAEL: Do you not?

SKINNER: No.

MICHAEL: Do you trust anybody?

SKINNER: I don't trust them.

MICHAEL: Do you think they'll beat you up, Skinner?

SKINNER: Maybe.

MICHAEL: Or shoot you?

SKINNER: Maybe.

MICHAEL: You really think they'd shoot you! You really do!

SKINNER: Yes. They're stupid enough. But as long as they've
only got people like you to handle, they can afford to be.
(LILY *returns.*)

LILY: That's better. Are we all ready?

MICHAEL: Come on.

LILY: You know where I live, young fella. Don't forget to bring
Norah over to see us.

MICHAEL: Promise.

LILY: And you'll call in any time you want a bite to eat.

SKINNER: I'll be there on the stroke of one every day.

LILY: You needn't bother your head. Just when you're stuck.
(*To Sir Joshua*) Good-bye, Mister.

MICHAEL: I'll go in front.

LILY: Good-bye, young fella.

MICHAEL: Good luck, Lily.

SKINNER: Shouldn't we go out singing 'We shall overcome?'

MICHAEL: I'm warning you, Skinner!

SKINNER: Do you not trust them?
(MICHAEL *leaves the parlour; his hands are above his head.*)

LILY: Lord, I enjoyed that. The crack was good. Wasn't the
crack good, Skinner?
(SKINNER *nods.*)

LILY: Good luck, son.

SKINNER: Good luck, Lily.
(*Pause. They are about to shake hands. Then* SKINNER *leans
forward and kisses her on the forehead.*)

LILY: Jesus, not since the chairman was courting me, have
I . . .
(*Pause. Then to shatter the moment* SKINNER *puts his hands
above his head and sings and dances:*)

SKINNER: 'As I walk along the Bois de Boulogne with an
independent air –'

MICHAEL: For Christ's sake!

LILY: Come on! Come on! Get to hell out of this damned place!
I hated it from the first moment I clapped eyes on it!
(LILY *leaves the parlour, her hands above her head.* SKINNER

switches off the light, closes the door, and joins them in the
passageway. All three have their hands above their heads. They
begin to move very slowly downstage in ritualistic procession.
The moment SKINNER *closes the door, the auditorium is filled*
with thundering, triumphant organ music on open diapason. It
is sustained for about fifteen seconds and then fades to
background as LIAM O'KELLY *of Telefis Eireann enters left*
with microphone in hand. He talks into the microphone in soft,
reverential tones.)

O'KELLY: I am standing just outside the Long Tower church.
And now the solemn requiem Mass, concelebrated by the
four Northern bishops is at an end, and the organ is playing
Bach's most beautiful, most triumphant and in a curious
way most appropriate *Prelude and Fugue No. 552*. And the
clouds that have overcast this bitterly cold and windswept
city of Derry this February morning can contain themselves
no longer, and an icy rain is spilling down on all those
thousands of mourners who couldn't get into the church
and who have been waiting here in silent tribute along these
narrow ghetto streets. But despite the rain, no one is
moving. They still stand, as they have stood for the past
two hours, their patient, drawn faces towards the church
door; and as one watches them, one wonders will this
enormous grief ever pass, so deeply has it furrowed the
mind of this ancient, noble, suffering city of St Colmcille.
And now the church doors are open and the first of the
cortège emerges. This is surely the most impressive
gathering of church and state dignitaries that this humble
parish of the Long Tower has ever seen. There is the
Cardinal Primate, his head stooped, looking grave and
weary; and indeed he must be weary because he flew in
from Rome only this morning in order to be here today.
And beside him I see Colonel Foley who is representing the
President. And immediately behind them are the members
of the hierarchy and the spiritual leaders of every order and
community in the country. And now the Taoiseach,
bare-headed, gently refusing an umbrella being offered by
one of the stewards; and flanking him are the leaders of the

167

two main opposition parties. Indeed I understand that the entire Dáil and Senate are here today. And if one were to search for a word that would best describe the atmosphere here today, the tenor of the proceedings, the attitude of the ordinary people, I think the word would be dignified. And now the first of the coffins. And all around me the men are removing their caps and some are kneeling on the wet pavements. This is the remains of Michael Joseph Hegarty. And immediately behind it the coffin of Elizabeth Doherty, mother of eleven children. And lastly the remains of Adrian Fitzmaurice – I beg your pardon – Adrian Fitzgerald, and this coffin is being carried by the Knights of Malta. And as the cortège passes me, the thousands on the footpaths move gently forward on to the road and take their place quietly among the mourners. I now hand you over to our unit in the cemetery.

(*He goes off. The music stops suddenly.* MICHAEL, LILY *and* SKINNER *now stand across the front of the stage, looking straight out. The* JUDGE *appears on the battlements.*)

JUDGE: In summary my conclusions are as follows:

1. There would have been no deaths in Londonderry on February 10 had the ban on the march and the meeting been respected, and had the speakers on the platform not incited the mob to such a fever that a clash between the security forces and the demonstrators was almost inevitable.

2. There is no evidence to support the accusation that the security forces acted without restraint or that their arrest force behaved punitively.

3. There is no reason to suppose that the soldiers would have opened fire if they had not been fired on first.

4. I must accept the evidence of eye-witnesses and various technical experts that the three deceased were armed when they emerged from the Guildhall, and that two of them at least – Hegarty and the woman Doherty – used their arms. Consequently it was impossible to effect an arrest operation. The detailed findings of this tribunal I will now pass on to the appropriate authorities.

(*The entire stage is now black, except for a battery of spotlights*

beaming on the faces of the three. Pause. Then the air is filled
with a fifteen-second burst of automatic fire. It stops. The three
stand as before, staring out, their hands above their heads.)

Black-out

Living Quarters was first produced by the Abbey Theatre, Dublin, on 24 March 1977. The cast was as follows:

SIR	Clive Geraghty
COMMANDANT FRANK BUTLER	Ray McAnally
HELEN KELLY	Fedelma Cullen
MIRIAM DONNELLY	Maire Hastings
BEN	Stephen Brennan
TINA	Bernadette Shortt
FATHER TOM CARTY	Michael O'hAonghusa
CHARLIE DONNELLY	Niall O'Brien
ANNA	Dearbhla Molloy
Direction	Joe Dowling

Set

Commandant Frank Butler's living quarters – a detached house close to a small military barracks in a remote part of County Donegal, Ireland.

The action takes place in the living-room and garden on a warm May evening and night. The living-room and garden have acting areas of almost equal size (left and right from the point of view of the audience).

The furnishings of the living-room are old and worn. Fireplace in the centre; an armchair on each side. The armchair left of the fireplace is of wicker. Small table, television set, sideboard on which are drinks. Some family photographs on the walls. On the mantelpiece a distinctive glass ornament with pendulous glass lobes. Door left of the fireplace leads to the kitchen off. Door right of the fireplace (used once in Act Two). A third door right leads to the hallway, which we see. Hallstand, small table, etc. A stairway

LIVING QUARTERS
after Hippolytus

for Seamus Deane

CHARACTERS

SIR
COMMANDANT FRANK BUTLER
HELEN KELLY
MIRIAM DONNELLY
BEN
TINA
FATHER TOM CARTY
CHARLIE DONNELLY
ANNA

rises from the hall. Another door (invisible and approximately opposite the fireplace) in the fourth, invisible, wall separating the living-room from the garden.

The garden begins at the front door and runs the full length of the side of the house, i.e. right across the front of the stage. In the garden a summer seat and some old deck chairs.

Down left, tucked into the corner, is a small, low footstool used only by Sir.

SIR: Middle-aged. Always in full control of the situation, of the other characters, of himself. His calm is never ruffled. He is endlessly patient and tolerant, but never superior. Always carries his ledger with him. Dressed in a dark lounge suit, dark tie, white shirt, black, highly polished shoes. *slick —*

COMMANDANT FRANK BUTLER: Tall, lean, military man in his early fifties. Grey hair, military moustache. Has been in the Irish army all his life. *3 SISTERS*

Four children by his first marriage:

HELEN KELLY: Twenty-seven, divorced; has been living in London for six years. An attractive woman with style and apparent self-assurance.

MIRIAM DONNELLY: Twenty-five, married to Charlie Donnelly; mother of three children. Plump, practical. Chain-smokes.

BEN: Twenty-four, hesitant, nervous, with a volatile face. Miriam describes him as a 'mother's boy'.

TINA: Eighteen, the youngest, 'the pet of the family', fresh, warm, eager.

FATHER TOM CARTY: Sixty-four, chaplain to the camp, with the rank of commandant. A self-aware man with a professional, breezy manner. (Preferably overweight.)

CHARLIE DONNELLY: Early thirties; Miriam's husband; court clerk; cautious and proper; always with a raincoat across his arm. Views the Butler family with smiling caution.

ANNA: Early twenties; Frank's second wife; mature, intelligent, passionate, direct in speech and manner.

Time: the present – in Ireland. *1977*

3 SISTERS ⟨ HELEN / MIRIAM 175 / ~~DONNELL~~ / TINA / BEN

Priest

Tom — pp 179-180 — Persona/role/identity, etc.
"electric", "stereotype"
"intense pain", not "experience it"

"the outsider who represents the society
they'll begin to feel alienated
from."

After "the point of no return", "they'll
hear is their own persistent inner
voices"

p 207-208 — Grace always available — CHOICE
is the gift X purchased for us.

p 219-220 — The ferrule

Charlie — "a spectator", not "a participant" —
Can't speak properly
"Marius actions like a voyeur." (209)

[handwritten: knee → house - living quarters]

[handwritten: Nora's name is Louise Hogan]

SIR *sits on his stool down left, his ledger closed on his knee. Nobody else on stage.*

[handwritten: like the narrator in Lover - both Parts.]

SIR: The home, the house, the living-quarters of Commandant Frank Butler, OC of B Company of the 37th Battalion of the Permanent Defence Forces. It is here on May 24th some years ago that our story is set, as they say – as if it were a feast laid out for consumption or a trap waiting to spring. And the people who were involved in the events of that day, although they're now scattered all over the world, every so often in sudden moments of privacy, of isolation, of panic, they remember that day, and in their imagination they reconvene here to reconstruct it – what was said, what was not said, what was done, what was not done, what might have been said, what might have been done; endlessly raking over those dead episodes that can't be left at peace.
(He rises and moves to centre stage.)
But reverie alone isn't adequate for them. And in their imagination, out of some deep psychic necessity, they have conceived this (*ledger*) – a complete and detailed record of everything that was said and done that day, as if its very existence must afford them their justification, as if in some tiny, forgotten detail buried here – a smile, a hesitation, a tentative gesture – if only it could be found and recalled – in it must lie the key to an understanding of *all* that happened. And in their imagination, out of some deep psychic necessity, they have conceived me – the ultimate arbiter, the

[handwritten left margin: life = feast ~ trap?]

[handwritten right margin: Imagination]

[handwritten: ✳]

[handwritten: IMAGINATION]

[handwritten: The play]

[handwritten: ✳ ✳]

[handwritten: some deep psychic necessity]

powerful and impartial referee, the final adjudicator, a kind
of human Hansard who knows those tiny little details and
interprets them accurately. And yet no sooner do they
conceive me with my authority and my knowledge than
they begin flirting with the idea of circumventing me, of
foxing me, of outwitting me. Curious, isn't it? But to get
back to that day.
(*He moves into the living-room, which now lights up.*)
May 24th; Commandant Frank Butler's home just outside
the village of Ballybeg; a remote and run-down army camp in
the wilds of County Donegal; and a day of celebration
because Commandant Butler and his company have returned
in triumph after five months service with the United Nations
in the Middle East. And their return is triumphant because
in their last week of duty, at an outpost called Hari, (*Reads*)
'while under siege and heavily outnumbered by guerillas
they responded gallantly, Commandant Butler behaving
with outstanding courage and selflessness, personally
exposing himself to heavy and persistent fire to carry nine of
his wounded men to safety.' And this evening top army brass
and politicians and local dignitaries have gathered here to
celebrate the triumphant return and to honour the
triumphant Commandant. So much for the occasion.
And hovering in the wings, once more reconvened in
recollection to take yet another look at the events of that
day, is the Butler family.
(*He now moves around the living-room and addresses the family
off.*)
Are we all set? Good. Now – you've all been over this
hundreds, thousands of times before. So on this
occasion – with your co-operation, of course – what I would
like to do is organize those recollections for you, impose a
structure on them, just to give them a form of sorts.
Agreed? Excellent! Naturally we'll only get through a tiny
portion of all that was said and done that day; but I think
we should attempt some kind of chronological order; and I
promise you that the selection I make will be as fair and as
representative as possible. So I'll call you as I require you

178

and introduce you then. Agreed? Fine! (*Opens ledger.*) Let's
see. 'Helen arrives' – we'll not go back as far as that. 'Anna
takes up her dress skirt. Tina prepares lunch' – we can skip
all that. Yes – let's begin here: 'It is late afternoon. Anna is
in bed. Tina is sponging her father's dress suit. In the camp
Frank Butler is greeting his distinguished guests. Helen is
out for a walk. Miriam has gone to the mess for a carton of
ice cream. Ben is washing a shirt in his caravan in the sand
dunes.' So. We require only Tina at the moment. And
remember – it's all here, every single syllable of it. But if
you wish to speak your thoughts as well – by all means.
Thank you. Thank you.
> (SIR *looks around the set and goes to adjust the position of the*
> *garden seat.* TOM *enters.*)

TOM: Sir.

SIR: (*Busy*) What is it, Father?   *PRIEST*

TOM: I don't suppose it would be a breach of secrecy or
etiquette if I – if you were to let me know how I'm
described there, would it? You know – something to hang
the cap on – 'good guy', 'funny guy', 'bit of a gossip'.
Which of my many fascinating personas should I portray?

SIR: (*Still busy*) You'll be yourself, Father.

TOM: Of course. Naturally. But you've a description there,
haven't you? And an objective view would be a help.

SIR: I don't think so.

TOM: As chaplain I've a right to – (*Pleasant again*) Please.

SIR: I think you shouldn't.

SIR: Please.

> (SIR *regards him calmly.*)

SIR: Very well.

TOM: (*Breezily*) Soldier – man of God – friend of the boys – you
name it.

SIR: 'Father Thomas Carty, sixty-four years of age, chaplain,
Commandant, close friend of the Butler family.'

TOM: (*Saluting*) Yours truly.

> (ANNA *enters in her dressing-gown. She stands at a distance*
> *and watches this scene.*)

SIR: 'Married Frank and Louise –'

TOM: May the Lord have mercy on her.

SIR: '–baptized their children and grandchildren: and six months ago married Frank again–to Anna.'

TOM: Indeed. A happy day.

SIR: 'The children used to call him Uncle–Uncle Tom–'

TOM: (*Delighted*) Tina still does–occasionally.

SIR: ' "Is Uncle Tom coming with us?" they'd say. And he did. Always. Everywhere. Himself and the batman–in attendance.'

TOM: That's one way of–

SIR: '–and that pathetic dependence on the Butler family, together with his excessive drinking make him a cliché, a stereotype. He knows this himself–'

TOM: Cliché? For God's sake–!

SIR: '–but he is not a fool. He recognizes that this definition allows him to be witness to their pain but absolves him from experiencing it; appoints him confidant but acquits him of the responsibility of conscience–'

TOM: That's not how–! O my God . . .

SIR: 'As the tale unfolds they may go to him for advice, not because they respect him, consider him wise–'

TOM: (*Sudden revolt*) Because they love me, that's why! They love me!

SIR: '–but because he is the outsider who represents the society they'll begin to feel alienated from, slipping away from them.'

TOM: (*Beaten*) Outsider?

(ANNA *goes to* TOM *and puts her arm around him.*)

SIR: 'And what he says won't make the slightest difference because at that point–the point of no return–they'll be past listening to anybody. At that point all they'll hear is their own persistent inner voices–' And so on and so forth.

TOM: (*On point of tears*) O my God–O my God–

SIR: It's your role.

TOM: No, it's not. No, no, no, it's not.

SIR: And to have any role is always something.

(ANNA *begins to lead* TOM *away.*)

When you've thought about it, you'll agree with me.

TOM: No, no, no–

180

SIR: And you'll do it.

TOM: No, no –

SIR: Oh, yes, you'll do it. Now I think everything's in position.
(CHARLIE *enters. Almost furtive. Almost ingratiating.*)

CHARLIE: By the way, Sir –

SIR: You're not needed, Charlie.

CHARLIE: Because I'm not one of the family?

SIR: Because we're beginning in the afternoon.

CHARLIE: But I *was* there that night, you know, and –

SIR: Early afternoon, Charlie.

CHARLIE: But I *did* come – about half eleven – to pick up Miriam.

SIR: I know.

CHARLIE: And I would have been here earlier, only I had to
leave the baby-sitter home.

SIR: I know.

CHARLIE: And if I'm nervous, she's late – I mean to say, if I'm
late, she's nervous.

SIR: I know.

CHARLIE: But I did get here before midnight. And doesn't that
make me a witness? Relevant, material, as we say.

SIR: Charlie, if I need you, I'll call you.

CHARLIE: Tell you what: supposing I just sat about, you know,
and looked on, I'd –

SIR: There are no spectators, Charlie. Only participants.

CHARLIE: Promise you – wouldn't open my mouth –

SIR: If your turn comes, I'll call you.

CHARLIE: Could keep an eye on the ledger for you.

SIR: Charlie.

CHARLIE: Oh, well – see you later – good luck.
(*He leaves.*)

SIR: And now to begin. The Butler home. Early evening of May
24th.
(*He sits on his low stool. Lights change.* TINA *enters from
kitchen. The jacket of her father's dress suit is lying across an
ironing-board and she is carrying a bowl of water to clean stains.
We can hear in the far distance a military band playing.* TINA
listens to the music for a few seconds and then hums the melody.)

SIR: Tina, the youngest of the four Butler children. The pet of

181

the family. Singing because her father is back from the
Middle East and because she has never seen such
excitement in the camp before. Her life up to this has been
protected and generally happy and content. True, her
mother died. But that was six years ago. And Tina loves her
stepmother, Anna, at least as much as she loved her
mother.'

(HELEN *enters left and crosses slowly to the garden seat right.
She is carrying a bunch of May flowers. As she passes the
living-room* TINA *sees her. She calls out.*)

TINA: Helen!

HELEN: Hello.

TINA: It's like a carnival, isn't it?

HELEN: Yes.

TINA: The Number One Army Band – first time ever in
Ballybeg!

HELEN: I know.

TINA: Did you have a swim?

HELEN: What?

TINA: Did you swim?

HELEN: Paddled.

TINA: Oh, you're daring!

HELEN: I am.

TINA: Was it cold?

HELEN: Can't hear you. Come on out – it's glorious.

TINA: When I finish this.

(HELEN *places the flowers on the seat and picks up the broken
ones.* TINA *exits to the kitchen.*)

SIR: 'The eldest of the family – Helen. Twenty-seven and
divorced. When she was nineteen and impetuous and
strong-willed, she married Private Gerry Kelly, her father's
batman, despite her mother's bitter and vicious opposition.
The marriage lasted a few months. Private Kelly deserted
and vanished. And Helen went to London. This is only her
second time home since then. The last time was for her
mother's funeral.'

(HELEN *stands still.*)

HELEN: When I got off the bus and walked in there this

182

morning the room was still stifling with her invalid's smell. Strange, wasn't it? And small things I thought I'd forgotten: her tiny, perfect, white teeth; the skin smooth and shiny over the arthritic knuckles; her walking-stick hooked on the back of the wicker chair. And that glass ornament on the mantelpiece that trembled when she screamed at me – (*Calmly, flatly*) 'You can't marry him, you little vixen! *Noblesse oblige!* D'you hear – *noblesse oblige!*'

SIR: She never spoke to you again?

HELEN: No.

SIR: Nor to him?

HELEN: Never to him.

SIR: Do you still feel anger?

HELEN: No, not a bit, I think. Not a bit.

SIR: And him – how real is he?

HELEN: Gerry? That's over.

SIR: Altogether?

HELEN: I'm wary. I'm controlled. I discipline myself.

SIR: Then this homecoming was a risk?

HELEN: In a way.

SIR: A test? A deliberate test?

HELEN: Perhaps.

SIR: And you're surviving it?

HELEN: I'm surviving it.

SIR: All right, Helen, you've tested yourself and you've paid your respects to your father. You could leave now.

HELEN: No. I'll see it through.

SIR: Your discipline may not hold.

HELEN: How can I be sure that I want it to?

SIR: Only you can answer that.

(*She suddenly busies herself with the flowers.* MIRIAM *comes briskly through the front door, the hall, into the living-room.*)

MIRIAM: O my God – that heat!

(*Once in the living-room* MIRIAM *gets three plates from the sideboard and begins dividing the carton of ice cream she has brought home.*)

SIR: 'Miriam – the middle daughter. Married to Charlie Donnelly, clerk of the district court. She has three children.

She is thinking of them.'

MIRIAM: They should be arriving home from school just about now. I hope they don't feel altogether abandoned.

SIR: She hasn't seen them for three hours.

MIRIAM: I gave them soup and sandwiches and a bar of chocolate each for lunch; and Mrs Moyne'll have a hot meal ready for them when they get back. And she'll stay with them until Charlie gets home from the court in Glenties. Then he'll leave her home and come back and make them liver and bacon for their tea. And then he'll go and collect her again and she'll get them porridge and bread and jam for supper and put them to bed.

SIR: They are not neglected children.

MIRIAM: Then he'll come and collect me and we should be home soon after midnight. He doesn't like hanging about here – no more than I do myself.

SIR: 'Before she married, Miriam was a nurse.'

MIRIAM: All the same it's a big day for Papa and I'm glad I came. God, wouldn't the kids love some of this ice cream!

(SIR *looks at the audience and spreads his hands.*)

MIRIAM: (*Calling*) Who's for ice cream? Anyone for ice cream?

TINA: (*From kitchen*) Me!

(MIRIAM *carries the tray of dishes out to the garden.*)

MIRIAM: Ice cream, Helen?

HELEN: Lovely.

MIRIAM: Did you ever see the likes of that crowd milling about the gates?

HELEN: I came up the back way.

MIRIAM: TV cameras and reporters and what-not. And Sergeant Burke trying to control the traffic and looking as if he was going to cry. And that mad wife of his with her hair dyed a bright orange, beside herself with excitement and blowing kisses into all the nobs' cars as they pass through the gate. Sweet God – bedlam! And all the buckos from the village – the Morans and the Sharkeys and all that gang – all squinting and gleeking and not missing a bar. Oh, but there'll be tales to be told for years to come.

(TINA *has joined them.*)

TINA: (*To* MIRIAM) Did you get the May flowers?

MIRIAM: Not me – her ladyship here.

HELEN: Aren't they pretty?

TINA: Remember – we used to gather great armfuls of them and
put them up on the May altar on the landing.

MIRIAM: In jam jars. (*Passes plate.*) Here.

TINA: And bundles of bluebells that would go limp overnight
and hang over the sides.

HELEN: The smell of them through the house – a sickly smell,
wasn't it?

TINA: And us kneeling on the lino for the prayers and easing up
one knee and then the other with the pain. Do you
remember, Helen?
(*Very brief pause.*)

HELEN: That meadow beyond the school's full of flowers.

MIRIAM: What meadow's that?

TINA: Phil the Butcher's field.

HELEN: Phil Boyle and Mary! I saw him watching me from
behind the byre, but I couldn't remember his name.

MIRIAM: Baldy Phil and Hairy Mary – I never could enjoy meat
from that place.

TINA: Did you not speak to him?

HELEN: No, he wouldn't remember me now.

TINA: 'Course he would.

MIRIAM: God, they must be ancient, that pair.

TINA: D'you remember – Mammy used to send us for eggs every
Saturday morning –

MIRIAM: 'You're to say: "A dozen eggs for *Commandant* Butler,
please" ' – hoping to get them cheap!

TINA: And if Ben came with us, Mary'd always give him a huge
kiss.

MIRIAM: A rub of her beard!

TINA: And he always cried and then she'd give him a duck egg
for himself and Daddy used to say he cried just to get the
duck egg – d'you remember?

MIRIAM: Oh, sweet God!

TINA: D'you remember, Helen?
(*As* HELEN *passes her she hugs her briefly. Pause.*)

185

HELEN: Yes. Yes, I remember.

MIRIAM: God bless Mammy and make her healthy again. God bless Daddy and have him transferred to Dublin.

TINA: We all had that bit.

MIRIAM: God bless Uncle Tom and make him a good priest. God bless Helen, Ben and Tina. And God bless me and give me bigger thighs than Josie McGrenra. And I got them.

TINA: What's this my rhyme was? God bless Mammy, Daddy, Uncle Tom, Helen, Miriam, Ben and Stinky Bum Blue.

MIRIAM: Who?

TINA: A rag doll. Still have her. God bless the Irish army and make it strong and brave.

(MIRIAM and HELEN laugh.)

HELEN: Tina!

TINA: That's true. And look at Daddy! And God bless me and take me up to heaven before my tenth birthday.

MIRIAM: Weren't you lucky you were ignored!

(HELEN and TINA speak together.)

HELEN: ⎫ Does he come –?

TINA: ⎭ What did you –?

TINA: Sorry – go ahead.

HELEN: I was just going to ask you, do you see Ben often?

TINA: You know Ben.

MIRIAM: Yes!

TINA: Whenever he takes the notion. When Daddy was out in the Middle East he called in maybe a couple of times a week. But now that he's back –

MIRIAM: Did you know that Charlie got him a job driving the mobile library? Surely to God that wasn't too taxing on him. And he stuck it for how long? Four days. Walked out without as much as a by your leave. Left the bloody library van sitting out in the bogs beyond Loughcrillan. Oh, that fella!

HELEN: Do they speak at all?

TINA: Daddy and him? When they meet. If they have to.

HELEN: I thought I might have run into him when I was down at the shore. Where has he got his caravan?

TINA: God knows where you'd find him. Sometimes he works

186

on the boats. Or does odd days labouring. And then he
disappears for weeks – I don't know where he
goes – Scotland – Dublin. But he always comes back.
Always.

MIRIAM: Like malaria.

TINA: But if he's around and hears you're here he'll be sure to
call.

HELEN: I hope so.

MIRIAM: Listen to me – let there be no romantic auld chat about
brother Ben. He's a wastrel – a spoiled mother's boy. And if
he turns up today to ruin the biggest event in Father's life
I'll soon send him packing. So. (*Lights a cigarette.*) Sure
you're not smoking?

HELEN: Positive.

TINA: Three years off – isn't she great?

MIRIAM: Magnificent. Tell us about London.

HELEN: It's all right. The same office job, the same landlady
since I went there.

MIRIAM: Digs or a flat?

HELEN: Digs.

TINA: Mrs Zimmermann from Zürich.

HELEN: If she thinks I need cheering up she says: 'Come and
have a cup of coffee with me, Mrs Kelly. I have a most
funny joke to impart to you.'

MIRIAM: (*Finishing ice cream.*) That was good. Does she feed
you well?

HELEN: Very well.

TINA: And her four cats and her seventeen canaries and her son,
a medical student.

MIRIAM: How do you know all that?

TINA: We write occasionally.

MIRIAM: If the Donnellys get a card at Christmas they feel
honoured.

HELEN: We're finished with cats and canaries and we're into
Pekinese dogs now. And the son's a successful young
doctor –

TINA: Jean.

HELEN: Jean – with a large practice. And the confidential stories

187

she insists on telling me about him and his private life and his patients – I can't stop her.

TINA: Is he handsome?

HELEN: In a way.

MIRIAM: Well?

HELEN: And married.

MIRIAM: Bugger him – that's him scrubbed. Oh, isn't that just perfect.

(TINA *and* MIRIAM *stretch out in the sun.* HELEN *sits upright.*)

TINA: It's almost too hot for me.

MIRIAM: Don't know when I sunbathed last.

TINA: Glorious.

MIRIAM: We'll come out in blisters.

TINA: Yes, nurse.

MIRIAM: Any olive oil in the house?

TINA: Kitchen.

MIRIAM: Where?

TINA: Bottom press.

MIRIAM: I suppose you wouldn't go for it?

TINA: Too lazy.

MIRIAM: Me, too. God, the big snout'll be like a beacon.

(TINA *laughs.*)

We get one hot day every five years and it goes to our heads.

Oh, perfect – perfect –

(HELEN *looks at them for a few seconds. Then, very suddenly, she goes down to* SIR. *Addresses him in urgent undertones.*)

HELEN: It's not right! It's not right!

SIR: Yes, it is.

HELEN: No, it's not. It's distorted – inaccurate.

SIR: I would tell you. Trust me.

HELEN: The whole atmosphere – three sisters, relaxed, happy, chatting in their father's garden on a sunny afternoon. There was unease – I *remember* – there were shadows we've got to acknowledge them!

SIR: Why?

HELEN: Because they were part of it.

188

SIR: Don't you think they're aware of them? They're thinking
the very same thing themselves.

(HELEN *looks up at her sisters.*)

Believe me – it's exactly right. (*Pause.*) Go on – join them
again.

(HELEN *goes back. Stands looking at them.*)

TINA: (*Her eyes closed*) Do you have to go back tomorrow?

HELEN: Afraid so.

TINA: Hardly worth your while for one night, was it?

HELEN: I've paid my respects to the Commandant.

TINA: When you phoned you were coming he was really
thrilled.

HELEN: And I saw you two, didn't I?

MIRIAM: A sight that has driven strong men to distraction.
(*She sits up.*) God, that's too much for me. And you met our
new stepmother.

TINA: (*Sitting up*) And she liked her – didn't you, Helen? So
there!

MIRIAM: So what?

TINA: So she thinks she's beautiful – that's what. And so do I.

MIRIAM: All I ever said –

HELEN: Shhh!

MIRIAM: Damn the hair I care if she hears me or not. I just
think she's far too young for him and that the quiet of this
backwater'll drive her bonkers. You and her and a batman
running this house – I mean what the hell do you *do* all
day?

TINA: She loves Ballybeg – she told me.

MIRIAM: As for himself, you'd hardly describe him as a court
jester, would you? I mean he's set in his ways and damned
selfish and bossy and –

TINA: Selfish? After the way he nursed Mammy for years?

MIRIAM: So well he might.

TINA: What does that mean?

HELEN: Will you both keep your voices down!

TINA: (*To* HELEN) What does she mean by that?

MIRIAM: That this bloody wet hole ruined her health and that
he wouldn't accept a transfer – always waiting for the big

189

promotion that would be worthy of him and that never came. Clonmel, Templemore, Mullingar, Kilkenny – they all came up at different times and he wangled his way out of them – not important enough for Commandant Butler. Well, he'll probably get what he wants as a result of this ballyhoo and I wish him luck – I really do – himself and his child bride. I'd strip in a minute, only those Sharkey stallions would be sure to be peeping over that hedge.

TINA: What any of us thinks isn't important. What is important is that he loves her and she loves him.

MIRIAM: Mother of God! Would you grow up, child.

TINA: And they're perfectly happy together.

MIRIAM: Married for five months and out of that they've been together all of what? – ten days?

TINA: Amn't I right, Helen?

MIRIAM: Unless the daily love letters count – do they?

TINA: Amn't I right, Helen?

MIRIAM: How would she know? She's a stranger here.
(*Suddenly sorry, she jumps up and kisses* HELEN.) Sorry, sorry sweetie – I didn't mean that. Really. I'm a coarse bitch. Always was. You know that. Sorry. (*She sits down again.*) As mother used to say – (*Grand accent*) 'Miriam, you're neither a Butler nor a Hogan. I'm afraid you're just – pure Ballybeg.'
(HELEN *and* TINA *laugh.* MIRIAM *closes eyes again.*)
Not a day passes but I thank God for that eejit, Charlie Donnelly.
(*Military music in the distance – the same piece as before.*)
She always called him 'Charles'. But I think she liked him.

TINA: Of course she did.

MIRIAM: But how could she? Maybe because his Uncle Mickey was land steward to the Duke of Abercorn.
(*They listen to the music.* MIRIAM *hums with it.*)

TINA: I suppose you never hear from your Gerald, Helen?

HELEN: 'My' Gerald?

TINA: Gerald, then.

HELEN: No.
(MIRIAM *sits up.*)

190

MIRIAM: I hope to God the kids have the sense to have on their
sun hats.
TINA: And no idea where he is?
HELEN: None.
(HELEN *rises and gathers her flowers.*)
MIRIAM: Wouldn't you think that aul' band would have a
second tune!
TINA: Daddy said someone saw him recently in Liverpool.
HELEN: Really.
MIRIAM: Should be called the Only One Army Band.
TINA: Whoever it was said he had a beard.
HELEN: They go so limp in the sun, don't they?
TINA: Do you ever think of him at all, Helen?
(HELEN *passes* TINA *on her way into the living-room; as
before, she hugs her briefly, only this time almost shaking her.
As she hugs her*:)
HELEN: For God's sake, Tina darling, will you—
MIRIAM: Oh, smart, smart, smart!
TINA: I thought she might like to—
MIRIAM: You thought! (*Calmer*) Come on—we'd better get
Pop's duds laid out for him. (*She sings the military music
loudly as she gathers the plates. She and* TINA *go into the
living-room.* HELEN *is putting the flowers in water.*) Be
marvellous, wouldn't it, if you turned a nice golden colour
like those women in the travel brochures? God, aul'
Charlie'd go off the head altogether! (*To* TINA) Are his
black shoes ready?
TINA: Not yet.
MIRIAM: I'll do them and you do the suit—okay? (*To* HELEN)
The years may have passed but we're still Daddy's little
beavers!
TINA: (*To* HELEN—*in apology*) Helen, I—I'm—
MIRIAM: (*Catching her arm*) Get me the shoe polish, duckie, will
you? You keep changing where you keep things in this
damned house.
(MIRIAM *polishes the shoes.* TINA *presses the suit.* HELEN *goes
out to the garden.* FRANK *enters by front door. Dressed in
commandant's UN uniform. Carrying two bottles. He pauses in*

191

the hall, looks up the stairs, calls gently.)

FRANK: Anna?

SIR: 'Commandant Frank Butler.'

FRANK: Anna?

SIR: 'Twelve months ago a widower, commandant of a remote
barracks, surrendering hope. Today a young wife, the Hero
of Hari, and certain promotion.' (*To* FRANK) 'Outstanding
courage and selflessness' – is that accurate?
(FRANK *shrugs.*)

SIR: You're nervous.

FRANK: Yes.

SIR: Of what?

FRANK: I don't know.

SIR: Can it be to do with Anna?

FRANK: Yes. Maybe. I don't know. With myself. I'm jittery for
some reason.

SIR: That's understandable.

FRANK: And unhappy. Suddenly unhappy. Profoundly
unhappy.

SIR: It's the tension.

FRANK: Yes?

SIR: And all the fuss. All those people.

FRANK: I suppose so.

SIR: But remember – they're here to honour you.

FRANK: I know that.

SIR: So keep calm. Keep cool.

FRANK: Yes.

SIR: Everything's running smoothly. Everything's in hand.

FRANK: Yes, yes. Everything's in hand.
(*He goes quickly into the living-room.*)
Anna must be asleep. We'll give her another quarter of an
hour – it's going to be a tiring evening for her. (*Hands the
bottles to* TINA.) These are for later, in case we have some
people back. Leave them on the sideboard. Did the cuff
links turn up?

TINA: In the jacket pocket.

FRANK: I thought you said you looked there.
(*To* MIRIAM) Are those ready?

192

MIRIAM: Another minute, Commandant, sir.

FRANK: (*To* TINA) And Anna's stuff – her dress and all
that – that's all arranged?

TINA: Lying on the bed in Ben's old room. Everything's
perfect. Stop fussing, Daddy.

FRANK: No, I'll tell you what you can do: give her another ten
minutes and then bring her a cup of tea.

TINA: What about yourself?

FRANK: I think I'll take a drink instead – no, maybe I shouldn't.
Yes, I'll take a cup of tea, too.

MIRIAM: What are they all at over there?

FRANK: Standing around, talking, drinking.

MIRIAM: Isn't it time you changed?

FRANK: I know. And I've still to get a speech ready.

TINA: Helen'll help you.

MIRIAM: (*Offering the shoes*) There you are.

FRANK: I don't want them just now, do I?

(MIRIAM *makes a face.*)

(*To* TINA) Where is Helen?

TINA: In the garden. (*Calls*) Helen! Daddy wants – !

FRANK: Shhh – Anna. I can go out, can't I?

(*He goes out to the garden.* MIRIAM *looks up at the ceiling.*)

MIRIAM: God, isn't he a charmer! Sooner you nor me,
daughter.

(MIRIAM *goes into the kitchen. After a time* TINA *joins her.*)

HELEN: See the conquering hero comes;
Sound the trumpets, beat the drums.

FRANK: Hah!

HELEN: (*Offering a flower*) For the Hero of Hari.

FRANK: Thank you.

(*As he accepts it he leans over her as if he is about to kiss her
forehead, hesitates, then quickly:*)

Did you see the heading in today's *Donegal Enquirer*?

HELEN: No.

FRANK: It's above the photograph taken at the airport
yesterday – 'President Greets Humble Hannibal.'
(*They both laugh. He sits beside her.*)
God, I feel so ancient, Helen.

HELEN: It'll soon be over.

FRANK: Walking over here from the camp, d'you know what I was thinking: what has a lifetime in the army done to me? Wondering have I carried over into this life the too rigid military discipline that – that the domestic life must have been bruised, damaged, by the stern attitudes that are necessary over – I suppose what I'm saying is that I'm not unaware of certain shortcomings in my relationships with your mother and with Ben; and indeed with you when you and Gerald decided to –

HELEN: The past's over, Father. And forgotten.

FRANK: That's true. Over and forgotten. (*Then briskly – to their mutual relief*) Any good at writing after-dinner speeches?

HELEN: Expert. What kind?

FRANK: Short and brilliant. And modest.

HELEN: Let's see. 'Gentlemen, I want to welcome you most sincerely, and even more sincerely to congratulate you on finding your way here.'

FRANK: Ah-ha!

HELEN: 'I will not dwell on the modest part I played in the event which the world now calls the Siege of Hari –'

FRANK: I certainly will.

HELEN: '– and which brought fame and honour not only to United Nations troops everywhere –'

FRANK: But also –

HELEN: '– to this country and to our own illustrious army.'

FRANK: Hear, hear; hear, hear.

HELEN: 'As for my own paltry part –'

FRANK: Silence! Silence!

HELEN: '– as I carried each of those nine men back to safety –'

FRANK: '– across those burning desert wastes –'

HELEN: '– my one sustaining thought was –'

FRANK: (*Quickly*) Do you know what it was?

HELEN: '– that you'd make me chief of staff as from this moment.'

FRANK: And why not?

HELEN: There you are – nothing to it.

FRANK: I knew you'd be good.

194

HELEN: Pleasure.
> (*Pause.*)

FRANK: When's your flight tomorrow?

HELEN: Eleven.

FRANK: I'll get someone to drive you to Derry.

HELEN: I enjoy the bus.

FRANK: I'm delighted you came, Helen. And very, very
grateful.

HELEN: A big occasion. A national hero.

FRANK: For a day.

HELEN: And some time before I go you must tell me exactly
what happened. All I know is what I've read in the papers.

FRANK: I'll post you a copy of the reports I've got to make out
for GHQ.

HELEN: Will you?

FRANK: Promise.
> (*Again a silence. And as before he stretches across instinctively
> to catch her hand. She looks at him. A moment of
> embarrassment. He pats her hand briskly instead.*)

Well, at least they're seeing the place at its best.

HELEN: That's true.

FRANK: In weather like this you forget how grim it can be.
When you heard about Anna and me—

HELEN: Yes?

FRANK: Were you hurt?

HELEN: Why would I be hurt?

FRANK: That I hadn't told you about it in advance.

HELEN: No, not at all.

FRANK: We told nobody. It was all very—at my time of day I
thought—just Anna and myself, and Tom. I suppose I
should have told Tina, being in the house and all, but I
knew Tina wouldn't mind. And I was on the point of
phoning you one night but we decided—I felt—it would be
better to present you all with the *fait accompli*. Very
impressive little ceremony it was, too; quiet, you know,
simple; very—that little Franciscan church in Dublin—the
one along the quay. Full of atmosphere; lovely. And we
came straight back here intending to take a honeymoon

195

later. And then, as you know, no sooner am I back than I'm off for five months. So in a way we still haven't had a honeymoon – you're sure you didn't mind?

HELEN: Positive.

FRANK: As soon as the fuss dies down we'll head off somewhere.

HELEN: So you should.

FRANK: France, maybe.

HELEN: You deserve a holiday.

FRANK: Or Italy. Somewhere. (*Pause.*) Have you and she had a chance to talk yet?

HELEN: For half an hour or so.

FRANK: Oh, good, good – yes?

HELEN: We had lunch together.

FRANK: Yes?

HELEN: Then I set her hair for her.

FRANK: Yes?

HELEN: Haven't you seen it?

FRANK: (*Sudden rush*) Isn't she beautiful, Helen? Isn't she beautiful?

HELEN: Yes.

FRANK: Yes, and warm and open and refreshing. And so direct – so direct – so uncomplicated. Anything she thinks – whatever comes into her head – straight out – it must come straight out – just like that. So unlike us: measured, watching, circling one another, peeping out, shying back. *(Ango-Irish!)*

HELEN: Is that us?

FRANK: Oh, yes, that's us – you, me, your mother –

HELEN: Tina?

FRANK: Tina's special, you know that; Tina's a baby.

HELEN: Is she? And Miriam?

FRANK: All right – maybe not Miriam.

HELEN: And Ben?

FRANK: I know nothing about him. But my mascot – I call her my mascot. A good name for her, isn't it? – whatever she is, it's there before you. And from the moment I met her – and I can say this to you, Helen: you're the only person I could

196

She's an outsider too!

Excludes:
- Tina
- Miriam
- Ben

say this to without embarrassment . . . There! You see!
Typical! You're withdrawing!

HELEN: I'm not! – I'm not!

FRANK: Yes, you are. And now I'm embarrassed. It's a family –

HELEN: Go on. Say what you were going to say.

FRANK: I can't now.

HELEN: Say it, Father.

(*Pause.*)

FRANK: (*Simply*) What I was going to say is that for the first
time in my life I am profoundly happy. (*Pause.*) And now
you're thinking there's no fool like an old fool.

HELEN: No.

FRANK: (*Quickly*) Infinitely happier than I ever was with your
mother. Is that a despicable thing to say? No, it's not. It's
the truth. During all those years of illness she was patient
and courageous and admirable. And I responded to that as
best I could. Despite what Ben thinks, I did my best. But it
had all withered into duty, Helen. There was no joy – the
joy had gone. And that's what Anna did – she restored joy
to me – she animated me again. If I'm a hero
today – whatever that silly word means – it is because of her.

HELEN: I'm sure that's true, Father.

FRANK: And nothing would give me more pleasure than to
bestow some of that joy on you.

HELEN: Me?

FRANK: If I could.

HELEN: Why me?

FRANK: Because I have a superabundance and because I sense a
melancholy about my first child.

(TINA *enters living-room with tray.*)

TINA: (*Calls*) Tea, everybody!

FRANK: If that's not too arrogant of me – is it? (*He looks at her.
Pause.*) And now you're convinced I'm an old fool, aren't
you?

HELEN: You keep looking for reassurance, hero.

FRANK: (*Rising briskly*) Do I? – it must be – because I need it.
God, look at the time – and I've still to get dressed.

(FRANK *goes quickly into the living-room.* TINA *is about to*

bring a cup of tea upstairs.)
Did you wake her up yet?
TINA: On my way.
FRANK: Take the suit with you, too.
(He sits and changes his shoes. TOM *enters the hall carrying a camera.)*
TOM: Hannibal!
FRANK: I can see that's going to stick.
TOM: *(Breezy, confident to* SIR) You were right – I'll do it.
SIR: I knew you would.
TOM: But maybe not as you think. You just can't label a man a cliché and write him off.
SIR: The assessment isn't mine.
TOM: Just watch and you'll see. You may be surprised.
SIR: I'm watching.
    *(*TINA *goes into the hall.)*
TOM: Tina, my love, are they ready?
TINA: Almost. You're looking great, Uncle Tom.
TOM: Feeling terrific, thank the Lord, terrific.
    *(*TINA *goes upstairs.* TOM *goes into the living-room.* MIRIAM *enters from the kitchen.)*
Is this all the length you are?
FRANK: Aren't you dressing?
TOM: I'm not one of the big shots. And how are you, Miriam?
MIRIAM: Great, thanks, Father.
FRANK: Are they getting restless over there?
TOM: Just waiting breathlessly in the ante-room to get a glimpse of you.
FRANK: Go to hell.
TOM: *(To* MIRIAM) Hoping to touch his sleeve as he passes.
FRANK: *(Leaving)* Give him a drink, Miriam.
TOM: The way he said that you'd think my tongue was hanging out. Nothing for me, thanks.
MIRIAM: It's a thirsty day.
TOM: Honestly. How's Charlie?
MIRIAM: Great.
TOM: Pity you didn't bring the kids – they'd have enjoyed the band.

MIRIAM: Isn't there chaos enough? Have you seen Helen yet?

TOM: Where?

MIRIAM: Here.

TOM: She's not!

MIRIAM: Arrived this morning.

TOM: Well, good Lord! Why did nobody tell me? (*He goes out to the garden.*) I've only just heard.

HELEN: Father Tom! It's good to see you!
(*He embraces her.*)

TOM: It's great to see you, Helen. How *are* you? Show me – you've lost weight.

HELEN: I don't think so – have I?

TOM: The answer I want is: as a matter of fact I have, Uncle Tom, and so have you. *Sug. entered.*
(*They both move into the living-room.*)

HELEN: Well, as a matter of fact, Father –

TOM: Don't tell me. I know. I know.

MIRIAM: Looking powerful, isn't he?

HELEN: You are.

TOM: I'm grotesque. Food, drink and sloth – they're killing me. The question is: will I survive until next November?

HELEN: Why then?

TOM: That's when I retire. And even if I last six months more, what's to become of me then? Kicked out of the only world I've known for forty years – I'll be lost. D'you know who I met the other day? Jackie Sheridan – Daddy knows him – chaplain down at Athlone all his life. Retired last year; living with a widowed sister in Waterford. And d'you know what he does to pass the time? Studies all the death notices in the morning paper and spends the rest of the day writing letters of condolence to the relatives. Black strangers! Honestly. Terrifying, isn't it? What d'you think of Anna?

HELEN: That was always an old trick of yours.

TOM: Trick? Trick? What trick?

HELEN: The disarming chatter and then the sudden, probing question.

MIRIAM: She's wise to you, Father Tom.

TOM: (*To* MIRIAM, *who is laughing*) Is that fair? D'you think

199

that's fair? (*To* HELEN) Well, I think she's terrific. And
sure the world knows Frank's terrific.

HELEN: So they'll make a terrific couple.

TOM: (*To* MIRIAM) Lord, hasn't she got sharp!

MIRIAM: England smartens them up all right.

TOM: I didn't mean that at all.

HELEN: Yes, you did.

TOM: Tell me, girls, I want your advice. The powers that be
have some kind of a notion that on a night like this I always
get plastered.

MIRIAM: Tch-tch-tch.

TOM: Wait – wait – wait! Now – should I confirm that notion for
them? Or should I stay sober and confound them? I could,
you know.

HELEN: Confirm them?

TOM: Confound them!

MIRIAM: Do that then, Father.

TOM: Should I?

MIRIAM: Anything to confound them.

TOM: That's it then. Settled. (*To* HELEN) What are you looking
sceptical about?

HELEN: Not a thing – not a thing.

(FRANK *enters in his dress uniform.* TINA *behind him.*)

FRANK: Anna'll be down in a minute.

(*The following lines* – MIRIAM's, TOM's, HELEN's,
TINA's – *all overlap.*)

MIRIAM: (*Clapping*) Well – well – well – well!

TOM: Ah, the prince himself!

HELEN: Very smart – very smart indeed!

TINA: Three cheers for the hero!

TOM: (*Sings*) For he's a jolly good fellow –

FRANK: Stop – stop – stop – stop – stop!

ALL TOGETHER: For he's a jolly good fellow;
    For he's a jolly good fellow;
    And so say all of us.

TOM: Everybody outside for a picture!

TINA: A photo – hurrah – hurrah – hurrah – a photo!

(*They move to the garden – talking – still singing/humming 'Jolly*

200

Good Fellow'. Comments like: 'My God, look at my dress',
'Anybody got a comb?', 'You're fine', 'Where do you want us to
stand?' etc., etc.)

TOM: Over here, please, everybody. You in the middle, Frank.
Miriam, you and Tina on one side.

FRANK: Where? Here?

TOM: A bit to the left.

FRANK: Here?

TOM: That's the right.

FRANK: It's *my* left.

TOM: No wonder you could never march!

TINA: What about me?

TOM: Fine where you are.

MIRIAM: Not a word – the cap's still over the lens.

HELEN: It's not!

TOM: You're quite right – so it is! (*Takes it off.*) That'll be a
help.

MIRIAM: Maybe – maybe.

TOM: A little tighter in, Helen, please. Good, good. At ease,
Frank.

FRANK: I am at ease.

TOM: Are you? Look at me. Big smile, everybody.

THE PICTURE!

ANNA'S ENTRANCE

(*The group is facing almost straight out.* ANNA *in a long
dressing-gown comes downstairs and into the living-room. She
looks around.*)

ANNA: (*Softly*) Frank? (*She looks out, sees the photographing,
stands watching.*)

TINA: Cheese – isn't that what you say?

HELEN: *Noblesse oblige.*

MIRIAM: Oh, very posh. Is that a London one?

ANNA: (*More loudly*) Frank!

FRANK: Come on, Tom. Get a move on.

SIR: 'She calls Frank twice. But Frank does not hear her. And
she goes back to her room and cries.'

TOM: Little tighter in, love.

TINA: Me?

TOM: No, Miriam. Tight in – perfect!

ANNA: Look at them – tight – tight – tight – arms around one

201

another – smiling. No, I won't go back to my room and cry. I'll tell them now!

(SIR *gets quickly to his feet and goes to* ANNA)

SIR: They won't hear you now.

ANNA: They will! They will!

SIR: Anna, believe me –

(*She rushes away from him and out to the garden where she stands facing the group.* SIR *looks on patiently. She is almost hysterical.*)

TOM: Frank.

FRANK: What?

TOM: This way.

FRANK: I'm glaring at you, for God's sake!

TOM: That's what I'm saying. Will you stop it! Now – terrific – Commandant Butler and his beautiful family.

MIRIAM: He really means me.

ANNA: (*Trying to control herself*) Listen to me, all of you. You, too, Chaplain.

MIRIAM: No film in the camera.

TINA: I'm going to laugh.

ANNA: When you were away, all those months I was left alone here –

TOM: Great – don't move – terrific. And another.

ANNA: Listen to me, Frank!

FRANK: (*To* TOM) No, no, no, no.

TOM: One more – just one more – that's all.

ANNA: I had an affair with your son, Ben – with your brother, Ben! An affair – an affair – d'you hear!

TOM: Even closer together.

MIRIAM: Thanks be to God Charlie isn't watching this caper.

ANNA: An affair, d'you hear – out of loneliness, out of despair, out of hate! And everybody in the camp knows – everybody except the Butlers!

(TINA *can control her laughter no longer – she explodes.*)

TOM: Terrific, Tina! Everybody join in!

(*The laughter is infectious. They laugh so much we can hardly hear what they are saying.*)

MIRIAM: *Noblesse oblige!*

TOM: Lovely, Frank.

HELEN: Is there really no film in it?

TINA: Hold me up! Hold me up!

TOM: (*Clicking, clicking*) Terrific, terrific! Stay where you are!
(ANNA *is staring at the others as if she had come out of a
dream.* SIR *goes to her and takes her arm, leading her off.*)

SIR: I told you, didn't I? 'Frank does not hear her and she goes
back to her room and cries.'

ANNA: (*Crying*) It wasn't despair.

SIR: I know.

ANNA: And it wasn't hate – no, not hate for him.

SIR: You'll tell us later.

ANNA: It wasn't even loneliness –

SIR: Later – later – you'll do it *later* exactly as it's here. Now go
back to your room.

ANNA: I'm sorry.

SIR: No harm done.

ANNA: Did I mess it all up?

SIR: You shuffled the pages a bit – that's all. But nothing's
changed.
(*Throughout this* ANNA–SIR *exchange the others have stood
with frozen smiles. Now that* ANNA *has gone off they are
released again.*)

TOM: There! Thank you – thank you – thank you.

FRANK: Right – off we go, Tom. Let's move – let's move.
(FRANK *goes into the house and hall. The others drift into the
living-room.*)

TOM: (*Camera*) Can I leave this here?

TINA: I'll look after it.

HELEN: When will we get copies?

MIRIAM: Have you never seen his pictures?

FRANK: (*Calling upstairs*) Anna! We're all set.

MIRIAM: If you get a word with the Taoiseach, Father, tell him
we're still waiting for the sewage out at Killclooney.

TOM: The very first thing I'll say to him.

MIRIAM: Just to give him an appetite.
(ANNA *comes downstairs.* FRANK *stands at the bottom with his
hands outstretched.*)

FRANK: Beautiful.

ANNA: I'm nervous, Frank.

FRANK: You are beautiful. (*Calls*) Look! Everybody look! Look what I'm bringing to the reception!

(*The others move out to the hallway.*)

TOM: Terrific, Anna, terrific!

HELEN: ⎤ Lovely, Anna. It's a beautiful dress. You did the
MIRIAM: ⎬ hair very well. Those are lovely shoes. Lovely
TINA: ⎦ Lovely.

FRANK: And look – look – (*jewellery*). And this, isn't this elegant (*Dress*)?

ANNA: Frank, I –

FRANK: And what about that (*hair*)? Your handiwork, isn't it, Helen?

HELEN: You're going to be late, Father.

FRANK: Let them wait.

ANNA: Please, Frank.

FRANK: All in all – beautiful!

ANNA: Please –

FRANK: And she says she's nervous! My darling, they'll never have seen a sight like it in the mess – in any mess – in all their puny lives. (*Briskly*) We're away. Don't wait up for me.

(BEN *enters left. Very diffident, very hesitant, as if he might turn and run away. He looks into the living-room – but the others have now moved out to the front of the house.*)

TOM: We're off. God bless.

HELEN: ⎤ Have a good time. Confound them, Father Tom.
MIRIAM: ⎬ Enjoy yourselves. Make a good speech, Daddy.
TINA: ⎦ Don't eat too much, Anna.

(*They are all off stage now – except* HELEN, *who is standing at the front door.*)

FRANK: Are we taking my car or yours?

TOM: It doesn't matter – either.

TINA: Take your own, Daddy.

(*The car moves off. We hear* TINA *and* MIRIAM *calling goodbyes.* HELEN *waves from the door.* BEN *moves closer to the house.* HELEN *turns and comes into the living-room.*)

204

SIR: 'Benedict Butler – Ben – twenty-four years of age. Only son of Frank and Louise. His father wanted him to go for a commission, but his mother wanted him to be a doctor. Was a first-year medical student at University College, Dublin, when his mother died.'

BEN: (*Softly*) Helen.

(HELEN *is standing looking at the photographs on the mantelpiece. She has her back to him.*)

SIR: 'Shortly after her death his health broke down and he never went back to college. Now fully recovered; the only after-effect being a stammer which afflicts him occasionally when he is tense.'

BEN: Helen.

SIR: 'As he looks into the living-room he imagines for a second that the figure at the mantelpiece is his mother.'

BEN: She had her back to me. She didn't hear me. And I stood outside in the garden and just watched her. Everything – her hair, her neck, her shoulders, the way she moved her arms – precisely as I remembered.

(HELEN *is now fingering the glass ornament.*)

Not a sound except the tap-tap-tap of her stick as she moved about. And for a second my heart expanded with an immense remembered love for her, and then at once shrank in terror of her. And then suddenly she turned and came towards the open door, and I saw it wasn't – it w-w-w-wasn't –

(HELEN *has turned and has moved to the open door. She is startled to see a man staring in at her.*)

HELEN: Who – ? (*Loud*) Ben!

(*He responds as if someone – a stranger – had called him.*)

BEN: (*Quickly, confused*) Yes? Yes?

(HELEN *runs out and throws her arms around him.*)

HELEN: ⎫(*Overlapping*) Oh – Ben, Ben, Ben, Ben, Ben!
BEN: ⎭ Yes? Yes? Yes? Yes? Yes?

SIR: (*Rising*) Thank you. (*Claps his hands twice to interrupt the action.*) That's fine – that's fine. We're moving along very nicely. (*Sees that* BEN *and* HELEN *are still locked in an embrace.*)

SIR: Thank you.

(*They separate.*)

Yes, very nicely indeed.

(*As soon as he claps his hands*, TINA, ANNA, FRANK *and* TOM *appear.*)

Now, we'll leave it there, I think, and move straight on to the point when –

ANNA: 'The point of no return'.

SIR: The – ?

ANNA: It's your phrase; you used it to Father Tom.

SIR: 'The point of no return' – you're quite right; so I did. Wasn't that very histrionic of me! Oh, no; heavens, no. We're nowhere near that – that decisive point yet.

ANNA: Then let's skip all the rest and go straight to it.

SIR: You've already been naughty and attempted that, Anna!

ANNA: Because it's the essence of it all, isn't it?

SIR: Well, of course we can do that. But if we do, then we're bypassing all that period when different decisions *might* have been made. Because at the point we've arrived at now, many different conclusions would have been possible if certain things had been said or done or left unsaid and undone. And at this point it did occur to many of you to say certain things or to omit saying certain things. And it is the memory of those lost possibilities that has exercised you endlessly since and has kept bringing you back here, isn't that so?

TOM: I'm sure he's right.

SIR: For example, Helen, you did think of spending the night with Charlie and Miriam.

HELEN: We've already been over all that.

SIR: We have indeed. And what you said was, 'No, I'll see it through.'

HELEN: Yes, I stayed; and I saw it through; and I didn't survive the test. And I've cracked up three times since. Now are you content?

SIR: It's your content we're talking about. And Ben, at this point you still had time to join your friends on the salmon boat.

206

ARE THE OPTIONS OPEN?
FREEDOM OF CHOICE !
vs. FATE?

BEN: Am I complaining? Am I?

SIR: But the thought did occur to you. And they didn't set out for – what? – another hour at least. So if you would like to explore that area of –

BEN: Just stick to the f-f-f-facts.

SIR: But that is a fact. And every time you get drunk, it's the one thing you keep talking about.

BEN: What happened happened. Leave it at that.

SIR: As you wish. As for yourself, Anna, you could have resolved – sitting up at that top table in the mess – bored by the talk around you – you could still have resolved to live with your secret –

ANNA: 'Live with my secret'! For God's sake!

SIR: Be fair, Anna. You did think of it. In which case Frank's life would have stayed reasonably intact. Oh, there were many, many options still open at this stage.

TOM: I agree completely.

(TOM *is ignored*.)

TINA: For me, too?

SIR: Not for you Tina, I'm afraid. You had no choice. That night you were faced with the inevitability of growing up. But that's all – well, almost all.

TOM: He's absolutely right – about the rest of us, I mean.

(*No one listens to him, either here or later when he preaches*.)

SIR: As for yourself, Frank –

(FRANK *holds up his hands*.)

FRANK: You're in command, Sir.

SIR: At this point, indeed at any point, you could well have –

FRANK: Please – please. I did what I had to do. There was no alternative for me. None. What I had to do was absolutely clear-cut. There was never any doubt in my mind.

SIR: I'm afraid that's true, Frank.

FRANK: So carry on as you think best, Sir. I'm in your hands.

SIR: Very well. Let's proceed. Let's leap ahead to – yes, several hours later.

TOM: Our options are still open – he's perfectly right.

SIR: And for this episode I think I need only Helen and Ben and Tina.

207

TOM: I'm not a sermonizing kind of fellow – good Lord, you know me better than that –
(*The others begin to drift away, each encased in his privacy.*)
– but I've got to speak what I know to be true, and that is that grace is available to each and every one of us if we just ask God for it –
SIR: Yes – here we are.
TOM: – which is really the Christian way of saying that our options are *always* open. Because that is the enormous gift that Christ purchased for us – the availability of choice and our freedom to choose.
(*He stops and looks around.* SIR *is poised with his finger on his ledger – he has all the time in the world.* ANNA *and* FRANK *have gone.* HELEN, BEN *and* TINA *have not heard a word he has said. His rally falters.*)
So that what I'm saying is – is that at this point there isn't necessarily an incompatability between your attitude, Sir and my own –
SIR: Good. 'It is 1.45 a.m. and –'
TOM: And, Sir.
(SIR *looks at him.*)
(*Forced roguishness*) Keep watching – you're going to be surprised.
(*He leaves.*)
SIR: 'It is 1.45 a.m. and Miriam and Charlie are at home, in bed. Charlie is sleeping. Miriam is staring at the ceiling. In the camp the reception is just over. Frank Butler and the Minister of Defence and the Chief of Staff are standing in a corner, conversing privately. Father Tom is in the car park, searching his pockets for car keys. Anna is standing alone at the mess waiting for Frank. In the Butler living-room –'
(*He breaks off because his eye catches* CHARLIE, *dressed as usual, tiptoeing across the stage.* CHARLIE *senses the silence, smiles at* SIR, *touches his forehead with his index finger.*)
CHARLIE: (*Confidentially*) Carry on – pay no attention to me – I'll just nip over here – look on from that corner.
(*He begins walking again.*)
SIR: I'm sorry.

208

CHARLIE: Fascinating to watch people – observe them, you
know – just like in the courts – as long as you're not involved
yourself – how the other half lives sort of thing.
SIR: It is 1.45 a.m. You arrived at 11.30 and left with Miriam.
CHARLIE: Honest to God, you won't hear a cheep out of –
SIR: You're at home in bed. You're asleep and Miriam's awake.
CHARLIE: I know the reason for that! If she's sleeping she can't
think. (*Pause.*) I mean to say – if she's thinking she can't
sleep. (*Begins moving.*) Just for this next piece –
SIR: Good night, Charlie.
   (CHARLIE *stops.*)
Good night.
   (CHARLIE *looks at him, sees he is adamant, and leaves.*)
'In the Butler living-room the doors and windows are wide
open because the night is sultry. Helen and Ben have a few
drinks together.'
I'll leave it to yourselves.
   (*He retires to his stool. The lights change. The lights from the
   living-room spill out to the garden.* BEN *and* HELEN *are slightly
   intoxicated and completely relaxed. This must not be played as
   a drunk scene, but lightly, full of laughter.* BEN *is striding
   about with a glass in his hand, a cigarette in his mouth. The
   diffident, uncertain* BEN *is suddenly voluble. The scene is
   played in almost constant movement – around the living-room,
   out in the garden, around the garden. Wherever* BEN *and*
   HELEN *go,* TINA *follows. But their accord, their intimacy,
   excludes her.*)
BEN: Follow behind me, keep me in sight, and I'll lead you there.
HELEN: I'm on your heels.
BEN: Right. Do you happen to remember a place by the name of
Carrickfad?
HELEN: Carrickfad! Do I remember Carrickfad!
BEN: Good. So you pass Carrickfad. Turn right at the old
coastguard station. Pass the old lime kiln. Pass the old
rectory.
HELEN: Ruins – ruins – ruins!
BEN: Cross the wooden bridge and straight down that track
until you come to the ring fort –

HELEN: On your left when you're facing the sea.

BEN: Turn left there, carry on for three-quarters of a mile until you come to the sand dunes –

HELEN: In Culhame.

BEN: Culhame is correct. But you have still to find my hermitage. Now, when you get to the foot of the sand hills, you stop, face north-north-west and look straight ahead; and if you've very good eyesight you'll see rising out of the bent the roof of a little blue caravan.

HELEN: (*To* TINA) 'A secret place', he says!

BEN: And there I can be consulted any morning between the hours of nine and eleven, except on those occasions when I'm off lecturing.

(*He goes out to the garden.* HELEN *follows. Then* TINA.)

HELEN: Secret! I could make my way there now – in the dark!

TINA: I was never there.

HELEN: Didn't we spend every Sunday in the summer sliding down those same dunes!

TINA: Had you great fun?

BEN: And when I'm travelling abroad I can usually be contacted at the nearest Salvation Army hostel. You know, we old army types – a great freemasonry. (*Calls in the direction of camp.*) My greetings, Chief of Staff, Adjutant General and Quartermaster General! God bless you, Number One Army Band!

HELEN: They've left hours ago, clown!

BEN: And warmest wishes to you, magazine, parade square and flagpole!

HELEN: D'you remember the day the two of us climbed up on to the roof of the old coastguard station?

BEN: A mad, mad pair!

TINA: Was Miriam with you?

BEN: Mad!

HELEN: She went to the top of the walls but didn't go up on to the roof.

TINA: And what happened?

HELEN: (*To* BEN) Tell her what happened!

BEN: What happened was that we were stuck up there for six hours.

HELEN: Right!

BEN: The pair of us clinging to two charred rafters.

HELEN: Remember them groaning!

BEN: Rigid with fright – couldn't move either forward or back in case they'd snap.

HELEN: Mother calling up, 'Don't wriggle, Ben. Don't wriggle!'

BEN: I was shaking with *cold*. And if I opened my eyes I could see Father directly below me. And cute enough, I remember thinking: if the rafter does snap, he'll break my fall.

HELEN: O my God.

TINA: How did you get down?

BEN: It took a full detachment of engineers – scaffolding, generators, arc lights – the biggest peacetime operation ever mounted by Western Command. And an ambulance –

HELEN: Two ambulances!

BEN: And that old MO – Colonel – ?

HELEN: Hayes.

BEN: That's him. 'Where the hell are the blankets?'

HELEN: What a day – what a day!

TINA: You must have had a lot of fun.

HELEN: I don't know what I'm laughing at. I thought I was finished.

BEN: I pointed it out to Anna about a month ago – one day we were out at the caravan – and told her the whole escapade; but somehow there was none of the terror, none of the delight. (*Goes inside.*) Now I have a feeling that if my commandant father knew I was here, he'd rush home and throw his arms around me and say, 'Welcome, son. Help yourself to a drink.'

(HELEN *goes inside.* TINA *follows.*)

HELEN: Part of him probably wants to.

BEN: Offer me a drink?

HELEN: You know very well.

BEN: 'A large whiskey, Sir? Thank you very much, Sir. You're altogether too kind.'

211

HELEN: And if he did?
  (*Pause as* BEN *pours a drink.*)
BEN: Too late – too late.
HELEN: But if he did?
BEN: We're long beyond that.
HELEN: What if he did?
BEN: What if he did? After all that's been said?
HELEN: Despite all that.
BEN: The day she died I called him a murderer.
HELEN: Six years have passed.
BEN: And he hit me – don't you remember? – he hit me!
HELEN: That's all over.
BEN: Years, years of hostility.
HELEN: That fades.
BEN: Does it?
HELEN: You know it does.
BEN: You can preserve it.
  (*He goes outside again. She follows. As before,* TINA *tags along.*)
HELEN: Why would you want to?
BEN: In case you'd forget.
HELEN: No!
BEN: Out of a sense of loyalty.
HELEN: To whom?
BEN: You can embalm it consciously, deliberately –
HELEN: That would be wrong.
BEN: – in acts of terrible perfidy –
HELEN: You wouldn't do that, Ben.
BEN: – which you do in a state of confusion, out of some vague
  residual passion that no longer fires you; hitting out,
  smashing back, not at what's there but at what you think
  you remember; and which you regret instantly – oh, yes,
  yes, yes, never underestimate the regret. But then it's too
  late, too late – the thing's preserved in perpetuity – as
  Charlie would say.
HELEN: You shouldn't drink.
BEN: So as we used to say – put that in your pipe and smoke it.
HELEN: (*To* TINA) Going off his head in that hermitage of his.

212

BEN: Helen.

HELEN: You *are* drunk.

BEN: Sister Helen.

HELEN: Sit down on that seat.

BEN: Helen Sarah Fidelma. *— the actress's name: Fedelma Cullen?!*

HELEN: H. S. F. – yes, I remember.

TINA: What was that?

HELEN: Horrible Smelly Feet.

TINA: I never heard that before!

HELEN: He used to drive me mad with that.

TINA: I'm going to remember that – H. S. F.!

BEN: I want to tell you something.

HELEN: You're getting silly.

BEN: I am not. And I want to tell you something.

HELEN: (*To* BEN) Give me a cigarette.

TINA: No, Helen, no!

HELEN: Just one.

BEN: Honourable Sincere Friend. *this is from 1 connection.*

TINA: Don't, Helen, please.

BEN: We'll both have one.

TINA: You'll regret it, Helen.

BEN: I've something to say to you.

HELEN: Is it important?

BEN: Very important – vitally important – and you'll know it's important.

HELEN: How?

BEN: Because I'll probably start stammering in the middle of it! *seems clear!*
(*They all laugh at this.*)

HELEN: Give me a light.

TINA: I'm disappointed in you, Helen.

HELEN: (*Mocking*) She's disappointed in me! Now I'm really upset. (*To* BEN) D'you remember – out in the turf shed – passing the cigarette from one to the other and it hot with sucking!

BEN: What I'm going to tell you is a big secret.

HELEN: I hate secrets.

BEN: No, not really a secret.

HELEN: Make up your mind.

BEN: More a confidence than a s-s-s-secret.
 (*They all laugh.*)
HELEN: You faked that!
BEN: I did not!
HELEN: You did – to hook me!
TINA: Tell us your secret.
BEN: May I confide my confidence?
HELEN: You may not.
BEN: I'm going to tell you.
HELEN: I don't want to hear it.
BEN: Helen –
HELEN: Everybody tells me their confidences.
BEN: Please –
HELEN: I'm sick of their confidences.
BEN: It's about –
HELEN: (*Covering her ears*) No, no, no, no!
TINA: (*Laughing*) Tell me, Ben! Tell me!
BEN: It has to do with my embalming job.
HELEN: Can't hear a word you're saying!
BEN: (*Shouts*) And with my profound regrets.
HELEN: We all have our regrets. Look after your own.
BEN: I'll shock you, Helen.
 (HELEN *takes her hands away from her ears. The atmosphere suddenly changes: the laughing is finished.*)
HELEN: (*Imperious*) I want a cup of coffee! He needs a cup of coffee! Go and make it for me, Tina!
BEN: Mother's voice – exactly!
TINA: I want to hear what Ben's –
HELEN: (*Calmer*) Would you, darling, please?
 (*She looks firmly at* TINA *until* TINA *finally gives way and goes into the living-room. She is about to go into the kitchen but hesitates to listen.*)
On a night like this you can hear the sea breaking on the Tor Mor.
BEN: (*Quiet, urgent*) I've got to tell you, Helen.
HELEN: You've 'got to' nothing.
BEN: When you wanted to talk about your Gerry I listened to you.

HELEN: Years ago. For God's sake, you're a man now!

BEN: I was the one carried your messages.

HELEN: Stop bleating! Stop snivelling!

BEN: Stood watching outside the gym hall when you and he were inside. Warned you that night the two of you took the jeep and went to the dance in Omagh—

HELEN: And stood there at Mother's side—and held her hand—held her hand as if you were her husband, while he stood at the door with his cap in his hand, trembling, the fool, trembling because the Commandant's wife was quizzing him in her quiet and most reasonable voice about his 'educational background' and his father's 'profession' and his 'prospects in his chosen career'—Private Gerald Kelly, batman—*my* Gerry—*my* Gerry. And all the time you stood beside her in that wicker chair, facing him, stroking her hand. *You* did, Ben; yes, you. And d'you know what he did when he came outside? Gerald Kelly—the defiant, the reckless, the daredevil Gerry Kelly? He cried, Ben. Yes; like a child. Gerry Kelly cried. Yes. He cried. Yes.
(*She goes to the other end of the garden. She cries quietly.* BEN *goes to her.*)

BEN: I'm sorry, Helen.

HELEN: (*Simply*) Sorry? What's sorry? 'Never underestimate the regret.' Is that what you said? I've lost him. She killed him. He's gone. Do I love Gerry Kelly still? I thought I'd squeezed every drop of him out of me. But now I know I haven't forgotten a second of him.

BEN: Helen—
(*Pause. Then* SIR *rises and moves forward.*)

SIR: Thank you. We've got quite a bit done. I'd say the back's broken.
(*To audience*) We'll resume again in approximately— what?—fifteen minutes.

Quick Black

ACT TWO

Only MIRIAM *is on stage, sitting in the wicker chair, reading the* Donegal Enquirer, *eating a slice of cake, an empty coffee mug beside her.*

Great bursts of laughter come from the kitchen. And as the other characters come on they carry with them an air of good humour – a gaiety, or, as SIR *calls it, a 'giddiness' that permeates the beginning of this sequence, right up until the arrival of* SIR. *They are dressed as we saw them at the end of Act One, except* FRANK, *who is in desert uniform.* TINA, *laughing, opens the kitchen door.*

TINA: There's a few cream cakes left. Do you want one?

MIRIAM: Don't tempt me.

TINA: Or a doughnut?

MIRIAM: Please. I'm up to here. What are they laughing at?

TINA: Father Tom's telling stories about when he was a curate in Yorkshire.

MIRIAM: God, weren't we reared on them!

TINA: Daddy says he makes them up as he goes along.

MIRIAM: Listen to this – from the *Enquirer* – 'Commandant Butler's eldest daughter, Christina, is in London –'

TINA: Me!

MIRIAM: 'His youngest daughter, Helen, lives at home.'

TINA: Sure they never get anything right, that crowd.

MIRIAM: But wait till you hear this. 'And another daughter is married to Mr Charles Donnelly, who is popular in the legal and sporting life of Donegal. As a young man he was a well known amateur high-jumper and is the father of three children!'

TINA: (*Laughing*) I'm away back to London.

(*She returns to the kitchen.*)

MIRIAM: High-jumper – sweet God. Amateur – my foot!

(*She continues reading.* BEN *enters left, singing, and meets* ANNA, *who enters from upstage – throughout this sequence none*

216

of the characters obeys the conventions of the set. They meet in the garden area.)

BEN: We're not late, are we?

ANNA: I don't think so.

BEN: I suppose he'd be out clapping his hands for us. Come along, children, come along, come along.

(She sits on the garden seat.)

You're eager to get it over with, aren't you?

ANNA: At the beginning I was. Now I don't care. Are you?

BEN: I don't give a damn about anyone or anything. I feel . . . flushed, giddy . . . I feel euphoric.

(ANNA laughs.)

ANNA: 'Euphoric'!

BEN: I do. I haven't felt like this since—*(Stops)*

ANNA: When?

BEN: I can tell you exactly—six years ago, October 19th—the day of my mother's funeral. That's when. That afternoon. After we had come back from the cemetery. Shocking, isn't it?

ANNA: Tell me about it.

BEN: Nothing much to tell. We were all in there *(living-room)*—it was pouring with rain—there were some visitors—the girls were crying—everybody was whispering. And suddenly I had to rush out of the room because I was afraid I'd burst out singing or cheer or leap into the air. Honestly. Walked across the sand hills for maybe a couple of hours—I don't remember. Anyhow until that madness passed.

ANNA: Was it madness?

(Pause. He looks at her quickly. Then resumes as before.)

BEN: And then I came back. Guilty as hell and soaked to the skin. *(Smiling)* And assumed the grief again—a greater grief, a guilty grief. All very strange.

ANNA: Are you going to sing for us now?

BEN: Sing, dance, anything you like.

(He does a few extravagant leaps around the stage, singing a few lines of 'I'm singing in the rain' at the same time. In the middle of his performance MIRIAM shouts out.)

MIRIAM: Ben, will you—for the love of God!

ANNA: *(When he finishes)* Very good. Very impressive.

217

(He flops down beside her.)

BEN: I really am giddy now!

ANNA: I think you should stick to the fishing all the same.

BEN: What are you going to do – when it's all over?

ANNA: An aunt of mine has a café in New Jersey. She always
wanted me over. So I'll stay with her for six months – until
I've saved some money. Then I'll move on to San Francisco
or Los Angeles; more likely San Francisco.

BEN: Just like that?

ANNA: Yes.

BEN: Have you any relatives in California?

ANNA: No.

BEN: Do you know anybody there?

ANNA: No one.

BEN: God, I wish I could be as decisive as that.

ANNA: What'll you do?

BEN: When this is all over? Oh, I'll – I suppose I'll head off, too.

ANNA: To America?

BEN: Not America. America's too – too foreign for me. Scotland.
England, maybe. Somewhere. Who knows?

ANNA: But you'll keep coming back here, won't you?
(Great laughter from the kitchen.)

BEN: Are you laughing at me, too?

ANNA: But that's what you'll do, isn't it?
(BEN leaps up.)

BEN: Let's go and see what's so funny.

ANNA: Oh, Ben, there's one thing I'd like you to do for me –

BEN: Yes?

ANNA: If you would.

BEN: What's that?

ANNA: You look startled.

BEN: Why should I look startled? What is it?

ANNA: I left a pair of old flat shoes in the caravan – I think
they're in that press under the sink. And a blue and white
scarf – it's hanging behind the door.

BEN: I'll get them for you.

ANNA: That's all.

BEN: Fine.

(*She goes up to him and kisses him lightly on the forehead.*)

ANNA: Dismiss.

BEN: (*Uneasy laugh*) What's that for?

ANNA: Our attempt at a love affair.
(*Laughter from kitchen.*)

BEN: What do you mean – attempt?

ANNA: That's what it was, wasn't it? (*She takes his arm and leads him into the living-room.*) Come on – we're missing the fun.
(*As they enter, the others –* FRANK, TOM, TINA, HELEN *– emerge from the kitchen. Now that they are all together the euphoric atmosphere is heightened.*)

FRANK: I don't believe a word of it, Tom!

TOM: Would I tell a lie, Helen?

HELEN: I keep telling you – I believe you.

FRANK: He now suddenly remembers that Canon Bradshaw had a wooden leg!

MIRIAM: God forgive you, Father Tom!

TOM: May I be called before my Maker.

ANNA: Who's Canon Bradshaw?
(FRANK *is standing beside* ANNA, *his arm casually around her shoulders.*)

FRANK: An eccentric parish priest he had when he was a curate in Hull.

TOM: A terrific yoke made from parana pine and treated with linseed oil. And he had two types of ferrule that he could screw into the bottom: one was brass that he used to polish every Friday night when he was doing the candlesticks –

HELEN: He's remembering more details.

MIRIAM: More lies.

BEN: Let him tell the story.

FRANK: (*To* ANNA) This was his first post.

TOM: – and the other ferrule was wooden and covered with black astrakhan –
(*Great laughter.*)

BEN: Astrakhan?

TOM: Just like a drumstick.

MIRIAM: This is all new! Canon Bradshaw used to be a cripple in a wheelchair!

219

TOM: God's my judge. And he'd use the wooden one when he'd be saying mass upstairs in the oratory. And when he'd come to the Sanctus he'd suddenly kick out backways, just like a donkey, and bang the bell three times with the astrakhan head.

BEN: Boom-boom-boom.

(*Laughter.*)

FRANK: Tom! Tom!

TINA: When did he use the brass one?

HELEN: You're encouraging him.

MIRIAM: Try to stop him.

TOM: He used the brass one —

MIRIAM: This is definitely a lie.

TOM: No. He used the brass one for walking, of course. And for beating carpets.

(*Again they all laugh.*)

I know — I know — no one ever believes me.

HELEN: All that laughing — my sides are sore.

FRANK: We're all sore. What has made all of us so frivolous?

MIRIAM: Listen — listen — listen — have you all seen this (*paper*)?

BEN: What is it?

FRANK: Yes, study that. I look very distinguished in that.

TINA: I think so too, Daddy.

FRANK: (*To* ANNA) Have you seen it?

ANNA: It's very good.

BEN: Let me see.

MIRIAM: Make up captions for the two of them as they shake hands. What's the President thinking? What's Father thinking?

TOM: Hannibal's old eyes; and the way he's leaning slightly backwards. You're thinking: the cute hawk smells the brandy off my breath!

HELEN: Very good. Anna?

ANNA: Show me.

FRANK: You be careful now.

ANNA: The President's saying to himself: my God, I've forgotten! Footman, Batman, Butler — what's the man's *name*?

FRANK: If you want to know he called me Francis.

220

BEN: I know what he's thinking: today's Monday – this must be the Italian equestrian team.

MIRIAM: And what's Father thinking?

FRANK: You'd never guess.

HELEN: Tell us.

MIRIAM: I know – I know: he keeps calling me corporal – have I been demoted?

FRANK: Wrong – wrong – all wrong.

HELEN: All right – we give up – you tell us.

FRANK: I will not.

MIRIAM: Go. Go on.

SEVERAL TOGETHER: Come on, Father. Tell us. Tell us. We're dying to know.

FRANK: No.

TOM: He can't tell because it's obscene.

FRANK: As a matter of fact –

HELEN: Well?

FRANK: (*To* ANNA) I was looking for you in the crowd.
(*This is greeted with clapping and with joking 'ohs' and 'ahs'.*) That's the truth.

TOM: In that case, and with that set to your jaw your caption should read: 'If she's not here, I'll shoot her!'
(*As he goes off*) Anybody for more coffee? My wonderful coffee?

SEVERAL TOGETHER: No! No! No! No! No! No!

TOM: All right. All right.
(FRANK *takes advantage of the chorus to catch* ANNA *by the hand and lead her out to the garden. As he leads her out:*)

FRANK: Tom and his silly stories. He can spin them out for hours on end. (*He catches both her hands and holds her at arm's length.*) Let me look at you. My God, how I missed you. Were they kind to you when I was away? Does the family overwhelm you? Did you miss me? Let me look at you. Let me look at my beautiful, beautiful mascot.

ANNA: What do you see?

FRANK: What's the serious face for?

ANNA: Tell me what you see, Frank.

FRANK: I see youth, beauty, directness, simplicity. My wife.

ANNA: Anything else?

FRANK: An ageing man trembling before her.

ANNA: Why is he trembling?

FRANK: With intensity. With uncertainty. Because he has never
had joy like this. Because he is afraid that somehow he can't
cope with so great a joy because he is an ageing man.

ANNA: She is trembling too –

(*He puts his fingers across her lips.*)

FRANK: Because he wants to smother her, wash her in words of
love, but he can't because he has no fluency in love words
and he's afraid she won't understand that –

(*Again she tries to speak and again he stops her.*)

No, no, no. And he's trembling because he's afraid she'll
tire of a man so staid, so formal, so ponderous – tire of his
earnestness – my God of this! – tire of this solemn, abject
display that is the only method he knows. But you'd tell me
if I ever began to disgust you, wouldn't you, Anna? Yes,
you would. You'd have nothing to say – those eyes would
tell me. (*Quick laugh.*) I've a confession to make. Let's sit
down.

(*They sit on the summer seat.*)

There are nine men in this country who know everything
about you!

ANNA: What men?

FRANK: The men that I rescued in the desert. Each time I
crawled back to base with a man on my back – each trip
took about half an hour – I told him about you – everything
about you – your hair, your neck, your shoulders, the way
you laugh – everything. Luckily most of them were too ill to
listen. Not that that made any difference – I'd have told
them anyway. And one of them – fellow called Driscoll, lost
both his legs – I had to carry him like a baby – he kept
moaning and crying for his mother and I heard myself
shouting to him, 'Shut up, Driscoll! I'm talking to you
about my Anna! So shut up! Shut up!' And he did. And he
listened. So you probably saved Driscoll's life – just as you
have saved mine.

(MIRIAM *comes out.*)

MIRIAM: D'you know what Charlie was saying? You should put down spuds in this garden next year. Great for killing weeds.

ANNA: Where's Father Tom?

(BEN, HELEN and TINA come out to the garden.)

MIRIAM: In the kitchen, I think.

HELEN: You don't want more of his coffee, do you?

(Laughter.)

BEN: Every time I hear Uncle Tom mention coffee I think of that famous picnic years ago —

HELEN: On Portnoo pier!

BEN: That's it.

MIRIAM: And the two flasks! Oh, sweet Saviour!

FRANK: He'll hear you, Miriam.

TINA: What was that? What happened?

FRANK: It's a bit unkind to poor Tom.

BEN: Poor Tom! I might have been killed.

MIRIAM: (To ANNA) We all drove out to Portnoo this Sunday — oh, thirteen — fourteen years ago —

BEN: I was twelve at the time.

FRANK: (To ANNA) The place with the lookout post on the hill above it.

HELEN: (To ANNA) Haven't you been there?

ANNA: Yes, yes, I know it.

MIRIAM: And Mammy sat with a rug round her knees and the rest of us had a swim and then we spread the cloth out on the pier for the picnic and Uncle Tom had his stuff and we had ours. And it must have been the month of June because I have a distinct memory that it was the first strawberries we'd had that season and Mammy had a carton of cream, fresh cream, and a carton of ice cream, and you know that sensation when you taste the first fresh strawberries of the season — just like the first new spuds — only lighter and —

BEN: Tell the story, will you?

HELEN: We had just begun to eat —

MIRIAM: When suddenly Ben began behaving very strangely.

TINA: Oh, *that* story!

(SIR enters; listens to the story and reacts to it as the others do.

223

As the narrative unfolds, BEN *acts the part he played.*)

BEN: Hic-hup-hic-hic-hic.

MIRIAM: Staggering across the cloth and kicking over the cups and the strawberries and the ice cream; and of course Mammy began to panic –

FRANK: (*To* ANNA) We can laugh at it now.

HELEN: 'Epilepsy! My baby boy's got epilepsy!'

TINA: The twelve-year-old baby!

FRANK: It was very frightening.

MIRIAM: And then he fell on his face and started vomiting and Mammy began to cry and Tina started to scream –

TINA: No wonder!

MIRIAM: All into the car – back home like the hammers of hell – and you know those roads along the Gweebarra –

FRANK: She knows them.

HELEN: (*To* BEN) You'd passed out at that stage and uncle Tom was praying in your ear –

MIRIAM: Straight into sick-quarters – frantic phone calls – doctors and nurses summoned –

ANNA: What was it? What had happened?

MIRIAM: What had happened was that little Christina here –

TINA: I was six at the time!

MIRIAM: – had switched Uncle Tom's flask and our flask –

BEN: (*To* TINA) Monster!

MIRIAM: – and poor Mammy had given Ben a cup of neat whiskey!

ANNA: No!

HELEN: Almost killed him.

BEN: He was never the same since.

ANNA: Oh, poor Tom!

BEN: Oh, poor me!

MIRIAM: And of course he could never own up.

HELEN: Did he know?

MIRIAM: Did he know! Course he knew!

FRANK: The sequel's the best part. Tell her that.

HELEN: That bit's not true, Father.

FRANK: Is it not?

MIRIAM: Doesn't matter if it's true or not – it's part of the

Butler lore.

ANNA: What's the sequel?

MIRIAM: Ben claims that—

BEN: I do not!

MIRIAM: All right—it is said that when he was lying in sick-quarters after he'd had his stomach pumped—

FRANK: Shhhh!

MIRIAM: —Uncle Tom came to see him.

BEN: That bit's true.

MIRIAM: —leaned over him, caught him by the throat, and said, 'Touch my flask again and I'll break your bloody neck!' (*They all laugh at this. Then continue talking in undertones.* CHARLIE *enters and stops beside* SIR *who is laughing too.*)

CHARLIE: What's all the laughing about?

SIR: Sorry?

CHARLIE: What are they laughing at?

SIR: They are happy.

CHARLIE: *They* are?

SIR: Yes.

CHARLIE: They know what's going to happen, don't they?

SIR: They know.

CHARLIE: So what are they happy about?

SIR: There's always a gaiety at this stage.

CHARLIE: At what stage?

(SIR *is walking towards the family. He is smiling. He does not look at* CHARLIE.)

SIR: Sorry?

CHARLIE: What episode is that?

SIR: Look at them—they're so happy.

CHARLIE: When is this supposed to have taken place?

SIR: Yes, I'm afraid they've taken a few liberties.

CHARLIE: Is this in your book?

SIR: Some of it is, Charlie. And I'm afraid some of it is the wishful thinking of lonely people in lonely apartments. But they're always being true to themselves. And even if they've juggled the time a bit, they're doing no harm. We mustn't be impatient with them.

CHARLIE: Cracked, that family. Bloody cracked. Always was.

225

And it's the same with my woman every time she gets back among them – she's as bad as they are. Look at her for God's sake! I don't see much of that side of her when she's at home, I can tell you.

(*He leaves quickly.* SIR *now joins the others.*)

TINA: Here's Sir!

SIR: Carry on – carry on – don't let me interrupt.

FRANK: Just recalling a family outing.

SIR: Yes.

MIRIAM: A picnic years ago.

SIR: The famous day at Portnoo – I know – I know.

(*The gaiety ebbs quickly away.*)

HELEN: I don't think we ever went back there, did we?

BEN: I didn't.

HELEN: Not as a family group.

MIRIAM: Not for a picnic.

HELEN: Certainly not for a picnic.

TINA: I was there one day last Easter. By myself.

FRANK: And Anna and I have gone a few times, haven't we?

ANNA: Where to?

FRANK: Portnoo.

ANNA: Yes – once or twice.

FRANK: Just for the run. But no picnic, I'm afraid.

SIR: It's a pretty place, Portnoo.

FRANK: Lovely on a good day.

SIR: Beautiful. And across the bay there's an attractive little island.

FRANK: Inniskeel – is that what it's called?

SIR: That's it.

FRANK: Yes.

SIR: And when the tide's out, you can walk out to it – out to the island.

FRANK: So I believe – I've never done that.

SIR: Actually you don't walk out from Portnoo. You go from Narin just over the road.

FRANK: I see. No, I've never done that.

SIR: Yes. A pretty place, Portnoo. Very pretty place.

(*Pause.*)

226

ANNA: Shouldn't we get on with it?

SIR: Take your time – I'm in no hurry.

FRANK: Perhaps we should.

SIR: There's no rush.

MIRIAM: Yes, let's start.

FRANK: I think we should.

SIR: If you would like to make a fresh pot of tea or – ?

ANNA: Let's start! Let's start!

SIR: Whatever you say . . .

FRANK: Yes, the sooner the better.

SIR: Very well. (*Opens his ledger.*) Where would you like to resume? (*Waits – no answers.*) Anyone got any preference? (TOM *bursts in from the kitchen.*)

TOM: I've remembered another use he had for that brass ferrule. You know how people in chapel like to sit spread out in those long pews? Well, he used to go hopping up along the aisle and whatever unfortunate was at the end of the seat he'd prod him – (*Sees* SIR.) Oh! You're back!

SIR: Only a few minutes – that's all.

TOM: (*Looking around*) Are we ready to – to go?

SIR: If you are.

TOM: Me. Oh, I'm – certainly, certainly. Any time you're ready, I'm – I'm – (*He fades out.*)

SIR: If no one else has any suggestions, may I propose that we do the reasonable thing – in other words carry on almost immediately after we left off; that is to say, just before the return of Frank and Anna and Tom from the reception. Does that suit everybody?

(*No answers.*)

And Tom!

TOM: Sir?

SIR: (*Smiling*) I'll keep watching.

TOM: (*Uneasily*) Oh yes, yes, do – do that.

(TOM *exits quickly – in his confusion going off left instead of right.*)

SIR: Not that way, Tom. Over this – (TOM *has gone.*) I don't think we need those things, do we? (*He picks up empty coffee mugs, the* Enquirer; *adjusts the chairs.*)

227

MIRIAM: I'm not needed, am I?

SIR: Not for the time being, thank you. Nor Helen, nor Tina. (*Looking round the set.*) That's more like it, isn't it?

(SIR *returns to his stool.* HELEN *and* TINA *and* MIRIAM *move off. Then* ANNA. *Finally* FRANK. FRANK *is thinking himself back to the scene that* SIR *has called for. As he passes* BEN:)

BEN: Talking about that silly picnic—

FRANK: (*To himself*) Let's see. We left the mess. I drove. Anna was beside me. Tom was in the back—

BEN: No, no, the Portnoo picnic—coming home in the car—you were driving and I was lying across Mother's lap—I suppose I was drunk, for God's sake—

FRANK: (*Only now aware of him*) What's that?

BEN: And you k-k-k-—and you kept—

SIR: 'It is now 3.45 a.m. —'

BEN: My head was on your knees—and you had one hand on the driving wheel—and your other hand kept s-s-s-s-—your other hand kept—

SIR: Frank.

FRANK: Sir?

SIR: You're off at this point.

FRANK: Yes, I know that. (*Irritably to* BEN.) What is it? What is it?

BEN: With your other hand, your free hand, all the way home you kept stroking my face, my face, my cheeks, my forehead—

SIR: Gentlemen, I'm sorry. I must insist.

FRANK: (*To* BEN) Not now, later, please—

BEN: But what I want to tell you, Father, and what I want you to know is that I—

FRANK: (*Leaving*) Some other time.

SIR: 'It is now 2.45 a.m. Tina is sleeping in bed. Helen is getting her case ready. Frank, Anna and Tom are driving home from the reception—Frank and Anna in front, Tom in the back—'

(*He is interrupted by* TOM, *who has discovered that he exited the wrong way. He is now crossing in front of* SIR.)

TOM: Sorry—sorry—beg your pardon.

SIR: Take your time. No rush.

TOM: Looking for matches.

SIR: And did you get some?

(TOM *taps his jacket pocket.*)

Fine – fine. No hurry. We've all the time in the world.
(*Calls*) Ready now, Frank?

FRANK: (*Off*) Yes.

SIR: (*Calls*) And Anna?

ANNA: (*Off*) Ready.

SIR: Good. Where was I? Ah – ' – Tom in the back. Ben is alone
in the living-room. He is moving around.' And that seems
to be all the directions I've got. A bit abrupt, isn't it? Could
you carry on from there? Thank you.
(*He sits on his stool. The lights change.* BEN *is alone in the
living-room.*)

BEN: There was a fellow in my class at UCD; Sproule – Harry
Sproule; from Tipperary. Horsey people. Had a brother
doing arts and another doing law at the same time. And
each had a flat of his own. And the three of them never met
during term – not even once. Didn't even travel together.
Strange, wasn't it? Harry Sproule. (*He fingers the ornament.*)

HELEN: (*Off*) What's that?

BEN: Called his father and mother by their Christian names.
Spoke of them warmly – as if they were friends of the
family. (*Pause.*) Did you ever think what it must have been
like for Anna coming into our family? (*He circles around the
wicker chair, looking at it.*)

HELEN: (*Off*) I can't hear you.

BEN: (*Not as loud*) With our bloody boring reminiscences and
our bloody awareness and our bloody quivering
sensibilities. There must be another way of ordering close
relationships, mustn't there? (*Shouts*) Mustn't there?
(HELEN *enters. A cigarette in her mouth. Very brisk. She lifts a
book and then goes to the radiator, where her tights are spread.*)

HELEN: Mustn't there what?

BEN: I'm saying we're a very closely knit family.

HELEN: I don't know. Are we? I suppose so. Does it matter?
Tights drying on a radiator and no heating on!

BEN: Maybe I should go now, Helen. *# Choice to stay.*

HELEN: Go where?

BEN: Leave. Before they get back.

HELEN: Whatever suits you.

BEN: I'd just like to see him for one minute, give him my congratulations and then clear off.

HELEN: (*Firmly*) Listen to me. You'll stay where you are. When he comes you'll shake his hand, say your piece, and then leave. Right? Can't wear these tomorrow.

Decisions

BEN: I think I'll take a drink. No, maybe I shouldn't. You'll be here, won't you?

HELEN: What do you want me to do, Ben? Stand at your side and hold your hand and stroke it?
(*She runs upstairs.*)

BEN: Helen, I've already apologized –
(*But she is gone. He is wretched.*)
God! (*Rehearsing*) Congratulations, Sir, I'm really proud of – (*Pause.*) Very well done, Frank. Great work.
Splendid – (*Pause.*) When I heard it on the radio, Father, I was so th-th-th-th-thrill – Oh Christ!
(*The voice of* TOM *off. Approaching, singing very slowly and very drunkenly.*)

TOM: We're here because we're here because we're here because we're here.
(BEN *rushes to the drinks. Uncorks a bottle, puts it to his head, corks it again. Then sits in the armchair right of fireplace.* TOM *arrives at the front door. He knocks loudly on it three times.* BEN *leaps up instinctively, nervously – then sits again.*)
Right door – wrong house.
(*He stands back and examines the façade.*)
Right house – wrong door.
(*He begins singing again. Comes into the garden doing an absurd advancing-retreating dance as he crosses the stage. Finally, very shortly after* ANNA's *entrance, he falls into a deck chair and falls asleep. While* TOM *is dancing,* ANNA *enters. She goes straight into the living-room. At first she does not see* BEN.)

BEN: You're very late.

230

ANNA: What are you doing here?

BEN: Just to congratulate –

ANNA: Get out! Get out!

BEN: What's wrong?

ANNA: My head's splitting – that's what's wrong! I'm at my wits' end – that's what's wrong!

(FRANK *enters the hallway. He is elated, assured, exuding confidence.*)

FRANK: Helen! Helen!

ANNA: Get out, Ben, for God's sake!

(*Before* BEN *can make up his mind,* FRANK *enters.*)

FRANK: I know she won't have gone to bed. She may have – (*He stops suddenly when he sees* BEN. *They stand looking at one another. Pause.*)

BEN: I was passing and I just dropped in . . .

FRANK: Yes?

(*Pause.*)

BEN: I heard all about it on the radio and read all the stuff in the papers – and for your sake I was really very – it was just great. (*Holds out his hand.*) Congratulations.

FRANK: (*Very formally*) Thank you.

(*Then suddenly* FRANK *opens his arms and embraces* BEN *warmly.*)

Ben! Thank you, son. Thank you.

(HELEN *enters from kitchen.*)

Do you see who's here?

HELEN: Naturally.

FRANK: Naturally.

HELEN: Well – how did it go? (*To* ANNA) Had you a great night? (*To* FRANK) You have news! I know by your face you have news!

FRANK: I had a wonderful night.

HELEN: Great.

(*He catches* HELEN *in his arms and swings her round.*)

FRANK: And I have wonderful news!

HELEN: (*To* ANNA) Tell me! (*To* FRANK) Tell me – tell me – tell me –

FRANK: Have a guess.

HELEN: Guess! How can I guess!?

FRANK: But first we'll have a celebration drink. (*Looking at* BEN.) A double celebration. (*Looking at* ANNA.) A treble celebration.

ANNA: Where's Father Tom?

FRANK: Who cares?

HELEN: (*To* ANNA) He's being transferred, isn't he?

FRANK: Yes, he's being transferred.

BEN: Wonderful.

FRANK: Where would you like him to be transferred to?

HELEN: Where? Where?

FRANK: Guess.

HELEN: Ah, Father—

FRANK: Take your choice.

HELEN: Tell us! Athlone?

FRANK: Anywhere you like.

HELEN: Ben, where? (*To* FRANK) I know! Cork!

FRANK: Cork's for talkers.

BEN: You're going to Galway.

FRANK: Galway's for ageing men.

HELEN: Limerick!

FRANK: Good God! Never Limerick!

HELEN: Where else?—where else?—it's not! It couldn't be!

FRANK: Couldn't be what?

HELEN: Dublin?

FRANK: Dublin it is.

HELEN: Oh, Father!
(*She kisses him.*)

FRANK: (*To* ANNA) And tell them the rest.

ANNA: Better look out for Father Tom.
(*She goes out to the garden.*)

FRANK: You are in the presence of Lieutenant-Colonel Frank Butler—

HELEN: Lieutenant—?

FRANK: Administrative Officer, GHQ, Parkgate Street, Dublin City.

HELEN: You're taking a hand at us, Father!

FRANK: Nothing's official yet. But when the Chief tells the
Taoiseach in your presence how highly he considers you
and then in the next breath talks about certain vacancies,
you know it's in the bag.

HELEN: I'm going to waken Tina – phone Miriam –

FRANK: Later – later – later. Let's savour it ourselves first.

BEN: (*Looking around*) So you'll be leaving here.

FRANK: At last, at long last, and without one regret. To Dublin.

HELEN: To the Hero and to Anna.

BEN: To you, Father.

FRANK: Hold on – where's Anna?

HELEN: In the garden.

(*He goes to the door and looks out to the garden.* ANNA *is
crouched beside* TOM, *trying to waken him.*)

FRANK: Let him sit there for God's sake. Come inside and
celebrate with the family.

TOM: (*Suddenly awake, sings*) We're here because we're here
because we're here because we're here –

HELEN: So that's the condition.

ANNA: (*To* TOM) Come inside and lie down for a while.

FRANK: You're a bloody useless slob, Tom. Pull yourself
together, man.

HELEN: How did Anna enjoy it?

(FRANK *turns back into the living-room.* ANNA *gets* TOM *to his
feet and they make their way slowly into the room,* TOM *singing
intermittently.*)

FRANK: Anna? Anna was – what's the word? – the cynosure of all
eyes. Radiant, that's what Anna was, sitting there beside
me, basking in the glory. And the compliments – my God!
The Taoiseach called her – incidentally that was by far the
best speech of the night. And astonishingly well
informed – named every one of the soldiers I had saved and
a few personal comments about several of them. And when
he was talking about me – well, he was so effusive and so
generous that I was almost embarrassed. Talked about
'quiet heroes from quiet places' and 'men whose full
development blossomed only in full manhood'. Really
eulogistic stuff. Very satisfying.

233

HELEN: And Anna?

BEN: Sit over here, Father.

FRANK: That's the state he was in after the first course.

HELEN: What did he say about Anna?

FRANK: Oh, Anna? What's this he called you? – a real tongue-twister – 'the Commandant's comely, composed and curvaceous consort' – at which the men just *howled*. Didn't they?

ANNA: Yes.

FRANK: Would you like to try that one, Ben?

BEN: (*Quickly*) You're okay, Father. You're fine. That's it.

ANNA: (*To* BEN) Could I get him something?

FRANK: Let him sleep it off. He's beyond sobering.

TOM: (*Suddenly awake*) Where's Helen? Want to 'pologize to Helen –

HELEN: Hello, Father.

TOM: (*Rising*) – 'pologize to Helen – privately – in here, Helen, in here. (*Staggers into the kitchen.*)

FRANK: Ignore him.

HELEN: Poor old Tom.

FRANK: But the highlight of the evening, Helen – I was presented with an illuminated address by the people of Ballybeg!

TOM: (*Off*) Helen!

FRANK: The people of Ballybeg – my God! A parchment this length, all the colours of the rainbow, and a photo of me stuck crookedly on the top; and read out before everybody by that pompous T. D. – McLaughlin, McLucas, what's his name.

HELEN: That was nice of them.

FRANK: D'you think so? Yes, I suppose the intention was good. But being publicly addressed by the people of Ballybeg – 'you are our most illustrious citizen' sort of stuff – my God they don't know me and we don't know them! But you'll enjoy this – you really will. Must have left it out in the car. Hold on a second.

TOM: (*Off*) Helen!

FRANK: I know him in this mood. Ignore him.

234

(FRANK *leaves*.)

HELEN: Have you ever seen him so elated! I'm delighted for him. (*She kisses* ANNA.) For both of you. Was it exhausting? Are you falling apart?

TOM: (*Off*) Helen!

HELEN: O my God. (*Calls*) Coming! Coming!
(*She goes into the kitchen. Pause.*)

ANNA: I can take no more of it.

BEN: If you just –

ANNA: I'm going to clear out in the morning.

BEN: Leave him?

ANNA: Didn't you hear him? 'I – I – I – I – I.' And how they howled – oh, how they howled – after sniggering behind their hands all night.

BEN: At him?

ANNA: Him – me – what matter? I can stand no more. I've got to go.

BEN: Just walk out?

ANNA: I've got to.

BEN: Oh, Anna, you can't do that –

ANNA: Why not?

BEN: That – that would kill him – he'd never understand.

ANNA: All right – I'll make him understand. You want him to understand?

BEN: What I'm saying is that you just can't walk out without –

ANNA: Fine. I'll tell him about us first.

BEN: Anna –

ANNA: You want him to understand?

BEN: Will you please –

ANNA: Do you think for one second he's not going to hear?

BEN: For Christ's sake –

ANNA: That the good people of Ballybeg or his own staff aren't going to let him know somehow?

BEN: You won't!

ANNA: Make up your mind! Is he not going to understand because he's not told? Or is he going to understand because he'll be told by them or by me – or by you, Ben?

BEN: Nobody need say anything. I'll clear out in –

235

ANNA: Yes, you'll clear out – typical Ben! What about me?

BEN: I'm warning you, Anna.

ANNA: Don't wag your finger at me!

BEN: If you tell him –

ANNA: Tell him – don't tell him – either way I'm leaving.

BEN: I'm saying n-n-n-nothing. I promise you that. Nothing. Nothing. Nothing.

ANNA: In that case I'll tell him. He deserves that much from me.

BEN: You're a heartless bitch!

(*Enter* HELEN *and* TOM, *arm in arm.*)

HELEN: Poor Father Tom. D'you know what that was all about? He officiated at all the Butler weddings and all the Butler baptisms but he didn't officiate at Helen's wedding, even though Helen asked him, because Louise disapproved and he hadn't the courage to stand up to Louise and it has been on his conscience ever since and that's why he's drunk tonight – otherwise he'd be cold sober. So.

TOM: Am I forgiven, Helen?

HELEN: Nothing to forgive, Father.

TOM: You know something, Helen?

HELEN: What's that, Father?

TOM: I'm no damn good, Helen. No damn good at all. I'm – I'm a washout, Helen.

HELEN: Indeed you're not.

TOM: You can't fool me, Helen, I know. I *know*.

HELEN: You're fine, Father.

TOM: And I'm forgiven?

HELEN: Completely.

(*He slumps into a seat.*)

TOM: Thanks be to God.

(*Almost immediately he is asleep.*)

HELEN: There you are – instant absolution!

(FRANK *enters reading in mock heroic style from the parchment. He begins at the front door.*)

FRANK: 'We, the people of Ballybeg, learn with great pride and great delight of the heroic deeds of Commandant Frank Butler' – Lieutenant-Colonel Butler, if you don't mind,

236

Ballybeg – 'who is an honoured and distinguished member of our parish and whose family the people of Ballybeg have always held in the highest esteem.'

HELEN: Read it properly, Father. Don't make a mock of it.

FRANK: 'We have always known the Hero of Hari' – Who's that? I beg your pardon – 'to have been an officer of exemplary habit and behaviour, a citizen of outstanding probity – '

ANNA: Frank.

FRANK: ' – and a father and a family man' – I like this – 'of noblest Christian integrity and rectitude.'

ANNA: Frank.

FRANK: Get down on your knees. 'We are confirmed in our estimate, therefore, when the fame of his heroic actions spread out across the face of – '

ANNA: I've something to say to you, Frank.

(*He stops and looks at her.* TINA *comes sleepily downstairs in her dressing-gown and is about to enter when she hears* ANNA's *voice. She stands outside the living-room door.*)

I am not going to Dublin with you.

FRANK: Nobody's going anywhere, my darling, until official confirmation comes.

ANNA: Then – any time – I'm not going to Dublin – I'm not going anywhere with you.

(*Pause.*)

FRANK: What is the matter, my love?

ANNA: Are you deaf? Are you stupid? Don't you understand simple words?

(*As he puts out his hand to her.*) Don't – don't – don't touch me! I'm leaving you, Frank – can't you understand that? Leaving you – leaving you – is that simple enough?

(*Very long pause during which* FRANK, *puzzled, studies her face for clues.*)

HELEN: I think she's –

FRANK: What is wrong, Anna?

HELEN: (*To* ANNA) You've had a very tiring –

FRANK: (*Firmly*) Please, Helen. (*Quietly to* ANNA.) Why are you leaving me, Anna? Is it something that I have said?

(ANNA *turns away from him because she is crying. She shakes her head.*)

FRANK: Is it something that I have done?

(ANNA *shakes her head.*)

HELEN: Anna –

FRANK: (*Very sharply*) Helen, please. (*Again quietly to* ANNA) Is it something that I have not done?

(ANNA *shakes her head.*)

Then why are you leaving me, Anna?

ANNA: You were so long away –

FRANK: Five months.

ANNA: And we'd been together such a short time –

FRANK: Ten days.

ANNA: (*Quickly*) And I tried to keep you, to maintain you in my mind – I tried, Frank, I tried. But you kept slipping away from me. I searched Tina for you, and Miriam, but you weren't in them. And then I could remember nothing – only your uniform, the colour of your hair, your footstep in the hall – that's all I could remember – a handsome, courteous, considerate man who had once been kind to me and who wrote me all those simple, passionate letters – too simple, too passionate. And then Ben came. And I found you in him, Frank.

FRANK: Found me?

ANNA: I was lost.

(FRANK *looks at her, then at* BEN, *then back to her.*)

FRANK: Are you telling me that you and he – ?

ANNA: We had an affair! We were lovers, Ben and I! And everybody in the camp knows! Everybody in Ballybeg knows! Everybody except the Butlers! That's what I'm telling you! We had an affair!

(TINA *gives a short cry – unheard in the living-room – and rushes upstairs.*)

HELEN: O Ben! – you? – O God!

(*She turns away from him.* FRANK *goes to* TOM *and puts his hand on the Chaplain's shoulder.*)

FRANK: (*Softly*) Chaplain – Chaplain.

TOM: Mmmm?

238

FRANK: Help, Chaplain.

TOM: (*Wakening*) Wha' – wha' – what's that?

FRANK: Advice, counsel, help, Chaplain.

TOM: What's the trouble, Frank?

FRANK: I need help, Tom.

TOM: Terrific, Frank – just terrific – terrific.

FRANK: What does a man do, Tom?

TOM: Yes, sir – yes, sir – just terrific.

FRANK: What should a man do?

(TOM *is asleep again.* FRANK *looks at him. Then very slowly he walks around the room as if he were trying to remember something.*) (*Finally, conversationally*) You know, when I think about it – my God, how she must have suffered. Not that I was insensitive to it – far from it; I used to try to imagine what it was like. I would close my eyes and attempt to invest my body with pain, willing it into my joints, deliberately desiring the experience. But it's not the same thing – not the same thing at all – how could it be? Because it cannot be assumed like that – it has got to be organic, generated from within. And the statistics are fascinating too – well, no, not fascinating – how could they be fascinating; but interesting, interesting. It starts around forty; it's estimated that five to six per cent of the population is affected; and women are three times more susceptible than men. But there you are – she was outside the general pattern. What age was she? Helen was what? – three? – four? – so she can't have been more than twenty-eight or twenty-nine. And she had a very brief introductory period, as they call it. Within six months the hands and feet were swollen and within twelve months the spine was affected. So that within no time at all the fibrous tissues had replaced the normal tissues and when that happens you have at least a partial disorganization of the joints and sometimes complete ankylosis – yes, you'd think I was an authority –

HELEN: Father –

FRANK: – and of course we attempted everything that was available – physiotherapy, teeth, tonsils, surgery, gold injections, aspirin courses, codeine courses. We even went

to a quack in Kerry who promised us that before we'd be
halfway home every swelling would have disappeared. And
the cortisone era—my God, the miracle era—the cure for
everything. And she responded so wonderfully to it at
first—absolutely no pain. She was even able to throw away
the stick for a couple of weeks. But it was an illusion—an
illusion. Back came the pain, worse than ever. Much, much
worse. My God, how she suffered. My God, how she
suffered. (*He stops and looks at each person in the room. Then
he looks out at* SIR, *whom he now addresses loudly, very
deliberately, and with conscious formality. He is very calm and
very controlled.*) Sir.
(SIR *speaks quietly and does not raise his eyes from the ledger.*)
SIR: Frank.
FRANK: I wish to protest, Sir. I wish to lodge a formal protest.
SIR: Yes, Frank.
FRANK: I am quite calm. And I am not bleating. I am not
snivelling.
SIR: No, Frank.
FRANK: But there are certain things that as a soldier—as a
man—I wish to state.
SIR: Yes, Frank.
FRANK: Yes, you did say we could speak our thoughts. That
was established at the outset, wasn't it? Well, I wish to
protest against my treatment. I wish to say that I consider I
have been treated unfairly.
SIR: (*Looking up*) Frank, I—
FRANK: No, I'm not addressing you, Sir; I'm not addressing
them; I suppose I'm not addressing anybody. And I am
fully aware that protesting at this stage is pointless—
pointless.
SIR: You can—
FRANK: No, no, no, of course it is. Absolutely pointless. The
ledger's the ledger, isn't it? Nothing can be changed now—
not a thing. But an injustice *has* been done to me, Sir, and
a protest must be made. I don't claim that I have been
blameless. Maybe my faults have been greater than most.
But it does seem—well, spiteful that when a point is reached

240

in my life, and late in my life, when certain modest ambitions are about to be realized, when certain happinesses that I never experienced are suddenly about to be attainable, it does seem spiteful that these fulfilments should be snatched away from me – and in a particularly wounding manner. Yes, I think that is unfair. Yes, that is unjust. And that is why I make this formal protest, Sir. Against an injustice done to me. Because I have been treated unfairly, Sir – that is all. (*He stops and looks around at the others – all isolated, all cocooned in their private thoughts. He opens his mouth as if he is about to address them, but they are so remote from him that he decides against it. He turns slowly and begins to walk up stage.*)

SIR: Frank!

(FRANK *ignores the call and goes through the door right off the fireplace, closing it behind him – this is the only time this door is used. Pause. Suddenly* TOM, *now sober, jumps to his feet. He is very agitated, and when he looks at the others, so contained, so remote, his panic increases. He goes to* BEN.)

TOM: You're not going to let him go, are you? You're going to stop him, aren't you? For God's sake, Ben, you've got to stop him! (BEN *remains encased and intact in his privacy.* TOM *looks to* HELEN *and goes to her.*)

You know what's going to happen! You know what he's going to do! Stop him. Helen! Stop him! Stop him! (*She looks at him as if he were a stranger.*)

Don't you hear what I'm saying – he has got to be stopped! (HELEN *looks away from him.* TOM *now addresses them all.*) How can you all sit there! You know what he's going to do! (*No one responds.* TOM *now looks to* SIR – *and rushes to him. He is about to cry with panic and despair.*)

You're going to stop him, aren't you, Sir? Yes, you're the one who can save him. You're not going to let him do that to himself – no, no, you're not.

SIR: The ledger can't be –

TOM: What can the ledger not be? – to hell with the ledger – that's what I say – to hell with that corrupt ledger.

SIR: Tom, sit down –

TOM: Great – great – 'Tom, sit down' – you know what Frank's

241

going to do and all you can say is 'Tom, sit down'.

SIR: Sit down and keep quiet.

TOM: I will not sit down and I will not keep quiet! My friend, Frank, has gone into that back room and not one of you is going to –

SIR: Shut up! Now!

TOM: I will –

SIR: You had your opportunities and you squandered them.

TOM: I never had –

SIR: Many opportunities, many times. You should have spoken then. We'll have none of your spurious concern now that it's all over. So sit down and shut up!

TOM: (*Suddenly deflated*) If I had – sometimes, I – I always tried to – Oh, my Jesus –
(*For a few seconds his mouth keeps opening and shutting, but no words come. He looks at the others. Pause. Then he shuffles over to* ANNA, *sits beside her, put his arm round her, and rests his face on her shoulders. His body shakes as he cries quietly. Pause. Then suddenly* TINA *comes stumbling down the stairs in a panic and rushes into the living-room. She is in a frenzy and looks around wildly. Then:*)

TINA: (*Shouts*) Daddy-Daddy-Daddy-Daddy!
(SIR *leaps to his feet.*)

SIR: (*Tense whisper*) Not yet! Tina! Not yet!
(*She freezes. Pause. Then a single revolver shot off.* TINA's *hands go up to her face. She screams. Silence. Pause.* SIR *sits again. Then very slowly, the others relax and emerge from their cocoons. Cigarettes are lit. A sense of relief. Serenity. The remaining sequence must not be played in a sad, nostalgic mood.* MIRIAM *enters in coat and headscarf.* TOM, *now fully sober, sits with his arms around* ANNA. *From his stool* SIR *watches this slow awakening. Then he rises, stretching his arms, smiling.*)

SIR: Well – well – well – well – well – well – well. (*He goes into the living-room.*) That wasn't too bad, was it?
(*No one answers – they are still not quite out of their reveries. He goes to* TINA, *catches her chin and wags it.*)
And how are you? All right?

(*She smiles and nods.*)

(*To all*) That wasn't too bad after all now, was it? No, of course it wasn't. (*To* HELEN) And you with your worries that things were being 'distorted' – (*To* ANNA) – and you afraid that you'd 'messed it all up' – (*To both*) I told you, didn't I? Incidentally, Anna, we made a mistake, you and I – well me, really.

ANNA: What was that?

SIR: I never introduced you! You're the only person who wasn't introduced. (*Opening ledger.*) So let's rectify that – right?   *Why?*

ANNA: No, please, Sir –

SIR: But I *want* to –

ANNA: Please. It doesn't matter now, not in the least. It's of no importance now.

SIR: I'm sorry. My mistake.

ANNA: It doesn't matter.

SIR: As you wish. (*He leafs through the ledger.*) I'm sure you're all tired, so what I think we'll do is go straight to the postscript and wind it up with that. 'Not yet, Tina! Not yet! – Single revolver shot – etc., etc. – ' We've been through all that –

TOM: There was never any doubt in my mind that it was an unfortunate accident. Never. And I said that at the inquest. I mean we were such terrific friends all our lives – no one was going to tell me that Frank Butler took – that it wasn't an accident. And I saw to it that my friend was buried with the full rites of the Church. I saw to that. It was the least I could do for my friend, Frank Butler – my terrific friend, Frank.

(SIR *has been waiting patiently for this to end.*)

SIR: Yes. A brief enough postscript as it happens. 'Funeral on Friday afternoon. The following morning Charlie Donnelly arrived with a van and removed all the furnishings – ' By the way, where is Charlie? Charlie!

(*He goes off left to look for him.*)

MIRIAM: I was worried about the children – you know – what I'd tell them.

TOM: Naturally. And how are the kids?

MIRIAM: I'd given them corn flakes and a fry for their
breakfast–they're a great crowd for fries–and they were
sitting round the table eating like nobody's business and I
said quietly, 'Your Granda's dead,' I said. 'Your Granda's
gone to Heaven to join your Grandma,' I said. And when
they began to cry I said, 'Don't cry for your Granda,' I
said. 'Your Granda was a good man and a brave man. Ask
anybody,' I said, 'and they'll tell you how good and brave
your Granda was.' Wasn't I right, Father?

TOM: God have mercy on his good soul.

MIRIAM: And they listened to me. You should have seen them.
They did–they listened–and they stopped crying. But he
was a good man, you know–a good man and a brave man.
No–a great man and a brave man.
(*She moves slowly off right.*)

SIR: (*Off left*) Charlie! Charlie!

TOM: You're going back to London, aren't you?

HELEN: Tomorrow afternoon.

TOM: Tina's going with you?

HELEN: Yes.

TOM: You'll look after her well, Helen, won't you? It's a big city
and she's never been away from home and–

TINA: Don't worry about me. I'll be all right. I can look after
myself.

TOM: You'll be in digs with Helen–that's good. And she'll get
you fixed up in a job.

TINA: I'm not a child, Father. I'm almost nineteen.

TOM: All the same, my love–

TINA: (*Bitterly*) Why the sudden concern about me? Why all the
platitudes? You're the one in trouble, Father–not me.
(*She goes off quickly.*)

HELEN: She didn't mean that, Father. She's upset. Tina!
(*She follows* TINA *off.* SIR *enters.*)

BEN: (*Urgently*) Remember just before that last sequence?

SIR: (*Consulting ledger*) Mm?

BEN: I was going to say something to him and you interrupted.

SIR: (*Not listening*) Yes–yes–
(TOM *looks around, then drifts aimlessly off.*)

BEN: Maybe I had some intimation of a moment being missed for ever – because there was the sudden necessity to blurt out, to plunge some oversimplification into him before it was too late. And what I was going to say to him was that ever since I was a child I always loved him and always hated her – he was always my hero. And even though it wouldn't have been the truth, it wouldn't have been a lie either: no, no; no lie.

SIR: I see.

BEN: But I suppose it was just as well it wasn't said like that because he could never receive that kind of directness, and I suppose I could never have said it. But I just hope – I just hope he was able to sense an expression of some k-k-k-k- – of some kind of love for him – even if it was only in my perfidy –

(*He goes off slowly.*)

SIR: Yes. (*Back to ledger.*) '– removed all the furnishings.' Yes. 'That afternoon Helen and Tina flew to London, where they now live in different flats and seldom meet. Tina works as a waitress in an all-night café and Helen has had to give up her office job because of an acute nervous breakdown. Ben went to Scotland. He came back after seven months. He has been jailed twice for drunk and disorderly behaviour. Father Tom has retired and is living in a nursing-home in County Wicklow. He has difficulty walking and spends most of his time in bed.'

(CHARLIE'*s brisk entrance interrupts the reading.*)

CHARLIE: Sorry – sorry – sorry – you were looking for me?

SIR: It doesn't matter, Charlie. We're just finishing up.

CHARLIE: If I'm here, I'm not wanted. (*Pause.*) I mean to say – if I'm wanted I'm not here. (*Laughs in surprise.*) Dammit, they're both right! First time that ever happened! Isn't that a good one! Where's the missus?

SIR: She left a few minutes ago.

CHARLIE: Oh-ho! Better catch up with her or there'll be hair flying. See you. Good luck – good luck. (*Pauses at exit.*) When do I clear out this stuff?

SIR: Saturday.

245

CHARLIE: Morning or afternoon?

SIR: Morning.

CHARLIE: Bang goes the sleep-in. Oh, well, good to get it all out of the road. Luck.

(*He leaves.*)

SIR: Goodbye, Charlie. Now – ' – spends most of his time in bed. Mrs Butler, Anna, emigrated to America. She lived with an aunt in New Jersey for six months and then went to Los Angeles, where she works in the office of a large insurance company – '

(*He breaks off because he is aware that the place is not empty. Then he sees ANNA.*)

Oh, you're still here. Heavens, I thought I was alone for a minute. Just the two of us. Not much point in continuing, is there?

ANNA: Yes – go on. Please go on.

SIR: With this?

ANNA: Please.

SIR: There's only – what? – two or three lines left.

ANNA: Even so.

SIR: 'She shares an apartment with an English girl and they go on holidays together. She owns a car and is thinking of buying an apartment of her own. She has never returned to Ireland.' And that's it.

ANNA: That's all?

SIR: That's all I've got here.

ANNA: Are you sure?

SIR: Blank pages.

ANNA: I see.

(*She gets up and begins to move off.*)

SIR: Did you expect there'd be something more?

ANNA: I just wondered – that's all.

SIR: Is there something missing?

ANNA: No. Not a thing. Not a single thing.

SIR: Ah. Good. Good. All right, Anna?

(*But she has gone. He shrugs his shoulders and closes the book. He takes a last look round the set and begins to leave. As he leaves, bring down the lights.*)

246

▲▲▲▲▲▲▲▲▲▲▲▲▲▲▲▲▲▲▲▲▲▲▲▲▲▲▲▲▲▲▲▲▲▲▲▲▲▲▲

ARISTOCRATS

▲▲▲▲▲▲▲▲▲▲▲▲▲▲▲▲▲▲▲▲▲▲▲▲▲▲▲▲▲▲▲▲▲▲▲▲▲▲▲

for **K.H.H.**
with affection and gratitude

CHARACTERS

WILLIE DIVER
TOM HOFFNUNG
UNCLE GEORGE
CASIMIR
ALICE
EAMON
CLAIRE
JUDITH
FATHER
(ANNA'S VOICE)

Aristocrats was first performed in the Abbey Theatre, Dublin, on Thursday, 8 March 1979. The cast was as follows:

WILLIE DIVER	Niall O'Brien
TOM HOFFNUNG	Kevin McHugh
UNCLE GEORGE	Bill Foley
CASIMIR	John Kavanagh
ALICE	Dearbhla Molloy
EAMON	Stephen Rea
CLAIRE	Ingrid Craigie
JUDITH	Kate Flynn
FATHER	Geoff Golden
ANNA'S VOICE	Kathleen Barrington

Direction	Joe Dowling
Setting and costumes	Wendy Shea
Lighting	Leslie Scott

The text was first published by the Gallery Press, Dublin, in 1980.

Set

Most of the action takes place outside the south side of the house. Most recently it was a lawn that has not been cared for in years. Before that it was a grass tennis court and before that a croquet lawn – but no trace of these activities remains.

The lawn stretches right across the full front of stage and upstage left (left and right from point of view of audience) where it halts at a tall grey gable with uncurtained windows.

Upstage left is a gazebo with a pagoda roof and badly weather-beaten. A rusty iron seat inside. The gazebo is made of wood and is about to collapse.

A small room – the study – occupies upstage right. One step up
into it from the lawn. And it is separated from the lawn by two
invisible walls. On the third wall, parallel to the front of stage, is
an early Victorian writing desk. The fourth wall, at right angles
to front of stage, has a huge marble fireplace. In front of the
fireplace is a *chaise-longue*. In the centre of this study a small
table, etc., etc., sufficient furnishings to indicate when the Hall
flourished and to suggest its present decline.

Downstage right is a broken sundial mounted on a stone
plinth. *~ The time is out of joint .*

Time and place: summer, mid-1970s. Ballybeg Hall, the home
of District Justice O'Donnell, a large and decaying house
overlooking the village of Ballybeg, County Donegal, Ireland. *Ballybeg Hall !*

Music (all works by Chopin, written for piano)

Act One
Scherzo No. 2 in B flat minor, Op. 31
Ballade in G minor, Op. 23
Waltz in G flat major. Op. 70, No. 1
Sonata no. 3 in B minor, Op. 58 (Third Movement only: Largo)
Waltz in A flat major (Posth.)
Waltz in E flat major (Posth.)

Act Two
Étude in E major, Op. 10, No. 3
Nocturne in F sharp major, Op. 15, No. 2

Act Three
Sonata No. 2 in B flat minor, Op. 35 (Third Movement: middle
section only)
Ballade in A flat major, Op. 47

ACT ONE

Early afternoon on a very warm summer day.

*The opening bars of Scherzo No. 2 in B flat minor fill the study
and the lawn, then fade to background.*

TOM HOFFNUNG *is seated at the table in the study, copying the
titles of books into his notebook. He is a quiet, calm, measured
American academic in his mid-fifties.*

Inside the door leading out to the hall is WILLIE DIVER. *He is in
his mid-thirties and is from the village. He is standing on a chair and
attaching a small speaker to the door frame (he is standing on his
jacket to protect the seat of the chair).*

Both men work for a few seconds in silence.

Now UNCLE GEORGE *enters from the hall. He is in his late
seventies, a brother of Father's. Panama hat, walking stick, very old
and creased off-white linen suit with an enormous red silk
handkerchief spilling out of the breast pocket, trousers stopping well
above his ankles. His mouth never stops working, vigorously
masticating imaginary food. All his gestures are informed with great
energy, as if he were involved in some urgent business.*

*He is half-way across the study before he realizes that there are
other people in the room. Then he stops, stands still, stares at them.*

TOM: Hi!

    (Pause.)

WILLIE: Hello, Mister George.

TOM: Come right through. I'm almost finished here.

    (GEORGE *hesitates—then turns and exits through the door.*)

TOM: That's the third time he's attempted to come in here.

    Maybe I should go somewhere else.

WILLIE: Not at all. He dodges about like that all the time.

TOM: Does he never speak?

WILLIE: They say he does. I never heard him.

TOM: And he's a brother of the District Justice—is that correct?

WILLIE: That's it. Fierce man for the booze when he was only a
young fella – drunk himself half-crazy. Then all of a sudden
packed it in. And stopped speaking.

TOM: I wonder why.

WILLIE: They say about here that when he wasn't going to be
asking for drink, he thought it wasn't worth saying
anything. But brains – d'you see Mister George? – the
smartest of the whole connection, they say.
(*He gets down from the chair, removes his jacket, carefully rubs
the seat with his sleeve.*)

WILLIE: Could you give us a second, Tom?

TOM: How's it going?

WILLIE: Nearly finished now.
(TOM *joins him at the door.*)

TOM: Judith's really going to be pleased with this.

WILLIE: Do you think so?

TOM: Sure she will. What can I do?

WILLIE: Show her this when she comes down, will you? There's
a volume control at the side here – loud or soft, whatever
way she wants it.

TOM: Right.

WILLIE: And if she wants to turn it off altogether, there's a
switch at the bottom here – d'you see?

TOM: Got it.

WILLIE: I haven't put it up too high for her, have I? What
d'you think?

TOM: Looks about right to me.

WILLIE: An ugly-looking aul' yoke in a room like this, isn't it?

TOM: You wouldn't notice it. It's a good job, Willie.

WILLIE: Indeed and it's rough enough. But it'll save her
running up and down them stairs every turnabout.

TOM: Is it on now?

WILLIE: I've still to connect it to the lead from the bedroom.
Hold on a minute.
(WILLIE *goes out to the hall.* TOM *returns to the table. Just
before he sits down,* CASIMIR *enters left, carrying deck-chairs.*
CASIMIR *is the only son of the house; in his thirties. Despite the
heat he is wearing a knitted V-neck pullover under his sports*

254

jacket. One immediately gets a sense that there is something different about him – as he says himself, 'peculiar'. But what it is, is elusive: partly his shyness, partly his physical movements, particularly the way he walks – rapid, jerky, without ease or grace – partly his erratic enthusiasm, partly his habit of suddenly grinning and giving a mirthless 'ha-ha' at unlikely times, usually when he is distressed. But he is not a buffoon nor is he 'disturbed'. He is a perfectly normal man with distinctive and perhaps slightly exaggerated mannerisms. He now stands at the step just outside the study and talks to TOM.)

CASIMIR: Claire.

TOM: Yeah.

CASIMIR: Playing the piano.

TOM: Sure.

CASIMIR: My sister Claire.

TOM: I know.

CASIMIR: Welcome home recital for me.

TOM: Some welcome.

CASIMIR: Dexterity – simplicity – passion – Claire has everything.

TOM: She certainly –

(*But* CASIMIR *has gone and now stands in the middle of the lawn.*)

CASIMIR: Claire!

CLAIRE: Yes?

CASIMIR: Play the G minor Ballade.

(*The music stops.*)

CLAIRE: Which?

CASIMIR: The G minor.

CLAIRE: I'm not in the mood for that, Casimir.

CASIMIR: Special request. Please.

CLAIRE: Just a bit of it, then.

(*He stands listening. She begins in the middle of the Ballade in G minor, Op. 23 just immediately before the molto crescendo, after three fz bars.*)

CASIMIR: Yes-yes-yes-yes-yes!

(*He sings a few bars with the piano, conducting at the same time – he is radiant with delight. Then he returns to the step.*)

255

CASIMIR: The G minor. Wonderful, isn't it?

TOM: Yeah.

> (CASIMIR *sings a few more bars.*)

CASIMIR: When I think of Ballybeg Hall it's always like this: the sun shining; the doors and windows all open; the place filled with music.

> (*He is suddenly off again – left – for more deck-chairs. The sound of static from the speaker. Then* FATHER's *laboured breathing.* TOM *listens.*) [Static | Father's breathing]

JUDITH: That's the best lunch you've had in days. Let me wipe your chin.

> (FATHER's *incoherent mumbling.*)

near the? speaker

JUDITH: It's very warm. I don't think you need this quilt, do you?

> (*Incoherent mumbling.* TOM *goes to the speaker. He stands listening.*)

JUDITH: Oh, Father, you've soiled your pyjamas again! Why didn't you tell me?

FATHER: Judith?

JUDITH: Come on. Let's get them changed.

FATHER: Where's Judith?

JUDITH: I'm Judith.

FATHER: Where's Judith?

JUDITH: I'm here beside you, Father.

FATHER: Where's Claire?

JUDITH: In the drawing-room.

FATHER: Where's Claire?

JUDITH: Can't you hear her? She's playing the piano for you. Lift your leg, Father.

FATHER: Where's Alice?

JUDITH: Everybody's here.

FATHER: Where's Casimir?

JUDITH: Everybody's at home. They're all downstairs.

FATHER: Where's Anna?

JUDITH: Anna's in Africa – you know that. Now – the other leg. Father please, I can't get them off unless you help me.

FATHER: Where's Judith? Where's Claire? Where's Casimir? Where's Alice? Where's –

JUDITH: They're all here. They're all downstairs.

FATHER: Let me tell you something in confidence: Judith betrayed the family.

JUDITH: Did she?

FATHER: I don't wish to make an issue of it. But I can tell you confidentially – Judith betrayed us.

JUDITH: That's better. Now you're more comfortable.

FATHER: Great betrayal; enormous betrayal.

JUDITH: Let me feel those tops. Are they wet, too?

FATHER: But Anna's praying for her. Did you know that?

JUDITH: Yes, I know, Father.

FATHER: Anna has the whole convent praying for her.

JUDITH: Now let's get these clean ones on. Lift this leg again.

FATHER: Where's Judith? Where's Alice? Where's Casimir? Where's Claire?

(WILLIE *returns, carrying a parcel of two bottles of whiskey.* TOM *pretends to consult his notebook.*)

WILLIE: That's her hooked up. Any sound out of her?

TOM: Yeah; something was said a moment ago. Seems to be working fine.

(WILLIE *examines the speaker.*)

WILLIE: Aye, it should be. She'd need to have this whole house rewired – half of them fittings is dangerous.

TOM: Is she aware of that?

WILLIE: Sure it would cost her a fortune. Tell her I'll take a run in later and sink them bare wires. And I'll leave this (*parcel*) here for her. A drop of whiskey. I thought maybe, you know, with the family back home and all, she might be a bit short. They come last night, didn't they?

TOM: And a late night it was, too. This'll be very welcome. You'll be going to the wedding, won't you?

WILLIE: Me? Oh damn the fear.

TOM: Will you not?

WILLIE: Not at all; that'll be a family affair. What about yourself?

TOM: I leave tomorrow.

WILLIE: They'll manage without us, (*Leaving*) Well . . .

TOM: Okay, Willie. You'll be back later?

257

WILLIE: Aye, sometime. And tell her, too – them groceries she wanted – I left them in the pantry.

TOM: I'll tell her.

(*Father's voice suddenly very loud and very authoritative.*)

FATHER: Are you proposing that my time and the time of this court be squandered while the accused goes home and searches for this title which he claims he has in a tin-box somewhere?

(WILLIE *is startled and delighted.*)

WILLIE: Himself by Jaysus!

JUDITH: Now this leg – that's it – that's great.

FATHER: And that we sit in this freezing court until he comes back? Is that what you propose, Sergeant?

JUDITH: Raise your body just a little.

FATHER: Because I can tell you I won't have it – I will not have it!

WILLIE: Himself by Jaysus, guldering away!

JUDITH: That's more comfortable.

FATHER: We're all petrified in this place as it is – really petrified. And I will not endure it a second longer. Case dismissed. Court adjourned.

JUDITH: Now over on your side and I'll tuck you in and you'll sleep for a while.

(*A few short mumbling sounds from* FATHER; *then silence.*)

WILLIE: D'you hear that for a voice, eh? By Jaysus, isn't he a powerful fighting aul' man all the time, eh?

TOM: Would you believe it! I've been here four days and I've never seen him yet.

WILLIE: Sure he hasn't been down the stairs since the stroke felled him. But before that – haul' your tongue, man – oh be Jaysus he was a sight to behold – oh be Jaysus!

(CASIMIR *has entered left with more deck-chairs which he sets up on the lawn. He now enters the study.*)

CASIMIR: Always Chopin – the great love of her life. She could play all the nocturnes and all the waltzes before she was ten. We thought we had a little Mozart on our hands. And on her sixteenth birthday she got a scholarship to go to Paris. But Father – you've met Father?

258

TOM: Actually I— *mimicking dad?*

CASIMIR: 'An itinerant musician? (*Wagging finger.*) Ho-ho-
ho-ho-ho.' Wasn't that naughty of him? (*Sees* WILLIE.) Ah!
(*There is a brief, awkward pause—*WILLIE *smiling, expecting
to be recognized,* CASIMIR *staring blankly.* WILLIE *finally
approaches gauchely.*)

WILLIE: How are you, Casimir?

CASIMIR: Yes? Yes? Who have we here?

WILLIE: No, you wouldn't remember me.

CASIMIR: Should I? Should I? Yes, of course I should.

WILLIE: It's—

CASIMIR: Don't—don't tell me—let me guess. I have it—it's
Deegan, the jarvey! Am I right?

WILLIE: Jackie Deegan.

CASIMIR: There you are!

WILLIE: Deegan, the car-man; that's right; he's dead; I'm
Diver.

CASIMIR: Diver?

WILLIE: From the back shore.

CASIMIR: Ah.

WILLIE: Willie Diver.

CASIMIR: Ah.

WILLIE: Tony Diver's son—the Slooghter Divers. I used to be
about the gate-lodge when my Uncle Johnny was in it.
(*Pause.*) Johnny MacLoone and my Auntie Sarah. (*Pause.*)
That's going back a fair few years now. My Uncle Johnny's
dead, too—Jaysus he must be dead thirty years now.
(*Pause.*) I seen you this morning from the upper hill—I've
the land all took from Judith.

TOM: And Willie's just rigged up this thing so that your father
can be heard down here now.

CASIMIR: What's that?

TOM: A baby-alarm. Won't that be a help?

CASIMIR: Ah yes; splendid, splendid.

TOM: Save Judith running up and down the stairs.

CASIMIR: Of course; indeed; wonderful; splendid; great idea.

WILLIE: I mind one day Casimir and me—we were only cubs
this size at the time—the pair of us got into a punt down at

259

the slip and cast off – d'you mind? – and be Jaysus didn't the tide carry us out.

CASIMIR: Good Lord! Were we drowned?

WILLIE: Damn the bit of us: the wind carried us back in again. Nobody knew a damn thing about us except ourselves.

CASIMIR: Well, wasn't that wonderful. Ha-ha. (*Suddenly shakes* WILLIE*'s hand.*) Marvellous to see you again. It's so good to be back again. Do you know how long it's been since I was home last? – eleven years. Now, if you'll pardon me – I'm the chef for today!

WILLIE: Surely to God, Casimir.

(CASIMIR *is off again – this time to the gazebo where he finds a few more faded seats which he carries out to the lawn.*)

WILLIE: Same aul' Casimir.

TOM: Is he?

WILLIE: When he'd come home on holidays from the boarding school, sometimes he'd walk down the village street, and we'd all walk in a line behind him, acting the maggot, you know, imitating him. And by Jaysus he never thought of looking round.

TOM: That expression – you've taken the land from Judith – what does it mean?

WILLIE: She has nobody to work it so she lets it out every year.

TOM: How many acres are there?

WILLIE: I could hardly tell you. It's all hill and bog.

TOM: So you lease it?

WILLIE: I sort of take it off her hands – you know.

TOM: And you till it?

WILLIE: I footer about. I'm no farmer.

TOM: But it's profitable land?

WILLIE: Profitable? (*Laughs.*) If you've a pair of wellingtons, we'll walk it some day.

(*He goes off towards the hall.* CASIMIR *is arranging the seats into a wide arc. The music suddenly stops.*)

CLAIRE: Casimir!

(CASIMIR *stops working.*)

CASIMIR: Hello-hello.

CLAIRE: Where are you?

CASIMIR: On the tennis-court – just beside the net.

CLAIRE: Can you hear me?

CASIMIR: Clearly.

CLAIRE: I've a test for you: what's the name of this?

(CASIMIR *is suddenly excited, suddenly delighted. He rushes to the step.*)

CASIMIR: A test! She's testing me! A game we played all the time when we were children!

CLAIRE: Casimir!

(*He runs back to the centre of the lawn.*)

CASIMIR: Go ahead! I'm ready! I'm waiting!

(*He stands poised, waiting. His eyes are shut tight. His fists clenched on his chest. To himself as he waits in suspense:*)

CASIMIR: Ha-ha. Good Lord – good Lord – good Lord – good Lord – good Lord –

(*The music begins: Waltz in G flat major, Op. 70, No. 1.*)

CASIMIR: Oh-oh-oh-it's-it's-it's – (*To himself*) – the McCormack Waltz! (*Clapping his hands in relief and delight and now shouting*) The McCormack Waltz! Right, Claire? Full marks? Amn't I right?

CLAIRE: Can't hear you.

CASIMIR: You can hear me very well. That's it. I know. I *know*.

(*He runs into the study.*)

CASIMIR: Got it! The McCormack Waltz! It's the G flat major actually but we call it the McCormack because one night John McCormack, Count John McCormack, you know who I'm talking about? – the tenor? – of course you do! – well, Father had something to do with McCormack getting the papal knighthood – some French cardinal Father knew in the Vatican – and because of that Father and McCormack became great friends.

(*TOM begins writing in his notebook.*)

TOM: Casimir, this is precisely the material I – may I jot down? –

(*But CASIMIR is now back at the door and clapping his hands.*)

CASIMIR: Bravo, Claire darling! Bravo, bravo, bravo!

(*Now he is back into the centre of the room again.*)

CASIMIR: Anyhow McCormack was staying here one night and

261

*

Mother was in one of her down periods and my goodness
when she was like that—oh, my goodness, poor Mother, for
weeks on end how unhappy she'd be.

TOM: She was forty-seven when she died?

CASIMIR: Forty-six.

TOM: Had she been ill for long? Was it sudden?

(*Pause.*) ×× *Distracts question*

CASIMIR: Anyhow, this night Claire played that waltz, the G
flat major, and McCormack asked Mother to dance and she
refused but he insisted, he insisted, and finally he got her to
the middle of the floor and he put his arm around her and
then she began to laugh and he danced her up and down the
hall and then in here and then out to the tennis-court and
you could hear their laughing over the whole house and
finally the pair of them collapsed in the gazebo out there.
Yes—marvellous! The McCormack Waltz!

TOM: Approximately what year was—

CASIMIR: A great big heavy man—oh, yes, I remember McCormack—I remember his enormous jowls trembling—but
Mother said he danced like Nijinsky. (*Suddenly aware.*) I'm
disturbing your studies, amn't I?

TOM: Actually you're—

CASIMIR: Of course I am. Give me five minutes to make a call
and then I'll leave you absolutely in peace.
(*As he goes to the phone—an old style phone, with a handle at
the side—below the fireplace, he picks up a cassette player from
the mantelpiece.*)

CASIMIR: Do you know what I did last night even before I
unpacked? I made two secret tapes of her to bring back to
Helga and the children, just to prove to them how splendid
a pianist she really is.

TOM: Have they never been to Ireland?

(*Momentary pause.*) × ×

CASIMIR: And I'm going to play them this afternoon while
we're having the picnic. And I've another little surprise up
my sleeve too; *after* we've eaten, I've got a tape that Anna
sent me last Christmas!

TOM: Very nice.

CASIMIR: A really tremendous person, Anna. Actually her name in religion is Sister John Henry and she chose that name because John Henry Newman – you know? – the cardinal? – Cardinal Newman? – of course you do – well, he married Grandfather and Grandmother O'Donnell – in this very room as a matter of fact – special dispensation from Rome. But of course we think of her as Anna. And the tape she sent me has a message for every member of the family. And it'll be so appropriate now that we're all gathered together again.

(*As he is saying the last few words he is also turning the handle on the phone.*)

FATHER: Don't touch that!

(CASIMIR *drops the phone in panic and terror.*)

CASIMIR: Christ! Ha-ha. O my God! That – that – that's –

TOM: It's only the baby-alarm.

CASIMIR: I thought for a moment Father was – was – was –

TOM: Maybe I should turn it down a bit.

CASIMIR: God, it's eerie – that's what it is – eerie – eerie –

(*The phone suddenly rings – and his panic is revived. He grabs it.*)

CASIMIR: Hello? Hello? Hello? Yes, I did ring, Mrs Moore. I'm sorry, I'm sorry, I'm very sorry. Could you try that call to Germany for me again? The number is Hamburg – Sorry, sorry, yes of course I gave it to you already; I am sorry – Yes, I'll hold on – (*To* TOM *who is watching him*) Helga, my wife – my wife Helga – to let her know I've arrived safely—she worries herself sick if I don't – (*Into phone*) Yes, just for the wedding on Thursday, to give Claire away, and then straight off again. Yes, indeed I'll tell her that, Mrs Moore. Thank you, thank you. (*To* TOM) Was always terrified of her, absolutely terrified; postmistress in Ballybeg ever since – Yes, yes, I'll hold on.

(TOM *fingers the limp servant's bell beside the fireplace.*)

TOM: When did they go out of action?

CASIMIR: What's that?

TOM: The bells.

CASIMIR: Oh I suppose when there was nobody to ring them.

263

Or nobody to obey them. She ought to be at home now.
(CLAIRE *begins playing another nocturne.* ALICE *enters. In her
mid-thirties. She is hungover after last night. As she enters she
touches her cheek which has a bruise mark on it.*)

ALICE: Morning, everybody.

TOM: It's afternoon, Alice.

ALICE: Is it?

(*She blows a kiss to* CASIMIR. *He blows one back.*)

ALICE: Am I the last down?

TOM: Just about. Is Eamon still asleep?

ALICE: He was up and about hours ago. He's gone down to the
village to visit his grandmother.

TOM: And how are you today?

ALICE: I misbehaved very badly last night, did I?

TOM: Not at all. You just sat there by yourself, singing nursery
rhymes.

ALICE: That's alright. Tom, isn't it?

TOM: Correct.

ALICE: Dr Thomas Hoffnung from Chicago.

TOM: You see – you were in great shape.

CASIMIR: Hoffnung's the German word for hope. So your
name's really Tom Hope. Terrific name, Alice, isn't it? –
Tom Hope! Calling Hamburg.

ALICE: What?

CASIMIR: Helga.

ALICE: Give her my love.

CASIMIR: She's in terrific form today.

ALICE: Is she?

CASIMIR: Claire.

ALICE: Oh – yes, yes. (*She shades her eyes with her hand and looks
outside.*) Is it cold?

TOM: No, it's a beautiful day.

(*She sits on top of the step and holds her head in her hands.*
TOM *moves back to* CASIMIR *who is anchored by the phone.*)

TOM: Perhaps you could confirm a few facts for me, Casimir.
This is where Gerard Manley Hopkins used to sit – is that
correct?

CASIMIR: Look at the arm-rest and you'll see a stain on it.

264

TOM: Where?

CASIMIR: The other arm – at the front.

TOM: Got it.

CASIMIR: He used to recite 'The Wreck of the *Deutschland*' to Grandmother O'Donnell and he always rested his teacup just there; and one afternoon he knocked it over and burned his right hand very severely.

(TOM *is writing all this information down.*)

TOM: That would have been about – ?

CASIMIR: Shhhh. Yes, Mrs Moore? Sorry, sorry? Yes-yes-yes – of course – thank you – thank you. (*He hangs up.*) Something wrong with the lines. Can't even get the Letterkenny exchange. Poor old Helga'll think I've deserted her. Tell me again, Tom – I'm ashamed to say I've forgotten – what's the title of your research?

TOM: I can hardly remember it myself.

CASIMIR: No, no, please, please.

TOM: 'Recurring cultural, political and social modes in the upper strata of Roman Catholic society in rural Ireland since the act of Catholic Emancipation.'

CASIMIR: Good heavens. Ha-ha.

TOM: I know. It's awful. I apologize.

CASIMIR: No, no, no, don't apologize. It sounds very – it sounds – Alice, isn't it very, very? – Right, let's be systematic. Judith has shown you the family records and the old estate papers, hasn't she?

TOM: Yeah.

CASIMIR: And you've seen all the old diaries in the library?

TOM: That's all covered.

CASIMIR: Splendid, splendid. So what you want now is – well, what?

TOM: Family lore, family reminiscences. For example, where did this (*crucifix*) come from?

CASIMIR: Cardinal O'Donnell; present from Salamanca. No relation, just a great family friend. And a Donegal man, of course; a neighbour, almost. Remember him, Alice?

ALICE: Who?

CASIMIR: Cardinal O'Donnell.

265

ALICE: Do I remember him? He must be dead seventy years.

CASIMIR: He's not.

ALICE: At least.

CASIMIR: Is he? Ah. Good heavens. I suppose you're right. In that case. Well, let's see what else we have. Oh, yes, everything has some association. Hopkins you know. (TOM *begins writing again.*)

TOM: Got that.

CASIMIR: And this is Chesterton.

TOM: Sorry?

CASIMIR: G. K. Chesterton.

TOM: The ashtray?

CASIMIR: The footstool.

TOM: Foot –

CASIMIR: He was giving an imitation of Lloyd George making a speech and he lost his balance and – Kraask! – Bam! – Smaak! – Boom! – down on his back across the fender. And you know the weight of Chesterton – he must be twenty stone! The fender's still dented, isn't it, Alice?

ALICE: Yes.
(*She goes out to the lawn and sits on one of the deck-chairs.* CLAIRE *begins to play Sonata No. 3 in B minor, Op. 58 – Third Movement.*)

CASIMIR: Sprained elbow and bruised ribs.

TOM: Great.

CASIMIR: Laid up in the nursery for five days.

TOM: That could have been when? – doesn't matter – I'll check it out. How often did he visit Ballybeg Hall?

CASIMIR: Oh, I've no idea – often, often, often – oh, yes. And Father and Mother spent part of their honeymoon with him in England, (*To* ALICE) didn't they? – (*Sees she is gone.*) Oh, they were very close friends. Father wanted me to be christened Gilbert Keith but Mother insisted on Casimir – he was a Polish prince – Mother liked that. And this (*chaise-longue*) is Daniel O'Connell, The Liberator – tremendous horseman, O'Connell – see the mark of his riding-boots? And that's the fifty-eight –

TOM: The clock?

266

CASIMIR: Chopin sonata – third movement.

TOM: Oh.

CASIMIR: And this (*candlestick*) is George Moore, the writer – I wonder why that's George Moore. And this (*book*) is Tom Moore – you know – Byron's friend – (*Sings*) 'Believe me if all those endearing young charms which I gaze on so fondly today'. And this (*Bible*) is Hilaire Belloc; wedding present to Father and Mother. And this is Yeats. And –

TOM: What's Yeats?

CASIMIR: This cushion (*on chaise-longue*).

TOM: Cushion – Yeats –

CASIMIR: Oh, he was – he was just tremendous, Yeats, with those cold, cold eyes of his. Oh, yes, I remember Yeats vividly.

TOM: That would have been when you were? –

CASIMIR: On one occasion sat up three nights in succession, just there, on Daniel O'Connell, with his head on that cushion and his feet on Chesterton, just because someone had told him we were haunted. Can you imagine! Three full nights! But of course we weren't haunted. There was never a ghost in the Hall. Father wouldn't believe in ghosts. And he was quite peeved about it; oh, quite peeved. 'You betrayed me, Bernard,' he said to Father. 'You betrayed me', and those cold eyes of his burning with –
    (*He breaks off suddenly because* CLAIRE *has switched from the Sonata to a waltz – A flat major (Posth.) – 'The Bedtime Waltz'.*)

CASIMIR: Listen! Listen! The Bedtime Waltz! Oh, that's my favourite – that's easily my favourite.
    (*He joins* ALICE *outside.*)

CASIMIR: Alice, do you know what that is?

ALICE: (*Sings*) 'Now off to bed, my darlings
    It's time to say goodnight'
    (CASIMIR *and* ALICE *sing together.*)
    'So up the stairs, my sweethearts
    And soon you'll be sleeping tight.'
    (TOM *has joined them outside.*)

CASIMIR: Beautiful, isn't it? Oh, that's easily my favourite; oh, easily, easily. The Bedtime Waltz. It's the A flat major actually but we call it The Bedtime – don't we, Alice ? – because as soon as Mother'd begin to play it, we'd have to dash upstairs – remember? – dash upstairs and wash ourselves and say our night prayers and be in bed before she'd finished. Isn't it so beautiful? (*Sings*) 'Now off to bed, my darlings . . .'

(*They all listen to the music for a few moments.*)

CASIMIR: My God, isn't she playing well? The impending marriage – that's what it is: the concentration of delight and fear and expectation. And Judith tells me she's been in really bubbling humour for months and months – not one day of depression. Not even one; maybe she's grown out of it. Isn't it marvellous? May I tell you something, Tom? We always said among ourselves, Judith and Alice and I – isn't this true, Alice?

ALICE: Isn't what true?

CASIMIR: We always said – well, no, it was never quite expressed; but we always, you know, we always suspected – amn't I right, Alice?

ALICE: What are you saying, Casimir?

CASIMIR: Just that we always thought that perhaps Claire darling was the type of girl, you know, the kind of girl – we always had the idea that our little Claire was one of those highly sensitive, highly intelligent young girls who might choose – who might elect to remain single in life. Ha-ha. That's what we thought. Isn't that true, Alice?

ALICE: And we were wrong.

CASIMIR: Indeed we were wrong! Thank goodness we were wrong! Not that she isn't an attractive girl, a *very* attractive girl – isn't she attractive, Tom? – don't you find Claire attractive?

ALICE: For God's sake, Casimir –

CASIMIR: What's wrong with that? Tom finds little Claire attractive or he doesn't find her attractive?

TOM: She's a very personable young lady.

CASIMIR: Personable – that's the word – an excellent word – personable. Of course she is. And such a sweet nature. And her young man, I gather, is an exceptionally fine type. You've met him, Tom, have you?

TOM: Just once – briefly.

CASIMIR: I'm really looking forward to meeting him. Aren't you, Alice? A mature man who neither smokes nor drinks and –

ALICE: A middle-aged widower with four young children.

CASIMIR: That's fine – that's fine. Claire is exceptionally good with children. Judith told me that when she was giving those piano lessons to the children in the village –

ALICE: What lessons? What children?

CASIMIR: All last winter she went every evening to five or six houses until – you know – poor old Claire – the old trouble – over-anxiety, that's all it is basically, I'm sure that's all it is – and when she had to give it up, I'm sure she missed the pin-money – I mean she must have – what was I talking about? Yes, all those children. Judith wrote and told me they were devoted to her – Judith told me that. And her young man, Jerry, runs a very successful greengrocer's business and he has a great white lorry with an enormous plastic banana on top of the cab and he supplies wonderful fresh vegetables to all the hotels within a twenty-mile radius and he's also an accomplished trumpet player and they play duets together. Good. Good. It all sounds just – just – just so splendid and so – so appropriate. Everything's in hand. Everything's under control. I'm so happy, so happy for her. Ha-ha.

(*His head rotates between* ALICE *and* TOM *in very rapid movements, staring at them with his fixed, anguished smile. Silence. Then suddenly the music changes – a waltz – E flat major (Posth.).).)

CASIMIR: Dance with me, Alice.

ALICE: Casimir.

CASIMIR: (*Shouts*) Clever, clever, Claire! Bravo! (*To* ALICE) Please.

ALICE: Not now.

CASIMIR: In celebration.

ALICE: You never could dance.

269

CASIMIR: Try me – come on – come on!
ALICE: Please. I'm –
(*He grabs her hands and pulls her to her feet.*)
CASIMIR: One-two-three
One-two-three –
ALICE: For God's sake –
CASIMIR: One-two-three
One-two-three
ALICE: Casimir!
CASIMIR: (*Sings*) Alice and Casimir
Alice and Casimir
Alice and Casimir
One-two-three
One-two-three –
(*He is now dancing with the reluctant* ALICE *and singing so loudly that he does not hear the phone ring.*)
TOM: Your call, Casimir!
CASIMIR: Over and round again
Back and forth, down again –
TOM: Casimir!
CASIMIR: Isn't she terrific! And an even better ballet dancer, and she has certificates in French to prove it!
TOM: Call to Hamburg!
CASIMIR: What?
TOM: Germany!
(CASIMIR *stops suddenly. He hears the phone now. The high spirits vanish instantly.*)
CASIMIR: God – Helga – that'll be Helga! Ha-ha.
(*He runs into the study and grabs the phone.*)
CASIMIR: Halloh? Halloh? Helga? Bist du da, Helga? Halloh? Halloh?
(ALICE *flops into a seat.*)
TOM: I'm sorry I can't dance.
ALICE: Thank God for that. Is that whiskey I saw in there?
TOM: Can I get you some?
ALICE: Would you, please?
(TOM *goes into the study and picks up the drinks tray.*)
CASIMIR: Yes, yes, I'm holding, Mrs Moore, I'm holding.

(*To* TOM) Terrific!

TOM: You're through?

CASIMIR: Yes.

TOM: Good.

CASIMIR: To Letterkenny. (*Into phone*) Very well, thank you, Mrs Moore – they're all very well. And how is Mr Moore keeping? Oh, good Lord, I never heard that – six years ago? Oh, good heavens, I'm very sorry – (*To* TOM) Ha-ha.

(TOM *carries the tray outside.*)

ALICE: Has he got through?

TOM: I think not quite.

ALICE: Sometimes when I ring home from London it takes me two hours.

TOM: Hey, you've hurt your cheek.

ALICE: Have I? Must have bumped into something last night. It's not sore. Have a drink yourself.

TOM: I will, thanks. Do you come home often?

ALICE: You're not going to interrogate me again, are you?

TOM: Would you mind?

ALICE: I don't know any answers.

TOM: When you were growing up, did you mix at all with the local people?

ALICE: We're 'local people'.

TOM: Sure; but you're gentry; you're big house.

ALICE: Eamon's local – Eamon's from the village.

TOM: But as kids did you play with other Ballybeg kids?

ALICE: We were sent off to boarding-school when we were seven or eight.

TOM: Casimir, too?

ALICE: He went to the Benedictines when he was six.

TOM: Wow. And afterwards?

ALICE: After we left boarding-school? Judith and Claire and I went to a convent in Carcassone – a finishing school – and became . . . young ladies (*Raises glass*), didn't we?

TOM: Indeed. And Casimir?

ALICE: Began law in the family tradition but always hated books. So he left home – went to England – worked at various 'genteel' jobs. Then he met Helga and she took him

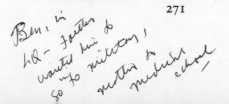

off to Germany. I think he works part-time in a food-processing factory – I don't want to ask him. Helga's the real bread-winner: she's a cashier in a bowling alley. Anything else?

TOM: Tell me about Eamon.

(*She rises and fills her glass again.*)

ALICE: Didn't we talk about that last night?

TOM: Briefly.

ALICE: What did I tell you?

(*He consults his notebook.*)

TOM: 'Poised for a brilliant career in the diplomatic service when –'

ALICE: 'Poised for a –' I never said that!

TOM: I'm quoting you.

ALICE: I *must* have been drunk.

TOM: Then the civil rights movement began in the North in '68. The Dublin government sent him to Belfast as an observer and after a few months observing and reporting he joined the movement. Was sacked, of course. Moved to England and is now a probation officer with the Greater London Council. Right?

ALICE: Listen – Claire's tired at last.

TOM: What was your father's attitude?

ALICE: To Eamon?

TOM: To the civil rights campaign.

ALICE: He opposed it. No, that's not accurate. He was indifferent: that was across the Border – away in the North.

TOM: Only twenty miles away.

ALICE: Politics never interested him. Politics are vulgar.

TOM: And Judith? What was her attitude? Was she engaged?

ALICE: She took part in the Battle of the Bogside. Left Father and Uncle George and Claire alone here and joined the people in the streets fighting the police. That's an attitude, isn't it? That's when Father had his first stroke. And seven months later she had a baby by a Dutch reporter. Does that constitute sufficient engagement?

(*They are interrupted by the sound of laughter and horse-play from the hall.*)

CLAIRE: Give me that, Eamon!

EAMON: Jump for it!

CLAIRE: I'm warning you!

CASIMIR: Shhhh – please!

EAMON: Jump-jump-jump-jump-jump!

CLAIRE: Eamon, I'm telling you! –

EAMON: Doesn't it suit me?

(*They burst into the study* – EAMON *wearing the head-dress of Claire's wedding outfit. She is trying to recover it.* EAMON *is in his thirties.* CLAIRE, *the youngest daughter, is in her twenties. At this moment she is in one of her high moods: talkative, playful, energetic. On other occasions she is solitary and silent and withdrawn. They are now in the study.*)

CLAIRE: Beautiful on you. Now give it back to me at once!

CASIMIR: Please – please.

EAMON: Sorry.

CASIMIR: Hamburg.

EAMON: What?

CASIMIR: Helga.

EAMON: Ah. (*To* CLAIRE) Behave yourself.

CASIMIR: Looking marvellous.

EAMON: Me?

CASIMIR: Splendid.

EAMON: Hungover.

CASIMIR: You weren't drunk.

CLAIRE: He was full.

EAMON: Great cure this morning.

CASIMIR: The A flat major, Claire? The Bedtime – wasn't I right?

CLAIRE: Full marks.

(EAMON *suddenly stoops down to the level of the mouthpiece of the phone and speaks rapidly into it.*)

EAMON: 'Mrs Moore isn't poor – '

CASIMIR: Eamon – !

EAMON: 'Mrs Moore's a rich aul' hoor!'

CASIMIR: Oh, God!

CLAIRE: Troublemaker! Come on!

EAMON: See you outside, Casimir.

273

CASIMIR: No, nothing, Mrs Moore – I didn't speak – sorry – sorry –

(CLAIRE *has* EAMON *by the arm and drags him outside. As he goes he bumps into the chaise-longue, the table, etc. As he does:–*)

EAMON: Begging your pardon, your eminence, your worship, your holiness – sorry, Shakespeare, Lenin, Mickey Mouse, Marilyn Monroe –

(*They are now out on the lawn.*)

EAMON: Like walking through Madame Tussaud's, isn't it, Professor? Or a bloody mine-field?

(CLAIRE *grabs her head-dress from his head.*)

CLAIRE: Thank you.

EAMON: Won't she be a beautiful bride?

TOM: Certainly will.

CLAIRE: Lucky for you it's not soiled.

ALICE: Let's see it, Claire.

CLAIRE: I'm going to shorten that net.

ALICE: Very smart. Did you get it in Derry?

CLAIRE: Judith made it. And the dress. And her own outfit, too. Economy.

ALICE: It's very pretty.

CLAIRE: Did you know that on the morning Grandmother O'Donnell got married the whole village was covered with bunting and she gave a gold sovereign to every child under twelve? And the morning Mother got married she distributed roses to everyone in the chapel. I was wondering what I could do – what about a plastic bag of vegetables to every old-age pensioner? I suppose it'll soon be lunch-time, won't it?

TOM: That was great music.

(*She looks directly at him and does not speak. He feels he has to add something.*)

Really wonderful. I enjoyed it. Really great.

CLAIRE: No, it wasn't.

TOM: I thought it was.

CLAIRE: I'm only a good pianist. I'm not a great pianist. I thought I was once. But I know I'm not.

EAMON: (*To* TOM) So there!

274

ALICE: Is this what you're going to shorten?

CLAIRE: Maybe. I don't know. What do you think?

ALICE: Let's see it on.

EAMON: (*To* ALICE) Granny sends her warmest love.
> (ALICE *turns away from him.*)
> She was disappointed you weren't with me but I said you
> had a headache. That wasn't a lie, was it?
> (ALICE *ignores him. She addresses* CLAIRE.)

ALICE: Maybe a fraction of an inch; but I like it as it is.

EAMON: Down in the village visiting my grandmother,
> Professor.

TOM: So I understand.

EAMON: Reared me from a pup, you might say. When I was
> three, the family had to emigrate to Scotland for work and I
> was left behind with granny. (*Arms around* CLAIRE.) Her
> very special love to you, she says. And she's sending up a
> small present tomorrow.

CLAIRE: I called in with her the day before yesterday.

EAMON: And brought her yellow roses.

CLAIRE: But I can't persuade her to come to the wedding.

EAMON: All she wanted is to be asked. And you were wearing a
> white cotton dress and a pale-blue headscarf and you looked
> like an angel. (*He hugs her briefly and releases her.*) Over the
> years, Professor, I've lusted after each of the three
> O'Donnell girls in turn. (*Sees the drink.*) Where was this
> hidden? I thought we guzzled every drop of booze in the
> house last night?

TOM: Willie brought it.

EAMON: Willie who?

CLAIRE: Willie who!

TOM: Willie Diver.

EAMON: Of course. Willie Slooghter, the ardent suitor. Sorry I
> missed him.

TOM: He'll be back later. He was putting up the baby-alarm for
> Judith. See – on the door-frame.

CLAIRE: That's going to be a great help.
> (EAMON *raises his glass to the speaker.*)

EAMON: The judicial presence restored. District Justice

275

O'Donnell, Sir, welcome downstairs again. (*To* CLAIRE)
Is it true that Willie practically haunts the place?

CLAIRE: A little bit, I'm afraid. But he's very helpful to Judith;
and very generous.

(CLAIRE *now sits and begins to sew her head-dress.* ALICE
drifts upstage and sits alone in the gazebo. TOM *sits close to the
sun-dial and glances through his notes.*)

EAMON: Always was. One civil and one decent man. (*Drinks.*)
Your good health, William. D'you know what someone in
the pub was telling me this morning? He has five hundred
slot-machines in amusement arcades all round the country.
Can you imagine? He'd be worth a fortune if he looked
after them but he never goes near them! I'm sorry – Claire?
(*Offering a drink.*)

CLAIRE: The doctor doesn't allow me to take alcohol when I'm
on sedatives.

EAMON: Aren't you a wise and obedient girl. Professor?

TOM: It's Tom. I'm okay.

EAMON: That's someone you should meet.

TOM: Who's that?

EAMON: My grandmother. You'd find her interesting. Worked
all her life as a maid here in the Hall.

TOM: In the Hall? Here?

EAMON: Didn't you know that? Oh, yes, yes. Something like
fifty-seven years continuous service with the District Justice
and his wife, Lord have mercy on her; and away back to the
earlier generation, with his father, the High Court judge
and his family. Oh, you should meet her before you leave –
a fund of stories and information.

TOM: She sounds –

EAMON: Carriages, balls, receptions, weddings, christenings,
feasts, deaths, trips to Rome, musical evenings,
tennis – that's the mythology I was nurtured on all my life,
day after day, year after year – the life of the
'quality' – that's how she pronounces it, with a flat 'a'. A
strange and marvellous education for a wee country boy,
wasn't it? No, not an education – a permanent
pigmentation. I'll tell you something, Professor: I know

276

more about this place, infinitely more, here and here. (*Head and heart.*) than they know. Sure? (*Drink*) You'll enjoy this. (*Now to* ALICE *up in the gazebo.*) Telling the professor about the night I told granny you and I were getting married. (*To* TOM) Not a notion in the world we were going out, of course. My God, Miss Alice and her grandson! Anyhow. 'Granny,' I said this night, 'Alice and I are going to get married.' 'Alice? Who's Alice? Alice Devenny? Alice Byrne? Not Alice Smith!' 'Alice O'Donnell.' 'What Alice O'Donnell's that?' 'Alice O'Donnell of the Hall.' A long silence. Then: 'May God and his holy mother forgive you, you dirty-mouthed upstart!' (*Laughs.*) Wasn't that an interesting response? As we say about here: Now you're an educated man, Professor – what do make of that response?

TOM: Oh boy.

EAMON: 'Oh boy'?

TOM: What do you make of it?

EAMON: Would you like to meet her?

TOM: That would be –

EAMON: I'm sure I could manage to squeeze an appointment.

TOM: Actually I'm leaving to- –

EAMON: She'd love to talk to you; I know she would.

TOM: Perhaps some other –

EAMON: She's crazy about Americans. She has a sister a waitress in the Bronx and a picture of Tom Mix above her bed. Hello, Uncle George. Sit down and give us a bit of your crack.
(*This to* UNCLE GEORGE *who has entered left – his usual entrance, finding himself in the middle of the group before he is aware that they are there. As before he stands and stares and then retreats the way he came.*)

EAMON: There goes one happy man.
(CASIMIR *has hung up and now stands at the study-lawn door.*)

CASIMIR: Can't get past Letterkenny. But they'll keep trying.

EAMON: Casimir? (*Drink.*)

CASIMIR: Later, perhaps. Now be patient for another few minutes and I'll bring out a beautiful picnic lunch.

CLAIRE: Do you need any help?

277

CASIMIR: Me? Didn't I tell you what the boys call me? The kinder mädchen.

CLAIRE: What's that? (*To* TOM) What does that mean?

TOM: Is it the . . . children's maid? The nanny?

CASIMIR: Well, yes, I suppose that's the literal translation but in this context it means – it means – well, it's really a kind of comical, affectionate term. They like to pull my leg, you know. Contrary to popular opinion the German temperament is naturally very – very frivolous and very, *very* affectionate. Where's Alice?

ALICE: Hello.

CASIMIR: What are you hiding there for? *(at the Gazebo)*

ALICE: Getting drunk.

CASIMIR: Now you're being frivolous. Right – ten minutes at the outside.

(*He goes back into the study and off into the hall.*)

TOM: The telephone system here is really unsatisfactory, isn't it?

EAMON: All a game.

TOM: In what way?

EAMON: Casimir pretending he's calling Helga the Hun. All a game. All a fiction.

ALICE: Oh shut up!

EAMON: No one has ever seen her. We're convinced he's invented her.

(TOM *laughs uncertainly.*)

TOM: Is he serious, Claire?

EAMON: And the three boys – Herbert, Hans and Heinrich. And the dachshund bitch called Dietrich. And his job in the sausage factory. It has the authentic ring of phoney fiction, hasn't it?

CLAIRE: Don't listen to him, Tom.

(ALICE *has come down from the gazebo to fill her glass.*)

ALICE: What's your phoney fiction?

EAMON: That I'm a laughing broth of an Irish boy. (*To* TOM) What was the word you used a few minutes ago – that yoke in there – what did you call it? A baby –?

TOM: Baby-alarm.

EAMON: That's it – baby-alarm.

278

TOM: You place a small microphone above a baby's cot so that if it cries –

EAMON: I know – I know how it works. No practical experience of course – have we, love? Just that I find the name curious. Good luck. Yes, I suppose baby-alarm has an aptness in the circumstances. But there's another word – what's the name I'm looking for? – what do you call the peep-hole in a prison door? Judas hole! That's it. Would that be more appropriate? But then we'd have to decide who's spying on whom, wouldn't we? No; let's keep baby-alarm. Gentler. (*Laughs.*) 'Baby-alarm' – yes, I like baby-alarm. (*To* ALICE) Shouldn't you go easy on that?

No kids

ALICE: Shut up.

EAMON: (*To* TOM) Less than twenty-four hours away from temperate London and already we're reverting to drunken Paddies. Must be the environment, mustn't it? Man-a-dear but that's a powerful aul' lump of a summer's day.
(TOM *is looking at his notes.* ALICE *has gone back to the gazebo.* EAMON *crosses to* CLAIRE *who is sewing and sits beside her. He puts his arm round her.*)

EAMON: I'm talking too much, amn't I? (*Pause.*) I always talk too much in this house, don't I? Is it because I'm still intimidated by it? (*Pause.*) And this was always a house of reticence, of things unspoken, wasn't it?
(*She looks at him and smiles. He touches her chin.*)
Keep your peace, little wise one. (*He removes his arm from round her.*) Judith tells me I'm proposing the toast to the groom's family.

CLAIRE: You know Jerry, don't you?

EAMON: Not very well. He was that bit older. (*Aware*) Well – a few years – and when you're young it seems a lot.
(*She takes his glass and drinks.*)
Hey! What about those pills?

CLAIRE: I haven't taken today's yet.

EAMON: Why not?

CLAIRE: You know his sister, Ellen?

EAMON: Yes.

CLAIRE: Do you like her?

279

EAMON: Ellen has her own ways.

CLAIRE: She'll be living in the house with Jerry and me.

EAMON: For a while, maybe. Ellen'll marry and move out.

CLAIRE: No, she won't move out. And she won't marry now – she's almost fifty-four – she's only a year younger than Jerry. And the house is hers. And yesterday she said to me that she'll carry on as usual – doing the cooking and the housework. So I'll have nothing to do. A life of leisure. Maybe take the children for walks – she suggested that. But that's all. The whole day idle. And he's getting me a car next Christmas so that I won't even have to walk. Next time you're back I'll have put on ten stone!

EAMON: I thought Jerry would want a working wife?

CLAIRE: Oh, yes. He's buying a piano so that I can teach the children to play. Maybe one of them will become a concert pianist?

(*She gets up and moves across the lawn.*)

EAMON: What the hell's keeping Casimir with the grub?

(*He rises and pours himself another drink.*)

EAMON: God bless Willie Diver. Did you know I was his best man? My God, *that* was a wedding. I was seventeen, Willie was eighteen, and Nora Sheridan, known locally as Nora the Nun – for reasons of Irish irony, Professor – Nora was thirty if she was a day. And at seventeen I thought: My God, lucky aul' Slooghter, marrying the village pro, my God he'll be getting it morning, noon and night and what more could a man want! But of course the marriage lasted five months and the brave Nora cleared off with a British soldier stationed in Derry and was never seen again and aul' Willie was back with the rest of us hoping to get it maybe once a year on St Patrick's night with big Tessie Mulligan if you promised to take her and her twin sister to the pig co-op dance. Isn't life full of tiny frustrations, Professor? And how's the research going?

TOM: Satisfactorily.

EAMON: Are you writing a book?

TOM: Eventually.

EAMON: About?

TOM: I'm not going to bore you with my theories.

280

EAMON: Please. (*To* ALICE) We're captivated – aren't we, love?

TOM: Alice is not captivated.

EAMON: Alice reveals her passion in oblique ways.

TOM: I'd really rather not –

EAMON: But I'm interested; I'm genuinely interested. Please.

TOM: Well, when we talk about the big house in this country, we usually mean the Protestant big house with its Anglo-Irish tradition and culture; and the distinction is properly made between that tradition and culture and what we might call the native Irish tradition and culture which is Roman Catholic.

EAMON: With reservations – yes. So?

TOM: So what I'm researching is the life and the life-style of the Roman Catholic big house – by no means as thick on the ground but still there; what we might call a Roman Catholic aristocracy – for want of a better term.

EAMON: No, no, it's a good term; I like the term. The Professor's talking about you, love!

TOM: And the task I've set myself is to explore its political, cultural and economic influence both on the ascendancy ruling class and on the native peasant tradition. Over the past one hundred and fifty years – in fact since Catholic emancipation – what political clout did they wield, what economic contribution did they make to the status of their co-religionists, what cultural effect did they have on the local peasantry?

EAMON: The Professor's talking about me, love! And Ballybeg Hall's your prototype?

TOM: No, just one example.

EAMON: And what conclusions have you reached?

TOM: None yet, Eamon. I'm still digging.

EAMON: Ah. Let's see can we help the Professor. What were the questions again? What political clout did they wield? (*Considers. Then sadly shakes his head.*) What economic help were they to their co-religionists? (*Considers. Then sadly shakes his head.*) What cultural effect did they have on the local peasantry? Alice? (*Considers. Then sadly shakes his head.*) We agree, I'm afraid. Sorry, Professor. Bogus thesis.

No book.

TOM: Okay. So no book.

EAMON: But you'll go ahead all the same, won't you?

TOM: I may well be so obtuse.

(CASIMIR *enters the study, carrying a large tray. As he crosses towards the lawn he chants*:)

CASIMIR: What we are about to receive is a magnificent lunch which will be served on the lawn and it has been prepared specially and with meticulous care by –

(*He is now on the lawn and is about to put the tray on the ground when his chant is interrupted by* FATHER's *clear and commanding voice.*)

FATHER: Casimir!

(CASIMIR *jumps to attention; rigid, terrified.*)

CASIMIR: Yes sir!

FATHER: Come to the library at once. I wish to speak to you.

(CASIMIR *now realizes that the voice has come from the speaker.*)

CASIMIR: Christ . . . oh-oh-oh my God . . . Ha-ha. Isn't that a very comical joke – I almost stood to attention – I almost stood –

(*He looks round at the others who are staring at him. He tries to smile. He is totally lost. He looks at the tray; then sinks to the ground with it, ending in a kneeling position.*)

CASIMIR: That's the second time I was caught – the second time –

(JUDITH *enters with the tea-pot. The eldest of the O'Donnell family: almost forty. She is dressed in old working clothes. Her appearance is of little interest to her.*)

JUDITH: Did you bring the sugar and the sandwiches, Casimir? I've got the tea here.

FATHER: At once, Sir. And bring your headmaster's report with you. I intend to get to the bottom of this.

CASIMIR: Judith?

JUDITH: What is it?

CASIMIR: Judith?

(*She goes quickly outside, gets down beside him and takes him in her arms. He is crying now.*)

282

CASIMIR: I'm sorry – I'm sorry – I'm very sorry.

JUDITH: It's all right.

CASIMIR: I'm very sorry, very sorry.

JUDITH: Everything's all right – everything's fine.

CASIMIR: I don't think it's fair, Judith.

JUDITH: Shhhhh.

CASIMIR: That's the second time I was caught by it. It's not fair – it's not fair.

JUDITH: Shhhhh.

CASIMIR: Ha-ha. It's not fair.

(*She rocks him in her arms as if he were a baby. The others look away. Bring lights down slowly.*)

ACT TWO

About an hour later.

   The remains of the lunch are scattered over the lawn: dishes, linen napkins, food, some empty wine bottles.

   The sun, the food, the wine have taken their toll: EAMON *is sprawled on the grass, dozing.*

   JUDITH, *her eyes closed, her face tilted up to the sun, is smoking a cigarette.*

   WILLIE *is sitting on the step immediately above and behind her.*

CLAIRE *is sitting apart from the others, close to the sundial.* TOM *is in the gazebo, reading a newspaper but aware of what the others are doing.*

   CASIMIR *is crawling around on his hands and knees, moving along very slowly and feeling the ground very carefully with his finger-tips. He is totally concentrated on this strange task. (He is looking for the holes left by croquet hoops; on the same site as the vanished tennis-court.)*

   Only ALICE *is lively. She has had a little too much to drink and she is pacing about, glass in hand, occasionally making giddy, complicated little steps with her feet.*

ALICE: I know you're paying no attention to me – old Alice is a

little tiddly, isn't she? But what I'm suggesting is very
sensible. The meal will be over at half one or two; and the
happy couple will drive off into eternal bliss. And what's to
become of the rest of us? Sit looking at one another with
melancholy faces? Sleep? Talk about old times? Listen to
Father on the baby-alarm? (*Short giggle – then remorse. To*
CASIMIR.) Apologies. Withdraw that. That was unkind. So
what do we do? My suggestion is – no, it's a formal
proposal, Madam Chairman (*Judith*) – I put it to your
worship that we all head off somewhere and have some fun
ourselves. You'll drive us, Willie, won't you?

WILLIE: Surely to God. Anywhere you want.

ALICE: All set, then. Where'll we go? Glencolmcille! Who's
for –

(JUDITH *sits up very quickly and lifts the writing pad at her*
side i.e. her list of wedding preparations.)

JUDITH: Willie isn't free to go anywhere.

(ALICE *grimaces extravagantly behind her back.*)

ALICE: Oooooh. So Willie isn't free. All right, we'll club
together and rent a car – no, *I'll* rent a car and you'll all be
my guests. Is that a unanimous verdict?

JUDITH: Let's get back to these things.

ALICE: And we'll bring our court clerk with us and every word
we utter will be carefully recorded.

JUDITH: Where had we got to? Any word from the
photographer?

WILLIE: He'll be there at the chapel and then he'll come up
here afterwards.

ALICE: God help the poor man if he thinks he's heard one word
of truth since he came here. Is he in the library?

TOM: Careful, Alice: I'm here.

ALICE: All you're hearing is lies, my friend – lies, lies, lies.

TOM: What's the truth?

ALICE: Later in the day and alcoholic Alice'll tell all.

JUDITH: I've asked one of the Moloney girls to look after Father
while we're at the church. Are you busy that morning?

WILLIE: Doing nothing.

JUDITH: Could you run her up? About half nine?

284

WILLIE: No bother.

JUDITH: Thanks.

ALICE: Well, if none of you want to come with me, as Sister
  Thérèse used to say – remember her strange English? –
  'Boo-gar the whole lot of you!'
  (*She slumps into a chair and closes her eyes.*)

Sister Thérèse

JUDITH: Food – that's all got except for the ham.

CASIMIR: Hurrah!
  (CASIMIR's *sudden triumphant exclamation startles everybody.*
  EAMON *wakens, startled.*)

CASIMIR: There you are! Knew they were here!

EAMON: God.

CASIMIR: There! Look – look – look!
  (*He has a finger stuck into the ground.*)

ALICE: Good old Casimir!

CASIMIR: Now if there's one there, there must be another
  somewhere beside it.
  (*He bends over to his search again.* EAMON *gets to his feet.*)

EAMON: What is he at? Who's missing?

JUDITH: What's the position about the flowers, Claire?

CASIMIR: Here it is! (*He stands up.*) You see – I remember it.
  Distinctly! (*He marks the spot with a napkin.*) That means
  that there must be another one – (*He strides across the
  lawn*) – somewhere about here. (*He grins at* EAMON.) Amn't
  I right?

EAMON: I'm sure you are.

CASIMIR: Seven in all – isn't that it?

EAMON: At least.

CASIMIR: No, no, just seven; and the peg in the middle.
  (*He suddenly drops on his hands and knees again and begins
  groping.*)

EAMON: Who is Peg?

JUDITH: Claire!

CLAIRE: Sorry?

JUDITH: The flowers arrive on the last bus tomorrow night?

CLAIRE: (*Vague, indifferent*) I think so.

JUDITH: And Jerry'll collect them and bring them up here?

CLAIRE: Yes . . . probably . . . I suppose so.

285

JUDITH: Claire, it's –

WILLIE: I'll remind him this evening.

JUDITH: Would you?

WILLIE: And if he's busy I'll collect them.

> (EAMON *picks up the cassette and switches it on – Étude Op.
> 10, No. 3 in E major. He sings with it in a parody of the
> Crosby style of the late 1940s.*)

Eamun parodies the music

EAMON: 'So deep is the night –'

> (CASIMIR, *automatically, without looking up.*)

CASIMIR: Terrific. The E major Étude – right, Claire?

EAMON: F major.

> (CASIMIR *sits up.*)

Doesn't know E from F

CASIMIR: Are you – ? No, it's the – Ah, you're taking a hand at
me, Eamon! I know you are. Ha-ha. Very good. Very
comical.

> (*He bends to his search again.*)

EAMON: 'No moon tonight; no friendly star to guide me on my
way – boo-be-doo-ba-ba-de-ba . . .'

> (*He pours himself a drink.*)

JUDITH: What arrangement have you come to with Miss Quirk,
Claire?

CLAIRE: No arrangement.

JUDITH: Is she going to play or is she not?

CLAIRE: I told you all I know. I met her by accident.

JUDITH: And what did she say?

CLAIRE: All she said was 'I play the harmonium at every
wedding in Ballybeg'.

ALICE: (*Eyes closed*) Who? Miss Quirk? O my God!

CLAIRE: I don't care. Let her play if she wants.

JUDITH: Did she ask you what music you wanted?

CLAIRE: You know very well she can play only two pieces.

ALICE: Tom Hoffnung!

TOM: Hello?

ALICE: Before you leave you should meet Miss Quirk.

TOM: Yeah?

ALICE: She's the Scott Joplin of Donegal.

JUDITH: (*To* WILLIE) I suppose I'll have to pay her something?

WILLIE: I'll look after it. You can square with me later.

Miss Quirk

(EAMON *is wandering around, glass in hand. He sings with the tape again, inventing the words he has forgotten.*)

EAMON: 'And so am I, lonely and forgotten by the stream . . .'
(*To* WILLIE) Remember dancing to that in the Corinthian in Derry?

WILLIE: Every Friday night.

EAMON: The steam rising out of us from getting soaked cycling in on the bikes.

WILLIE: And the big silver ball going round and round up on the ceiling. Jaysus.

EAMON: Tommy McGee on the sax; Bobby Kyle on piano; Jackie Fogarty on drums; young Turbet on clarinet.

WILLIE: And slipping out to the cloakroom for a slug out of the bottle.

EAMON: And the long dresses – the New Look – isn't that what it was called?

WILLIE: Oh Jaysus.

EAMON: (*To* JUDITH) Remembrance of things past.

JUDITH: (*To* WILLIE) Is that coffee stone cold?
(WILLIE *rises immediately.*)

WILLIE: If there's any left in it.
(*He goes to the remains of the picnic.*)

EAMON: Do you remember the night we sneaked out to the Corinthian on my uncle's motor-bike?

JUDITH: Yes.

EAMON: We were still sitting over there (*in the gazebo*) when the sun came up.

CASIMIR: Here we are! Two more holes! Corner number two! All agreed?
(*He stands up, marks the position with a napkin as before, and goes to another part of the lawn.*)

EAMON: You wore your mother's silver tiara in your hair. Do you remember?

JUDITH: Yes.

EAMON: Everything?

CASIMIR: So that number three must be about – here.
(*He drops on his hands and knees again and begins groping.*)

ALICE: (*Eyes closed*) I have it on very good authority that in the

287

privacy of her digs Miss Quirk plays the ukulele and sings dirty songs.

EAMON: There was a hedgehog caught in the tennis-net. He had rolled himself up into a ball and his spikes were up against danger. Like me, you said. Do you remember?

JUDITH: Yes.

EAMON: And I asked you to marry me.

ALICE: I'm ashamed to say I like dirty songs, Tom.

EAMON: And you said yes.

JUDITH: Where had we got to? – taxis. What about taxis, Willie?

WILLIE: You'll need only two. The car that leaves Jerry at the chapel then comes up here for you and Claire; and it waits here until the other car has headed off with the rest of the family and then it follows on. (*He returns with a cup of coffee.*) There's a wee drop in it – it's not too bad. They were good times, Eamon, eh?, them nights in the Corinthian.

EAMON: They were good times, Professor.

TOM: What were?

EAMON: Plebeian past times. Before we were educated out of our emotions.
(*He switches up the volume of the cassette while he sings again.*)

EAMON: 'So deep is the night, ba-ba-dee-boo-ba-ba-ba-ba . . .'
(*He reduces the volume again.*)

JUDITH: I think we have enough wine.

ALICE: I hope there's plenty wine.

WILLIE: (*To* ALICE) I left in two cases – is that enough?
(ALICE *now opens her eyes and sits forward.*)

ALICE: Good ole Willie! (*Sings*) 'Drink to me only with thine eyes –'
(*Immediately* EAMON *begins singing.*)

EAMON: 'Boo-ba-de-boo-ba-ba'

ALICE: 'And I will pledge with mine'.
(CASIMIR, *without interrupting his search, joins* ALICE.)
    'Or leave a kiss within the cup
    And I'll not ask for wine.'
(ALICE *sits back, closes her eyes and continues humming.*)

288

EAMON: (*To* TOM) Recognize it?

TOM: Elizabethan. Is it Ben Jonson?

EAMON: The very buck. Used to nip into the scullery and recite it to granny.

TOM: I think perhaps I should check that.

EAMON: Would I tell you a lie?

FATHER: I have considered very carefully everything I have heard and I must now ask you to – I must request – I must – I – I . . .
(*The suddenness and authority of father's voice create a stillness, almost an unease. Nobody speaks for a few seconds.*)

JUDITH: He's very restless today.

CASIMIR: I wasn't caught that time – no, no! I wasn't caught that time – ha-ha!

FATHER: Judith!
(CASIMIR *stiffens.*)

FATHER: Judith? Judith? Where's Judith? Jud-ith!

ALICE: Stay where you are. I'll go.
(*She rises.*)

JUDITH: It's all right. He probably wants nothing at all.
(JUDITH *goes off quickly.* ALICE *walks about. She is slightly unsteady.*)

ALICE: But I would like to go – I would like to help. Why won't she let me help? When I went up to see him last night just after I arrived, I got such a shock – he's so altered. Isn't he altered? I mean he was always such a big strong man with such power, such authority; and then to see him lying there, so flat under the clothes, with his mouth open –
(CASIMIR *stands up. He has been listening to* ALICE *and the vigour of his announcement this time is forced.*)

CASIMIR: The third! There you are! Number three! (*He marks it as before.*) Only one more to get.
(*He crosses the lawn to the fourth corner but does not go down on his hands and knees. He stands listening to* ALICE.)

ALICE: I caught his face between my hands – isn't that right, Casimir? You were there beside me – and I held it like that. And it was such a strange sensation – I must never have touched his face before – is that possible never to have

289

touched my father's face? And it seemed so small between my hands; and it was so cool and his beard so rough and I felt so – so equal to him. (*She begins to cry.*) And then he opened his eyes. And he didn't recognize me – isn't that right, Casimir? And that's when I began to cry. He didn't know me. He didn't know you either, Casimir, did he?

CASIMIR: No.

ALICE: He didn't know me either. It was so strange – your own father not knowing you. He didn't know you either, Casimir, did he?

CASIMIR: No.

ALICE: His own flesh and blood. Did he know you, Willie?

WILLIE: Well, you see like, Alice, I'm not his son.

ALICE: That's true. And that's when I began to cry. I'm sorry – I'm sorry – I know I'm slightly drunk but I'm still capable of – of – of –

(EAMON *offers her Judith's coffee – she brushes past him.*)

ALICE: I want a drink. Who's hidden the drink? Where's the drink all hidden? (*She finds it and helps herself.*) Oh dear, dear God.

EAMON: 'Boo-ba-de-ba-ba-ba-ba; boom-boom-boom' . . .

(EAMON *moves over beside* CLAIRE. CASIMIR *gets down on his hands and knees again.* ALICE *drops into a seat and closes her eyes.*)

EAMON: Whatever he's looking for, he deserves to find it.

CLAIRE: The remains of an old croquet court.

EAMON: Ah. Before my time.

(*A new tape begins: Nocturne in F sharp major, Op. 15, No. 2.* CLAIRE *is fingering a gold watch.*)

EAMON: Present from Jerry?

CLAIRE: For my last birthday.

EAMON: Very handsome, isn't it?

JUDITH: Is something wrong?

CLAIRE: Yes.

FATHER: Judith?

JUDITH: I'm here beside you.

CLAIRE: And I told you, didn't I – he's getting me a car for Christmas.

290

JUDITH: What's the matter?

EAMON: Lucky you.

FATHER: Judith?

JUDITH: What is it?

CLAIRE: And he's had the whole house done up from top to bottom. New carpets everywhere – even in the kitchen. I helped Ellen choose them.

JUDITH: Are you cold? Do you want the quilt on again?

(*Without any change in her tone, and smiling as if she were chatting casually,* CLAIRE *continues.*)

CLAIRE: I'm in a mess, Eamon.

JUDITH: You're upset today.

CLAIRE: I don't know if I can go on with it.

JUDITH: You got your pills, didn't you?

FATHER: Judith betrayed the family – did you know that?

JUDITH: Yes. Now – that's better.

FATHER: Great betrayal; enormous betrayal.

JUDITH: Let me feel those tops.

FATHER: But Anna's praying for her. Did you know that?

JUDITH: Yes, I know that, Father.

CLAIRE: Listen to them! (*Short laugh.*) It goes on like that all the time, all the time. I don't know how Judith stands it. She's lucky to be so . . . so strong-minded. Sometimes I think it's driving me mad. Mustn't it have been something trivial like that that finally drove mother to despair? And then sometimes I think: I'm going to miss it so much. I'm so confused, Eamon.

EAMON: Aren't we all confused.

CLAIRE: But if you really loved someone the way you're supposed to love someone you're about to marry, you shouldn't be confused, should you? Everything should be absorbed in that love, shouldn't it? There'd be no reservations, would there? I'd love his children and his sister and his lorry and his vegetables and his carpets and everything, wouldn't I? And I'd love all of him, too, wouldn't I?

(EAMON *puts his arm round her.*)

CLAIRE: That's one of the last nocturnes he wrote.

EAMON: Is it?

CLAIRE: Why does he not see that I'm in a mess, Eamon?

EAMON: You don't have to go on with it, you know.

(CASIMIR *is suddenly and triumphantly on his feet again.*)

CASIMIR: Number four! There you are! The complete croquet court! See, Eamon? Look, Claire! I remember! I knew!

(CLAIRE *jumps up. She is suddenly vigorous, buoyant, excited. Her speech is rapid.*)

CLAIRE: Come on – who's for a game?

CASIMIR: Me-me-me!

CLAIRE: Give me a mallet.

(CASIMIR *mimes giving her one.*)

CASIMIR: There you are.

CLAIRE: Is this the best you have?

CASIMIR: It's brand new – never been used.

CLAIRE: Where are the hoops?

CASIMIR: All in position. Just a second. (*He drops three more napkins in the centre of the court.*) That's it. This one (*centre napkin*) is the peg.

CLAIRE: And the balls?

CASIMIR: At your feet.

CLAIRE: Right.

CASIMIR: Who goes first?

CLAIRE: The bride-to-be – who else?

CASIMIR: Wonderful! Off you go. Ladies and gentlemen – please – give the players room. Thank you. Thank you.

CLAIRE: First shot of the game.

CASIMIR: And a beautiful, beautiful shot it is. Now for the champion.

(*This imaginary game and their exchanges about it continue during the following sequences.* EAMON *rises; switches off the cassette; picks up a bottle of wine and a glass; drifts across the lawn. As he passes* WILLIE:)

EAMON: 'Ba-ba-de-boo-ba-ba'. Many hedgehogs about now?

WILLIE: What?

EAMON: Hedgehogs – you know – (*He mimes one*) – many of them about?

WILLIE: How the hell would I know about hedgehogs?

292

EAMON: 'Ba-ba-de-boo-ba-ba – Ba-ba-boo . . .'

WILLIE: Hedgehogs! Jaysus!

(WILLIE *goes to the croquet court and watches the game.*)

CASIMIR: That was good – that was very good.

CLAIRE: That was brilliant.

CASIMIR: But watch this. This is how it's really done. Aaaaaah!

(ALICE *opens her eyes, sits forward, and watches* CLAIRE *and* CASIMIR *in bewilderment.*)

CLAIRE: That ball hit your leg.

CASIMIR: It did not.

CLAIRE: I saw it – you winced.

CASIMIR: (*To* ALICE) Did the ball hit my leg?

ALICE: What?

CASIMIR: Did you see me wince?

CLAIRE: You did. I saw you. I saw you.

ALICE: What are you doing?

CASIMIR: Croquet. (*To* CLAIRE) My turn – right?

CLAIRE: I'll let you off this time. (*To* ALICE) Keep an eye on him – he cheats.

ALICE: Where are the – ?

CLAIRE: But he's still not winning. (*To* CASIMIR) And watch where you're swinging that mallet.

ALICE: Oh my God.

(*She closes her eyes and sinks back in her seat. The game continues.* UNCLE GEORGE *enters the study – his usual entrance – and is out on the lawn before he discovers it is occupied. He stops, looks around.*)

WILLIE: Hello, Mr George.

(UNCLE GEORGE *goes back into the study – and off.*)

EAMON: Hello, Uncle George. Goodbye, Uncle George. Not one of you is aware that on the day of our wedding Uncle George shook my hand and spoke seven words. And the seven words he spoke were: 'There's going to be a great revolution.' And I thought that after all those years of silence and contemplation that must be a profound remark. (EAMON *is now beside* TOM. *He sits very close to him and smiles warmly at him.*) Wasn't I a fool?

TOM: Were you?

293

EAMON: I'm wiser now.

TOM: Good.

EAMON: And I've solved your problem.

TOM: Which one's that, Eamon?

EAMON: Your book.

TOM: Have I a problem?

EAMON: It has to be a fiction – a romantic fiction – like Helga the Hun.

TOM: Yeah?

EAMON: A great big block-buster of a gothic novel called *Ballybeg Hall – From Supreme Court to Sausage Factory*; four generations of a great Irish Catholic legal dynasty; the gripping saga of a family that lived its life in total isolation in a gaunt Georgian house on top of a hill above the remote Donegal village of Ballybeg; a family without passion, without loyalty, without commitments; administering the law for anyone who happened to be in power; above all wars and famines and civil strife and political upheaval; ignored by its Protestant counterparts, isolated from the mere Irish, existing only in its own concept of itself, brushing against reality occasionally by its cultivation of artists; but tough – oh, yes, tough, resilient, tenacious; and with one enormous talent for – no, a *greed* for survival – that's the family motto, isn't it? – *Semper permanemus*. Don't for a second underestimate them. What do you think?

TOM: It's your fiction.

EAMON: A bit turgid – yes – I can see that. (*Suddenly happy again.*) But the romantic possibilities are there – oh, yes, by God. Mother for example. Make Mother central.

ALICE: Leave Mother out of it.

EAMON: Why?

ALICE: You really are a bastard!

EAMON: Because I see Mother as central?

ALICE: For Christ's sake!

EAMON: Trust me – I'm an ex-diplomat.

ALICE: Trust you!

EAMON: Yes, I have pieties, too. (*To* TOM) She was an actress.

Remember of Bar's motor.

Did you know that? No, you didn't – that little detail was
absorbed into the great silence. Yes; travelling round the
country with the Charles Doran Company. Spotted by the
judge in the lounge of the Railway Hotel and within five
days decently wed and ensconced in the Hall here and
bugger poor aul' Charles Doran who had to face the rest of
rural Ireland without a Colleen Bawn! And a raving beauty
by all accounts. No sooner did Yeats clap eyes on her than a
sonnet burst from him – 'That I may know the beauty of
that form' – Alice'll rattle it off for you there. Oh, terrific
stuff. And O'Casey – haven't they told you that one? – poor
O'Casey out here one day ploughterin' after tennis balls and
spoutin' about the workin'-man when she appeared in the
doorway in there and the poor creatur' made such a
ramstam to get to her that he tripped over the Pope or Plato
or Shirley Temple or somebody and smashed his bloody
glasses! The more you think of it – all those
calamities – Chesterton's ribs, Hopkins's hand, O'Casey's
aul' specs – the County Council should put up a sign outside
that room – Accident Black Spot – shouldn't they? Between
ourselves, it's a very dangerous house, Professor.

TOM: What have you got against me, Eamon?

EAMON: And of course you'll have chapters on each of the
O'Donnell forebears: Great Grandfather – Lord Chief
Justice; Grandfather – Circuit Court Judge; Father – simple
District Justice; Casimir – failed solicitor. A fairly rapid
descent; but no matter, no matter; good for the book;
failure's more lovable than success. D'you know, Professor,
I've often wondered: if we had had children and they
wanted to be part of the family legal tradition, the only
option open to them would have been as criminals,
wouldn't it? (*Offering the bottle*) There's enough here for
both of us. No? (*He pours a drink for himself.*) After we went
upstairs last night, Alice and I, we had words, as they say.
She threw a book at me. And I struck her. You've noticed
her cheek, haven't you? No one else here would dream of
commenting on it; but you did, didn't you? And she didn't
tell you, did she? Of course she didn't. That's why she's

295

Crystal Fox

similar to Wedding Day Speech p. 274

freezing me. But she'll come round. It'll be absorbed.
Duty'll conquer.

TOM: I don't want to hear about your –

EAMON: What have I got against you?

TOM: Yes. You're the only member of the family who has
been . . . less than courteous to me since I came here. I
don't know why that is. I guess you resent me for some
reason.

(EAMON *considers this. He is not smiling now.*)

EAMON: Nervous; that's all. In case – you'll forgive me – in case
you're not equal to your task. In case you'll loot and run.
Nervous that all you'll see is – (*Indicates the croquet
game*) – the make-believe.

(JUDITH *enters the study. As she does, the phone rings. She
answers it.*)

EAMON: No, I don't resent you, Professor. I'm sure you're an
honest recorder. I'm nervous of us; we don't pose to our
best advantage.

JUDITH: Casimir!

CASIMIR: Hello?

CLAIRE: I have you on the run now.

CASIMIR: You certainly have not.

JUDITH: Phone, Casimir!

(*His usual response to this.*)

CASIMIR: The phone! – Helga – that'll be Helga – sorry – sorry –
excuse me – sorry –

(*As he rushes into the study he trips on the step.*)

CASIMIR: I beg your pardon – forgive me –

(*He rushes on in.*)

CLAIRE: You play for him until he comes back, Willie.

WILLIE: Me?

CLAIRE: There's nothing to it.

WILLIE: Aw, g'way out of that.

CLAIRE: Come on. You start over there.

WILLIE: Sure I mean to say –

CLAIRE: You aim for that post first and then you drive the ball
through the hoop over in that far corner.

CASIMIR: Hello? Hello? Hello?

296

(WILLIE *looks round at the others. He is embarrassed and afraid of being laughed at – particularly by* EAMON – *so he laughs foolishly.*)

WILLIE: Me playing croquet – and nothing to play with! Jaysus! Sure I never even seen the game in my –

CLAIRE: You've been watching us, haven't you? (*Thrusts a mallet into his hand.*) Go on! All you do is hit the ball. It's very simple.

WILLIE: All the same you feel a bit of an eejit – (*To* EAMON) They have me playing croquet now, Eamon! Without balls nor nothin'! Jaysus!

EAMON: Go ahead, William. Take the plunge. Submit to baptism. You'll never look back.

WILLIE: I couldn't –

CLAIRE: If you're going to play, will you play!

CASIMIR: Halloh? Halloh? Helga? Wer spricht dort, bitte? (WILLIE *hesitates. Then suddenly flings off his jacket, spits on his hands and rubs them together.*)

WILLIE: Right – right – I'll play – indeed and I'll play – where's the ball? – Give us a mallet – out of my road – where do I begin? Let me at it.
(*As before keep up the dialogue during the* CLAIRE–WILLIE *game.* JUDITH, *who has been tidying in the study, now comes out.*)

EAMON: How is he?

JUDITH: All right. I think. It might be just the heat. (*He gives her his glass.*) What about you?
(*He looks around – finds another.*)

EAMON: Here we are.

CLAIRE: Very good, Willie. You're getting the hang of it.

WILLIE: Am I? By Jaysus maybe I am too.
(EAMON *sits beside* JUDITH. *She is aware he is looking at her.*)

JUDITH: It's almost warm. (*Pause.*) I get sleepy if I take more than one glass. (*Pause.*) This must be my third today.
(ALICE *moves in her seat.*)

ALICE: Oh, that's very nice.

JUDITH: She's got older looking.

EAMON: Yes.

297

JUDITH: Has it become a real problem?

EAMON: When is a problem a real problem?

JUDITH: I suppose when you can't control it.

EAMON: She was fine until November, dry for almost eighteen months. Since then she's been in hospital twice. And I knew this trip would be a disaster.

JUDITH: I tried to talk to her last night –

EAMON: About her drinking?

JUDITH: No, no; about London. I was suggesting she get a job. She said none of us was trained to do anything. And she's right – we're not. Anyhow she cut me off. But she was always closer to Claire; and Casimir, of course.

EAMON: We live in a damp basement flat about half the size of the morning-room. I'm out all day and a lot of nights. It's a very lonely life for her. You'll miss Claire.

JUDITH: Yes.

EAMON: She won't be far away.

JUDITH: That's true.

EAMON: Just you and Father.

JUDITH: And Uncle George.

EAMON: And Uncle George.

JUDITH: Yes.

EAMON: It'll be a quiet house.

JUDITH: We manage.

WILLIE: Go on – go on – go on – go on.

EAMON: You said that morning you'd marry me.

JUDITH: We manage because we live very frugally. There's Father's pension; and I get some money from letting the land; and I grow all the vegetables we use; and I enjoy baking –

EAMON: Why did you change your mind?

JUDITH: So that apart from doctor's bills the only expenses we have are fuel and electric and the phone. And I'm thinking of getting rid of the phone. It's used very little anyhow.

EAMON: You never told me why.

WILLIE: You missed it! You missed it!

CLAIRE: I did not!

WILLIE: You weren't within a bloody mile of it! Ha-ha-ha-ha.

298

JUDITH: And I have Willie. I don't think I could manage
without Willie's help. Yes, I probably could. Yes, of course
I would. But he's the most undemanding person I know.
Some intuitive sense he has: he's always there when I want
him. And everything he does is done so simply, so easily,
that I almost take him for granted.

EAMON: Judith, I—

(*She closes her eyes and her speech becomes tense and deliberate,
almost as if she were talking to herself.*)

JUDITH: Listen to me, Eamon. I get up every morning at 7.30
and make breakfast. I bring Father his up first. Very often
the bed's soiled so I change him and sponge him and bring
the clothes downstairs and wash them and hang them out.
Then I get Uncle George his breakfast. Then I let the hens
out and dig the potatoes for the lunch. By that time Claire's
usually up so I get her something to eat and if she's in one
of her down times I invent some light work for her to do,
just to jolly her along, and if she's in one of her high times
I've got to try to stop her from scrubbing down the house
from top to bottom. Then I do out the fire, bring in the
turf, make the beds, wash the dishes. Then it's time to
bring Father up his egg-flip and shave him and maybe
change his clothes again. Then I begin the lunch. And so it
goes on and on, day after day, week after week, month after
month. I'm not complaining, Eamon. I'm just telling you
my routine. I don't even think of it as burdensome. But it
occupies every waking moment of every day and every
thought of every day. And I know I can carry on—happily
almost, yes almost happily—I know I can keep going as long
as I'm not diverted from that routine, as long as there are
no intrusions on it. Maybe it's an unnatural existence. I
don't know. But it's my existence—here—now. And there is
no end in sight. So please don't intrude on it. Keep out of
it. Now. Altogether. Please.

(*She lights a cigarette. Pause.*)

EAMON: Whatever the lady wants.

(TOM *joins them.* EAMON *rises and flashes a radiant smile at
him.*)

[handwritten margin note: ✳ Sounds like Chekhov]

299

EAMON: *Semper permanemus.* (*Almost into Tom's face as he shuffles past him.*) 'Ba-doo-be-da-da-da-ba-dab . . .'
(*TOM ignores him. EAMON picks up an empty wine bottle and examines it with excessive interest.*)

TOM: I've some packing to do. Thank Casimir for lunch, will you?

JUDITH: Yes.

TOM: I'd be careful of that sun. You should have your head covered.
(*He goes off right. WILLIE is down on his hunkers, fanning an imaginary ball through an imaginary hoop.*)

WILLIE: Come on, my wee darling, come on, come on, come on, another inch, another wee fraction – And it's through! I've won! I've won!
(*He is elated with his triumph. His elation is genuine – not part of the make-believe. And his triumph has given him a confidence. He reaches for his jacket and swaggers off the court with great assurance.*)

CLAIRE: It's not over yet.

WILLIE: Over! Finished! You're bet! Pack it in! I won, Eamon!

CLAIRE: I've one more shot –

WILLIE: Bet to the ropes! Your tongue's hanging out! Throw in the towel! Aul' Slooghter won hands down! Up the back shore boys!

CLAIRE: Watch this, Willie.

WILLIE: I'm watching nothing! The game's over! (*To EAMON*) What do you make of that, lad, eh?

EAMON: 'So deep is the n-n-n-n-night . . .'

CLAIRE: It's through, Willie.

WILLIE: Takes an aul' Diver every time!
(*ALICE is awakened by the noise. WILLIE pursues EAMON.*)

WILLIE: Never had a mallet in my hand before! Never stood on a croquet court before! Bloody good, eh?

EAMON: 'Terrific'. (*He gives one of Casimir's grins.*) A real insider now, Willie.

WILLIE: Give us a slug of something there – I'm as dry as a lime-kiln. What's in that?
(*EAMON hands him the empty wine bottle.*)

EAMON: Here.

WILLIE: Jaysus, that's empty!

EAMON: Imagine it's full. Use your peasant talent for fantasy, man.

(CASIMIR *has finished his call. He comes outside. He is uneasy but tries to hide it.*)

CASIMIR: Well. That's that job done. Glad to get that off my mind. What's been happening out here?

JUDITH: Did you get through?

CASIMIR: Little Heinrich I was speaking to actually – he's the baby – he's seven – little Heinrich. Helga's out at one of her SG meetings. Ha-ha.

ALICE: What's her SG?

CASIMIR: The Spiritualisten Gruppe – she's a spiritualist, Helga – table-rapping, seances, all that stuff – total believer. They meet every fortnight; and they're so passionate about it – oh, my goodness, you've no idea how passionate. I pretend I'm sympathetic – you know – domestic harmony – ha-ha. So that's where she is now – at her SG meeting.

JUDITH: I'm sure Heinrich misses you.

CASIMIR: Oh yes – oh yes. But the line was bad. And the trouble is, you see, the trouble is his English is as bad as my German – if that's possible! No problem, no problem at all when we're together – I mean we can smile and make signs and stagger on; but it's so difficult on the phone. And of course Helga's right – I mean they've got to be a little German family, haven't they? After all they're German, aren't they? So. Yes, they're all fine, thank goodness. Fine. He said to tell you all 'Grüsse' – that's the German for – for 'regards' – 'salutations' – oh, he's a very intelligent young man; very independent; very self-contained. I really must make one more big effort with my German.

JUDITH: Time we cleared this mess up.

CASIMIR: No, no; not yet. I've a great treat for all of you – Anna's tape!

ALICE: I forgot about that.

CASIMIR: Could you all gather round and I'll play the tape

301

Anna sent me last Christmas. Messages for everybody! A
real, real treat!

WILLIE: Maybe I should go and leave yous to –

CASIMIR: Go? For heaven's sake! I'd be deeply offended if you
left. And so would Anna.

(*He begins to arrange the seats in a wide arc facing out. The
others help him and begin picking up the remains of the picnic.
As they do this work the following passages overlap.*)

JUDITH: (*To* CLAIRE) What tape is this?

CLAIRE: I don't know. Never heard of it.

ALICE: (*To* WILLIE) How did it go?

WILLIE: What?

ALICE: That mad game you were playing.

WILLIE: I won.

ALICE: How do you know when you lose?

CASIMIR: Would you sit here, Eamon?

EAMON: Anywhere you like.

CASIMIR: Splendid. Where's Tom?

JUDITH: Gone to do some packing. He said thank you for the
lunch.

CASIMIR: I don't suppose he'd be very interested. (*As he
switches tapes.*) Disposing of you temporarily, Claire. But
don't worry – we'll reinstate you.

(*Everyone is in position.* CASIMIR *stands before them, the
cassette in his hand. He is happy to be master of ceremonies.*)

CASIMIR: Good. Fine. Splendid. Are we all settled? Well,
before I begin, may I explain to our guest here –

CLAIRE: Who's the guest?

ALICE: I'm the guest.

CASIMIR: Willie's our guest – and a very welcome guest he is,
too. (ALICE *claps.*) And I just wish to explain to him that
little Anna joined the convent twenty years ago, when she
was only seventeen –

ALICE: Eighteen.

CASIMIR: – and that apart from one visit home she's been in
Africa ever since; so that her knowledge of our lives is
perhaps slightly – hasn't kept pace perhaps with the way –

ALICE: For God's sake just play it, Casimir.

302

CASIMIR: Yes. Ah. Yes. Play it. Indeed I –

JUDITH: Shhhh!

CLAIRE: What?

JUDITH: Listen! (*They all listen for a moment.*) Sorry. Thought I heard Father. Go ahead.

CASIMIR: Should I get Uncle George out?

ALICE: Casimir!

CASIMIR: Sorry – sorry – no point at all, is there? Yes. Are we all ready? Splendid. Sister John Henry. Little Anna.
(*He places the cassette on the lawn and switches it on. Anna's voice is a child's voice. She speaks slowly and distinctly as if she were reading from a school-book.*)

ANNA: Hello Daddy and Judith and Alice and Casimir and little Claire.

ALICE: Hello, Anna.

ANNA: This is Anna speaking to you all the way from St Joseph's mission in Kuala in Zambia. I hope you are all together when this is being played because I am imagining you all sitting before a big log fire in the drawing-room – Daddy spread out and enjoying his well-earned relaxation after his strenuous day in court and the rest of you sitting on the rug or around the Christmas tree in the north window.
(*ALICE has been trying to attract Claire's attention – she wants her glass refilled. But CLAIRE does not notice her. Finally she has to whisper: –*)

ALICE: Claire.

CASIMIR: Shhh.

ALICE: Just a drop.
(*CLAIRE fills the glass.*)

ANNA: How are you all? May I wish each and every one of you – and you, too, dear Nanny – are you there, Nanny?

ALICE: Sorry, sister.

ANNA: – may I wish you all a holy and a happy Christmas and all of God's peace and content for the New Year.

ALICE: Amen.

ANNA: Later in the tape Reverend Mother who is here beside me will say a few words to you and after that you will hear

303

my school choir singing some Irish songs that I have taught them –

ALICE: God!

ANNA: – and some African songs they have taught me.

ALICE: Good God!

ANNA: I hope you will enjoy them. But first I wish to speak to my own dear Daddy. How are you, Daddy? I ought to be cross with you for never writing to me but I know how busy you always are providing for us, and Judith tells me in her letters that you are in very good health. So thank God for that.

(FATHER *enters the study. An emaciated man; eyes distraught; one arm limp; his mouth pulled down at one corner. A grotesque and frightening figure. He is dressed only in pyjamas. The tops are buttoned wrongly and hang off his shoulders; the bottoms about to slip off his waist. He moves very slowly – one step at a time – through the study. He is trying to locate where Anna's voice is coming from – his distraught eyes are rolling round the room. When he speaks his voice is barely audible.*)

FATHER: Anna?

ANNA: But before I go any further, I'm going to play the violin for you – a little piece you always liked me to play for you: The Gartan Mother's Lullaby. Do you remember it?

FATHER: (*Slightly louder*) Anna?

ANNA: So this is my Christmas present to you, my dear Daddy. I hope you like it.

(*She plays a few bars of the music – the playing of a child. Now* FATHER *is almost at the study door. He raises his head and emits an almost-animal roar.*)

FATHER: Annaaaaaaaaaaaa!

(*The listeners outside do not react for a second. Then they panic.* ALICE *grabs the cassette to switch it off – and instead turns the volume up so that the tape's scream and* FATHER's *roar overlap for a few seconds. They all leap to their feet – chairs are overturned – but seem to be incapable of action.* CASIMIR *is on his knees, transfixed, immobile.* CLAIRE *is on the point of hysteria.* FATHER's *roar stops. Saliva is dribbling from his mouth. He begins to sink to the ground.* EAMON, *who is furthest away from him, is the first to move. He runs to* FATHER *and catches him as he collapses so that they both sink to the ground together. Now the tape is silenced.* EAMON *screams at the others – screams as if his own life depended on it.*)

EAMON: Doctor! Call the doctor! For Christ's sake, will someone call the doctor!

Black-out

ACT THREE

Early afternoon two days later.

The seats and deck-chairs as before.

EAMON *is sitting on the step.* TOM *is changing the film in his camera.* CASIMIR, *his hands behind his back, is restlessly pacing round the perimeter of the tennis-court.*

All three are dressed in lounge suits – they have recently returned from Father's funeral.

We can hear CLAIRE *playing the piano – Sonata No. 2 in B flat minor, Op. 35, middle section of Third Movement (i.e. portion between 'Dead March' statements – omit 'Dead March'). It will be necessary to repeat this music which runs up to the entrance of* ALICE *and* JUDITH.

CASIMIR: (*Pacing*) He was by no means a skilful tennis player, Father, but oh my goodness he was very consistent and very determined. (*Halts.*) Alice and I would be over there and he would be here. And before he served he always went through a long ritual of placing his toe precisely on the edge of the line (*He demonstrates*), moving it and adjusting it for maybe twenty seconds until he had it exactly where he wanted it – as if the whole game depended on the exact placing of his toe. (*Paces again.*) And of course this always sent Alice and me into fits of secret giggling, so that when he finally did serve, we were never able to return the ball and so he thought he was a much

305

better player than he really was! Yes. Wonderful, wasn't it? (*Halts.*) Oh but God help you if he caught you laughing – oh-ho-ho-ho. (*Paces again.*) Just about this time we should all have been sitting down at the wedding reception – (*Looks at watch.*) – yes, just about now. Funny, isn't it? The B flat minor Sonata – that was Grandfather O'Donnell's favourite. Probably because he actually heard Chopin play it.

TOM: Who heard Chopin?

CASIMIR: Grandfather. Haven't I told you that story?

TOM: No.

(CASIMIR *comes down stage.*)

CASIMIR: Oh, yes. At a party in Vienna – a birthday party for Balzac. Everybody was there: Liszt and George Sand and Turgenev and Mendelssohn and the young Wagner and Berlioz and Delacroix and Verdi – and of course Balzac. Everybody. It went on for days. God knows why Grandfather was there – probably gate-crashed. Anyhow that's what Chopin played.

TOM: Your grandfather, Casimir?

CASIMIR: Grandfather O'Donnell; a great traveller; Europe every year.

TOM: But he wouldn't have been a contemporary of these people, would he?

CASIMIR: Would he not?

TOM: You must mean your great-grandfather, don't you?

CASIMIR: Do I? Great-grandfather O'Donnell then. Yes, you're right: he lived in Europe for six months one time to escape the fever that followed the famine here. A party in Vienna. The expression became part of the family language: anything great and romantic and exciting that had happened in the past or might happen in the future, we called it 'a party in Vienna' – yes. Very beautiful, isn't it? And there was another detail about that party: Chopin was playing that sonata and Balzac began to sing it and Grandfather told Balzac to shut up and Chopin said, 'Bravo, Irishman! Bravo!' Grandfather, of course, was thrilled. Isn't it beautiful, Eamon?

306

EAMON: Yes.

CASIMIR: (*Pacing again*) Chopin died in Paris, you know, and when they were burying him they sprinkled Polish soil on his grave. (*Pause.*) Because he was Polish. Did you notice how she went straight to the piano the moment we came back? Like a homing instinct; yes. I often wonder how far she might have gone if father hadn't thwarted her. Oh, I'm afraid he was more than naughty about that; oh, yes. Oh, I'm afraid he was adept at stifling things. I'm grateful to you for staying over, Tom.

TOM: Not at all.

CASIMIR: I appreciate it very much.

TOM: The least I could do.

CASIMIR: Is your father dead?

TOM: Yeah.

(CASIMIR *goes to him and very formally shakes his hand.*)

CASIMIR: I'm very, very sorry.

TOM: Thank you.

CASIMIR: It is a great loss.

TOM: Indeed.

CASIMIR: When did he die?

TOM: When I was three months old.

CASIMIR: Good Lord.

(*He begins pacing again.*)

TOM: A few details, Casimir; perhaps you could help me with them?

CASIMIR: Yes?

TOM: You mentioned that your mother played the piano – (*Producing notebook*) – where are we? – yeah – you talked about her playing a waltz at bedtime.

CASIMIR: The A flat major – oh, yes, that's *my* favourite; that's easily my favourite.

TOM: You're sure about that?

CASIMIR: That The Bedtime's the A flat major? Oh, I'm –

TOM: No, no; that your mother did play the piano.

(CASIMIR *halts.*)

TOM: Just that I inferred from something Judith said in passing that your mother did not in fact play.

CASIMIR: Judith said that?

TOM: What I understood was –

CASIMIR: You must have taken her up wrong, Tom. Oh, yes, Mother was a splendid pianist. By no means as talented as little Claire; but very competent. And a lovely singer. Oh, yes. Her favourite piece was a song called *Sweet Alice*. And Father hated it – hated it. 'Rubbish' he called it. 'Vulgar rubbish'. So that she never sang it when he was around. Oh, yes, she had lots of songs like that from her childhood. Do you know that song, Eamon?

EAMON: (*Sings*) 'Do you remember –'
(CASIMIR *joins him.*)
'. . . Sweet Alice, Ben Bolt?
Sweet Alice with hair so brown?'

CASIMIR: That's it – that's it! It's not insensitive of us to sing just after Father's funeral, is it? Ha-ha. Anyway. I remember when she'd sing *Sweet Alice* she seemed to become very, very young again and very, very beautiful, as if the song restored to her something she had lost, something that had withered in her . . . Oh, yes, she was a very talented pianist.

TOM: I'm sure I misunderstood Judith. It's of no importance. I'll check it again. And the other query was –
(*He consults his notebook again; hesitates; decides not to pursue the enquiry; closes the book and puts it in his pocket.*)

TOM: Yeah; that's okay; that can wait, too. No more problems.

CASIMIR: What was the other query?

TOM: Question mark after Yeats; that's all.

CASIMIR: What about him?

TOM: Just that you said you remember him sitting in –

CASIMIR: Oh my goodness yes; oh, he was just tremendous, Yeats, with those cold, cold eyes of his. Oh, yes, I remember Yeats vividly.

TOM: Sure.

CASIMIR: What's the question mark for?

TOM: It's of no significance. I think I got myself a little confused here, too. Doesn't matter.

CASIMIR: What's the confusion?

308

(*The music stops.* TOM *produces his notebook again.*)

TOM: Well, you were born on 1st April, 1939.

CASIMIR: Good heavens – don't I know! All Fools Day! Yes?

TOM: And Yeats died the same year. Two months earlier. I've
double checked it. (*He looks up from his notes.* CASIMIR *is
staring at him. Pause.*) I make little mistakes like that all the
time myself. My mother worked for the Bell Telephone
Company and until I went to high school I thought she
worked for a Mr Bell who was my uncle for God's sake . . .
It's a natural misunderstanding, that's all . . . I mean a man
like Yeats is a visitor to your home, a friend of the family,
you hear a lot of talk about him, and naturally after a time,
naturally you come to think you actually . . . I've some
correspondence to catch up with. Forgive me.

(*He goes into the study and off.* CASIMIR *grimaces at* EAMON.)

CASIMIR: Ha-ha. It was very kind of Tom to stay over. I
appreciate that very much. (*Begins pacing again.*) Father
would have been so pleased by that funeral today – no, not
pleased – gratified. The packed chapel; the music; that
young curate's fine, generous panegyric and he didn't know
Father at all, Judith says. Then down through the village
street – his village, his Ballybeg – that's how he thought of
it, you know, and in a sense it was his village. Did you
know that it used to be called O'Donnellstown? Yes, years
and years ago. How simple it all was this time, wasn't it?
You remember Mother's funeral, don't you? – all that
furtiveness, all that whispering, all those half-truths. We
didn't know until the very last minute would they allow her
a Christian burial at all because of the circumstances –
remember? But today it was – today was almost . . . festive
by comparison, wasn't it? Every shop shut and every blind
drawn; and men kneeling on their caps as the hearse
passed; and Nanny sobbing her heart out when the coffin
was being lowered – did you see her? – of course you
did – you were beside her. All that happened, didn't it,
Eamon? All that happened? Oh, yes, he would have been so
gratified.

EAMON: There are certain things, certain truths, Casimir, that

309

are beyond Tom's kind of scrutiny.

(*The same sonata music begins again.*)

CASIMIR: Oh, there are. Oh, yes, there are – aren't there? Yes – yes. I discovered a great truth when I was nine. No, not a great truth; but I made a great discovery when I was nine – not even a great discovery but an important, a very important discovery for me. I suddenly realized I was different from other boys. When I say I was different I don't mean – you know – good Lord, I don't for a second mean I was – you know – as they say nowadays 'homo-sexual' – good heavens I must admit, if anything, Eamon, if anything I'm – (*Looks around.*) – I'm vigorously hetero-sexual ha-ha. But of course I don't mean that either. No, no. But anyway. What I discovered was that for some reason people found me . . . peculiar. Of course I sensed it first from the boys at boarding-school. But it was Father with his usual – his usual directness and honesty who made me face it. I remember the day he said to me: 'Had you been born down there' – we were in the library and he pointed down to Ballybeg – 'Had you been born down there, you'd have become the village idiot. Fortunately for you, you were born here and we can absorb you.' Ha-ha. So at nine years of age I knew certain things: that certain kinds of people laughed at me; that the easy relationships that other men enjoy would always elude me; that – that – that I would never succeed in life, whatever – you know – whatever 'succeed' means –

EAMON: Casimir –

CASIMIR: No, no, please. That was a very important and a very difficult discovery for me, as you can imagine. But it brought certain recognitions, certain compensatory recognitions. Because once I recognized – once I acknowledged that the larger areas were not accessible to me, I discovered – I had to discover smaller, much smaller areas that were. Yes, indeed. And I discovered that if I conduct myself with some circumspection, I find that I can live within these smaller, perhaps very confined territories without exposure to too much hurt. Indeed I find that I can experience some happiness and perhaps give a measure of happiness, too. My great discovery. Isn't it so beautiful? (*Music.*) Somehow the hall doesn't exist without him. (*He begins pacing again.*) We must have a talk some time, Eamon.

IMPORTANT TRANSITION

EAMON: Yes.

CASIMIR: I don't think we ever had a talk, you and I, had we?

EAMON: I don't think so.

CASIMIR: I'd really like to talk to you because I think you—I think you understand . . . (*He gestures towards the house*) . . . what it has done to all of us.

EAMON: I don't know about that.

CASIMIR: Oh, yes, you do. I know you do. And you would tell me about your work and about London and I would tell you about my boys and about Hamburg. Will you, Eamon, please?

EAMON: Of course.

CASIMIR: Good. Great. Next time we meet. We even have our agenda all ready, haven't we? When I went up to see him the evening I arrived—was it only two days ago?—I stood looking down at him and I remembered a poem called *My Father Dying*, and the last lines go:

author?

TRADITIONS
TRANSITIONS
TRANSLATIONS

> 'But on any one
> of these nights soon
> for you, the dark will not crack with dawn
> And then I will begin
> with you that hesitant conversation
> going on and on and on.'

Something disquieting about that line 'going on and on and on', isn't there? Ha-ha.

(JUDITH *and* ALICE *enter.* CASIMIR *resumes pacing.* JUDITH *in a dark dress and carrying Alice's case.* ALICE *with coat and handbag. They deposit these things in the study.*)

ALICE: Thanks. Just leave it there.

JUDITH: When's your bus?

ALICE: We've another fifteen or twenty minutes yet.

JUDITH: Willie'll be here. He said he'll run you down.

ALICE: That'd be handy.

(They both come out to the lawn.)

ALICE: There's tea in there if you want it.

EAMON: None for me.

ALICE: Casimir?

CASIMIR: Not at the moment, thank you.

JUDITH: Did you get your flight fixed up?

CASIMIR: Mrs Moore did all the phoning, made all the arrangements. She was wonderful.

JUDITH: Does Helga know?

CASIMIR: I sent her a telegram. I should be home at midnight.

(EAMON touches ALICE's cheek with his index finger.)

EAMON: It's healed.

ALICE: Is it?

EAMON: Almost.

ALICE: I heal quickly.

EAMON: Sorry.

ALICE: I've packed your things.

EAMON: Thanks.

ALICE: Have you the tickets?

(He taps his jacket pocket.)

ALICE: I'll be glad to be home, if it's only to get a sleep. *(Aloud)* Tom hasn't left yet, has he?

JUDITH: He's in the library; some dates he wants to check again.

EAMON: 'Check', 'recheck', 'double-check', 'cross-check'.

JUDITH: He's talking about waiting over until the morning.

EAMON: Wasn't he lucky to be here for Father's death? I suppose he'll interpret that as 'the end of an epoch'.

JUDITH: Isn't it?

EAMON: Is it?

CASIMIR: He's from Chicago, he tells me. And I suspect he may be a very wealthy man: his uncle owns the Bell Telephone Company.

EAMON: He should never have been let set foot here.

JUDITH: He asked my permission.

EAMON: To pry?

JUDITH: To chronicle.

EAMON: Ah.

312

JUDITH: To record the truth.

EAMON: Better still. And you said, 'Go ahead, stranger'.

JUDITH: Is there something to hide?

(EAMON *spreads his hands.*)

JUDITH: Besides – it's my home.

(*Brief pause. Then quickly.*)

ALICE: It wasn't exactly the biggest funeral ever seen in Ballybeg, was it?

CASIMIR: Did you notice – the whole village closed down.

ALICE: For the minute it took the hearse to pass through. And as Sister Thérèse would say: 'The multitude in the church was a little empty, too.'

CASIMIR: I thought the requiem mass very moving.

ALICE: Until Miss Quirk cut loose. For God's sake did nobody tell her it wasn't the wedding?

JUDITH: She would have played anyway.

ALICE: But maybe not *This Is My Lovely Day.* Or is that one of the two pieces?

JUDITH: You might have got *Bless This House.*

ALICE: Father would not have been amused. Casimir, will you please stop prowling around?

CASIMIR: Oh. Sorry – sorry.

(*He sits – as if he were about to take off again.*)

ALICE: Who was the man standing just behind Willie at the graveside? – glasses, pasty-looking, plump, bald. I noticed him in the chapel, too; in the front pew on the men's side.

EAMON: Jerry.

ALICE: Who?

EAMON: Jerry McLaughlin.

ALICE: Who's Jerry Mc – ? Not – !

(EAMON *nods.*)

ALICE: For God's sake! But that man could be her father, Judith!

JUDITH: Easy.

(*The music stops suddenly. Silence.*)

ALICE: She couldn't have heard me, could she?

CLAIRE: Casimir!

313

CASIMIR: Hello-hello.

CLAIRE: What's the name of this?

ALICE: (*Relieved*) God.

(CASIMIR *leaps up*.)

CASIMIR: A test! She's testing me again! (*Shouts*.) Go ahead!
I'm ready! I'm waiting!

(*He moves upstage and stands poised, waiting. His eyes are shut
tight, etc. etc. as before. The music is the Ballade in A flat
major, Op. 47*.)

ALICE: You never told me he was like that.

JUDITH: Like what?

ALICE: That's an elderly man. (*To* EAMON) Did you know he
was like that?

CASIMIR: Good Lord – good Lord – good Lord – good Lord –

ALICE: She's only – what? – twenty-seven? – twenty-eight?

CASIMIR: I know it – I know it so well – but what is it? – what *is*
it? –

ALICE: Thank God the wedding's postponed for three months.
Maybe she'll come to her senses in the meantime. How
could the poor child marry a man like that, for God's sake?

JUDITH: I've no idea. (*Rises*.) There are some things we've got
to get settled before you all leave. (*Shouts*.) Claire, could
you come out for a few minutes?

ALICE: So that's Jerry McLaughlin.

EAMON: He looks older than he is.

JUDITH: Claire!

ALICE: O dear, dear, dear, dear, dear.

(*The music stops*. CASIMIR *comes downstage*.)

CASIMIR: (*To* EAMON) It's a sonata – a sonata – I know
that – either 58 or 59 – but which? – which?

EAMON: Don't ask me.

ALICE: (*To* EAMON) What age is he?

CASIMIR: Oh, Lord, I should know. Alice?

ALICE: What?

CASIMIR: 58 or 59?

ALICE: Is he serious?

CASIMIR: 59 – that's my guess.

ALICE: He's right.

CASIMIR: Am I?

ALICE: He must be that. Oh, the poor baby!

(CLAIRE *enters – she is not wearing mourning clothes.* ALICE *studies her face with anxious compassion.*)

CLAIRE: (*To* CASIMIR) Well?

CASIMIR: It's a sonata.

CLAIRE: Is it?

CASIMIR: Isn't it?

ALICE: Claire darling, that was just beautiful playing.

CLAIRE: Thanks.

CASIMIR: Yes; it's a sonata.

CLAIRE: So you've said.

CASIMIR: Is it not?

ALICE: Would you like to sit here, facing the sun?

CLAIRE: I'm fine. (*To* CASIMIR) You don't know!

JUDITH: Please, everybody –

CASIMIR: And it's either – and I'm not absolutely certain –

CLAIRE: You don't know!

JUDITH: Claire –

CASIMIR: It's either the –

JUDITH: May I – ?

CASIMIR: 58 – right?

JUDITH: Please may I speak?

CLAIRE: (*Whispers*) Wrong.

CASIMIR: (*Whispers*) 59?

JUDITH: Could I have a moment now that we're all here?

CASIMIR: Sorry – sorry. I beg your pardon, Judith.

CLAIRE: (*Whispers*) Completely wrong.

JUDITH: We haven't got all that much time. (*To* CASIMIR) Here's a seat.

(*He sits.* CLAIRE *grins at him behind Judith's back. He signals another answer. She rejects this, too. He is deflated.* ALICE *has not taken her eyes off* CLAIRE. *Now she goes to her.*)

ALICE: I got a glimpse of you coming down the aisle this morning and I had a sudden memory of you coming down on the morning of your first communion; and you looked exactly the same as you did then – not one day older – a beautiful little innocent child. Hasn't changed a bit, has she? (*She looks round for confirmation; but everyone is silent and waiting.*) What's wrong?

JUDITH: I would like to talk about what's to happen now that Father's gone – before you all leave.

ALICE: Sorry. Sorry. Of course. Go ahead.

JUDITH: I know he has left everything to the four of us – the house, the furnishings, the land. And the question is: what are we going to do?

ALICE: Well, as far as I'm concerned, my home's in London, Casimir's is in Hamburg, and this house is yours and Claire's. (*To* CASIMIR) Isn't that right?

CASIMIR: Oh, yes; oh, yes, indeed.

ALICE: Naturally we'll come back now and again. But the Hall must be your home. So the next time we're here we'll sign over to you whatever our share is – or better still have the papers drawn up and sent to us. The important thing is to have it all formal. (*To* CASIMIR) Don't you agree?

CASIMIR: I –

ALICE: (*To* JUDITH) I see no problem.

EAMON: What has Casimir to say?

CASIMIR: Me? Oh, yes, Alice is right, absolutely right. I mean I would hope to bring the boys over some time for a holiday – a short holiday – if I may. But I would be really happy for you to have it all, Judith – and Claire – oh, yes, very happy. You deserve it. It should be yours. It must be yours. Oh, yes.

ALICE: So. We're all agreed.

CASIMIR: One small thing: would it be possible – would you mind very much if I took that photo of mother in the silver frame – a keepsake, you know –

ALICE: That's the one on the drawing-room mantelpiece?

CASIMIR: Yes. It's really very small. But I would – I would really cherish that. If I may.

ALICE: And the sooner the place is in your names the better – before we all have a big row some day! And that's that. All settled. (*To* EAMON) Do we need to keep an eye on the time?

EAMON: Judith has other ideas, I think.

316

ALICE: Have you? What ideas?

JUDITH: Owning the place, going on living here – it's not as simple as it looks. In fact it's impossible.

ALICE: Why?

JUDITH: We can't afford it. You've forgotten – no, you've never known – the finances of this place. For the past seven years we've lived on Father's pension. That was modest enough. And now that's gone. The only other income is from the land and Willie takes that because no one else would; but that can't continue. So that from now on there's no money coming in. Last October when the storm lifted the whole roof off the back return I tried to get an overdraft from the bank. The manager was very sympathetic but he couldn't help – actually what he said was that the house was a liability.

EAMON: That's bloody –

JUDITH: Then I got a dealer down from Dublin to evaluate the library and some of the furniture. He offered me £70 for the grandmother clock and £90 for the whole library. So eventually Willie and I put up polythene sheets and nailed them to the rafters. And the floor in the morning-room has collapsed with dry-rot – haven't you seen it? – and every time there's heavy rain, we have to distribute – (*To* CLAIRE) how many is it? – seventeen buckets in the upstairs rooms to catch the water. And the only fire we had all last winter was in Father's bedroom. And on a day like this it looks so beautiful, doesn't it?
(*Short pause.*)

ALICE: Judith, God forgive us, we never for a second suspected –

JUDITH: That's just one side of the story.

ALICE: Oh but we can all help. We must. None of us is wealthy but the very least we can do is –

JUDITH: So there's no point in signing the place over to us – well over to me. I'm not going to go on living here. Maybe Claire –

CLAIRE: I'm getting out, too, amn't I? I'm getting married, amn't I?

317

ALICE: (*To* JUDITH) Where will you go? What will you do?

JUDITH: The first thing I'm going to do is take the baby out of the orphanage.

ALICE: Of course. Yes.

JUDITH: 'The baby' – he's seven now. (*To* CASIMIR) Do you know he's two days younger than your Heinrich? Where I'll go I haven't made up my mind yet. Willie has a mobile home just outside Bundoran. He has a lot of slot-machines around that area and he wants me to go there with him.

ALICE: That would be –

JUDITH: But he doesn't want the baby. So that settles that. Anyhow I've got to earn a living somehow. But the only reason I brought all this up is – what's to become of Uncle George?

EAMON: What you're saying is that after Claire's wedding – if you can wait that length – you're going to turn the key in the door and abandon Ballybeg Hall?

JUDITH: I'm asking –

EAMON: You know what will happen, don't you? The moment you've left the thugs from the village will move in and loot and ravage the place within a couple of hours. Is that what you're proposing? Oh, your piety is admirable.

JUDITH: I'm asking what's to become of Uncle George.

EAMON: Judith's like her American friend: the Hall can be assessed in terms of roofs and floors and overdrafts.

ALICE: Eamon –

EAMON: No, no; that's all it means to her. Well I know it's real worth – in this area, in this county, in this country. And Alice knows. And Casimir knows. And Claire knows. And somehow we'll keep it going. Somehow we'll keep it going. Somehow we'll –

ALICE: Please, Eamon.

(JUDITH *breaks down. Pause.*)

EAMON: Sorry . . . sorry . . . sorry again . . . Seems to be a day of public contrition. What the hell is it but crumbling masonry. Sorry. (*Short laugh.*) Don't you know that all that is fawning and forelock-touching and Paddy and shabby and greasy peasant in the Irish character finds a house like this irresistible? That's why we were ideal for colonizing.

318

Something in us needs this .(. . aspiration. Don't despise us – we're only hedgehogs, Judith. Sorry.
(*He goes to the gazebo.*)

ALICE: He hates going back to London. He hates the job. (*Pause.*) What is there to say? There's nothing to say, is there?

JUDITH: No.
(*Silence.* CLAIRE *rises and crosses the lawn. As she passes* CASIMIR: —)

CLAIRE: A ballade.

CASIMIR: Sorry?

CLAIRE: Ballade in A flat major.

CASIMIR: (*Indifferently*) Ah. Was it really? No, I'd never have got that. There you are. Never.
(*He gets up and begins his pacing. Pause.*)

ALICE: So the baby's seven now?

JUDITH: Eight next month.

ALICE: The woman in the flat above us has a little girl. She comes in to us every evening after school. Eamon buys her sweets. She's devoted to him. He's great with children.

JUDITH: Yes?

ALICE: Avril, Avril Harper. Lovely affectionate child.

JUDITH: What age is she?

ALICE: She's just eight.

JUDITH: They say that's a very interesting age.

ALICE: She's a very interesting child. And a very affectionate child.
(*The conversation dies again.* ALICE *rises.*)

CASIMIR: (*To* CLAIRE) There's still some clay on your shoes.

CLAIRE: Did you notice a wreath of red and yellow roses at the foot of the grave? That was from the children I taught last winter. There were five of them and they put their pocket money together to buy it. Wasn't that kind of them? And each of them came up to me in turn and shook my hand very formally and said how sorry they were. I asked them to be sure and visit me in my new home. They said they would. I made them promise. They said they would.
(*Another silence.*)

ALICE: Are you sure Willie's coming?

JUDITH: Yes; he knows; he'll be here.

ALICE: Time enough anyway.

CASIMIR: There was a telegram from the bishop, Judith.

JUDITH: Yes.

CASIMIR: Out on the hall table.

JUDITH: I saw it.

ALICE: What did it say?

CASIMIR: Deepest sympathy to you all and to George on your great loss – something like that.

JUDITH: We still haven't reached a decision about Uncle George.
(CASIMIR *suddenly stops pacing and exclaims – almost wails – in his panic.*)

CASIMIR: Oh my God!

CLAIRE: What?

CASIMIR: Oh good God!
(*He dashes into the study, as always tripping on the step and apologizing over his shoulder.*)

CASIMIR: Sorry – sorry – I beg your –
(*He rushes to the phone. His sudden departure shatters the mood.* EAMON *comes out of the gazebo. The others come together.*)

ALICE: What's wrong, Casimir?

EAMON: What happened?

JUDITH: Is he ill?

ALICE: I don't know. He suddenly bolted.

CLAIRE: Listen!

EAMON: Is he sick?

CLAIRE: Listen!

CASIMIR: Hello? Hello? Yes, Mrs Moore, it's me again. I'm afraid. I'm a nuisance, amn't I? That telegram I sent to Germany – Yes, yes, indeed the house will be lonely – Very nice sermon, indeed; very moving – I'll tell her that; of course I will; thank you very much –

ALICE: I thought he was going to be sick.

CASIMIR: That telegram I sent to Germany an hour ago, Mrs Moore – has it gone? Ah. Well, That's that – No, no, I'm not complaining – oh, no – I'm delighted, thank you, absolutely delighted, thank you . . .

(*He rings off and comes outside. He is thoroughly wretched. Everybody is staring at him. He manages one of his grins.*)

CASIMIR: Ha-ha. Oh good God.

ALICE: Is something wrong?

CLAIRE: What's the matter, Casimir?

CASIMIR: Sent a telegram to Helga. To let her know I'd be home tonight.

ALICE: And so you will.

CASIMIR: Yes.

JUDITH: What's wrong, Casimir?

CASIMIR: Tried to cancel it but it's gone. I told you she's a great believer in that spiritualist stuff – seances, ghosts, things – I told you that, didn't I? Yes, I did. Well, you see, I've only suddenly realized what I said in the telegram. What I said was: FATHER BURIED THIS MORNING ARRIVING HAMBURG MIDNIGHT TONIGHT. Ha-ha. Oh my God.

(*Their sympathy for his genuine anguish prevents them from laughing outright. But* CLAIRE *sniggers first – then* ALICE *– then they all collapse. And finally he joins them. Comments like 'Arriving Hamburg midnight tonight', 'I thought he was sick', 'He said "I'm absolutely delighted, Mrs Moore"', 'Poor Father in Germany'. In the middle of this release* UNCLE GEORGE *enters right in his usual manner.* ALICE *sees him first. She looks at him – then makes a sudden decision. She rushes to* EAMON.)

ALICE: Do me a favour, Eamon.

EAMON: What?

ALICE: A big favour – please.

EAMON: What is it?

ALICE: Uncle George – let us take him.

EAMON: To London?

ALICE: Please, Eamon.

EAMON: He wouldn't come.

ALICE: Let me try. Please.

EAMON: Would he come?

ALICE: (*Calls*) Uncle George!

(*He stops just as he is about to make his retreat. She goes to him.*)

ALICE: I want you to come to London with Eamon and me. You

wouldn't have to talk. You wouldn't ever have to say a word. But you'd be great company for me, just being there. I wouldn't be lonely if you were there with me.

(ALICE *reaches forward to catch his hand but withdraws again. Long pause. Then –*)

GEORGE: Haven't been in London since the year nineteen and ten; to be precise the week Edward the Seventh died. Saw it all. That's what *I* call a funeral.

ALICE: Will you come? Please.

(*Short pause.*)

GEORGE: Another visit's about due, I suppose. I'll pack.

(*He marches off the way he came.*)

ALICE: Thank you, Uncle George – thank you. (*Elated, to* EAMON) He's coming! (*To all*) He's coming with us to London! Do you mind?

EAMON: Where will he sleep?

ALICE: On the divan – anywhere – he won't mind – he never cared about his comfort. You're sure you don't mind?

EAMON: He'll be *my* keepsake.

(WILLIE *enters through the study.*)

WILLIE: Sorry I'm a bit late. Who needs a lift down to the bus?

ALICE: Thanks, Willie. I suppose we should start moving.

CASIMIR: Time enough yet, aren't we?

JUDITH: Anybody feel like something to eat?

WILLIE: No time for eating now.

JUDITH: (*To* EAMON) A cup of tea?

EAMON: No thanks.

JUDITH: A drink?

EAMON: Nothing.

ALICE: How long a delay have you in London before your Hamburg flight?

CASIMIR: An hour and a half.

ALICE: We'll stay with you at the airport and eat there.

JUDITH: (*To* WILLIE) Uncle George is going with Alice and Eamon.

WILLIE: Going where?

JUDITH: London.

WILLIE: You're joking me. Are you serious?

JUDITH: Yes.

WILLIE: Jaysus, he'll fair keep London in chat.

3 couples — cilu W. T.

> (*They are all seated again:* CLAIRE *close to* CASIMIR; WILLIE *beside* JUDITH; EAMON *on the ground at Alice's feet, his head resting against her leg; the three couples spread across the lawn. There is an unspoken wish to protract time, to postpone the final breaking up.* CASIMIR *picks up the cassette.*)

CASIMIR: What'll it be?

CLAIRE: Your pleasure.

CASIMIR: My pleasure – right.

CLAIRE: But not a test.

CASIMIR: Not a test; no more tests; just my pleasure.

> (*Pause.*)

WILLIE: They gave him a nice enough wee send off, didn't they?

JUDITH: Yes.

WILLIE: I was up in court before him once – did I ever tell you that one?

JUDITH: What was that?

WILLIE: First car I ever had. No tax, no insurance, no licence, no brakes, no nothing – buck all except that the damn thing kind of went. Jaysus. And I mind I swore a pack of lies to him.

JUDITH: Were you fined?

WILLIE: Let me off with a caution! He must have believed me. No, he didn't. Knew damn well I was a liar. He just pretended he believed me. Jaysus, he was a strange bird. How are you?

JUDITH: Slight headache. It's nothing.

WILLIE: I thought so – I was watching you in the chapel. Here.

JUDITH: What's that?

WILLIE: Aspirin. Got them on the way up.

JUDITH: Thanks. I'll take them later.

> (*Bedtime Waltz on the cassette.*)

WILLIE: I don't want to hustle yous; but if you're getting the 3.30 you'd need to start moving.

> (*Nobody hears him.*)

CASIMIR: You're too young to remember Mother singing that.

CLAIRE: Am I?

CASIMIR: Oh, yes; much too young.

CLAIRE: I think I remember her – I'm not sure. You'll come back again for my wedding, won't you?

CASIMIR: Wouldn't miss it for all the world. Three months time, isn't it?

CLAIRE: I wish it were tomorrow. I would love it would be tomorrow.

CASIMIR: Three months? Oh my goodness three months'll fly – just fly. We'll all be back again before you know. What's three months? Three months is nothing, nothing, nothing. (*Brief pause.*)

ALICE: What are you thinking?

EAMON: That in a way it's as difficult for me as it is for you.

ALICE: What is?

EAMON: Leaving; leaving for good. I know it's your home. But in a sense it has always been my home, too, because of granny and then because of you.

ALICE: I don't know what I feel. Maybe a sense of release; of not being pursued; of the possibility of – (*Short pause*) – of 'fulfilment'. No. Just emptiness. Perhaps maybe a new start. Yes, I'll manage.

EAMON: Because you're of that tradition.

ALICE: What tradition?

EAMON: Of discipline; of self-discipline – residual aristocratic instincts.

ALICE: I'm the alcoholic, remember.

EAMON: So was Uncle George – once.

ALICE: You and Judith always fight.

EAMON: No, we don't. When did you discover that?

ALICE: I've always known it. And I think it's because you love her. I think it's because you think you love her; and that's the same thing. No, it's even more disturbing for you. And that's why I'm not unhappy that this is all over – because love is possible only in certain contexts. And now that this is finished, you may become less unhappy in time.

EAMON: Have we a context?

ALICE: Let's wait and see.

324

WILLIE: Does nobody want to catch this bus?

JUDITH: Don't worry, Willie. They'll make it.

(CASIMIR *has been humming with the cassette. Now he stops.*)

CASIMIR: What you must all do – what you must all do very soon – is come to Hamburg for a holiday! Helga and I have some wonderful friends you'll enjoy meeting – novelists, poets, painters, musicians! – marvellous people! – and we'll have a great reunion of the whole family! It will be like old times! Everybody'll come next summer! Next summer in Hamburg!

EAMON: A party in Vienna.

CASIMIR: Yes, yes, yes indeed, Eamon! That's what it'll be – a party in Vienna!

(CLAIRE *switches off the cassette.*)

CLAIRE: (*Calmly*) I'm suddenly sick of Chopin – isn't that strange? Just suddenly sick of him. I don't think I'll ever play Chopin again.

(*Silence. Then* EAMON *begins to sing softly.*)

EAMON: 'Oh don't you remember Sweet Alice, Ben Bolt . . .'

WILLIE: I'm telling you, Eamon, that aul' bus isn't going to wait for you, you know.

ALICE: 'Sweet Alice with hair so brown . . .'

(EAMON *and* ALICE *sing together.*)

'She wept with delight when you gave her a smile
And trembled with fear at your frown . . .'

(*While they are singing the line above.*)

JUDITH: I keep thinking I hear sounds from that speaker.

(WILLIE *begins to rise.*)

WILLIE: I'll take it down now.

JUDITH: Don't touch it! (*Softer*) Not just now. Not just at this moment.

(CASIMIR *has walked round to* EAMON *and* ALICE *and sings with them. All three*:)

'In the old church yard in the valley, Ben Bolt
In a corner obscure and alone
They have fitted a slab of granite so grey
And sweet Alice lies under the stone . . .'

(*While they are singing,* UNCLE GEORGE *has entered the study.*

325

He puts his small case on the ground and his coat across a chair and sits with his hands on his lap. He has all the patience in the world. As he sings CASIMIR *glances over the house.* CLAIRE *begins to hum. One has the impression that this afternoon – easy, relaxed, relaxing – may go on indefinitely.*

WILLIE: I'm telling you – they're going to miss it!

JUDITH: No, they won't.

WILLIE: They're cutting it close then. Jaysus they're cutting it very close.

SINGERS: 'They have fitted a slab of granite so grey
And sweet Alice lies under the stone . . .'
(Before the song ends bring the lights down slowly to dark.)

▲▲▲

FAITH HEALER

▲▲▲

for Anne again

CHARACTERS

FRANK
GRACE
TEDDY

Faith Healer was first produced at the Longacre Theatre, New York, on 5 April 1979. The cast was as follows:

FRANK	James Mason
GRACE	Clarissa Kaye
TEDDY	Donal Donnelly

Direction	José Quintero

PART ONE

FRANK

The stage is in darkness. Brief pause.

Then out of this darkness comes FRANK's *incantation, 'Aberarder,
Aberayron . . .' At the end of the second line bring up lights very
slowly, first around him and then gradually on the whole set.
Throughout this opening incantation he is standing down stage left,
feet together, his face tilted upwards, his eyes shut tight, his hands in
his overcoat pockets, his shoulders hunched.**

*He is middle-aged; grey or greying; pale, lined face. The overcoat
is unbuttoned, the collar up at the back; either navy or black, and of
heavy-nap material; a good coat once but now shabby, stained,
slept-in. Underneath he is wearing a dark suit that is polished with
use; narrow across the shoulders; sleeves and legs too short. A soiled
white shirt. A creased tie. Vivid green socks.*

*Three rows of chairs – not more than fifteen seats in all – occupy
one third of the acting area stage left. These seats are at right-angles
to the audience.*

On the back drop is a large poster:

The Fantastic Francis Hardy

Faith Healer

One Night Only

*This poster is made of some fabric, linen perhaps, and is soiled and
abused.*

FRANK: (*Eyes closed*)
    Aberarder, Aberayron,

---

*Note: Stage directions have been kept to a minimum. In all four
parts the director will decide when and where the monologist sits,
walks, stands, etc.

Llangranog, Llangurig,
Abergorlech, Abergynolwyn,
Llandefeilog, Llanerchymedd,
Aberhosan, Aberporth . . .

All those dying Welsh villages. (*Eyes open.*) I'd get so tense
before a performance, d'you know what I used to do? As we
drove along those narrow, winding roads I'd recite the
names to myself just for the mesmerism, the sedation, of
the incantation –
Kinlochbervie, Inverbervie,
Inverdruie, Invergordon,
Badachroo, Kinlochewe,
Ballantrae, Inverkeithing,
Cawdor, Kirkconnel,
Plaidy, Kirkinner . . .

Welsh – Scottish – over the years they became
indistinguishable. The kirks or meeting-houses or
schools – all identical, all derelict. Maybe in a corner a
withered sheaf of wheat from a harvest thanksgiving of
years ago or a fragment of a Christmas decoration across a
window – relics of abandoned rituals. Because the people
we moved among were beyond that kind of celebration.

Hardly ever cities or towns because the halls were far too
dear for us. Seldom England because Teddy and Gracie
were English and they believed, God help them, that the
Celtic temperament was more receptive to us. And never
Ireland because of me –

I beg your pardon – *The Fantastic Francis Hardy, Faith
Healer, One Night Only.* (*A slight bow.*) The man on the
tatty banner. (*He takes off his overcoat, selects an end chair
from one of the rows, and throws the coat across it. This chair
and coat will be in the same position at the opening of Part
Four.*)

When we started out – oh, years and years ago – we used
to have *Francis Hardy, Seventh Son of a Seventh Son* across
the top. But it made the poster too expensive and Teddy
persuaded me to settle for the modest 'fantastic'. It was a
favourite word of his and maybe in this case he employed it

with accuracy. As for the Seventh Son – that was a lie. I was in fact the only child of elderly parents, Jack and Mary Hardy, born in the village of Kilmeedy in County Limerick where my father was sergeant of the guards. But that's another story . . .

The initials were convenient, weren't they? FH – Faith Healer. Or if you were a believer in fate, you might say my life was determined the day I was christened. Perhaps if my name had been Charles Potter I would have been . . . Cardinal Primate; or Patsy Muldoon, the Fantastic Prime Minister. No, I don't mock those things. By no means. I'm not respectful but I don't mock.

Faith healer – faith healing. A craft without an apprenticeship, a ministry without responsibility, a vocation without a ministry. How did I get involved? As a young man I chanced to flirt with it and it possessed me. No, no, no, no, no – that's rhetoric. No; let's say I did it . . . because I could do it. That's accurate enough. And occasionally it worked – oh, yes, occasionally it *did* work. Oh, yes. And when it did, when I stood before a man and placed my hands on him and watched him become whole in my presence, those were nights of exultation, of consummation – no, not that I was doing good, giving relief, spreading joy – good God, no, nothing at all to do with that; but because the questions that undermined my life then became meaningless and because I knew that for those few hours I had become whole in myself, and perfect in myself, and in a manner of speaking, an aristocrat, if the term doesn't offend you.

But the questionings, the questionings . . . They began modestly enough with the pompous struttings of a young man: *Am I endowed with a unique and awesome gift?* – my God, yes, I'm afraid so. And I suppose the other extreme was *Am I a con man?* – which of course was nonsense, I think. And between those absurd exaggerations the possibilities were legion. Was it all chance? – or skill? – or illusion? – or delusion? Precisely what power did I possess? Could I summon it? When and how? Was I its servant? Did

333

it reside in my ability to invest someone with faith in me or did I evoke from him a healing faith in himself? Could my healing be effected without faith? But faith in what? – in me? – in the possibility? – faith in faith? And is the power diminishing? You're beginning to masquerade, aren't you? You're becoming a husk, aren't you? And so it went on and on and on. Silly, wasn't it? Considering that nine times out of ten nothing at all happened. But they persisted right to the end, those nagging, tormenting, maddening questions that rotted my life. When I refused to confront them, they ambushed me. And when they threatened to submerge me, I silenced them with whiskey. That was efficient for a while. It got me through the job night after night. And when nothing happened or when something did happen, it helped me to accept that. But I can tell you this: there was one thing I did know, one thing I always knew right from the beginning – I always knew, drunk or sober, I always knew when nothing was going to happen.

Teddy. Yes, let me tell you about Teddy, my manager. Cockney. Buoyant. Cheerful. Tiny nimble feet. Dressed in cord jacket, bow-tie, greasy velour hat. I never knew much about his background except that he had been born into show business. And I never understood why he stayed with me because we barely scraped a living. But he had a devotion to me and I think he had a vague sense of being associated with something . . . spiritual and that gave him satisfaction. If you met him in a bar he'd hold you with those brown eyes of his. 'I've 'andled some of *the* most sensational properties in my day, dear 'eart, believe me. But I've threw 'em all up for Mr 'ardy 'ere, 'cos 'e is just the most fantastic fing you've ever seen.' And listening to him I'd almost forget what indeed he had given up to tour with us – a Miss Mulatto and Her Three Pigeons, and a languid whippet called Rob Roy who took sounds from a set of bagpipes. Humbling precedents, if I were given to pride. And he believed all along and right up to the end that somewhere one day something 'fantastic' was going to happen to us. 'Believe me, dear 'eart,' perhaps when we had barely enough petrol to take us to the next village, 'believe me, we are on the point of making a killing.' He was a romantic man. And when he talked about this killing, I had a fairy-tale image of us being summoned to some royal bedroom and learned doctors being pushed aside and I'd raise the sleeping princess to life and we'd be wined and dined for seven days and seven nights and sent on our way with bags of sovereigns. But he was a man of many disguises. Perhaps he wasn't romantic. Perhaps he knew that's what I'd think. Perhaps he was a much more perceptive man than I knew.

And there was Grace, my mistress. A Yorkshire woman. Controlled, correct, methodical, orderly. Who fed me, washed and ironed for me, nursed me, humoured me. Saved me, I'm sure, from drinking myself to death. Would have attempted to reform me because that was her nature, but didn't because her instincts were wiser than her impulses. Grace Dodsmith from Scarborough – or was it Knaresborough? I don't remember, they all sound so alike, it doesn't matter. She never asked for marriage and for all her tidiness I don't think she wanted marriage – her loyalty was adequate for her. And it was never a heady relationship, not even in the early days. But it lasted. A surviving relationship. And yet as we grew older together I thought it wouldn't. Because that very virtue of hers – that mulish, unquestioning, indefatigable loyalty – settled on us like a heavy dust. And nothing I did, neither my bitterness nor my deliberate neglect nor my blatant unfaithfulness, could disturb it.

We'd arrive in the van usually in the early evening. Pin up the poster. Arrange the chairs and benches. Place a table inside the door for the collection. Maybe sweep the place out. Gracie'd make tea on the primus stove. Teddy'd try out his amplifying system. I'd fortify myself with some drink. Then we'd wait. And wait. And as soon as darkness fell, a few would begin to sidle in –

Penllech, Pencader,
Dunvegan, Dunblane,

Ben Lawers, Ben Rinnes,
Kirkliston, Bennane . . .

Teddy and his amplifying system: I fought with him about
it dozens of times and finally gave in to him. Our row was
over what he called 'atmospheric background music'. When
the people would have gathered Teddy would ask them – he
held the microphone up to his lips and assumed a special,
reverential tone – he'd ask them to stay in their seats while I
moved among them. 'Everybody'll be attended to, dear
'eart. Relax. Take it easy. And when Mr 'ardy gets to you,
no need to tell 'im wot's bovvering you – Mr 'ardy knows.
Just trust 'im. Put yourself in 'is 'ands. And God bless you
all. And now, dear 'eart – Mr 'ardy, Faif 'ealer!' At which
point I'd emerge – and at the same moment Teddy'd put on
his record.

And as I'd move from seat to seat, among the crippled
and the blind and the disfigured and the deaf and the
barren, a voice in the style of the thirties crooned Jerome
Kern's song:

Lovely, never, never change,
Keep that breathless charm,
Won't you please arrange it,
'Cause I love you
Just the way you look tonight.

Yes; we were always balanced somewhere between the
absurd and the momentous.

(*Moving through seats*) And the people who came – what is
there to say about them? They were a despairing people.
That they came to me, a mountebank, was a measure of their
despair. They seldom spoke. Sometimes didn't even raise
their eyes. They just sat there, very still, assuming that
I divined their complaints. Abject. Abased. Tight. Longing
to open themselves and at the same time fearfully herding
the anguish they contained against disturbance. And they
hated me – oh, yes, yes, yes, they hated me. Because by
coming to me they exposed, publicly acknowledged, their
desperation. And even though they told themselves they
were here because of the remote possibility of a cure, they

336

knew in their hearts they had come not to be cured but for confirmation that they were incurable; not in hope but for the elimination of hope; for the removal of that final, impossible chance – that's why they came – to seal their anguish, for the content of a finality.

And they knew that I knew. And so they defied me to endow them with hopelessness. But I couldn't do even that for them. And they knew I couldn't. A peculiar situation, wasn't it? No, not peculiar – eerie. Because occasionally, just occasionally, the miracle would happen. And then – panic – panic – panic! Their ripping apart! The explosion of their careful calculations! The sudden flooding of dreadful, hopeless hope! I often thought it would have been a kindness to them not to go near them.

And there was another thing about them. When Teddy was introducing me, I would look at them and sometimes I got a strange sense that they weren't there on their own behalf at all but as delegates, *legati*, chosen because of their audacity; and that outside, poised, mute, waiting in the half-light, were hundreds of people who held their breath while we were in the locality. And I sometimes got the impression, too, that if we hadn't come to them, they would have sought us out.

We were in the north of Scotland when I got word that my mother had had a heart attack. In a village called Kinlochbervie, in Sutherland, about as far north as you can go in Scotland. A picturesque little place, very quiet, very beautiful, looking across to the Isle of Lewis in the Outer Hebrides; and we were enjoying a few days rest there. Anyhow, when the news came, Teddy drove me down to Glasgow. Gracie wanted to come with me and couldn't understand when I wouldn't take her. But she used her incomprehension as fuel for her loyalty and sent me off with a patient smile.

It was my first time home in twenty years. My father had retired and was living in a housing estate outside Dublin. When he opened the door he didn't recognize me – I had to tell him who I was. Then he shook my hand as if I were an

337

acquaintance and led me up to the bedroom.

She was exactly as I remembered her – illness hadn't ravaged her. Sleeping silently. Her skin smooth and girlish, her chin raised as if in expectation. Jesus, I thought, O my Jesus, what am I going to do?

'She looks nice,' he said.

'Yes,' I said. 'She looks great.'

He cleared his throat.

'She passed away quietly. You missed her by approximately one hour and ten minutes,' as if he were giving evidence. And then he cried.

And I felt such overwhelming relief that when he cried, I cried easily with him.

Twelve years later I was back in Ireland again; with Teddy and Gracie. Things had been lean for a long time. Or as Teddy put it, 'If we want to eat, we've got to open up new territory, dear 'eart. You've cured 'em all 'ere. Come on – let's go to the lush pickings of Ireland.' And I agreed because I was as heartsick of Wales and Scotland as they were. And the whiskey wasn't as efficient with the questions as it had been. And my father had died in the meantime. And I suppose because I always knew we would end up there. So on the last day of August we crossed from Stranraer to Larne and drove through the night to County Donegal. And there we got lodgings in a pub, a lounge bar, really, outside a village called Ballybeg, not far from Donegal Town.

There was no sense of home-coming. I tried to simulate it but nothing stirred. Only a few memories, wan and neutral. One of my father watching me through the bars of the day-room window as I left for school – we lived in a rented house across the street. One of playing with handcuffs, slipping my hands in and out through the rings. One of my mother making bread and singing a hymn to herself: 'Yes, heaven, yes, heaven, yes, heaven is the prize.' And one of a group of men being shown over the barracks – I think they were inspectors from Dublin – and my father saying, 'Certainly, gentlemen, by all means, gentlemen, anything

338

you say, gentlemen.' Maybe one or two other memories.
They evoked nothing.

When we came downstairs to the lounge in the pub we
got caught up in the remnants of a wedding party – four
young men, locals, small farmers, whose friend had just
gone off on his honeymoon a few hours earlier. Good suits.
White carnations. Dark, angular faces. Thick fingers and
black nails. For a while they pretended to ignore us. Then
Ned, the biggest of them, asked bluntly who we were and
what we were. Teddy told them. 'Dear 'eart . . . the . . .
most . . . sensational . . . fantastic.' And either at the
extravagance of the introduction or because of an unease
they suddenly exploded with laughter and we were
embraced. We formed a big circle and drank and chatted.
Gracie sang – 'Ilkley Moor'? – something like that. Teddy
entertained them with tales of our tours ranging from the
outrageous to the maudlin and ended with his brown eyes
moist with tears: 'Dear 'earts, the insights it 'as given me
into tortured 'umanity.' And I told myself that I was indeed
experiencing a home-coming. All irony was suspended.

Then suddenly a man called Donal who had scarcely
spoken up to this thrust a bent finger in front of my face
and challenged, 'Straighten that, Mr Hardy.' And the bar
went still.

I caught the finger between the palms of my hands and
held it there and looked into his face. Already he was
uneasy – he wanted to withdraw the challenge. He began to
stammer how the accident happened – something about a
tractor, a gearbox, a faulty setting. And as he spoke I
massaged the finger. And when he stopped talking I opened
my hands and released him. The finger was whole . . .

Badrallach, Kilmore,
Llanfaethlu, Llanfechell,
Kincardine, Kinross,
Loughcarron, Loughgelly . . .

We caroused right through the night. Toasts to the landlord
who claimed he met my father once and as the night went
on that they were close friends. Toasts to Teddy and

339

Gracie. Toasts to my return. To Donal's finger. Toasts to the departed groom and his prowess. To the bride and her fertility. To the rich harvest – the corn, the wheat, the barley. Toasts to all Septembers and all harvests and to all things ripe and eager for the reaper. A Dionysian night. A Bacchanalian night. A frenzied, excessive Irish night when ritual was consciously and relentlessly debauched.

Then sometime before dawn McGarvey was remembered. Their greatest, their closest friend McGarvey who in his time had danced with them and drunk with them and built roads with them and cut turf with them. McGarvey who ought to have been best man that day – my God, who else? – and who wasn't even at the wedding reception. And as they created him I saw McGarvey in my mind, saw his strained face and his mauve hands and his burning eyes, crouched in his wheelchair and sick with bitterness. Saw him and knew him before Teddy in his English innocence asked why he wasn't there; before Ned told us of the fall from the scaffolding and the paralysis. Saw him and recognized our meeting: an open place, a walled yard, trees, orange skies, warm wind. And knew, knew with cold certainty that nothing was going to happen. Nothing at all.

I stood at the window and watched them set off to fetch McGarvey. Four of them getting into a battered car; now serious and busy with good deeds; now being polite to one another, holding doors open, you sit in front, no you, no you. Then they were gone, the car sluggish under their weight.

Teddy lay slumped in a stupor in a corner. Gracie went round the tables, emptying ashtrays, gathering glasses and leaving them on the counter, straightening chairs. No intimation whatever of danger. I suggested she should go to bed and she went off. Why wouldn't she? – the housework was finished.

(*He comes right down, walking very slowly, until he is as close as he can be to the audience. Pause.*)

The first Irish tour! The great home-coming! The new beginning! It was all going to be so fantastic! And there I

340

am, pretending to subscribe to the charade. (*He laughs.*)
Yes; the restoration of Francis Hardy. (*Laughs again.*)

But we'll come to that presently. Or as Teddy would
have put it: Why don't we leave that until later, dear 'eart?
Why don't we do that? Why not?

Indeed.

(*He looks at the audience for about three seconds. Then quick
black.*)

PART TWO

GRACE

We discover GRACE HARDY *on stage, the same set as Part One,
with the rows of seats removed. She is sitting on a wooden chair
beside a small table on which are ashtrays, packets of cigarettes, the
remains of a bottle of whiskey, a glass.*

    *She is in early middle-age. Indifferent to her appearance and
barely concealing her distraught mental state. Smoking a
lot – sometimes lighting one cigarette from the other.*

GRACE: (*Eyes closed*)
    Aberarder, Aberayron,
    Llangranog, Llangurig,
    Abergorlech, Abergynolwyn,
    Penllech, Pencader,
    Llandefeilog, Llanerchymedd . . .
That most persistent of all the memories, (*Eyes open*) that
most persistent and most agonizing –

But I *am* getting stronger, I *am* becoming more
controlled – I'm sure I am. I measure my progress – a silly
index, I know, and he would certainly have scoffed at it –
but I can almost measure my progress by the number of
hours I sleep and the amount I drink and the number of
cigarettes I smoke. And, as they say, I've a lot to be
thankful for; I know I have. And I like living in London.

341

And the bedsitter's small but it's warm and comfortable.
And it's a pleasant walk to the library in Paddington where
I work four hours every morning. And on my way home, if
the day's fine, I usually go through the park. And at night I
listen to the radio or I read – oh, I read a lot – fiction,
romance, history, biography, whatever I take home with
me, whatever's handy; and I've begun to make a rug for the
hearth – I'll do a bit at that or maybe I'll try a new recipe or
read the paper or knit or – or – And on Thursday afternoons
I go to the doctor to get my pills renewed. He said to me
last week, he said to me, 'Of course you've had a traumatic
experience, Mrs Hardy; absolutely horrific. But it's
over – finished with. And you've really got to be stern with
yourself. You were a solicitor once, weren't you? Well,
what you must do now is bring the same mental rigour, the
same discipline to your recovery that you once brought to a
legal case.' And he looked so pleased with his analogy and
so clean and so pleasant and so efficient and, yes, so
innocent, sitting there behind his desk with his grey suit
and his college tie and his clear eyes and his gold pen
poised, and he meant so well and he was so patient and it
was all so simple for him; and I found myself nodding yes,
yes, yes to him, yes, yes; and I thought: That's how you
used to nod to Frank, too, especially in that last year – yes,
yes, yes, Frank, you know you can, Frank, I swear you
can – but he's watching me warily – nothing was simple for
him – he's watching me and testing me with his sly
questions and making his own devious deductions, probing
my affirmations for the hair crack, tuned for the least hint
of excess or uncertainty, but all the same, all the same
drawing sustenance from me – oh, yes, I'm sure of
that – finding some kind of sustenance in me – I'm
absolutely sure of that, because finally he drained me,
finally I was exhausted.

But I *am* making progress. And I suppose what I really
mean by that is that there are certain restricted memories
that I can invite now, that I can open myself fully to, like a
patient going back to solids. I can think about the night the

342

old farmer outside Cardiff gave him £200 for curing his limp – just handed him his wallet – and we booked into the Royal Abercorn and for four nights we lived like kings. And the weekend we spent one Easter walking in the Grampian mountains. I can think about that; yes, memories like that I can receive and respond to them. Because they *were* part of our lives together. But then as soon as I begin to open under them, just as soon as it seems that I'm beginning to come together again –

(*Eyes closed tight*) Abergorlech, Abergynolwyn,

    Llandefeilog, Llanerchymedd,

    Aberhosan, Aberporth . . .

It's winter, it's night, it's raining, the Welsh roads are narrow, we're on our way to a performance. (*Eyes open.*) He always called it a performance, teasing the word with that mocking voice of his – 'Where do I perform tonight?' 'Do you expect a performance in a place like this?' – as if it were a game he might take part in only if he felt like it, maybe because that was the only way he could talk about it. Anyhow Teddy's driving as usual, and I'm in the passenger seat, and he's immediately behind us, the Fantastic Francis Hardy, Faith Healer, with his back to us and the whiskey bottle between his legs, and he's squatting on the floor of the van – no, not squatting – crouched, wound up, concentrated, and happy – no, not happy, certainly not happy, I don't think he ever knew what happiness was – but always before a performance he'd be . . . in complete mastery – yes, that's close to it – in such complete mastery that everything is harmonized for him, in such mastery that anything is possible. And when you speak to him he turns his head and looks beyond you with those damn benign eyes of his, looking past you out of his completion, out of that private power, out of that certainty that was accessible only to him. God, how I resented that privacy! And he's reciting the names of all those dying Welsh villages – Aberarder, Aberayron, Llangranog, Llangurig – releasing them from his mouth in that special voice he used only then, as if he were blessing them or consecrating himself. And then, for him, I didn't exist. Many, many, many times I didn't exist for him. But before a performance this exclusion – no, it wasn't an exclusion, it was an erasion – this erasion was absolute: he obliterated me. Me who tended him, humoured him, nursed him, sustained him – who debauched myself for him. Yes. That's the most persistent memory. Yes. And when I remember him like that in the back of the van, God how I hate him again –

Kinlochbervie, Inverbervie,
Inverdruie, Invergordon,
Badachroo, Kinlochewe,
Ballantrae, Inverkeithing,
Cawdor, Kirkconnel,
Plaidy, Kirkinner . . .

(*Quietly, almost dreamily*) Kinlochbervie's where the baby's buried, two miles south of the village, in a field on the left-hand side of the road as you go north. Funny, isn't it, but I've never met anybody who's been to Kinlochbervie, not even Scottish people. But it *is* a very small village and very remote, right away up in the north of Sutherland, about as far north as you can go in Scotland. And the people there told me that in good weather it is very beautiful and that you can see right across the sea to the Isle of Lewis in the Outer Hebrides. We just happened to be there and we were never back there again and the week that we were there it rained all the time, not really rained but a heavy wet mist so that you could scarcely see across the road. But I'm sure it is a beautiful place in good weather. Anyhow, that's where the baby's buried, in Kinlochbervie, in Sutherland, in the north of Scotland. Frank made a wooden cross to mark the grave and painted it white and wrote across it *Infant Child of Francis and Grace Hardy* – no name, of course, because it was still-born – just *Infant Child*. And I'm sure that cross is gone by now because it was a fragile thing and there were cows in the field and it wasn't a real cemetery anyway. And I had the baby in the back of the van and there was no nurse or doctor so no one knew anything about it except Frank and Teddy and me. And there was no clergyman at

344

the graveside – Frank just said a few prayers that he made up. So there is no record of any kind. And he never talked about it afterwards; never once mentioned it again; and because he didn't, neither did I. So that was it. Over and done with. A finished thing. Yes. But I think it's a nice name, Kinlochbervie – a complete sound – a name you wouldn't forget easily . . . (*Tense again*) God, he was such a twisted man! With such a talent for hurting. One of his mean tricks was to humiliate me by always changing my surname. It became Dodsmith or Elliot or O'Connell or McPherson – whatever came into his head; and I came from Yorkshire or Kerry or London or Scarborough or Belfast; and he had cured me of a blood disease; and we weren't married – I was his mistress – always that – that was the one constant: 'You haven't met Gracie McClure, have you? She's my mistress,' knowing so well that that would wound me and it always did; it shouldn't have; I should have become so used to it; but it always did. And Teddy – Teddy wasn't just a fit-up man who was always in trouble with the police for pilfering but a devoted servant, dedicated acolyte to the holy man. It wasn't that he was simply a liar – I never understood it – yes, I knew that he wanted to hurt me, but it was much more complex than that; it was some compulsion he had to adjust, to refashion, to re-create everything around him. Even the people who came to him – they weren't just sick people who were confused and frightened and wanted to be cured; no, no; to him they were . . . yes, they were real enough, but not real as persons, real as fictions, his fictions, extensions of himself that came into being only because of him. And if he cured a man, that man became for him a successful fiction and therefore actually real, and he'd say to me afterwards, 'Quite an interesting character that, wasn't he? I knew that would work.' But if he didn't cure him, the man was forgotten immediately, allowed to dissolve and vanish as if he had never existed. Even his father, and if he loved anyone he loved his father, even he was constantly re-created, even after his death. He was in fact a storeman

345

in a factory in Limerick – I met him once, a nice old man; but Frank wasn't content with that – he made him a stonemason and a gardener and a bus-driver and a guard and a musician. It was as if – and I'm groping at this – but it seemed to me that he kept remaking people according to some private standard of excellence of his own, and as his standards changed, so did the person. But I'm sure it was always an excellence, a perfection, that was the cause of his restlessness and the focus of it.

We were in Wales when he got word of his father's death. He went home alone. And when he came back he spoke of the death as if it had been his mother's. 'She passed away quietly,' he said. 'I don't know how father'll manage without her.' And the point was his mother had been dead for years when I first met him. Oh, he was a convoluted man.

The first day I went to the doctor, he was taking down all the particulars and he said to me, 'And what was your late husband's occupation, Mrs Hardy?' 'He was an artist,' I said – quickly – casually – but with complete conviction – just the way he might have said it. Wasn't that curious? Because the thought had never occurred to me before. And then because I said it and the doctor wrote it down, I knew it was true . . .

I left him once. Yes; I left *him*! Up and left. God, when I think of it! We'd been married seven years at the time, and within that twelve months I'd had a pleurisy and then two miscarriages in quick succession and I suppose I was feeling very sorry for myself. And we'd been living that winter in a derelict cottage in Norfolk miles from anyone – it was really a converted byre. I remember kneeling before a tiny grate and crying because the timber was so wet the fire wouldn't light, and trying to get to sleep on a damp mattress on the floor. Anyway we'd had a fight about something silly; and I must have been very depressed or suddenly worked myself up into a stupid panic because on some mad impulse I tore a page off an old calendar and wrote on the back of it, 'Dear Frank I'm leaving you because I cannot endure the

346

depravity of our lives any longer do not follow me I love you deeply Grace.' Wasn't it awful! 'I love you deeply' – to a man like that. And 'Do not follow me' – do not follow me! – God, I had some kind of innocence then!

Anyhow I went home. For the first time and the last time. I got the night-crossing from Glasgow and then the bus to Omagh and walked the three miles out to Knockmoyle. I remember I stood at the gates for a while and looked up the long straight avenue flanked with tall straight poplars, across the lawn, beyond the formal Japanese garden and into the chaotic vegetable plot where my mother messed about and devoted her disturbed life to. It was Bridie, the housekeeper, who reared me; and mother in her headscarf and wellingtons was a strange woman who went in and out of the mental hospital.

Father was in the breakfast-room, in a wicker chair beside a huge fire, with a rug around his knees and his head slightly forward and staring straight in front of him just as he did when he was on the bench and hectoring a defendant. The stroke had spared his features and he looked so distinguished with his patrician face and his white hair perfectly groomed and his immaculate grey suit.

And I knocked on the table so that I wouldn't startle him and I said, 'It's me, Father. It's Grace.'

'What's that? Speak up!'

And I could hear old Bridie moving about the kitchen and I was afraid she'd hear me and come up and throw her arms around me before I'd have a chance to kiss him over and over again and say sorry and tell him how often I thought about him.

I moved round so that I was directly in front of him.

'It's Grace, Father.'

'Yes? Yes?'

'Grace – Gracie.'

'Raise your voice. You're mumbling.'

'Timmikins,' I said – that's what he used to call me when I was a child.

'Who?'

347

'Timmikins,' I said again.

'I know who it is,' he said.

'I came home to see you,' I said.

He gazed at me for a long, long time. And his mouth opened and shut but no sound came. And then finally and suddenly the words and the remembrance came together for him.

'You ran off with the mountebank.' And he wasn't accusing – all he wanted was corroboration.

'Frank and I got married,' I said.

'Yes, you ran off with the mountebank just after you qualified. And you killed your mother – you know that. But I told her you'd be back. Six months, I said; give her six months and she'll come crawling back.'

I was crouching in front of him and holding his cold hands and our faces so close that I could smell his breath.

'Father,' I said, 'Father, listen –'

But words were now spilling out of him, not angry words but the tired formula words of the judge sentencing me to nine months in jail but suspending the sentence because he understood I came from a professional family with a long and worthy record of public service and hoping that I would soon regret and atone for the blemish I had brought on that family and on my own profession and threatening that if I ever appeared before him again he would have no option but to send me to jail and impose the maximum penalty et cetera, et cetera, et cetera.

And as I watched him and listened to him and felt the darts of his spittle on my face, I had an impulse – and I thank God I resisted it – a calm, momentary impulse to do an ugly, shameful thing: I wanted to curse him – no, not curse him – assault and defile him with obscenities and to articulate them slowly and distinctly and brutally into his patrician face; words he never used; a language he didn't speak; a language never heard in that house. But even in his confusion he'd understand it and recognize it as the final rejection of his tall straight poplars and the family profession and his formal Japanese gardens. But more important, much, much more important, recognize it as my proud testament to my mountebank and the van and the wet timber and the primus stove and the dirty halls and everything he'd call squalor. But thank God I didn't do that. Instead – and he was still sentencing me – I just walked away. And I never saw him again. And he died before the year was over. And the next night I was back in the Norfolk byre, back on the damp mattress and kissing Frank's face and shoulders and chest and telling him how sorry I was; and he's drunk and giving me his sly smile and saying little. And then I was pregnant again and this time I held on to it for the full time. And that was the black-faced, macerated baby that's buried in a field in Kinlochbervie in Sutherland in the north of Scotland –

Badrallach, Kilmore,
Llanfaethlu, Llanfechell,
Kincardine, Kinross,
Loughcarron, Loughgelly . . .

(*At banner*) Faith healer – faith healing – I never understood it, never. I tried to. In the beginning I tried diligently – as the doctor might say I brought all my mental rigour to bear on it. But I couldn't even begin to apprehend it – this gift, this craft, this talent, this art, this magic – whatever it was he possessed, that defined him, that was, I suppose, essentially him. And because it was his essence and because it eluded me I suppose I *was* wary of it. Yes, of course I was. And he knew it. Indeed, if by some miracle Frank could have been the same Frank without it, I would happily have robbed him of it. And he knew that, too – how well he knew that; and in his twisted way read into it the ultimate treachery on my part. So what I did was, I schooled myself – I tried to school myself – to leave it to him and him with it and be content to be outside them. And for a time that seemed to work for both of us: we observed the neutrality of the ground between us. But as time went on and particularly in the last few years when he became more frantic and more truculent, he began to interpret my remove as resentment, even as hostility, or he pretended he

349

did – you could never be sure with him – and he insisted on dragging me into feud between himself and his talent. And then we would snarl and lunge and grapple at one another and things were said that should never have been said and that lay afterwards on our lives like slow poison. When his talent was working for him, the aggression wasn't quite so bitter – after he'd cured someone he'd be satisfied just to flaunt himself, to taunt me: 'And what does the legal mind make of all that? Just a con, isn't it? Just an illusion, isn't it?' And I'd busy myself putting away the chairs or taking down the banner. But when he couldn't perform – and in those last two years that became more and more frequent, the more desperate he became – then he'd go for me with bared teeth as if I were responsible and he'd scream at me, 'You were at your very best tonight, Miss O'Dwyer, weren't you? A great night for the law, wasn't it? You vengeful, spiteful bitch.' And I'd defend myself. And we'd tear one another apart.

As soon as we'd open the doors, that's where I'd take my seat, at a table if there was one, or if there wasn't, with a tray on my knee; because sometimes they'd pay on their way in, now and again far more than they could afford, I suppose in the hope that somehow it would sweeten Frank to them. And that's where I'd sit all through the performance and collect whatever they'd leave on the way out.

And when they'd all be seated – 'all'! Many a time we were lucky to have half-a-dozen – then Teddy'd put on the record, a worn-out hissing version of a song called 'The Way You Look Tonight'. I begged Frank to get something else, anything else. But he wouldn't. It had to be that. 'I like it,' he'd say, 'and it confuses them.'

Then Teddy'd come out and make his announcement.

And then Frank would appear.

I wish you could have seen him. It wasn't that he was a handsome man. He wasn't really. But when he came out before those people and moved among them and touched them – even though he was often half-drunk – he had a

350

special . . . magnificence. And I'd sit there and watch him and I'd often find myself saying to myself, 'Oh you lucky woman.' Oh, yes, oh, indeed, yes.

(*Sits and pours a drink*) I didn't want to come back to Ireland. Neither did Teddy. But he insisted. He had been in bad shape for months and although he didn't say it – he would never have said it – I knew he had some sense that Ireland might somehow recharge him, maybe even restore him. Because in that last year he seemed to have lost touch with his gift. And of course he was drinking too much and missing performances and picking fights with strangers – cornering someone in a pub and boasting that he could perform miracles and having people laugh at him; or else lying in the back of the van – we lived in it most of the time now – lying in the van and not speaking or eating for days.

But the real trouble was the faith healing. It wasn't that he didn't try – I suppose trying hadn't much to do with it anyway – but he tried too hard, he tried desperately, and usually nothing happened, nothing at all. I remember, just a few weeks before we came back, he met an old woman in an off-licence in Kilmarnock and he told her he could cure her arthritis. And he tried. And he failed. In the old days he wouldn't have given her another thought; but he became obsessed with that old woman, found out where she lived, went to her house again and again until finally her son-in-law threw him out and threatened to get the police for him.

So on the last day of August we crossed from Stranraer to Larne and drove through the night to County Donegal. And there we got lodgings in a pub, a lounge bar, really, outside a village called Ballybeg, not far from Donegal Town. (*She moves again.*) And the strange thing was that night began so well. I remember watching him and thinking: Yes, his sense was true, he *is* going to be restored here – he was so easy and so relaxed and so charming, and there was nobody more charming than him when he wanted to be. I could tell even by the way he was drinking – not gulping down the first three or four drinks as if they were

351

only preliminaries. And he chatted to the landlord and they talked about the harvest and about fishing and about the tourist trade. He even introduced me as his wife – God, I suppose that ought to have alerted me.

And there was a group of young men in the lounge, five of them, local men on their way home from their friend's wedding; and one of them, the youngest of them, was in a wheelchair. And they were sitting in a corner by themselves and you could tell they wanted to be left alone. And when I saw him go over to them I had a second of unease. But whatever it was he said to them, they smiled and shook hands with him and moved into the centre of the lounge and he called me over and we all sat round in a big circle and one of them ordered a drink and the landlord joined us and we just sat there and chatted and laughed and told stories and sang songs. Where was Teddy? (*Remembering*) Yes, he was there, too, just outside the circle, slightly drunk and looking a bit bewildered. And it began as such a happy night – yes, happy, happy, happy! The young men were happy. I was happy. And Frank – yes, yes, I know he was happy too. And then out of the blue – we were talking about gambling – Frank suddenly leaned across to one of the wedding guests, a young man called Donal, and said, 'I can cure that finger of yours.' And it was dropped as lightly, as casually, as naturally into the conversation as if he had said 'This is my round.' So naturally that the others didn't even hear it and went on talking. And he caught the twisted finger between his palms and massaged it gently and then released it and the finger was straight and he turned immediately to me and gave me an icy, exultant, theatrical smile and said, 'That's the curtain-raiser.'

And I knew at once – I knew it instinctively – that before the night was out he was going to measure himself against the cripple in the wheelchair.

And he did. Yes. Outside in the yard. I watched from an upstairs window. But that was hours later, just after day-break. And throughout the night the others had become crazed with drink and he had gone very still and sat with

his eyes half-closed but never for a second taking them off
the invalid.

Before they all went out to the yard – it was almost dawn
then – I gripped him by the elbow. 'For Christ's sake,
Frank, please, for my sake,' and he looked at me, no, not at
me, not at me, past me, beyond me, out of those damn
benign eyes of his; and I wasn't there for him . . .

Aberarder, Kinlochbervie,

Aberayron, Kinlochbervie,

Invergordon, Kinlochbervie . . . in Sutherland, in the
north of Scotland . . .

(*By rote*) But I *am* getting stronger. I *am* becoming more
controlled. I can measure my progress by the number of
hours I sleep and the amount I drink and – and –

O my God I'm in such a mess – I'm really in such a
mess – how I want that door to open – how I want that man
to come across that floor and put his white hands on my
face and still this tumult inside me – O my God I'm one of
his fictions too, but I need him to sustain me in that
existence – O my God I don't know if I can go on without
his sustenance.

(*Fade to black.*)

PART THREE

TEDDY

We discover TEDDY *on stage. He is probably in his fifties but it
would be difficult to pin-point his age accurately because he has a
showman's verve and perkiness that make him appear younger than
that.*

*He is wearing a bow-tie, checked shirt, smoking jacket/dressing
gown (short), house slippers.*

*We discover him sitting beside the table – the same small table as in
Part Two; but* TEDDY'S *chair is more comfortable than* GRACE'S.
He is listening to a recording of Fred Astaire singing 'The Way You

Look Tonight' – an old record-player and a very abused record.

Occasionally during his monologue he goes to a small locker – like a hospital locker – where he keeps his bottles of beer. Beside this locker is an empty dog-basket.

The poster is in the same position as in Part One and Part Two.

(No attempt has been made to write this monologue in the phonetic equivalent of Cockney/London English. But the piece must be played in that dialect.)

TEDDY *is sitting with his eyes closed, his head back, listening to the music.*

> *'Some day when I'm awf'ly low*
> *When the world is cold,*
> *I will feel a glow just thinking of you*
> *And the way you look tonight . . .'*

At the end of the first verse he opens his eyes, sees that his glass is empty, goes to the locker, gets a bottle of beer and comes back to his seat. Omit all the middle verses – go from the first verse to the last. As TEDDY *gets his drink he sings odd lines with the record.*

> *'Lovely, never, never change,*
> *Keep that breathless charm,*
> *Won't you please arrange it*
> *'Cause I love you*
> *Just the way you look tonight.*
> *Mm, mm, mm, mm,*
> *Just the way you look tonight.'*

TEDDY: What about that then, eh? Fred Astaire. Fantastic, isn't it? One of the greats, Freddy. Just fantastic. I could listen to that all day – (*Sings*) 'Just the way you look . . .' It was Gracie insisted on that for our theme music. And do you know why, dear heart? She wouldn't admit it to him but she told me. Because that was the big hit the year she and Frank was married. Can you imagine! But of course as time goes by she forgets that. And of course he never knows why it's our theme – probably thinks I've got some sort of a twisted mind. So that the two of them end up blaming *me* for picking it! But by that time I really like the tune, you know; and anyway it's the only record we have. So I keep

354

it. And old Teddy he's the only one of the three of us that
knows its romantic significance. I'll tell you something,
dear heart: spend your life in showbusiness and you become
a philosopher.

But it is a fantastic tune, isn't it? Did you ever look back
over all the great artists – old Freddy here, Lillie Langtry,
Sir Laurence Olivier, Houdini, Charlie Chaplin, Gracie
Fields – and did you ever ask yourself what makes them all
top-liners, what have they all got in common? Okay, I'll tell
you. Three things. Number one: they've got ambition this
size. Okay? Number two: they've got a talent that is
sensational and unique – there's only one Sir
Laurence – right? Number three: not one of them has two
brains to rub together. You think I'm joking? I promise
you. They know they have something fantastic, sure,
they're not that stupid. But what it is they have, how they
do it, how it works, what that sensational talent is, what it
all means – believe me, they don't know and they don't care
and even if they did care they haven't the brains to analyse
it.

Let me tell you about two dogs I had once. Okay? One
was a white poodle and she was so brilliant – I mean, that
dog she knew what you were thinking about before you
even thought about it yourself. Before I'd come home at
night, d'you know what that dog would do? She'd switch
on the electric fire, pull the curtains, and leave my slippers
and a bottle of beer sitting there beside my chair. But put
her in front of an audience – fell apart – couldn't do nothing.
Right. Now the other dog he was a whippet. Maybe you
remember him, Rob Roy, The Piping Dog? (*Brief pause.*)
Well, it was quite a few years ago. Anyway, you see that
whippet, he was fantastic. I mean to say, just tell me how
many times in your life has it been your privilege to hear a
three-year-old male whippet dog play 'Come Into The
Garden, Maud' on the bagpipes *and* follow for his encore
with 'Plaisir d'Amour'. Okay? Agreed. Sensational talent.
Ambition? I couldn't stop him rehearsing. Morning, noon
and night he'd sit there blowing the bloody thing and

working them bellows with his back leg – all night long if
I'd let him. That's all he lived for, being on top of the heap.
And brains? Had he brains, that whippet? Let me tell you.
I had that dog four and a half years, until he expired from
pulmonary exhaustion. And in all that time that whippet
couldn't even learn his name! I mean it. I mean apart from
his musical genius that whippet in human terms was
educationally subnormal. A retarded whippet, in fact. I'd
stub my toe against something, and I'd say 'God!', and
who'd come running to me, wagging his tail? I tell you: a
philosopher – that's what you become.

I'll give you another example. One of the best acts I ever
handled – Miss Mulatto and Her Pigeons. You see that kid?
D'you know what that kid could do? I swear to God this is
no lie, that kid talked pigeon! I swear. Fluent. That kid
could plant her pigeons all over the house – some here, some
there, some down there; and then she'd stand in the centre
of the stage and she'd speak to them in a great flood of
pigeon, you know – I can't do it, I can't even speak
English – but this flood of pigeon would come out of her.
And suddenly all those birds – a hundred and twenty of
them, I should know, six to a box, twenty boxes, that's
when I had to buy the van – all those birds would rise up
from all over the house and come flying in like a bloody
massive snowstorm and smother her on the stage. Fantastic.
Can you imagine it? Her being able to talk to every one of
them hundred and twenty birds and for all I know maybe
them all speaking different languages! I said to her once,
'Mary Brigid,' I said, that was her name, Mary Brigid
O'Donnell, I said, 'What do you say to them?' And she
tossed her head and she said, 'Say to them? How would I
know what I say to them, Teddy? I just make sounds at
them.' See? (*He touches his head.*) Nothing. Empty. But
what a talent! What an artist! And another thing, when
those birds all died that winter of '47 – all of them, just like
that, within twenty-four hours, we were in Crewe at the
time, the vet said it was galloping shingles – after those
birds died, Mary Brigid never worked again. I suppose it'd

356

be like as if . . . as if someone sat on Yehudi Menuhin's fiddle and smashed it. God! Bloody artists!

(TEDDY *disposes of the empty bottle and sings as he does.*)

'Oh, but you're lovely
With your smile so warm,
And your cheek so soft
There is nothing for me but to love you—'

I'll tell you something: if you're thinking of going into the promotion business, let me tell you something—I'll give you this for nothing—it's the best advice you'll ever get—and it has been the one ruling principle in all my years as a professional man: if you're going to handle great artists, you must handle them—believe me, I know what I'm talking about—you must handle them on the basis of a relationship that is strictly business only. Personally, in the privacy of your heart, you may love them or you may hate them. But that has nothing to do with it. Your client he has his job to do. You have your job to do. On that basis you complement each other. But let that relationship between you spill over into friendship or affection and believe me, dear heart, the coupon's torn. The one rule I've always lived by: friends is friends and work is work, and as the poet says, never the twain shall meet. Okay? Okay. (*Indicating poster*) Him? No, he was no great artist. Course he was no great artist. Never anything more than a mediocre artist. At best. Believe me. I should know, shouldn't I? Sure he had talent. Talent? He had more talent—listen to me—he had more talent than—and brains?—brains!—that's all the stupid bastard had was brains! For Christ's sake, brains! And what did they do for him, I ask you, all those bloody brains? They bloody castrated him—that's what they done for him—bloody knackered him! So what do you end up handling? A bloody fantastic talent that hasn't one ounce of ambition because his bloody brains has him bloody castrated! Tell me—go ahead—you tell me—you tell me—I genuinely want to know—what sort of act is that to work with, to spend your life with? How do you handle an act like that? You tell *me*. I never knew! I never learned! Oh,

357

for God's sake, no wonder I have ulcers!

(*Pause. Then softly*) But when his brain left him alone. When he was in form.

There was one night in particular. Wales it was. Village called Llanblethian. An old Methodist church that I get for ten bob. A week before Christmas.

And we're flat broke. And Frank, he's on two bottles of whiskey a day at this stage. And Gracie and him they've been fighting something terrible and she's disappeared off somewhere. And I've a pocketful of bills to pay.

Okay. Eight o'clock. I open the doors. I'm not exactly knocked down in the stampede. As a matter of fact, dear heart – nobody. God. And now it's snowing. I close the doors. Frank he's looking like he's about to die, and his hands and his shoulders they're shaking like this. 'Get me a drink,' he says. I pretend I don't hear him. The door's flung open. The stampede? (*He shakes his head.*) Gracie. 'Where's the genius?' she shouts. 'I came to see the great Irish genius. Where is he?' And he hears her and he screams, 'Get that bitch out! Get rid of that bitch!' 'Oh, he's here, is he?' she says. 'Physician, heal thyself!' she says with this great, mad, mocking voice. 'Out! Out!' he shouts. 'The genius!' she screams. 'Out! Out!' 'Genius!' And their voices they're echoing up through those dirty big oak rafters of the church so that it goes on and on and on . . . Oh, God, I mean to say, dear heart . . .

Finally – it must be near nine o'clock now – we're about to pack up and the door opens and in come ten people. I don't remember all the details now. There's two kids, I know; one of them has this great big lump on his cheek. And there's a woman with crutches. And there's another young woman with a crying baby in her arms. And there's a young man with dark glasses and one of those white sticks for blind people. Five or six others – I can't remember – I mean I didn't know then the kind of night it was going to be, did I? Oh, yes, and an old man, a farmer – he's lame – he's helped in by his daughter. And they all sit down. And I goes through my paces: Ladies and Gentlemen and et cetera and so on. And then I goes to Frank and I says, 'Okay, Frank?' And very slowly he straightens up and when I see his face I'm sure he's going to be sick and he doesn't answer me at all but sort of – you know – drifts past me and down to them and among them.

(*He slowly pours the remains of a bottle into his glass. Then takes a drink.*)

All I can say now is that it was . . . I mean I don't ask you to believe what happened. Quite honestly – and I don't say this with no belligerence – it makes no difference to me whether you believe me or not. But what happened that night in that old Methodist hall in the village of Llanbethian in Glamorganshire in Wales is that every single person in that church was cured. Ten people. All made right again. I'd seen him do fantastic things before but I'd never seen him do anything on that scale. Never. And I'll tell you a funny thing: there was no shouting or cheering or dancing with joy, nothing at all like that. Hardly a word was spoken. It was like as if not only had he taken away whatever it was was wrong with them, but like he had given them some great content in themselves as well. That sounds silly, doesn't it? But that's the way it seemed.

And when he had finished, they all got to their feet and shook his hand, one after the other, very formal like. And the old farmer, the one who'd been lame and had been helped in by his daughter, he made a little speech. He said, in that lilting Welsh accent – I can't do that neither – he said, 'Mr Hardy, as long as men live in Glamorganshire, you'll be remembered here.' And whatever way he said it, you knew it was true; and whatever way he said Glamorganshire, it sounded like the whole world. And then he took out his wallet and placed it on the table and he said, 'I hope I'm not insulting you, sir.' And they all went out.

(*Short pause*) That was one of the big nights, that was. I mean we were stunned – Gracie – me – Frank himself; we just stood looking at one another. I mean to say – ten people – all in a few minutes. And then he suddenly went crazy with delight. And he threw his arms around me and

kissed me on both cheeks. And then he ran down to Gracie
and caught her in his arms and lifted her up into the air and
danced her up and down the aisle of that old church and the
two of them sang at the top of their voices, 'Lovely, never
never change', trying to sing and dance and at the same
time breaking their sides laughing. And then he flung the
doors open and they ran outside and sang and danced in the
snow. What a pair! Oh my dear, what a pair! Like kids they
were. Just like kids. Then I heard the van starting up. But
by the time I got out they were gone. Just like that. Didn't
see them again for four days – what happened was they went
off to some posh hotel in Cardiff and lived it up until the
wallet was empty. Just like kids, you know. Thoughtless;
no thought for tomorrow. And no cruelty intended – oh no,
no cruelty. But at a time like that a bit thoughtless. And
that's understandable, too, after a night like that, isn't it?
Just a little bit thoughtless – that's all.

(*He goes to the locker for another bottle. As he goes*) What a
funny couple they were, though. Oh dear, what a funny
couple. I mean to spend the greater part of their lives
together, fighting as they did; and when I say fighting, I
mean really sticking the old knife in and turning it as hard
as they could. I never understood it – job for the
head-shrink, isn't it? – why two people should burn
themselves out in that way. Sure they could have split. Why
didn't they then? Don't ask me. For God's sake why didn't
I leave them and get myself something nice and simple and
easy like – like – like a whistling dolphin? And what was the
fighting all about in the end? All right you could say it was
because the only thing that finally mattered to him was his
work – and that would be true. Or you could say it was
because the only thing that finally mattered to her was
him – and I suppose that would be true, too. But when you
put the two propositions together like that – I don't
know – somehow they both become only half-truths, you
know.

Or maybe you could say that no artist should ever be
married. I've heard that theory, too; and after a lifetime in

the profession I would incline to the conclusion that that theory has quite a bit of validity in it. I mean look at Rob Roy, The Piping Dog. Just consider for one minute the fortune I could have made in stud fees when that dog was a household name. Queuing up with their bitches they were; queuing bloody up. Twenty nicker a throw they were offering me. I thought I was sitting on a gold-mine. Do you know what I did in anticipation of the fortune that was going to come pouring in? I got a fifteen-foot black Carrara marble headstone with gold lettering put up over my mother's grave. Set me back £214, that did. Okay – and what happened? – what happened every single time? I'll tell you. I come into the room here with a very beautiful and very sexy whippet bitch. He's just been rehearsing and he's lying there in that basket, gasping for breath. I say to him, 'Look at this then, old Rob. Who's good to you then, eh?' But he's temperamental – he won't look up. And the bitch, she's rolling her eyes and waggling all over and laughing like a bloody gypsy. 'Come on, boy,' I say, 'come on, come on. You've got a nice friend here.' And what does he do every time, every single time? He gets to his feet. He gives this great yawn. And then suddenly – just like that – goes for her throat! For her bloody *throat* for God's sake! Tries to tear her limb from bloody limb! Course he's stupid but he's not that stupid! I mean he knows what it's all about! My God he knows! My God, there's days he's so randy, that whippet, there's days I daren't strap the bloody bagpipes to him! And yet look what he does when it's bloody handed to him on a plate – some of the most beautiful whippet bitches in the country and every one of them crying out for it! Goes for her throat and tries to desecrate my mother's memory at the same time! Oh my God – artists! I ask you!

(*He gathers the empty bottles on the table and drops them into a waste-paper basket. As he does.*) Ups and downs – losses and gains – roundabouts and swings – isn't that it?

And if that night in Llanbethian was one of the high spots, I suppose the week we spent in that village in Sutherland was about as bad a patch as we ever struck. For

Gracie it was. Certainly for Gracie. And for me, too, I
think. Oh, that's going back a fair few years. About the time
he really began to lose control of the drinking. Anyway,
there we were away up in Sutherland – what *was* the name
of that village? Inverbuie? Inverbervie? Kinlochbervie?
– that's it! – Kinlochbervie! – very small, very remote, right
away up in the north of Sutherland, about as far north as you
can go in Scotland, and looking across at the Isle of Lewis in
the Outer Hebrides.

I'll always remember our first sight of that village. We
climb up this long steep hill through this misty fog and
when we get to the top we stop; and away down below us in
the valley – there's Kinlochbervie; and it is just bathed in
sunshine. First time we've seen the sun in about a month.
And now here's this fantastic little village sitting on the
edge of the sea, all blue and white and golden, and all lit up
and all sparkling and all just heavenly. And Gracie she
turns to me and she says, 'Teddy,' she says, 'this is where
my baby'll be born.' Even though she wasn't due for three
more weeks. But she was right. That's where the baby was
born.

Okay. We head down into the valley and just about two
miles out of the village the front axle goes thrackk! Terrific.
Frank, he's out cold in the back. So I leave Gracie
sunbathing herself on a stone wall and I hikes it into
Kinlochbervie to get help.

That was a Tuesday morning. The following Friday
we're still there, still waiting for a local fisherman called
Campbell who's out in his trawler to come back 'cause he's
the only local who owns a tractor and we're depending on
his mother who happens to be deaf as a post to persuade
him when he comes back to tow us the thirty-five miles to
the nearest village where there's a blacksmith but there's a
chance, too, that this blacksmith might not be at home
when we get there because his sister, Annie, she's getting
married to a postman in Glasgow and the blacksmith may
be the best man. One of those situations – you know.
(*Shouts*) 'Are you sure this blacksmith can fix axles, dear

362

heart?' 'Och, Annie, she's a beautiful big strong girl with brown eyes.'

Right. We hang about. And since funds are low – as usual – Gracie and Frank they sleep in the van and I'm kipping in a nearby field. I don't mind; the weather's beautiful. Saturday passes – no Campbell. Sunday passes – no Campbell. And then on Sunday evening . . . the baby's born.

(*Very slowly he goes for another beer, opens it, pours it. As he does this he whistles a few lines of 'The Way You Look Tonight' through his teeth. Then with sudden anger.*)

Christ, you've got to admit he really was a bastard in many ways! I know he was drinking heavy – I know – I know all that! But for Christ's sake to walk away deliberately when your wife's going to have your baby in the middle of bloody nowhere – I mean to say, to do that deliberately, that's some kind of bloody-mindedness, isn't it? And make no mistake, dear heart: it was deliberate, it was bloody-minded. 'Cause as soon as she starts having the pains, I go looking for him, and there he is heading up the hill, and I call after him, and I know he hears me, but he doesn't answer me. Oh, Christ, there really was a killer instinct deep down in that man!

(*Pause. He takes a drink, puts the glass down on the table and looks at it.*)

I don't know . . . I don't know how we managed. God, when I think of it. Her lying on my old raincoat in the back of the van . . . shouting for him, screaming for him . . . all that blood . . . her bare feet pushing, kicking against my shoulders . . . 'Frank!' she's screaming, 'Frank! Frank!' and I'm saying, 'My darling, he's coming – he's coming, my darling – he's on his way – he'll be here any minute' . . . and then that – that little wet thing with the black face and the black body, a tiny little thing, no size at all . . . a boy it was . . .

(*Pause.*) And afterwards she was so fantastic – I mean she was so bloody fantastic. She held it in her arms, just sitting there on the roadside with her back leaning against the

363

stone wall and her legs stretched out in front of her, just
sitting there in the sun and looking down at it in her arms.
And then after about half an hour she said, 'It's time to
bury it now, Teddy.' And we went into a nearby field and I
had to chase the cows away 'cause they kept following us
and I dug the hole and I put it in the hole and I covered it
up again. And then she asked me was I not going to say no
prayers over it and I said sure, why not, my darling, I said;
but not being much of a praying man I didn't know right
what to say; so I just said this was the infant child of
Francis Hardy, Faith Healer, and his wife, Grace Hardy,
both citizens of Ireland, and this was where their infant
child lies, in Kinlochbervie, in Sutherland; and God have
mercy on all of us, I said.

And all the time she was very quiet and calm. And when
the little ceremony was concluded, she put her two white
hands on my face and brought me to her and kissed me on
the forehead. Just once. On the forehead.

And later that evening I made a cross and painted it
white and placed it on top of the grave. Maybe it's still
there. You never know. About two miles south of the
village of Kinlochbervie. In a field on the left-hand side of
the road as you go north. Maybe it's still there. Could still
well be. Why not? Who's to say?

(*Pause.*) Oh, he came back all right; just before it was dark.
Oh, sure. Sober as a judge, all spruced up, healthy-looking,
sunburned, altogether very cocky; and full of old chat to me
about should we have a go in the Outer Hebrides or maybe
we should cross over to the east coast or should we plan a
journey even further north now that the weather was so
good – you know, all business, things he never gave a damn
about. And he seemed so – you know – so on top of things, I
thought for a while, I thought: My God, he doesn't know!
He genuinely doesn't know! But then suddenly in the
middle of all this great burst of interest I see him glancing
into the van with the corner of the eye – not that there was
anything to see; I had it all washed out by then – but it was
the way he done it and the way he kept on talking at the

same time that I *knew* that *he* knew; and not only that he knew but that he knew it all right down to the last detail. And even though the old chatter never faltered for a minute, whatever way he kept talking straight into my face, I knew too that – oh, I don't know how to put it – but I got this feeling that in a kind of way – being the kind of man he was – well somehow I got the feeling, I *knew* that he *had* to keep talking because he had suffered all that she had suffered and that now he was . . . about to collapse. Yeah. Funny, wasn't it? And many a time since then I get a picture of him going up that hill that Sunday afternoon, like there's some very important appointment he's got to keep, walking fast with his head down and pretending he doesn't hear me calling him. And I've thought maybe – course it was bloody minded of him! I'm not denying that! – but maybe being the kind of man he was, you know, with that strange gift he had, I've thought maybe – well, maybe he had to have his own way of facing things . . .

Oh, I don't know. None of my business, was it? None of my concern, thank the Lord, except in so far as it might affect the performance of my client. Listen to me, dear heart, I'll give you this for nothing, the best advice you'll ever get – the *one* rule I've always lived by: friends is friends and work is work and never the twain shall meet as the poet says. Okay? Okay.

(*With a glass in his hand he goes slowly up stage until he is standing beneath the poster. As he goes he hums the lines 'Some day when I'm awf'ly low, When the world is cold'. He reads.*) The Fantastic Francis Hardy, Faith Healer: One Night Only. Nice poster though, isn't it? A lifetime in the business and that's the only memento I've kept. That's a fact. See some people in our profession? – they hoard everything: press-clippings, posters, notices, photographs, interviews – they keep them all. Never believed in that though. I mean the way I look at it, you've got to be a realist, you know, live in the present. Look at Sir Laurence – you think he spends his days poring over old albums? No, we don't have time for that. And believe me

365

I've had my share of triumphs and my share of glory over the years; and I'm grateful for that. But I mean it doesn't butter no parsnips for me today, does it?

And do you know, dear heart, it was almost thrown out! Well, I mean it *was* thrown out – I just happened to spot it in this pile of stuff that Gracie's landlord had dumped outside for the dustmen. I'd come straight from the morgue in Paddington, and the copper there he'd given me her address; and there I was, walking along the street, looking for number 27; and there it is, lying on the footpath where her landlord had dumped it. I mean, if it had been raining, it would have been destroyed, wouldn't it? But there it was, neat as you like. And just as I was picking it up, this city gent he's walking past and he says, 'How dare you steal private property, Sir!' (*In a fury.*) And I caught him by the neck and I put my fist up to his face and I said to him, I said to him, 'You open your fucking mouth once more, mate, just once fucking more, and I'll fucking well make fucking sausage meat of you!'

(*Pause while he controls himself again*) If you'll pardon the language, dear heart. But I just went berserk. I mean half an hour before, this copper he'd brought me to Paddington and I'm still in a state of shock after that. And besides it's only – what? – twelve months since the whole County Donegal thing: that night in the Ballybeg pub and then hanging about waiting for the trial of those bloody Irish Apaches and nobody in the courtroom understands a word I'm saying – they had to get an interpreter to explain to the judge in English what the only proper Englishman in the place was saying! God!

And I'm still only getting over all that when this copper comes up here one morning while I'm shaving and I opens the door and he asks me my name and I tell him and then he says I'm to go to Paddington with him rightaway to . . .

(*He stops suddenly and stares for a long time at the audience. Then:–*) Tell you what – why don't I go back twelve months and tell you first about that night in Ballybeg? Why don't I do that? Why not? (*He gets another bottle, opens it, pours it.*)

366

It was the last day of August and we crossed from Stranraer to Larne and drove through the night to County Donegal. And there we got lodgings in a pub, a lounge bar, really, outside a village called Ballybeg, not far from Donegal Town.

(*He takes a drink and leaves the glass down. Pause.*) You see that night in that pub in Ballybeg? You know how I spent that night? I spent the whole of that night just watching them. Mr and Mrs Frank Hardy. Side by side. Together in Ireland. At home in Ireland. Easy; relaxed; chatting; laughing. And it was like as if I was seeing them for the first time in years and years – no! not seeing them but *remembering them* Funny thing that, wasn't it? I'm not saying they were strangers to me – strangers! I mean, Frank and Gracie, how could they be strangers to *me*! – but it was like as if I was seeing them as they were once, as they might have been all the time – like if there was never none of the bitterness and the fighting and the wettings and the bloody van and the smell of the primus stove and the bills and the booze and the dirty halls and that hassle that we never seemed to be able to rise above. Like away from all that, all that stuff cut out, this is what they could be.

And there they were, the centre of that big circle round that big lounge, everybody wanting to talk to them, them talking to everybody, now and then exchanging an odd private word between themselves, now and then even touching each other very easy and very casual.

And she was sitting forward in this armchair. And she was all animation and having a word with everybody and laughing all the time. And she was wearing this red dress. And her hair it was tied back with a black ribbon. And how can I tell you how fantastic she looked?

And then sometime around midnight someone said, 'Why don't you sing us a song, Gracie?' And as natural as you like, as if she done it every day of the week, she stood up and she sang an Irish song called 'Believe me if all those endearing young charms/Which I gaze on so fondly today' – Christ, I don't mean that's the title; that's the whole first verse for Christ's sake. And it wasn't that she was a sensational singer – no, no, she wasn't. I mean she had this kind of very light, wavery kind of voice – you know, like the voice of a kid of ten or eleven. But she stands up there in that Irish pub, in that red dress and with her hair all back from her face; and she's looking at him as she's singing; and we're all looking at her; and the song – it sort of comes out of her very simple and very sweet, like in a way not as if she's performing but as if the song's just sort of rising out of her by itself. And I'm sitting there just outside the circle, sitting there very quiet, very still. And I'm saying to myself. 'O Jesus, Teddy boy . . . Oh my Jesus . . . What are you going to do?'

And then I looks over at Frank – I mean I just happen to look over, you know the way you do – and there he is, gazing across at me. And the way he's gazing at me and the look he has on his face is exactly the way he looks into somebody he knows he's going to cure. I don't know – it's a hard thing to explain if you've never seen it. It's a very serious look and it's a very compassionate look. It's a look that says two things. It says: No need to speak – I know exactly what the trouble is. And at the same time it says: I am now going to cure you of that trouble. That's the look he gave me. He held me in that look for – what? – thirty seconds. And then he turned away from me and looked at her – sort of directed his look towards her so that I had to look at her too. And suddenly she is this terrific woman that of course I love very much, married to this man that I love very much – love maybe even more. But that's all. Nothing more. That's all. And that's enough.

And for the first time in twenty years I was so content – so content, dear heart, do you know what I done? I got drunk in celebration – slowly, deliberately, happily slewed! And someone must have carried me upstairs to bed because the next thing I know Gracie's hammering on my chest and shouting and sobbing, 'Get up, Teddy! Get up! Something terrible has happened! Something horrible!' (*Long pause as he goes and gets another beer.*)

368

But I was telling you about the poster and how it's lying on the street outside Gracie's digs. That's it. How I've just come from Paddington and how the copper he's given me her address. That's right – I've told you all that. Or to go back to the morning of that same day – twelve months exactly after that night in Ballybeg.

Okay. I'm shaving. Knock at the door. This copper. Asks me my name. I tell him. Asks me to come with him to the morgue in Paddington to identify a body. What body? Body of a lady. And I say what lady? And he says a Mrs Grace Hardy. And I say come off it, she's in Ireland, that's where I left her. And he says you must be mistaken, she's been in London for the past four months, living in digs in number 27 Limewood Avenue. Limewood Avenue! I mean this here is Limewood Grove! Limewood Avenue's just four streets away. And I say she's there now, is she? And he says no, she's dead, she's in the morgue. And I say you must be wrong, copper. And he says no mistake, she's dead, from an overdose of sleeping-tablets, and would I come with him please and make a formal identification.

So the copper he brought me in a van to Paddington – you know, just like our van; only his van I'm sure it's taxed and insured. But it's the same inside: two seats in the front, me driving, her beside me, and Frank in the back all hunched up with the bottle between his legs. And there she was. Gracie all right. Looking very beautiful. Oh my dear I can't tell you how beautiful she looked.

And the copper he said, 'Is that Grace Hardy?' 'It is,' I said. 'Did you know her well?' 'Oh, yes,' I said, 'a professional relationship going back twenty-odd years.' 'Cause that's what it was, wasn't it, a professional relationship? Well it certainly wasn't nothing more than that, I mean, was it?

(*He stands for some seconds just looking at the audience. Then he does not see them any more. He sits on his chair and puts on the record. After the first few lines fade rapidly to black.*)

369

PART FOUR

FRANK

FRANK

The poster is gone. The set is empty except for the single chair across which lies Frank's coat exactly as he left it in Part One.

We discover FRANK *standing down stage left, where we left him.*

In this final section FRANK *is slightly less aloof, not quite as detached as in Part One. To describe him now as agitated would be a gross exaggeration. But there should be tenuous evidence of a slightly heightened pulse-rate, of something approximating to excitement in him, perhaps in the way his mind leaps without apparent connection from thought to thought; and his physical movements are just a shade sharper.*

FRANK: (*Eyes shut*)
> Aberarder, Kinlochbervie,
> Aberayron, Kinlochbervie,
> Invergordon, Kinlochbervie . . . in Sutherland,
> in the north of Scotland . . .

(*He opens his eyes. A very brief pause. Then recovering quickly*) But I've told you all that, haven't I? – how we were holidaying in Kinlochbervie when I got word that my mother had died? Yes, of course I have. I've told you all that. (*Begins moving.*) A picturesque little place, very quiet, very beautiful, looking across to the Isle of Lewis . . . about as far north as you can go in . . . in Scotland . . . (*He keeps moving. As he does he searches his pockets. Produces a newspaper clipping, very tattered, very faded.*) I carried this around with me for years. A clipping from the *West Glamorgan Chronicle*. 'A truly remarkable event took place in the old Methodist church in Llanblethian on the night of December 21st last when an itinerant Irish faith

healer called Francis Harding . . .' For some reason they
never seemed to – (*He shrugs in dismissal*) '. . . cured ten
local people of a variety of complaints ranging from
blindness to polio. Whether these very astonishing cures
were effected by autosuggestion or whether Mr Harding is
indeed the possessor of some extra-terrestrial power . . .'
Nice word that. '. . . we are not as yet in a position to
adjudicate. But our preliminary investigations would
indicate that something of highly unusual proportions took
place that night in Llanblethian.'

'Unusual proportions' . . . (*Short laugh.*)

Never knew why I kept it for so long. Its testimony? I
don't think so. Its reassurance? No, not that. Maybe, I
think . . . maybe just as an identification. Yes, I think
that's why I kept it. It identified me – even though it got my
name wrong.

Yes, that *was* a strange night. One of those rare nights
when I could – when I could have moved mountains. Ten
people – one after the other. And only one of them came
back to thank me – an old farmer who was lame. I
remember saying to Gracie the next day, 'Where are the
other nine?' – in fun, of course; of course in fun. But she
chose to misunderstand me and that led to another row.

Yes; carried it for years; until we came back to Ireland.
And that night in that pub in Ballybeg I crumpled it up (*He
does this now*) and threw it away.

I never met her father, the judge. Shortly after Gracie
and I ran off together, he wrote me a letter; but I never met
him. He said in it – the only part I remember – he used the
phrase 'implicating my only child in your career of
chicanery'. And I remember being angry and throwing the
letter to her; and I remember her reading that line aloud
and collapsing on the bed with laughing and kicking her
heels in the air and repeating the phrase over and over
again – I suppose to demonstrate her absolute loyalty to me.
And I remember thinking how young she *did* look and how
cruel her laughter at him was. Because by then my anger
against him had died and I had some envy of the man who

371

could use the word 'chicanery' with such confidence.

I would have liked to have had a child. But she was barren. And anyhow the life we led wouldn't have been suitable. And he might have had the gift. And he might have handled it better than I did. I wouldn't have asked for anything from him – love, affection, respect – nothing like that. But I would have got pleasure just in looking at him. Yes. A child would have been something. What is a piece of paper? Or those odd moments of awe, of gratitude, of adoration? Nothing, nothing, nothing . . .

(*Looking around*) It was always like this – shabby, shabby, bleak, derelict. We never got that summons to Teddy's royal palace; not even to a suburban drawing-room. And it would have been interesting to have been just once – not for the pretensions, no, no, but to discover was it possible in conditions other than these, just for the confirmation that this despair, this surrender wasn't its own healing. Yes, that would have been interesting.

And yet . . . and yet . . .

(*Suddenly, rapidly*) Not for a second, not for a single second was I disarmed by the warmth and the camaraderie and the deference and the joviality and the joy and the effusion of that home-coming welcome that night in that pub in Ballybeg. No, not for a second. Of course I responded to it. Naturally I responded to it. And yes, the thought did cross my mind that at long last is there going to be – what? – a fulfilment, an integration, a full blossoming? Yes, that thought occurred to me. But the moment that boy Donal threatened me with his damned twisted finger, that illusion quickly vanished. And I knew, I knew instinctively why I was being hosted.

Aberarder, Kinlochbervie,
Aberayron, Kinlochbervie,
Invergordon, Kinlochbervie . . .

Where had we got to? Ah, yes – Teddy had been put to bed and Gracie had finished her housekeeping – I could hear her moving about upstairs; and the wedding guests had gone to get McGarvey. Only the landlord and myself in that huge, garish lounge.

I walked around it for a time.

I thought of Teddy asleep upstairs, at peace and reconciled at last. And I wondered had I held on to him out of selfishness, should I have attempted to release him years ago. But I thought – no; his passion was a sustaining one. And maybe, indeed, maybe I had impoverished him now.

And I thought of Gracie's mother and the one time we met, in Dublin, on her way back to hospital. We were in a restaurant together, the three of us, Gracie and she and I; and she never spoke until Gracie had gone off to pay the bill and then she said, 'I suffer from nerves, you know,' her face slightly averted from me but looking directly at me at the same time and smiling at me. I said I knew. I was afraid she was going to ask me for help. 'What do you make of that?' I said I was sure she would get better this time. 'You know, there are worse things,' she said. I said I knew that. 'Much, much worse,' she went on and she was almost happy-looking now. 'Look at her father – he is obsessed with order. That's worse.' I suppose so, I said. 'And Grace – she wants devotion, and that's worse still.' 'Is it?' I asked. 'And what do you want?' And before I could answer, Gracie came back, and the smile vanished, and the head dropped. And that was all. No request for help. And I never heard her voice again.

And I remembered – suddenly, for no reason at all – the day my father took me with him to the horse fair in Ballinasloe. And the only incident I remembered was that afternoon, in a pub. And a friend of my father's, Eamon Boyle, was with us; and the two men were slightly drunk. And Boyle put his hand on my head and said to my father, 'And what's this young man going to be, Frank?' And my father opened his mouth and laughed and said, 'Be Jaysus, Boyle, it'll be hard for him to beat his aul fella!' And for the first time I saw his mouth was filled with rotten teeth. And I remember being ashamed in case Boyle had seen them, too. Just a haphazard memory. Silly. Nothing to it. But for some reason it came back to me that night.

373

And I thought of the first big row Grace and I had. I don't know what it was about. But I know we were in Norfolk at the time, living in a converted byre. And she was kneeling in front of the grate, trying to kindle some wet timber; and I can't remember what I said but I remembered her reply; and what she said was: 'If you leave me, Frank, I'll kill myself.' And it wasn't that she was demented – in fact she was almost calm, and smiling. But whatever way she looked straight at me, without fully facing me, I recognized then for the first time that there was more of her mother than her father in her; and I realized that I would have to be with her until the very end.

(*He walks up stage. Pause*) I must have walked that floor for a couple of hours. And all the time the landlord never moved from behind the bar. He hadn't spoken since the wedding guests left. He wouldn't even look at me. I think he hated me. I know he did. I asked him for a last drink. Then he spoke in a rush: 'Get to hell out of here before they come back, Mister! I know them fellas – savage bloody men. And there's nothing you can do for McGarvey – nothing nobody can do for McGarvey. You know that.' 'I know that,' I said. 'But if you do nothing for him, Mister, they'll kill you. I know them. They'll kill you.' 'I know that, too,' I said. But he rushed into a back room.

I poured a drink for myself. A small Irish with an equal amount of water. The thought occurred to me to get drunk but I dismissed it as . . . inappropriate. Then I heard the car return and stop outside. A silence. Then Donal's head round the door.

'McGarvey's here. But he's shy about coming in. Come you out. They're waiting for you out there in the yard.'

'Coming,' I said.

(*He puts on the hat and overcoat and buttons it slowly. When that is done he goes on.*)

There were two yards in fact. The first one I went into – it was immediately behind the lounge – it was a tiny area, partially covered, dark, cluttered with barrels and boxes of empties and smelling of stale beer and toilets. I knew that

374

wasn't it.

Then I found a wooden door. I passed through that and there was the other, the large yard. And I knew it at once.

I would like to describe that yard to you.

It was a September morning, just after dawn. The sky was orange and everything glowed with a soft radiance – as if each detail of the scene had its own self-awareness and was satisfied with itself.

The yard was a perfect square enclosed by the back of the building and three high walls. And the wall facing me as I walked out was breached by an arched entrance.

Almost in the centre of the square but a little to my left was a tractor and a trailer. In the back of the trailer were four implements: there was an axe and there was a crowbar and there was a mallet and there was a hay-fork. They were resting against the side of the trailer.

In the corners facing me and within the walls were two mature birch trees and the wind was sufficient to move them.

The ground was cobbled but pleasant to walk on because the cobbles were smooth with use.

And I walked across that yard, over those worn cobbles, towards the arched entrance, because framed in it, you would think posed symmetrically, were the four wedding guests; and in front of them, in his wheelchair, McGarvey.

The four looked . . . diminished in that dawn light; their faces whiter; their carnations chaste against the black suits. Ned was on the left of the line, Donal on the right, and the other two, whose names I never knew, between them.

And McGarvey. Of course, McGarvey. More shrunken than I had thought. And younger. His hands folded patiently on his knees; his feet turned in, his head slightly to the side. A figure of infinite patience, of profound resignation, you would imagine. Not a hint of savagery. And Ned's left hand protectively on his shoulder.

And although I knew that nothing was going to happen, nothing at all, I walked across the yard towards them. And as I walked I became possessed of a strange and trembling

375

intimation: that the whole corporeal world – the cobbles, the trees, the sky, those four malign implements – somehow they had shed their physical reality and had become mere imaginings, and that in all existence there was only myself and the wedding guests. And that intimation in turn gave way to a stronger sense: that even we had ceased to be physical and existed only in spirit, only in the need we had for each other.

(*He takes off his hat as if he were entering a church and holds it at his chest. He is both awed and elated. As he speaks the remaining lines he moves very slowly down stage.*)

And as I moved across that yard towards them and offered myself to them, then for the first time I had a simple and genuine sense of home-coming. Then for the first time there was no atrophying terror; and the maddening questions were silent.

At long last I was renouncing chance.

(*Pause for about four seconds. Then quick black.*)

TRANSLATIONS

for Stephen Rea

CHARACTERS

MANUS
SARAH
JIMMY JACK
MAIRE
DOALTY
BRIDGET
HUGH
OWEN
CAPTAIN LANCEY
LIEUTENANT YOLLAND

Translations was first presented by Field Day Theatre Company in the Guildhall, Derry on Tuesday, 23 September 1980. The cast was as follows:

MANUS	Mick Lally
SARAH	Ann Hasson
JIMMY JACK	Roy Hanlon
MAIRE	Nuala Hayes
DOALTY	Liam Neeson
BRIDGET	Brenda Scallon
HUGH	Ray McAnally
OWEN	Stephen Rea
CAPTAIN LANCEY	David Heap
LIEUTENANT YOLLAND	Shaun Scott

Direction	Art O Briain
Design	Consolata Boyle
Design assistance	Magdalena Rubalcava
	Mary Friel
Lighting	Rupert Murray

Field Day Theatre Company was formed by Brian Friel and Stephen Rea. *Translations* was their first production.

The action takes place in a hedge-school in the townland of Baile Beag/Ballybeg, an Irish-speaking community in County Donegal.

ACT ONE	An afternoon in late August 1833.
ACT TWO	A few days later.
ACT THREE	The evening of the following day.

One interval – between the two scenes in Act Two.

(For the convenience of readers and performers unfamiliar with the language, roman letters have been used for the Greek words and quotations in the text. The originals, together with the Latin and literal translations, appear on pp. 449–50.)

Much ——— omen

manus

ACT ONE

The hedge-school is held in a disused barn or hay-shed or byre. Along the back wall are the remains of five or six stalls – wooden posts and chains – where cows were once milked and bedded. A double door left, large enough to allow a cart to enter. A window right. A wooden stairway without a banister leads to the upstairs living-quarters (off) of the schoolmaster and his son. Around the room are broken and forgotten implements: a cart-wheel, some lobster-pots, farming tools, a battle of hay, a churn, etc. There are also the stools and bench-seats which the pupils use and a table and chair for the master. At the door a pail of water and a soiled towel. The room is comfortless and dusty and functional – there is no trace of a woman's hand.

When the play opens, MANUS *is teaching* SARAH *to speak. He kneels beside her. She is sitting on a low stool, her head down, very tense, clutching a slate on her knees. He is coaxing her gently and firmly and – as with everything he does – with a kind of zeal.*

MANUS *is in his late twenties/early thirties; the master's older son. He is pale-faced, lightly built, intense, and works as an unpaid assistant – a monitor – to his father. His clothes are shabby; and when he moves we see that he is lame.*

SARAH's *speech defect is so bad that all her life she has been considered locally to be dumb and she has accepted this: when she wishes to communicate, she grunts and makes unintelligible nasal sounds. She has a waiflike appearance and could be any age from seventeen to thirty-five.*

JIMMY JACK CASSIE – *known as the* Infant Prodigy – *sits by himself, contentedly reading Homer in Greek and smiling to himself. He is a bachelor in his sixties, lives alone, and comes to these evening classes partly for the company and partly for the intellectual stimulation. He is fluent in Latin and Greek but is in no way pedantic – to him it is perfectly normal to speak these tongues. He*

383

never washes. His clothes – heavy top coat, hat, mittens, which he wears now – are filthy and he lives in them summer and winter, day and night. He now reads in a quiet voice and smiles in profound satisfaction. For JIMMY *the world of the gods and the ancient myths is as real and as immediate as everyday life in the townland of Baile Beag.*

MANUS *holds* SARAH'*s hands in his and he articulates slowly and distinctly into her face.*

MANUS: We're doing very well. And we're going to try it once more – just once more. Now – relax and breathe in . . . deep . . . and out . . . in . . . and out . . .
(SARAH *shakes her head vigorously and stubbornly.*)
MANUS: Come on, Sarah. This is our secret.
(*Again vigorous and stubborn shaking of* SARAH'*s head.*)
MANUS: Nobody's listening. Nobody hears you.
JIMMY: '*Ton d'emeibet epeita thea glaukopis Athene . . .*'
MANUS: Get your tongue and your lips working. 'My name –' Come on. One more try. 'My name is –' Good girl.
SARAH: My . . .
MANUS: Great. 'My name –'
SARAH: My . . . my . . .
MANUS: Raise your head. Shout it out. Nobody's listening.
JIMMY: '. . . *alla hekelos estai en Atreidao domois . . .*'
MANUS: Jimmy, please! Once more – just once more – 'My name –' Good girl. Come on now. Head up. Mouth open.
SARAH: My . . .
MANUS: Good.
SARAH: My . . .
MANUS: Great.
SARAH: My name . . .
MANUS: Yes?
SARAH: My name is . . .
MANUS: Yes?
(SARAH *pauses. Then in a rush.*)
SARAH: My name is Sarah
MANUS: Marvellous! Bloody marvellous!
(MANUS *hugs* SARAH. *She smiles in shy, embarrassed pleasure.*)

384

Did you hear that, Jimmy? – 'My name is Sarah' – clear as a bell.

(*To* SARAH) The Infant Prodigy doesn't know what we're at.

(SARAH *laughs at this.* MANUS *hugs her again and stands up.*) Now we're really started! Nothing'll stop us now! Nothing in the wide world!

(JIMMY, *chuckling at his text, comes over to them.*)

JIMMY: Listen to this, Manus.

MANUS: Soon you'll be telling me all the secrets that have been in that head of yours all these years. Certainly, James – what is it? (*To* SARAH) Maybe you'd set out the stools?

(MANUS *runs up the stairs.*)

SARAH: Wait till you hear this, Manus.

MANUS: Go ahead. I'll be straight down.

JIMMY: '*Hos ara min phamene rabdo epemassat Athene* –' 'After Athene had said this, she touched Ulysses with her wand. She withered the fair skin of his supple limbs and destroyed the flaxen hair from off his head and about his limbs she put the skin of an old man . . .'! The divil! The divil!

(MANUS *has emerged again with a bowl of milk and a piece of bread.*)

JIMMY: And wait till you hear! She's not finished with him yet!

(*As* MANUS *descends the stairs he toasts* SARAH *with his bowl.*)

JIMMY: '*Knuzosen de oi osse* –' 'She dimmed his two eyes that were so beautiful and clothed him in a vile ragged cloak begrimed with filthy smoke . . .'! D'you see! Smoke! Smoke! D'you see! Sure look at what the same turf-smoke has done to myself! (*He rapidly removes his hat to display his bald head.*) Would you call that flaxen hair?

MANUS: Of course I would.

JIMMY: 'And about him she cast the great skin of a filthy hind, stripped of the hair, and into his hand she thrust a staff and a wallet'! Ha-ha-ha! Athene did that to Ulysses! Made him into a tramp! Isn't she the tight one?

MANUS: You couldn't watch her, Jimmy.

JIMMY: You know what they call her?

MANUS: '*Glaukopis Athene.*'

JIMMY: That's it! The flashing-eyed Athene! By God, Manus, sir, if you had a woman like that about the house, it's not stripping a turf-bank you'd be thinking about – eh?

MANUS: She was a goddess, Jimmy.

JIMMY: Better still. Sure isn't our own Grania a class of a goddess and –

MANUS: Who?

JIMMY: Grania – Grania – Diarmuid's Grania.

MANUS: Ah.

JIMMY: And sure she can't get her fill of men.

MANUS: Jimmy, you're impossible.

JIMMY: I was just thinking to myself last night: if you had the choosing between Athene and Artemis and Helen of Troy – all three of them Zeus's girls – imagine three powerful-looking daughters like that all in the one parish of Athens! – now, if you had the picking between them, which would you take?

MANUS: (*To* SARAH) Which should I take, Sarah?

JIMMY: No harm to Helen; and no harm to Artemis; and indeed no harm to our own Grania, Manus. But I think I've no choice but to go bull-straight for Athene. By God, sir, them flashing eyes would fair keep a man jigged up constant! (*Suddenly and momentarily, as if in spasm,* JIMMY *stands to attention and salutes, his face raised in pained ecstasy.* MANUS *laughs. So does* SARAH. JIMMY *goes back to his seat, and his reading.*)

MANUS: You're a dangerous bloody man, Jimmy Jack.

JIMMY: 'Flashing-eyed'! Hah! Sure Homer knows it all, boy. Homer knows it all.

(MANUS *goes to the window and looks out.*)

MANUS: Where the hell has he got to?

(SARAH *goes to* MANUS *and touches his elbow. She mimes rocking a baby.*)

MANUS: Yes, I know he's at the christening; but it doesn't take them all day to put a name on a baby, does it?

(SARAH *mimes pouring drinks and tossing them back quickly.*)

MANUS: You may be sure. Which pub?

(SARAH *indicates.*)

MANUS: Gracie's?

(*No. Further away.*)

MANUS: Con Connie Tim's?

(*No. To the right of there.*)

MANUS: Anna na mBreag's?

(*Yes. That's it.*)

MANUS: Great. She'll fill him up. I suppose I may take the class then.

(MANUS *begins to distribute some books, slates and chalk, texts, etc., beside the seats.* SARAH *goes over to the straw and produces a bunch of flowers she has hidden there. During this:*)

JIMMY: '*Autar o ek limenos prosebe –* ' 'But Ulysses went forth from the harbour and through the woodland to the place where Athene had shown him he could find the good swineherd who – '*o oi biotoio malista kedeto*' – what's that, Manus?

MANUS: 'Who cared most for his substance'.

JIMMY: That's it! 'The good swineherd who cared most for his substance above all the slaves that Ulysses possessed . . .'

(SARAH *presents the flowers to* MANUS.)

MANUS: Those are lovely, Sarah.

(*But* SARAH *has fled in embarrassment to her seat and has her head buried in a book.* MANUS *goes to her.*)

MANUS: Flow-ers.

(*Pause.* SARAH *does not look up.*)

MANUS: Say the word: flow-ers. Come on – flow-ers.

SARAH: Flowers.

MANUS: You see? – you're off!

(MANUS *leans down and kisses the top of* SARAH's *head.*)

MANUS: And they're beautiful flowers. Thank you.

(MAIRE *enters, a strong-minded, strong-bodied woman in her twenties with a head of curly hair. She is carrying a small can of milk.*)

MAIRE: Is this all's here? Is there no school this evening?

MANUS: If my father's not back, I'll take it.

(MANUS *stands awkwardly, having been caught kissing* SARAH *and with the flowers almost formally at his chest.*)

MAIRE: Well now, isn't that a pretty sight. There's your milk. How's Sarah?

(SARAH *grunts a reply*.)

MANUS: I saw you out at the hay.

(MAIRE *ignores this and goes to* JIMMY.)

MAIRE: And how's Jimmy Jack Cassie?

JIMMY: Sit down beside me, Maire.

MAIRE: Would I be safe?

JIMMY: No safer man in Donegal.

(MAIRE *flops on a stool beside* JIMMY.)

MAIRE: Ooooh. The best harvest in living memory, they say; but I don't want to see another like it. (*Showing* JIMMY *her hands*.) Look at the blisters.

JIMMY: *Esne fatigata?*

MAIRE: *Sum fatigatissima.*

JIMMY: *Bene! Optime!*

MAIRE: That's the height of my Latin. Fit me better if I had even that much English.

JIMMY: English? I thought you had some English?

MAIRE: Three words. Wait—there was a spake I used to have off by heart. What's this it was? (*Her accent is strange because she is speaking a foreign language and because she does not understand what she is saying.*) 'In Norfolk we besport ourselves around the maypoll.' What about that!

MANUS: Maypole.

(*Again* MAIRE *ignores* MANUS.)

MAIRE: God have mercy on my Aunt Mary—she taught me that when I was about four, whatever it means. Do you know what it means, Jimmy?

JIMMY: Sure you know I have only Irish like yourself.

MAIRE: And Latin. And Greek.

JIMMY: I'm telling you a lie: I know one English word.

MAIRE: What?

JIMMY: Bo-som.

MAIRE: What's a bo-som?

JIMMY: You know—(*He illustrates with his hands*)—bo-som—bo-som—you know—Diana, the huntress, she has two powerful bosom.

MAIRE: You may be sure that's the one English word you would know. (*Rises*) Is there a drop of water about?

388

(MANUS *gives* MAIRE *his bowl of milk.*)

MANUS: I'm sorry I couldn't get up last night.

MAIRE: Doesn't matter.

MANUS: Biddy Hanna sent for me to write a letter to her sister in Nova Scotia. All the gossip of the parish. 'I brought the cow to the bull three times last week but no good. There's nothing for it now but Big Ned Frank.'

MAIRE: (*Drinking*) That's better.

MANUS: And she got so engrossed in it that she forgot who she was dictating to: 'The aul drunken schoolmaster and that lame son of his are still footering about in the hedge-school, wasting people's good time and money.'

(MAIRE *has to laugh at this.*)

MAIRE: She did not!

MANUS: And me taking it all down. 'Thank God one of them new national schools is being built above at Poll na gCaorach.' It was after midnight by the time I got back.

MAIRE: Great to be a busy man.

(MAIRE *moves away.* MANUS *follows.*)

MANUS: I could hear music on my way past but I thought it was too late to call.

MAIRE: (*To* SARAH) Wasn't your father in great voice last night?

(SARAH *nods and smiles.*)

MAIRE: It must have been near three o'clock by the time you got home?

(SARAH *holds up four fingers.*)

MAIRE: Was it four? No wonder we're in pieces.

MANUS: I can give you a hand at the hay tomorrow.

MAIRE: That's the name of a hornpipe, isn't it? – 'The Scholar In The Hayfield' – or is it a reel?

MANUS: If the day's good.

MAIRE: Suit yourself. The English soldiers below in the tents, them sapper fellas, they're coming up to give us a hand. I don't know a word they're saying, nor they me; but sure that doesn't matter, does it?

MANUS: What the hell are you so crabbed about?!

(DOALTY *and* BRIDGET *enter noisily. Both are in their twenties.* DOALTY *is brandishing a surveyor's pole. He is an*

389

open-minded, open-hearted, generous and slightly thick young man. BRIDGET *is a plump, fresh young girl, ready to laugh, vain, and with a countrywoman's instinctive cunning.* DOALTY *enters doing his imitation of the master.*)

DOALTY: Vesperal salutations to you all.

BRIDGET: He's coming down past Carraig na Ri and he's as full as a pig!

DOALTY: *Ignari, stulti, rustici* – pot-boys and peasant whelps – semi-literates and illegitimates.

BRIDGET: He's been on the batter since this morning; he sent the wee ones home at eleven o'clock.

DOALTY: Three questions. Question A – Am I drunk? Question B – Am I sober? (*Into* MAIRE'*s face*) *Responde – responde!*

BRIDGET: Question C, Master – When were you last sober?

MAIRE: What's the weapon, Doalty?

BRIDGET: I warned him. He'll be arrested one of these days.

DOALTY: Up in the bog with Bridget and her aul fella, and the Red Coats were just across at the foot of Croc na Mona, dragging them aul chains and peeping through that big machine they lug about everywhere with them – you know the name of it, Manus?

MAIRE: Theodolite.

BRIDGET: How do you know?

MAIRE: They leave it in our byre at night sometimes if it's raining.

JIMMY: Theodolite – what's the etymology of that word, Manus?

MANUS: No idea.

BRIDGET: Get on with the story.

JIMMY: *Theo – theos* – something to do with a god. Maybe *thea* – a goddess! What shape's the yoke?

DOALTY: 'Shape!' Will you shut up, you aul eejit you! Anyway, every time they'd stick one of these poles into the ground and move across the bog, I'd creep up and shift it twenty or thirty paces to the side.

BRIDGET: God!

DOALTY: Then they'd come back and stare at it and look at their calculations and stare at it again and scratch their heads. And cripes, d'you know what they ended up doing?

390

BRIDGET: Wait till you hear!

DOALTY: They took the bloody machine apart!

> (*And immediately he speaks in gibberish – an imitation of two very agitated and confused sappers in rapid conversation.*)

BRIDGET: That's the image of them!

MAIRE: You must be proud of yourself, Doalty.

DOALTY: What d'you mean?

MAIRE: That was a very clever piece of work.

MANUS: It was a gesture.

MAIRE: What sort of gesture?

MANUS: Just to indicate . . . a presence.

MAIRE: Hah!

BRIDGET: I'm telling you – you'll be arrested.

> (*When* DOALTY *is embarrassed – or pleased – he reacts physically. He now grabs* BRIDGET *around the waist.*)

DOALTY: What d'you make of that for an implement, Bridget? Wouldn't that make a great aul shaft for your churn?

BRIDGET: Let go of me, you dirty brute! I've a headline to do before Big Hughie comes.

MANUS: I don't think we'll wait for him. Let's get started.

> (*Slowly, reluctantly they begin to move to their seats and specific tasks.* DOALTY *goes to the bucket of water at the door and washes his hands.* BRIDGET *sets up a hand-mirror and combs her hair.*)

BRIDGET: Nellie Ruadh's baby was to be christened this morning. Did any of yous hear what she called it? Did you, Sarah?

> (SARAH *grunts: No.*)

BRIDGET: Did you, Maire?

MAIRE: No.

BRIDGET: Our Seamus says she was threatening she was going to call it after its father.

DOALTY: Who's the father?

BRIDGET: That's the point, you donkey you!

DOALTY: Ah.

BRIDGET: So there's a lot of uneasy bucks about Baile Beag this day.

DOALTY: She told me last Sunday she was going to call it Jimmy.

BRIDGET: You're a liar, Doalty.

DOALTY: Would I tell you a lie? Hi, Jimmy, Nellie Ruadh's aul fella's looking for you.

JIMMY: For me?

MAIRE: Come on, Doalty.

DOALTY: Someone told him . . .

MAIRE: Doalty!

DOALTY: He heard you know the first book of the Satires of Horace off by heart . . .

JIMMY: That's true.

DOALTY: . . . and he wants you to recite it for him.

JIMMY: I'll do that for him certainly, certainly.

DOALTY: He's busting to hear it.

(JIMMY *fumbles in his pockets.*)

JIMMY: I came across this last night – this'll interest you – in Book Two of Virgil's *Georgics*.

DOALTY: Be God, that's my territory alright.

BRIDGET: You clown you! (*To* SARAH) Hold this for me, would you? (*her mirror.*)

JIMMY: Listen to this, Manus. '*Nigra fere et presso pinguis sub vomere terra . . .*'

DOALTY: Steady on now – easy, boys, easy – don't rush me, boys –

(*He mimes great concentration.*)

JIMMY: Manus?

MANUS: 'Land that is black and rich beneath the pressure of the plough . . .'

DOALTY: Give *me* a chance!

JIMMY: 'And with *cui putre* – with crumbly soil – is in the main best for corn.' There you are!

DOALTY: There you are.

JIMMY: 'From no other land will you see more wagons wending homeward behind slow bullocks.' Virgil! There!

DOALTY: 'Slow bullocks'!

JIMMY: Isn't that what I'm always telling you? Black soil for corn. *That's* what you should have in that upper field of yours – corn, not spuds.

DOALTY: Would you listen to that fella! Too lazy be Jasus to wash himself and he's lecturing me on agriculture! Would you go and take a running race at yourself, Jimmy Jack Cassie! (*Grabs* SARAH.) Come away out of this with me, Sarah, and we'll plant some corn together.

MANUS: All right—all right. Let's settle down and get some work done. I know Sean Beag isn't coming—he's at the salmon. What about the Donnelly twins? (*To* DOALTY) Are the Donnelly twins not coming any more?

(DOALTY *shrugs and turns away.*)

Did you ask them?

DOALTY: Haven't seen them. Not about these days.

(DOALTY *begins whistling through his teeth. Suddenly the atmosphere is silent and alert.*)

MANUS: Aren't they at home?

DOALTY: No.

MANUS: Where are they then?

DOALTY: How would I know?

BRIDGET: Our Seamus says two of the soldiers' horses were found last night at the foot of the cliffs at Machaire Buidhe and . . . (*She stops suddenly and begins writing with chalk on her slate.*) D'you hear the whistles of this aul slate? Sure nobody could write on an aul slippery thing like that.

MANUS: What headline did my father set you?

BRIDGET: 'It's easier to stamp out learning than to recall it.'

JIMMY: Book Three, the *Agricola* of Tacitus.

BRIDGET: God but you're a dose.

MANUS: Can you do it?

BRIDGET: There. Is it bad? Will he ate me?

MANUS: It's very good. Keep your elbow in closer to your side. Doalty?

DOALTY: I'm at the seven-times table. I'm perfect, skipper.

(MANUS *moves to* SARAH.)

MANUS: Do you understand those sums?

(SARAH *nods: Yes.* MANUS *leans down to her ear.*)

MANUS: My name is Sarah.

(MANUS *goes to* MAIRE. *While he is talking to her the others swop books, talk quietly, etc.*)

MANUS: Can I help you? What are you at?

MAIRE: Map of America. (*Pause.*) The passage money came last Friday.

MANUS: You never told me that.

MAIRE: Because I haven't seen you since, have I?

MANUS: You don't want to go. You said that yourself.

MAIRE: There's ten below me to be raised and no man in the house. What do you suggest?

MANUS: Do you want to go?

MAIRE: Did you apply for that job in the new national school?

MANUS: No.

MAIRE: You said you would.

MANUS: I said I might.

MAIRE: When it opens, this is finished: nobody's going to pay to go to a hedge-school.

MANUS: I know that and I . . . (*He breaks off because he sees* SARAH, *obviously listening, at his shoulder. She moves away again.*) I was thinking that maybe I could . . .

MAIRE: It's £56 a year you're throwing away.

MANUS: I can't apply for it.

MAIRE: You *promised* me you would.

MANUS: My father has applied for it.

MAIRE: He has not!

MANUS: Day before yesterday.

MAIRE: For God's sake, sure you know he'd never –

MANUS: I couldn't – I can't go in against him.

(MAIRE *looks at him for a second. Then:–*)

MAIRE: Suit yourself. (*To* BRIDGET) I saw your Seamus heading off to the Port fair early this morning.

BRIDGET: And wait till you hear this – I forgot to tell you this. He said that as soon as he crossed over the gap at Cnoc na Mona – just beyond where the soldiers are making the maps – the sweet smell was everywhere.

DOALTY: You never told me that.

BRIDGET: It went out of my head.

DOALTY: He saw the crops in Port?

BRIDGET: Some.

MANUS: How did the tops look?

*"sweet smell" —
associated with
potato famine.*

BRIDGET: Fine – I think.

DOALTY: In flower?

BRIDGET: I don't know. I think so. He didn't say.

MANUS: Just the sweet smell – that's all?

BRIDGET: They say that's the way it snakes in, don't they? First the smell; and then one morning the stalks are all black and limp.

DOALTY: Are you stupid? It's the rotting stalks makes the sweet smell for God's sake. That's what the smell is – rotting stalks.

MAIRE: Sweet smell! Sweet smell! Every year at this time somebody comes back with stories of the sweet smell. Sweet God, did the potatoes ever fail in Baile Beag? Well, did they ever – ever? Never! There was never blight here. Never. Never. But we're always sniffing about for it, aren't we? – looking for disaster. The rents are going to go up again – the harvest's going to be lost – the herring have gone away for ever – there's going to be evictions. Honest to God, some of you people aren't happy unless you're miserable and you'll not be right content until you're dead!

DOALTY: Bloody right, Maire. And sure St Colmcille prophesied there'd never be blight here. He said:

The spuds will bloom in Baile Beag
Till rabbits grow an extra lug.

And sure that'll never be. So we're all right. Seven threes are twenty-one; seven fours are twenty-eight; seven fives are forty-nine – Hi, Jimmy, do you fancy my chances as boss of the new national school?

JIMMY: What's that? – what's that?

DOALTY: Agh, g'way back home to Greece, son.

MAIRE: You ought to apply, Doalty.

DOALTY: D'you think so? Cripes, maybe I will. Hah!

BRIDGET: Did you know that you start at the age of six and you have to stick at it until you're twelve at least – no matter how smart you are or how much you know.

DOALTY: Who told you that yarn?

BRIDGET: And every child from every house has to go all day, every day, summer or winter. That's the law.

395

DOALTY: I'll tell you something – nobody's going to go near them – they're not going to take on – law or no law.

BRIDGET: And everything's free in them. You pay for nothing except the books you use; that's what our Seamus says.

DOALTY: 'Our Seamus'. Sure your Seamus wouldn't pay anyway. She's making this all up.

BRIDGET: Isn't that right, Manus?

MANUS: I think so.

BRIDGET: And from the very first day you go, you'll not hear one word of Irish spoken. You'll be taught to speak English and every subject will be taught through English and everyone'll end up as cute as the Buncrana people.

(SARAH *suddenly grunts and mimes a warning that the master is coming. The atmosphere changes. Sudden business. Heads down.*)

DOALTY: He's here, boys. Cripes, he'll make yella meal out of me for those bloody tables.

BRIDGET: Have you any extra chalk, Manus?

MAIRE: And the atlas for me.

(DOALTY *goes to* MAIRE *who is sitting on a stool at the back.*)

DOALTY: Swop you seats.

MAIRE: Why?

DOALTY: There's an empty one beside the Infant Prodigy.

MAIRE: I'm fine here.

DOALTY: Please, Maire. I want to jouk in the back here.

(MAIRE *rises.*)

God love you. (*Aloud*) Anyone got a bloody table-book? Cripes, I'm wrecked.

(SARAH *gives him one.*)

God, I'm dying about you.

(*In his haste to get to the back seat,* DOALTY *bumps into* BRIDGET *who is kneeling on the floor and writing laboriously on a slate resting on top of a bench-seat.*)

BRIDGET: Watch where you're going, Doalty!

(DOALTY *gooses* BRIDGET. *She squeals. Now the quiet hum of work:* JIMMY *reading Homer in a low voice;* BRIDGET *copying her headline;* MAIRE *studying the atlas;* DOALTY, *his eyes shut tight, mouthing his tables;* SARAH *doing sums.*

After a few seconds:—

BRIDGET: Is this 'g' right, Manus? How do you put a tail on it?

DOALTY: Will you shut up! I can't concentrate!

(*A few more seconds of work. Then* DOALTY *opens his eyes and looks around.*)

False alarm, boys. The bugger's not coming at all. Sure the bugger's hardly fit to walk.

(*And immediately* HUGH *enters. A large man, with residual dignity, shabbily dressed, carrying a stick. He has, as always, a large quantity of drink taken, but he is by no means drunk. He is in his early sixties.*)

HUGH: *Adsum*, Doalty, *adsum*. Perhaps not in *sobrietate perfecta* but adequately *sobrius* to overhear your quip. Vesperal salutations to you all.

(*Various responses.*)

JIMMY: *Ave*, Hugh.

HUGH: James. (*He removes his hat and coat and hands them and his stick to* MANUS, *as if to a footman.*) Apologies for my late arrival: we were celebrating the baptism of Nellie Ruadh's baby.

BRIDGET: (*Innocently*) What name did she put on it, Master?

HUGH: Was it Eamon? Yes, it was Eamon.

BRIDGET: Eamon Donal from Tor! Cripes!

HUGH: And after the *caerimonia nominationis*—Maire?

MAIRE: The ritual of naming.

HUGH: Indeed—we then had a few libations to mark the occasion. Altogether very pleasant. The derivation of the word 'baptize'?—where are my Greek scholars? Doalty?

DOALTY: Would it be—ah—ah—

HUGH: Too slow. James?

JIMMY: *'Baptizein'*—to dip or immerse.

HUGH: Indeed—our friend Pliny Minor speaks of the *'baptisterium'*—the cold bath.

DOALTY: Master.

HUGH: Doalty?

DOALTY: I suppose you could talk then about baptizing a sheep at sheep-dipping, could you?

(*Laughter. Comments.*)

HUGH: Indeed – the precedent is there – the day you were appropriately named Doalty – seven nines?

DOALTY: What's that, Master?

HUGH: Seven times nine?

DOALTY: Seven nines – seven nines – seven times nine – seven times nine are – cripes, it's on the tip of my tongue, Master – I knew it for sure this morning – funny that's the only one that foxes me –

BRIDGET: (*Prompt*) Sixty-three.

DOALTY: What's wrong with me: sure seven nines are fifty-three, Master.

HUGH: Sophocles from Colonus would agree with Doalty Dan Doalty from Tulach Alainn: 'To know nothing is the sweetest life.' Where's Sean Beag?

MANUS: He's at the salmon.

HUGH: And Nora Dan?

MAIRE: She says she's not coming back any more.

HUGH: Ah. Nora Dan can now write her name – Nora Dan's education is complete. And the Donnelly twins? (*Brief pause. Then:–*)

BRIDGET: They're probably at the turf. (*She goes to* HUGH.) There's the one-and-eight I owe you for last quarter's arithmetic and there's my one-and-six for this quarter's writing.

HUGH: *Gratias tibi ago.* (*He sits at his table.*) Before we commence our *studia* I have three items of information to impart to you – (*To* MANUS) A bowl of tea, strong tea, black –
(MANUS *leaves.*)
Item A: on my perambulations today – Bridget? Too slow. Maire?

MAIRE: Perambulare – to walk about.

HUGH: Indeed – I encountered Captain Lancey of the Royal Engineers who is engaged in the ordnance survey of this area. He tells me that in the past few days two of his horses have strayed and some of his equipment seems to be mislaid. I expressed my regret and suggested he address you himself on these matters. He then explained that he

398

does not speak Irish. Latin? I asked. None. Greek? Not a
syllable. He speaks – on his own admission – only English;
and to his credit he seemed suitably verecund – James?

JIMMY: *Verecundus* – humble.

HUGH: Indeed – he voiced some surprise that we did not speak
his language. I explained that a few of us did, on occasion –
outside the parish of course – and then usually for the
purposes of commerce, a use to which his tongue seemed
particularly suited – (*Shouts*) and a slice of soda bread – and I
went on to propose that our own culture and the classical
tongues made a happier conjugation – Doalty?

DOALTY: *Conjugo* – I join together.

(DOALTY *is so pleased with himself that he prods and winks at*
BRIDGET.)

HUGH: Indeed – English, I suggested, couldn't really express us.
And again to his credit he acquiesced to my logic.
Acquiesced – Maire?

(MAIRE *turns away impatiently.* HUGH *is unaware of the*
gesture.)

Too slow. Bridget?

BRIDGET: *Acquiesco.*

HUGH: *Procede.*

BRIDGET: *Acquiesco, acquiescere, acquievi, acquietum.*

HUGH: Indeed – and Item B . . .

MAIRE: Master.

HUGH: Yes?

(MAIRE *gets to her feet uneasily but determinedly. Pause.*)

Well, girl?

MAIRE: We should all be learning to speak English. That's what
my mother says. That's what I say. That's what Dan
O'Connell said last month in Ennis. He said the sooner we
all learn to speak English the better.

(*Suddenly several speak together.*)

JIMMY: What's she saying? What? What?

DOALTY: It's Irish he uses when he's travelling around
scrounging votes.

BRIDGET: And sleeping with married women. Sure no woman's
safe from that fella.

399

JIMMY: Who-who-who? Who's this? Who's this?

HUGH: *Silentium!* (*Pause.*) Who is she talking about?

MAIRE: I'm talking about Daniel O'Connell.

HUGH: Does she mean that little Kerry politician?

MAIRE: I'm talking about the Liberator, Master, as you well know. And what he said was this: 'The old language is a barrier to modern progress.' He said that last month. And he's right. I don't want Greek. I don't want Latin. I want English.

(MANUS *reappears on the platform above.*)

I want to be able to speak English because I'm going to America as soon as the harvest's all saved.

(MAIRE *remains standing.* HUGH *puts his hand into his pocket and produces a flask of whiskey. He removes the cap, pours a drink into it, tosses it back, replaces the cap, puts the flask back into his pocket. Then:–*)

HUGH: We have been diverted – *diverto – divertere –* Where were we?

DOALTY: Three items of information, Master. You're at Item B.

HUGH: Indeed – Item B – Item B – yes – On my way to the christening this morning I chanced to meet Mr George Alexander, Justice of the Peace. We discussed the new national school. Mr Alexander invited me to take charge of it when it opens. I thanked him and explained that I could do that only if I were free to run it as I have run this hedge-school for the past thirty-five years – filling what our friend Euripides calls the '*aplestos pithos*' – James?

JIMMY: 'The cask that cannot be filled'.

HUGH: Indeed – and Mr Alexander retorted courteously and emphatically that he hopes that is how it will be run.

(MAIRE *now sits.*)

Indeed. I have had a strenuous day and I am weary of you all. (*He rises.*) Manus will take care of you.

(HUGH *goes towards the steps.* OWEN *enters.* OWEN *is the younger son, a handsome, attractive young man in his twenties. He is dressed smartly – a city man. His manner is easy and charming: everything he does is invested with consideration and enthusiasm. He now stands framed in the doorway, a travelling bag across his shoulder.*)

OWEN: Could anybody tell me is this where Hugh Mor
O'Donnell holds his hedge-school?

DOALTY: It's Owen – Owen Hugh! Look, boys – it's Owen
Hugh!

(OWEN *enters. As he crosses the room he touches and has a
word for each person.*)

OWEN: Doalty! (*Playful punch.*) How are you, boy? *Jacobe, quid
agis?* Are you well?

JIMMY: Fine. Fine.

OWEN: And Bridget! Give us a kiss. Aaaaaah!

BRIDGET: You're welcome, Owen.

OWEN: It's not – ? Yes, it *is* Maire Chatach! God! A young
woman!

MAIRE: How are you, Owen?

(OWEN *is now in front of* HUGH. *He puts his two hands on his*
FATHER's *shoulders.*)

OWEN: And how's the old man himself?

HUGH: Fair – fair.

OWEN: Fair? For God's sake you never looked better! Come
here to me.

(*He embraces* HUGH *warmly and genuinely.*) Great to see you,
Father. Great to be back.

(HUGH's *eyes are moist – partly joy, partly the drink.*)

HUGH: I – I'm – I'm – pay no attention to –

OWEN: Come on – come on – come on – (*He gives* HUGH *his
handkerchief.*) Do you know what you and I are going to do
tonight? We are going to go up to Anna na mBreag's . . .

DOALTY: Not there, Owen.

OWEN: Why not?

DOALTY: Her poteen's worse than ever.

BRIDGET: They say she puts frogs in it!

OWEN: All the better. (*To* HUGH) And you and I are going to
get footless drunk. That's arranged.

(OWEN *sees* MANUS *coming down the steps with tea and soda
bread. They meet at the bottom.*)

And Manus!

MANUS: You're welcome, Owen.

OWEN: I know I am. And it's great to be here. (*He turns round, arms outstretched.*) I can't believe it. I come back after six years and everything's just as it was! Nothing's changed! Not a thing! (*Sniffs.*) Even that smell – that's the same smell this place always had. What is it anyway? Is it the straw?

DOALTY: Jimmy Jack's feet.

(*General laughter. It opens little pockets of conversation round the room.*)

OWEN: And Doalty Dan Doalty hasn't changed either!

DOALTY: Bloody right, Owen.

OWEN: Jimmy, are you well?

JIMMY: Dodging about.

OWEN: Any word of the big day?

(*This is greeted with 'ohs' and 'ahs'.*)

Time enough, Jimmy. Homer's easier to live with, isn't he?

MAIRE: We heard stories that you own ten big shops in Dublin – is it true?

OWEN: Only nine.

BRIDGET: And you've twelve horses and six servants.

OWEN: Yes – that's true. God Almighty, would you listen to them – taking a hand at me!

MANUS: When did you arrive?

OWEN: We left Dublin yesterday morning, spent last night in Omagh and got here half an hour ago.

MANUS: You're hungry then.

HUGH: Indeed – get him food – get him a drink.

OWEN: Not now, thanks; later. Listen – am I interrupting you all?

HUGH: By no means. We're finished for the day.

OWEN: Wonderful. I'll tell you why. Two friends of mine are waiting outside the door. They'd like to meet you and I'd like you to meet them. May I bring them in?

HUGH: Certainly. You'll all eat and have . . .

OWEN: Not just yet, Father. You've seen the sappers working in this area for the past fortnight, haven't you? Well, the older man is Captain Lancey . . .

HUGH: I've met Captain Lancey.

OWEN: Great. He's the cartographer in charge of this whole area. Cartographer – James?

(OWEN *begins to play this game – his father's game – partly to involve his classroom audience, partly to show he has not forgotten it, and indeed partly because he enjoys it.*)

JIMMY: A maker of maps.

OWEN: Indeed – and the younger man that I travelled with from Dublin, his name is Lieutenant Yolland and he is attached to the toponymic department – Father? – *responde – responde!*

HUGH: He gives names to places.

OWEN: Indeed – although he is in fact an orthographer – Doalty? – too slow – Manus?

MANUS: The correct spelling of those names.

OWEN: Indeed – indeed!
   (OWEN *laughs and claps his hands. Some of the others join in.*)
   Beautiful! Beautiful! Honest to God, it's such a delight to be back here with you all again – 'civilized' people.
   Anyhow – may I bring them in?

HUGH: Your friends are our friends.

OWEN: I'll be straight back.
   (*There is general talk as* OWEN *goes towards the door. He stops beside* SARAH.)

OWEN: That's a new face. Who are you?
   (*A very brief hesitation. Then:–*)

SARAH: My name is Sarah.

OWEN: Sarah who?

SARAH: Sarah Johnny Sally.

OWEN: Of course! From Bun na hAbhann! I'm Owen – Owen Hugh Mor. From Baile Beag. Good to see you.
   (*During this* OWEN–SARAH *exchange.*)

HUGH: Come on now. Let's tidy this place up. (*He rubs the top of his table with his sleeve.*) Move, Doalty – lift those books off the floor.

DOALTY: Right, Master; certainly, Master; I'm doing my best, Master.
   (OWEN *stops at the door.*)

OWEN: One small thing, Father.

HUGH: *Silentium!*

OWEN: I'm on their pay-roll.
   (SARAH, *very elated at her success, is beside* MANUS.)

403

SARAH: I said it, Manus!

(MANUS *ignores* SARAH. *He is much more interested in* OWEN *now.*)

MANUS: You haven't enlisted, have you?!

(SARAH *moves away.*)

OWEN: Me a soldier? I'm employed as a part-time, underpaid, civilian interpreter. My job is to translate the quaint, archaic tongue you people persist in speaking into the King's good English.

(*He goes out.*)

HUGH: Move – move – move! Put some order on things! Come on, Sarah – hide that bucket. Whose are these slates? Somebody take these dishes away. *Festinate! Festinate!*

(MANUS *goes to* MAIRE *who is busy tidying.*)

MANUS: You didn't tell me you were definitely leaving.

MAIRE: Not now.

HUGH: Good girl, Bridget. That's the style.

MANUS: You might at least have told me.

HUGH: Are these your books, James?

JIMMY: Thank you.

MANUS: Fine! Fine! Go ahead! Go ahead!

MAIRE: You talk to me about getting married – with neither a roof over your head nor a sod of ground under your foot. I suggest you go for the new school; but no – 'My father's in for that.' Well now he's got it and now this is finished and now you've nothing.

MANUS: I can always . . .

MAIRE: What? Teach classics to the cows? Agh –

(MAIRE *moves away from* MANUS. OWEN *enters with* LANCEY *and* YOLLAND. CAPTAIN LANCEY *is middle-aged; a small, crisp officer, expert in his field as cartographer but uneasy with people – especially civilians, especially these foreign civilians. His skill is with deeds, not words.* LIEUTENANT YOLLAND *is in his late twenties/early thirties. He is tall and thin and gangling, blond hair, a shy, awkward manner. A soldier by accident.*)

OWEN: Here we are. Captain Lancey – my father.

404

LANCEY: Good evening.

(HUGH *becomes expansive, almost courtly, with his visitors.*)

HUGH: You and I have already met, sir.

LANCEY: Yes.

OWEN: And Lieutenant Yolland – both Royal Engineers – my father.

HUGH: You're very welcome, gentlemen.

YOLLAND: How do you do.

HUGH: *Gaudeo vos hic adesse.*

OWEN: And I'll make no other introductions except that these are some of the people of Baile Beag and – what? – well you're among the best people in Ireland now. (*He pauses to allow* LANCEY *to speak.* LANCEY *does not.*) Would you like to say a few words, Captain?

HUGH: What about a drop, sir?

LANCEY: A what?

HUGH: Perhaps a modest refreshment? A little sampling of our *aqua vitae?*

LANCEY: No, no.

HUGH: Later perhaps when –

LANCEY: I'll say what I have to say, if I may, and as briefly as possible. Do they speak *any* English, Roland?

OWEN: Don't worry. I'll translate.

LANCEY: I see. (*He clears his throat. He speaks as if he were addressing children – a shade too loudly and enunciating excessively.*) You may have seen me – seen me – working in this section – section? – working. We are here – here – in this place – you understand? – to make a map – a map – a map and –

JIMMY: *Nonne Latine loquitur?*

(HUGH *holds up a restraining hand.*)

HUGH: James.

LANCEY: (*To* JIMMY) I do not speak Gaelic, sir.

(*He looks at* OWEN.)

OWEN: Carry on.

LANCEY: A map is a representation on paper – a picture – you understand picture? – a paper picture – showing, representing this country – yes? – showing your country in

miniature – a scaled drawing on paper of – of – of –
(*Suddenly* DOALTY *sniggers. Then* BRIDGET. *Then* SARAH.
OWEN *leaps in quickly.*)

OWEN: It might be better if you *assume* they understand you –

LANCEY: Yes?

OWEN: And I'll translate as you go along.

LANCEY: I see. Yes. Very well. Perhaps you're right. Well.
What we are doing is this. (*He looks at* OWEN. OWEN *nods
reassuringly.*) His Majesty's government has ordered the first
ever comprehensive survey of this entire country – a general
triangulation which will embrace detailed hydrographic and
topographic information and which will be executed to a
scale of six inches to the English mile.

HUGH: (*Pouring a drink*) Excellent – excellent.

(LANCEY *looks at* OWEN.)

OWEN: A new map is being made of the whole country.

(LANCEY *looks to* OWEN: *Is that all?* OWEN *smiles
reassuringly and indicates to proceed.*)

LANCEY: This enormous task has been embarked on so that the
military authorities will be equipped with up-to-date and
accurate information on every corner of this part of the
Empire.

OWEN: The job is being done by soldiers because they are
skilled in this work.

LANCEY: And also so that the entire basis of land valuation can
be reassessed for purposes of more equitable taxation.

OWEN: This new map will take the place of the estate agent's
map so that from now on you will know exactly what is
yours in law.

LANCEY: In conclusion I wish to quote two brief extracts from
the white paper which is our governing charter: (*Reads*)
'All former surveys of Ireland originated in forfeiture and
violent transfer of property; the present survey has for its
object the relief which can be afforded to the proprietors
and occupiers of land from unequal taxation.'

OWEN: The captain hopes that the public will cooperate with
the sappers and that the new map will mean that taxes are
reduced.

HUGH: A worthy enterprise – *opus honestum*! And Extract B?

LANCEY: 'Ireland is privileged. No such survey is being undertaken in England. So this survey cannot but be received as proof of the disposition of this government to advance the interests of Ireland.' My sentiments, too.

OWEN: This survey demonstrates the government's interest in Ireland and the captain thanks you for listening so attentively to him.

HUGH: Our pleasure, Captain.

LANCEY: Lieutenant Yolland?

YOLLAND: I – I – I've nothing to say – really –

OWEN: The captain is the man who actually makes the new map. George's task is to see that the place-names on this map are . . . correct. (*To* YOLLAND.) Just a few words – they'd like to hear you. (*To class.*) Don't you want to hear George, too?

MAIRE: Has he anything to say?

YOLLAND: (*To* MAIRE) Sorry – sorry?

OWEN: She says she's dying to hear you.

YOLLAND: (*To* MAIRE) Very kind of you – thank you . . . (*To class*) I can only say that I feel – I feel very foolish to – to – to be working here and not to speak your language. But I intend to rectify that – with Roland's help – indeed I do.

OWEN: He wants me to teach him Irish!

HUGH: You are doubly welcome, sir.

YOLLAND: I think your countryside is – is – is – is very beautiful. I've fallen in love with it already. I hope we're not too – too crude an intrusion on your lives. And I know that I'm going to be happy, very happy, here.

OWEN: He is already a committed Hibernophile –

JIMMY: He loves –

OWEN: All right, Jimmy – we know – he loves Baile Beag; and he loves you all.

HUGH: Please . . . May I . . . ?

(HUGH *is now drunk. He holds on to the edge of the table.*)

OWEN: Go ahead, Father. (*Hands up for quiet.*) Please – please.

HUGH: And we, gentlemen, we in turn are happy to offer you our friendship, our hospitality, and every assistance that

407

you may require. Gentlemen – welcome!
(*A few desultory claps. The formalities are over. General conversation. The soldiers meet the locals.* MANUS *and* OWEN *meet down stage.*)

OWEN: Lancey's a bloody ramrod but George's all right. How are you anyway?

MANUS: What sort of a translation was that, Owen?

OWEN: Did I make a mess of it?

MANUS: You weren't saying what Lancey was saying!

OWEN: 'Uncertainty in meaning is incipient poetry' – who said that?

MANUS: There was nothing uncertain about what Lancey said: it's a bloody military operation, Owen! And what's Yolland's function? What's 'incorrect' about the place-names we have here?

OWEN: Nothing at all. They're just going to be standardized.

MANUS: You mean changed into English?

OWEN: Where there's ambiguity, they'll be Anglicized.

MANUS: And they call you Roland! They both call you Roland!

OWEN: Shhhhh. Isn't it ridiculous? They seemed to get it wrong from the very beginning – or else they can't pronounce Owen. I was afraid some of you bastards would laugh.

MANUS: Aren't you going to tell them?

OWEN: Yes – yes – soon – soon.

MANUS: But they . . .

OWEN: Easy, man, easy. Owen – Roland – what the hell. It's only a name. It's the same me, isn't it? Well, isn't it?

MANUS: Indeed it is. It's the same Owen.

OWEN: And the same Manus. And in a way we complement each other. (*He punches* MANUS *lightly, playfully and turns to join the others. As he goes.*) All right – who has met whom? Isn't this a job for the go-between?

(MANUS *watches* OWEN *move confidently across the floor, taking* MAIRE *by the hand and introducing her to* YOLLAND. HUGH *is trying to negotiate the steps.* JIMMY *is lost in a text.* DOALTY *and* BRIDGET *are reliving their giggling.* SARAH *is staring at* MANUS.)

ACT TWO

Scene i

The sappers have already mapped most of the area. YOLLAND's *official task, which* OWEN *is now doing, is to take each of the Gaelic names – every hill, stream, rock, even every patch of ground which possessed its own distinctive Irish name – and Anglicize it, either by changing it into its approximate English sound or by translating it into English words. For example, a Gaelic name like Cnoc Ban could become Knockban or – directly translated – Fair Hill. These new standardized names were entered into the Name-Book, and when the new maps appeared they contained all these new Anglicized names.* OWEN's *official function as translator is to pronounce each name in Irish and then provide the English translation.*

The hot weather continues. It is late afternoon some days later.

Stage right: an improvised clothes-line strung between the shafts of the cart and a nail in the wall; on it are some shirts and socks.

A large map – one of the new blank maps – is spread out on the floor. OWEN *is on his hands and knees, consulting it. He is totally engrossed in his task which he pursues with great energy and efficiency.*

YOLLAND's *hesitancy has vanished – he is at home here now. He is sitting on the floor, his long legs stretched out before him, his back resting against a creel, his eyes closed. His mind is elsewhere. One of the reference books – a church registry – lies open on his lap.*

Around them are various reference books, the Name-Book, a bottle of poteen, some cups, etc.

OWEN *completes an entry in the Name-Book and returns to the map on the floor.*

OWEN: Now. Where have we got to? Yes – the point where that
    stream enters the sea – that tiny little beach there. George!
YOLLAND: Yes. I'm listening. What do you call it? Say the Irish
    name again?

OWEN: Bun na hAbhann.

YOLLAND: Again.

OWEN: Bun na hAbhann.

YOLLAND: Bun na hAbhann.

OWEN: That's terrible, George.

YOLLAND: I know. I'm sorry. Say it again.

OWEN: Bun na hAbbann.

YOLLAND: Bun na hAbbann.

OWEN: That's better. Bun is the Irish word for bottom. And Abha means river. So it's literally the mouth of the river.

YOLLAND: Let's leave it alone. There's no English equivalent for a sound like that.

OWEN: What is it called in the church registry?

(*Only now does* YOLLAND *open his eyes.*)

YOLLAND: Let's see . . . Banowen.

OWEN: That's wrong. (*Consults text.*) The list of freeholders calls it Owenmore – that's completely wrong: Owenmore's the big river at the west end of the parish. (*Another text.*) And in the grand jury lists it's called – God! – Binhone! – wherever they got that. I suppose we could Anglicize it to Bunowen; but somehow that's neither fish nor flesh.

(YOLLAND *closes his eyes again.*)

YOLLAND: I give up.

OWEN: (*At map*) Back to first principles. What are we trying to do?

YOLLAND: Good question.

OWEN: We are trying to denominate and at the same time describe that tiny area of soggy, rocky, sandy ground where that little stream enters the sea, an area known locally as Bun na hAbhann . . . Burnfoot! What about Burnfoot?

YOLLAND: (*Indifferently*) Good, Roland, Burnfoot's good.

OWEN: George, my name isn't . . .

YOLLAND: B-u-r-n-f-o-o-t?

OWEN: Are you happy with that?

YOLLAND: Yes.

OWEN: Burnfoot it is then. (*He makes the entry into the Name-Book.*) Bun na hAbhann – B-u-r-n-

YOLLAND: You're becoming very skilled at this.

410

OWEN: We're not moving fast enough.

YOLLAND: (*Opens eyes again*) Lancey lectured me again last night.

OWEN: When does he finish here?

YOLLAND: The sappers are pulling out at the end of the week. The trouble is, the maps they've completed can't be printed without these names. So London screams at Lancey and Lancey screams at me. But I wasn't intimidated.

(MANUS *emerges from upstairs and descends.*)

'I'm sorry, sir,' I said, 'But certain tasks demand their own tempo. You cannot rename a whole country overnight.' Your Irish air has made me bold. (*To* MANUS) Do you want us to leave?

MANUS: Time enough. Class won't begin for another half-hour.

YOLLAND: Sorry — sorry?

OWEN: Can't you speak English?

(MANUS *gathers the things off the clothes-line.* OWEN *returns to the map.*)

OWEN: We now come across that beach . . .

YOLLAND: Tra — that's the Irish for beach. (*To* MANUS) I'm picking up the odd word, Manus.

MANUS: So.

OWEN: . . . on past Burnfoot; and there's nothing around here that has any name that I know of until we come down here to the south end, just about here . . . and there should be a ridge of rocks there . . . Have the sappers marked it? They have. Look, George.

YOLLAND: Where are we?

OWEN: There.

YOLLAND: I'm lost.

OWEN: Here. And the name of that ridge is Druim Dubh. Put English on that, Lieutenant.

YOLLAND: Say it again.

OWEN: Druim Dubh.

YOLLAND: Dubh means black.

OWEN: Yes.

YOLLAND: And Druim means . . . what? a fort?

OWEN: We met it yesterday in Druim Luachra.

YOLLAND: A ridge! The Black Ridge! (*To* MANUS) You see, Manus?

OWEN: We'll have you fluent at the Irish before the summer's over.

YOLLAND: Oh, I wish I were. (*To* MANUS *as he crosses to go back upstairs*) We got a crate of oranges from Dublin today. I'll send some up to you.

MANUS: Thanks. (*To* OWEN) Better hide that bottle. Father's just up and he'd be better without it.

OWEN: Can't you speak English before your man?

MANUS: Why?

OWEN: Out of courtesy.

MANUS: Doesn't he want to learn Irish? (*To* YOLLAND) Don't you want to learn Irish?

YOLLAND: Sorry – sorry? I – I –

MANUS: I understand the Lanceys perfectly but people like you puzzle me.

OWEN: Manus, for God's sake!

MANUS: (*Still to* YOLLAND) How's the work going?

YOLLAND: The work? – the work? Oh, it's – it's staggering along – I think – (*To* OWEN) – isn't it? But we'd be lost without Roland.

MANUS: (*Leaving*) I'm sure. But there are always the Rolands, aren't there?

(*He goes upstairs and exits.*)

YOLLAND: What was that he said? – something about Lancey, was it?

OWEN: He said we should hide that bottle before Father gets his hands on it.

YOLLAND: Ah.

OWEN: He's always trying to protect him.

YOLLAND: Was he lame from birth?

OWEN: An accident when he was a baby: Father fell across his cradle. That's why Manus feels so responsible for him.

YOLLAND: Why doesn't he marry?

OWEN: Can't afford to, I suppose.

YOLLAND: Hasn't he a salary?

OWEN: What salary? All he gets is the odd shilling Father throws

412

him – and that's seldom enough. I got out in time, didn't I?
(YOLLAND *is pouring a drink.*)
Easy with that stuff – it'll hit you suddenly.

YOLLAND: I like it.

OWEN: Let's get back to the job. Druim Dubh – what's it called in the jury lists? (*Consults texts.*)

YOLLAND: Some people here resent us.

OWEN: Dramduff – wrong as usual.

YOLLAND: I was passing a little girl yesterday and she spat at me.

OWEN: And it's Drimdoo here. What's it called in the registry?

YOLLAND: Do you know the Donnelly twins?

OWEN: Who?

YOLLAND: The Donnelly twins.

OWEN: Yes. Best fishermen about here. What about them?

YOLLAND: Lancey's looking for them.

OWEN: What for?

YOLLAND: He wants them for questioning.

OWEN: Probably stolen somebody's nets. Dramduffy! Nobody ever called it Dramduffy. Take your pick of those three.

YOLLAND: My head's addled. Let's take a rest. Do you want a drink?

OWEN: Thanks. Now, every Dubh we've come across we've changed to Duff. So if we're to be consistent, I suppose Druim Dubh has to become Dromduff.
(YOLLAND *is now looking out the window.*)
You can see the end of the ridge from where you're standing. But D-r-u-m- or D-r-o-m-? (*Name-Book*) Do you remember – which did we agree on for Druim Luachra?

YOLLAND: That house immediately above where we're camped –

OWEN: Mm?

YOLLAND: The house where Maire lives.

OWEN: Maire? Oh, Maire Chatach.

YOLLAND: What does that mean?

OWEN: Curly-haired; the whole family are called the Catachs. What about it?

YOLLAND: I hear music coming from that house almost every night.

413

OWEN: Why don't you drop in?

YOLLAND: Could I?

OWEN: Why not? We used D-r-o-m then. So we've got to call it D-r-o-m-d-u-f-f – all right?

YOLLAND: Go back up to where the new school is being built and just say the names again for me, would you?

OWEN: That's a good idea. Poolkerry, Ballybeg –

YOLLAND: No, no; as they still are – in your own language.

OWEN: Poll na gCaorach,

(YOLLAND *repeats the names silently after him.*)

Baile Beag, Ceann Balor, Lis Maol, Machaire Buidhe, Baile na gGall, Carraig na Ri, Mullach Dearg –

YOLLAND: Do you think I could live here?

OWEN: What are you talking about?

YOLLAND: Settle down here – live here.

OWEN: Come on, George.

YOLLAND: I mean it.

OWEN: Live on what? Potatoes? Buttermilk?

YOLLAND: It's really heavenly.

OWEN: For God's sake! The first hot summer in fifty years and you think it's Eden. Don't be such a bloody romantic. You wouldn't survive a mild winter here.

YOLLAND: Do you think not? Maybe you're right.

(DOALTY *enters in a rush.*)

DOALTY: Hi, boys, is Manus about?

OWEN: He's upstairs. Give him a shout.

DOALTY: Manus! The cattle's going mad in that heat – Cripes, running wild all over the place. (*To* YOLLAND) How are you doing, skipper?

(MANUS *appears.*)

YOLLAND: Thank you for – I – I'm very grateful to you for –

DOALTY: Wasting your time. I don't know a word you're saying. Hi, Manus, there's two bucks down the road there asking for you.

MANUS: (*Descending*) Who are they?

DOALTY: Never clapped eyes on them. They want to talk to you.

MANUS: What about?

414

DOALTY: They wouldn't say. Come on. The bloody beasts'll end up in Loch an Iubhair if they're not capped. Good luck, boys!

(DOALTY *rushes off.* MANUS *follows him.*)

OWEN: Good luck! What were you thanking Doalty for?

YOLLAND: I was washing outside my tent this morning and he was passing with a scythe across his shoulder and he came up to me and pointed to the long grass and then cut a pathway round my tent and from the tent down to the road – so that my feet won't get wet with the dew. Wasn't that kind of him? And I have no words to thank him . . . I suppose you're right: I suppose I couldn't live here . . . Just before Doalty came up to me this morning, I was thinking that at that moment I might have been in Bombay instead of Ballybeg. You see, my father was at his wits end with me and finally he got me a job with the East India Company – some kind of a clerkship. This was ten, eleven months ago. So I set off for London. Unfortunately I – I – I missed the boat. Literally. And since I couldn't face Father and hadn't enough money to hang about until the next sailing, I joined the army. And they stuck me into the Engineers and posted me to Dublin. And Dublin sent me here. And while I was washing this morning and looking across the Tra Bhan, I was thinking how very, very lucky I am to be here and not in Bombay.

OWEN: Do you believe in fate?

YOLLAND: Lancey's so like my father. I was watching him last night. He met every group of sappers as they reported in. He checked the field kitchens. He examined the horses. He inspected every single report – even examining the texture of the paper and commenting on the neatness of the handwriting. The perfect colonial servant: not only must the job be done – it must be done with excellence. Father has that drive, too; that dedication; that indefatigable energy. He builds roads – hopping from one end of the Empire to the other. Can't sit still for five minutes. He says himself the longest time he ever sat still was the night before Waterloo when they were waiting for Wellington to

415

make up his mind to attack.

OWEN: What age is he?

YOLLAND: Born in 1789 – the very day the Bastille fell. I've
often thought maybe that gave his whole life its character.
Do you think it could? He inherited a new world the day he
was born – The Year One. Ancient time was at an end. The
world had cast off its old skin. There were no longer any
frontiers to man's potential. Possibilities were endless and
exciting. He still believes that. The Apocalypse is just about
to happen . . . I'm afraid I'm a great disappointment to
him. I've neither his energy, nor his coherence, nor his
belief. Do I believe in fate? The day I arrived in
Ballybeg – no, Baile Beag – the moment you brought me in
here, I had a curious sensation. It's difficult to describe. It
was a momentary sense of discovery; no – not quite a sense
of discovery – a sense of recognition, of confirmation of
something I half knew instinctively; as if I had stepped . . .

OWEN: Back into ancient time?

YOLLAND: No, no. It wasn't an awareness of *direction* being
changed but of experience being of a totally different order.
I had moved into a consciousness that wasn't striving nor
agitated, but at its ease and with its own conviction and
assurance. And when I heard Jimmy Jack and your father
swapping stories about Apollo and Cuchulainn and Paris
and Ferdia – as if they lived down the road – it was then that
I thought – I knew – perhaps I could live here . . . (*Now
embarrassed*) Where's the pot-een?

OWEN: Poteen.

YOLLAND: Poteen – poteen – poteen. Even if I did speak Irish
I'd always be an outsider here, wouldn't I? I may learn the
password but the language of the tribe will always elude
me, won't it? The private core will always be . . . hermetic,
won't it?

OWEN: You can learn to decode us.

(HUGH *emerges from upstairs and descends. He is dressed for
the road. Today he is physically and mentally jaunty and
alert – almost self-consciously jaunty and alert. Indeed, as the
scene progresses, one has the sense that he is deliberately*

416

parodying himself. The moment HUGH *gets to the bottom of the steps* YOLLAND *leaps respectfully to his feet.*)

HUGH: (*As he descends*)

> Quantumvis cursum longum fessumque moratur
> Sol, sacro tandem carmine vesper adest.

I dabble in verse, Lieutenant, after the style of Ovid. (*To* OWEN) A drop of that to fortify me.

YOLLAND: You'll have to translate it for me.

HUGH: Let's see –

> No matter how long the sun may linger on his long and weary journey
> At length evening comes with its sacred song.

YOLLAND: Very nice, sir.

HUGH: English succeeds in making it sound . . . plebeian.

OWEN: Where are you off to, Father?

HUGH: An *expeditio* with three purposes. Purpose A: to acquire a testimonial from our parish priest – (*To* YOLLAND) a worthy man but barely literate; and since he'll ask me to write it myself, how in all modesty can I do myself justice? (*To* OWEN) Where did this (*drink*) come from?

OWEN: Anna na mBreag's.

HUGH: (*To* YOLLAND) In that case address yourself to it with circumspection. (*And* HUGH *instantly tosses the drink back in one gulp and grimaces.*) Aaaaaaagh! (*Holds out his glass for a refill.*) Anna na mBreag means Anna of the Lies. And Purpose B: to talk to the builders of the new school about the kind of living accommodation I will require there. I have lived too long like a journeyman tailor.

YOLLAND: Some years ago we lived fairly close to a poet – well, about three miles away.

HUGH: His name?

YOLLAND: Wordsworth – William Wordsworth.

HUGH: Did he speak of me to you?

YOLLAND: Actually I never talked to him. I just saw him out walking – in the distance.

HUGH: Wordsworth? . . . No. I'm afraid we're not familiar with your literature, Lieutenant. We feel closer to the warm Mediterranean. We tend to overlook your island.

YOLLAND: I'm learning to speak Irish, sir.

HUGH: Good.

YOLLAND: Roland's teaching me.

HUGH: Splendid.

YOLLAND: I mean – I feel so cut off from the people here. And I was trying to explain a few minutes ago how remarkable a community this is. To meet people like yourself and Jimmy Jack who actually converse in Greek and Latin. And your place names – what was the one we came across this morning? – Termon, from Terminus, the god of boundaries. It – it – it's really astonishing.

HUGH: We like to think we endure around truths immemorially posited.

YOLLAND: And your Gaelic literature – you're a poet yourself –

HUGH: Only in Latin, I'm afraid.

YOLLAND: I understand it's enormously rich and ornate.

HUGH: Indeed, Lieutenant. A rich language. A rich literature. You'll find, sir, that certain cultures expend on their vocabularies and syntax acquisitive energies and ostentations entirely lacking in their material lives. I suppose you could call us a spiritual people.

OWEN: (*Not unkindly; more out of embarrassment before* YOLLAND) Will you stop that nonsense, Father.

HUGH: Nonsense? What nonsense?

OWEN: Do you know where the priest lives?

HUGH: At Lis na Muc, over near . . .

OWEN: No, he doesn't. Lis na Muc, the Fort of the Pigs, has become Swinefort. (*Now turning the pages of the Name-Book – a page per name.*) And to get to Swinefort you pass through Greencastle and Fair Head and Strandhill and Gort and Whiteplains. And the new school isn't at Poll na gCaorach – it's at Sheepsrock. Will you be able to find your way?

(HUGH *pours himself another drink. Then:*–)

HUGH: Yes, it is a rich language, Lieutenant, full of the mythologies of fantasy and hope and self-deception – a syntax opulent with tomorrows. It is our response to mud cabins and a diet of potatoes; our only method of replying to . . . inevitabilities. (*To* OWEN) Can you give me the loan of half-a-crown? I'll repay you out of the subscriptions I'm collecting for the publication of my new book. (*To* YOLLAND) It is entitled: 'The Pentaglot Preceptor or Elementary Institute of the English, Greek, Hebrew, Latin and Irish Languages; Particularly Calculated for the Instruction of Such Ladies and Gentlemen as may Wish to Learn without the Help of a Master'.

YOLLAND: (*Laughs*) That's a wonderful title!

HUGH: Between ourselves – the best part of the enterprise. Nor do I, in fact, speak Hebrew. And that last phrase – 'without the Help of a Master' – that was written before the new national school was thrust upon me – do you think I ought to drop it now? After all you don't dispose of the cow just because it has produced a magnificent calf, do you?

YOLLAND: You certainly do not.

HUGH: The phrase goes. And I'm interrupting work of moment. (*He goes to the door and stops there.*) To return briefly to that other matter, Lieutenant. I understand your sense of exclusion, of being cut off from a life here; and I trust you will find access to us with my son's help. But remember that words are signals, counters. They are not immortal. And it can happen – to use an image you'll understand – it can happen that a civilization can be imprisoned in a linguistic contour which no longer matches the landscape of . . . fact. Gentlemen. (*He leaves.*)

OWEN: 'An *expeditio* with three purposes': the children laugh at him: he always promises three points and he never gets beyond A and B.

MANUS: He's an astute man.

OWEN: He's bloody pompous.

YOLLAND: But so astute.

OWEN: And he drinks too much. Is it astute not to be able to adjust for survival? Enduring around truths immemorially posited – hah!

YOLLAND: He knows what's happening.

OWEN: What is happening?

YOLLAND: I'm not sure. But I'm concerned about my part in it.

419

It's an eviction of sorts.

OWEN: We're making a six-inch map of the country. Is there something sinister in that?

YOLLAND: Not in—

OWEN: And we're taking place-names that are riddled with confusion and—

YOLLAND: Who's confused? Are the people confused?

OWEN: —and we're standardizing those names as accurately and as sensitively as we can.

YOLLAND: Something is being eroded.

OWEN: Back to the romance again. All right! Fine! Fine! Look where we've got to. (*He drops on his hands and knees and stabs a finger at the map.*) We've come to this crossroads. Come here and look at it, man! Look at it! And we call that crossroads Tobair Vree. And why do we call it Tobair Vree? I'll tell you why. Tobair means a well. But what does Vree mean? It's a corruption of Brian—(*Gaelic pronunciation*) Brian—an erosion of Tobair Bhriain. Because a hundred-and-fifty years ago there used to be a well there, not at the crossroads, mind you—that would be too simple—but in a field close to the crossroads. And an old man called Brian, whose face was disfigured by an enormous growth, got it into his head that the water in that well was blessed; and every day for seven months he went there and bathed his face in it. But the growth didn't go away; and one morning Brian was found drowned in that well. And ever since that crossroads is known as Tobair Vree—even though that well has long since dried up. I know the story because my grandfather told it to me. But ask Doalty—or Maire—or Bridget—even my father—even Manus—why it's called Tobair Vree; and do you think they'll know? I know they don't know. So the question I put to you, Lieutenant, is this: what do we do with a name like that? Do we scrap Tobair Vree altogether and call it—what?—The Cross? Crossroads? Or do we keep piety with a man long dead, long forgotten, his name 'eroded' beyond recognition, whose trivial little story nobody in the parish remembers?

YOLLAND: Except you.

420

OWEN: I've left here.

YOLLAND: You remember it.

OWEN: I'm asking you: what do we write in the Name-Book?

YOLLAND: Tobair Vree.

OWEN: Even though the well is a hundred yards from the actual
crossroads – and there's no well anyway – and what the hell
does Vree mean?

YOLLAND: Tobair Vree.

OWEN: That's what you want?

YOLLAND: Yes.

OWEN: You're certain?

YOLLAND: Yes.

OWEN: Fine. Fine. That's what you'll get.

YOLLAND: That's what you want, too, Roland.
(*Pause.*)

OWEN: (*Explodes*) George! For God's sake! *My name is not Roland!*

YOLLAND: What?

OWEN: (*Softly*) My name is Owen.
(*Pause.*)

YOLLAND: Not Roland?

OWEN: Owen.

YOLLAND: You mean to say – ?

OWEN: Owen.

YOLLAND: But I've been –

OWEN: O-w-e-n.

YOLLAND: Where did Roland come from?

OWEN: I don't know.

YOLLAND: It was never Roland?

OWEN: Never.

YOLLAND: O my God!
(*Pause. They stare at one another. Then the absurdity of the
situation strikes them suddenly. They explode with laughter.*
OWEN *pours drinks. As they roll about, their lines overlap.*)

YOLLAND: Why didn't you tell me?

OWEN: Do I look like a Roland?

YOLLAND: Spell Owen again.

OWEN: I was getting fond of Roland.

YOLLAND: O my God!

OWEN: O-w-e-n.

YOLLAND: What'll we write—

OWEN: —in the Name-Book?!

YOLLAND: R-o-w-e-n!

OWEN: Or what about Ol-

YOLLAND: Ol- what?

OWEN: Oland!

 (*And again they explode.* MANUS *enters. He is very elated.*)

MANUS: What's the celebration?

OWEN: A christening!

YOLLAND: A baptism!

OWEN: A hundred christenings!

YOLLAND: A thousand baptisms! Welcome to Eden!

OWEN: Eden's right! We name a thing and—bang!—it leaps into existence!

YOLLAND: Each name a perfect equation with its roots.

OWEN: A perfect congruence with its reality. (*To* MANUS) Take a drink.

YOLLAND: Poteen—beautiful.

OWEN: Lying Anna's poteen.

YOLLAND: Anna na mBreag's poteen.

OWEN: Excellent, George.

YOLLAND: I'll decode you yet.

OWEN: (*Offers drink*) Manus?

MANUS: Not if that's what it does to you.

OWEN: You're right. Steady—steady—sober up—sober up.

YOLLAND: Sober as a judge, Owen.

 (MANUS *moves beside* OWEN.)

MANUS: I've got good news! Where's Father?

OWEN: He's gone out. What's the good news?

MANUS: I've been offered a job.

OWEN: Where? (*Now aware of* YOLLAND.) Come on, man—speak in English.

MANUS: For the benefit of the colonist?

OWEN: He's a decent man.

MANUS: Aren't they all at some level?

OWEN: Please.

 (MANUS *shrugs.*)

422

[handwritten marginalia:] And God said... and it was. Silence → existence

He's been offered a job.

YOLLAND: Where?

OWEN: Well – tell us!

MANUS: I've just had a meeting with two men from Inis Meadhon. They want me to go there and start a hedge-school. They're giving me a free house, free turf, and free milk; a rood of standing corn; twelve drills of potatoes; and –
(*He stops.*)

OWEN: And what?

MANUS: A salary of £42 a year!

OWEN: Manus, that's wonderful!

MANUS: You're talking to a man of substance.

OWEN: I'm delighted.

YOLLAND: Where's Inis Meadhon?

OWEN: An island south of here. And they came looking for you?

MANUS: Well, I mean to say . . .
(OWEN *punches* MANUS.)

OWEN: Aaaaagh! This calls for a real celebration.

YOLLAND: Congratulations.

MANUS: Thank you.

OWEN: Where are you, Anna?

YOLLAND: When do you start?

MANUS: Next Monday.

OWEN: We'll stay with you when we're there. (*To* YOLLAND) How long will it be before we reach Inis Meadhon?

YOLLAND: How far south is it?

MANUS: About fifty miles.

YOLLAND: Could we make it by December?

OWEN: We'll have Christmas together. (*Sings*) 'Christmas Day on Inis Meadhon . . .'

YOLLAND: (*Toast*) I hope you're very content there, Manus.

MANUS: Thank you.
(YOLLAND *holds out his hand.* MANUS *takes it. They shake warmly.*)

OWEN: (*Toast*) Manus.

MANUS: (*Toast*) To Inis Meadhon.
(*He drinks quickly and turns to leave.*)

OWEN: Hold on – hold on – refills coming up.

MANUS: I've got to go.

OWEN: Come on, man; this is an occasion. Where are you rushing to?

MANUS: I've got to tell Maire.

(MAIRE *enters with her can of milk.*)

MAIRE: You've got to tell Maire what?

OWEN: He's got a job!

MAIRE: Manus?

OWEN: He's been invited to start a hedge-school in Inis Meadhon.

MAIRE: Where?

MANUS: Inis Meadhon – the island! They're giving me £42 a year and . . .

OWEN: A house, fuel, milk, potatoes, corn, pupils, what-not!

MANUS: I start on Monday.

OWEN: You'll take a drink. Isn't it great?

MANUS: I want to talk to you for –

MAIRE: There's your milk. I need the can back.

(MANUS *takes the can and runs up the steps.*)

MANUS: (*As he goes*) How will you like living on an island?

OWEN: You know George, don't you?

MAIRE: We wave to each other across the fields.

YOLLAND: Sorry-sorry?

OWEN: She says you wave to each other across the fields.

YOLLAND: Yes, we do; oh, yes; indeed we do.

MAIRE: What's he saying?

OWEN: He says you wave to each other across the fields.

MAIRE: That's right. So we do.

YOLLAND: What's she saying?

OWEN: Nothing – nothing – nothing. (*To* MAIRE) What's the news?

(MAIRE *moves away, touching the text books with her toe.*)

MAIRE: Not a thing. You're busy, the two of you.

OWEN: We think we are.

MAIRE: I hear the Fiddler O'Shea's about. There's some talk of a dance tomorrow night.

OWEN: Where will it be?

MAIRE: Maybe over the road. Maybe at Tobair Vree.

YOLLAND: Tobair Vree!

MAIRE: Yes.

YOLLAND: Tobair Vree! Tobair Vree!

MAIRE: Does he know what I'm saying?

OWEN: Not a word.

MAIRE: Tell him then.

OWEN: Tell him what?

MAIRE: About the dance.

OWEN: Maire says there may be a dance tomorrow night.

YOLLAND: (*To* OWEN) Yes? May I come? (*To* MAIRE) Would anybody object if I came?

MAIRE: (*To* OWEN) What's he saying?

OWEN: (*To* YOLLAND) Who would object?

MAIRE: (*To* OWEN) Did you tell him?

YOLLAND: (*To* MAIRE) Sorry-sorry?

OWEN: (*To* MAIRE) He says may he come?

MAIRE: (*To* YOLLAND) That's up to you.

YOLLAND: (*To* OWEN) What does she say?

OWEN: (*To* YOLLAND) She says—

YOLLAND: (*To* MAIRE) What-what?

MAIRE: (*To* OWEN) Well?

YOLLAND: (*To* OWEN) Sorry-sorry?

OWEN: (*To* YOLLAND) Will you go?

YOLLAND: (*To* MAIRE) Yes, yes, if I may.

MAIRE: (*To* OWEN) What does he say?

YOLLAND: (*To* OWEN) What is she saying?

OWEN: Oh for God's sake! (*To* MANUS *who is descending with the empty can.*) You take on this job, Manus.

MANUS: I'll walk you up to the house. Is your mother at home? I want to talk to her.

MAIRE: What's the rush? (*To* OWEN) Didn't you offer me a drink?

OWEN: Will you risk Anna na mBreag?

MAIRE: Why not.

(YOLLAND *is suddenly intoxicated. He leaps up on a stool, raises his glass and shouts.*)

YOLLAND: Anna na mBreag! Baile Beag! Inis Meadhon! Bombay! Tobair Vree! Eden! And poteen—correct, Owen?

OWEN: Perfect.

YOLLAND: And bloody marvellous stuff it is, too. I love it!
Bloody, bloody, bloody marvellous!
(*Simultaneously with his final 'bloody marvellous' bring up very
loud the introductory music of the reel. Then immediately go to
black. Retain the music throughout the very brief interval.*)

SCENE II

The following night.

*This scene may be played in the schoolroom, but it would be
preferable to lose – by lighting – as much of the schoolroom as
possible, and to play the scene down front in a vaguely 'outside' area.*

*The music rises to a crescendo. Then in the distance we hear
MAIRE and YOLLAND approach – laughing and running. They run
on, hand-in-hand. They have just left the dance. Fade the music to
distant background. Then after a time it is lost and replaced by guitar
music. MAIRE and YOLLAND are now down front, still holding
hands and excited by their sudden and impetuous escape from the
dance.*

MAIRE: O my God, that leap across the ditch nearly killed me.

YOLLAND: I could scarcely keep up with you.

MAIRE: Wait till I get my breath back.

YOLLAND: We must have looked as if we were being chased.
(*They now realize they are alone and holding hands – the
beginnings of embarrassment. The hands disengage. They begin
to drift apart. Pause.*)

MAIRE: Manus'll wonder where I've got to.

YOLLAND: I wonder did anyone notice us leave.
(*Pause. Slightly further apart.*)

MAIRE: The grass must be wet. My feet are soaking.

YOLLAND: Your feet must be wet. The grass is soaking.
(*Another pause. Another few paces apart. They are now a long
distance from one another.*)

YOLLAND: (*Indicating himself*) George.

426

(MAIRE *nods:* Yes-yes. *Then:*–)

MAIRE: Lieutenant George.

YOLLAND: Don't call me that. I never think of myself as Lieutenant.

MAIRE: What-what?

YOLLAND: Sorry-sorry? (*He points to himself again.*) George.

(MAIRE *nods:* Yes-yes. *Then points to herself.*)

MAIRE: Maire.

YOLLAND: Yes, I know you're Maire. Of course I know you're Maire. I mean I've been watching you night and day for the past –

MAIRE: (*Eagerly*) What-what?

YOLLAND: (*Points*) Maire. (*Points.*) George. (*Points both.*) Maire and George.

(MAIRE *nods:* Yes-yes-yes.)

I – I – I –

MAIRE: Say anything at all. I love the sound of your speech.

YOLLAND: (*Eagerly*) Sorry-sorry?

(*In acute frustration he looks around, hoping for some inspiration that will provide him with communicative means. Now he has a thought: he tries raising his voice and articulating in a staccato style and with equal and absurd emphasis on each word.*)

Every-morning-I-see-you-feeding-brown-hens-and-giving-meal-to-black-calf –(*The futility of it*) – O my God.

(MAIRE *smiles. She moves towards him. She will try to communicate in Latin.*)

MAIRE: *Tu es centurio in* – *in* – *in exercitu Britannico* –

YOLLAND: Yes-yes? Go on – go on – say anything at all – I love the sound of your speech.

MAIRE: – *et es in castris quae* – *quae* – *quae sunt in agro* –(*The futility of it*) – O my God.

(YOLLAND *smiles. He moves towards her. Now for her English words.*) George – water.

YOLLAND: 'Water'? Water! Oh yes – water – water – very good – water – good – good.

MAIRE: Fire.

YOLLAND: Fire – indeed – wonderful – fire, fire, fire – splendid – splendid!

427

MAIRE: Ah . . . ah . . .

YOLLAND: Yes? Go on.

MAIRE: Earth.

YOLLAND: 'Earth'?

MAIRE: Earth. Earth.

(YOLLAND *still does not understand.* MAIRE *stoops down and picks up a handful of clay. Holding it out.*) Earth.

YOLLAND: Earth! Of course – earth! Earth. Earth. Good Lord, Maire, your English is perfect!

MAIRE: (*Eagerly*) What-what?

YOLLAND: Perfect English. English perfect.

MAIRE: George –

YOLLAND: That's beautiful – oh, that's really beautiful.

MAIRE: George –

YOLLAND: Say it again – say it again –

MAIRE: Shhh. (*She holds her hand up for silence – she is trying to remember her one line of English. Now she remembers it and she delivers the line as if English were her language – easily, fluidly, conversationally.*)

George, 'In Norfolk we besport ourselves around the maypoll.'

YOLLAND: Good God, do you? That's where my mother comes from – Norfolk. Norwich actually. Not exactly Norwich town but a small village called Little Walsingham close beside it. But in our own village of Winfarthing we have a maypole too and every year on the first of May – (*He stops abruptly, only now realizing. He stares at her. She in turn misunderstands his excitement.*)

MAIRE: (*To herself*) Mother of God, my Aunt Mary wouldn't have taught me something dirty, would she?

(*Pause.* YOLLAND *extends his hand to* MAIRE. *She turns away from him and moves slowly across the stage.*)

YOLLAND: Maire.

(*She still moves away.*)

Maire Chatach.

(*She still moves away.*)

Bun na hAbhann? (*He says the name softly, almost privately, very tentatively, as if he were searching for a sound she might*

428

respond to. He tries again.) Druim Dubh?

(MAIRE *stops. She is listening.* YOLLAND *is encouraged.*)

Poll na gCaorach. Lis Maol.

(MAIRE *turns towards him.*)

Lis na nGall.

MAIRE: Lis na nGradh.

(They are now facing each other and begin moving – almost imperceptibly – towards one another.)

MAIRE: Carraig an Phoill.

YOLLAND: Carraig na Ri. Loch na nEan.

MAIRE: Loch an Iubhair. Machaire Buidhe.

YOLLAND: Machaire Mor. Cnoc na Mona.

MAIRE: Cnoc na nGabhar.

YOLLAND: Mullach.

MAIRE: Port.

YOLLAND: Tor.

MAIRE: Lag.

(She holds out her hands to YOLLAND. *He takes them. Each now speaks almost to himself/herself.)*

YOLLAND: I wish to God you could understand me.

MAIRE: Soft hands; a gentleman's hands.

YOLLAND: Because if you could understand me I could tell you how I spend my days either thinking of you or gazing up at your house in the hope that you'll appear even for a second.

MAIRE: Every evening you walk by yourself along the Tra Bhan and every morning you wash yourself in front of your tent.

YOLLAND: I would tell you how beautiful you are, curly-headed Maire. I would so like to tell you how beautiful you are.

MAIRE: Your arms are long and thin and the skin on your shoulders is very white.

YOLLAND: I would tell you . . .

MAIRE: Don't stop – I know what you're saying.

YOLLAND: I would tell you how I want to be here – to live here – always – with you – always, always.

MAIRE: 'Always'? What is that word – 'always'?

YOLLAND: Yes-yes; always.

MAIRE: You're trembling.

YOLLAND: Yes, I'm trembling because of you.

MAIRE: I'm trembling, too.

   (*She holds his face in her hand.*)

YOLLAND: I've made up my mind . . .

MAIRE: Shhhh.

YOLLAND: I'm not going to leave here . . .

MAIRE: Shhh – listen to me. I want you, too, soldier.

YOLLAND: Don't stop – I know what you're saying.

MAIRE: I want to live with you – anywhere – anywhere at
   all – always – always.

YOLLAND: 'Always'? What is that word – 'always'?

MAIRE: Take me away with you, George.

   (*Pause. Suddenly they kiss.* SARAH *enters. She sees them. She
   stands shocked, staring at them. Her mouth works. Then almost
   to herself.*)

SARAH: Manus . . . Manus!

   (SARAH *runs off. Music to crescendo.*)

ACT THREE

The following evening. It is raining.

   SARAH *and* OWEN *alone in the schoolroom.* SARAH, *more waiflike than ever, is sitting very still on a stool, an open book across her
knee. She is pretending to read but her eyes keep going up to the room
upstairs.* OWEN *is working on the floor as before, surrounded by his
reference books, map, Name-Book, etc. But he has neither
concentration nor interest; and like* SARAH *he glances up at the
upstairs room.*

   After a few seconds MANUS *emerges and descends, carrying a
large paper bag which already contains his clothes. His movements
are determined and urgent. He moves around the classroom, picking
up books, examining each title carefully, and choosing about six of
them which he puts into his bag. As he selects these books:–*

OWEN: You know that old limekiln beyond Con Connie Tim's
   pub, the place we call The Murren? – do you know why it's
   called The Murren?

430

(MANUS *does not answer.*)

I've only just discovered: it's a corruption of Saint Muranus. It seems Saint Muranus had a monastery somewhere about there at the beginning of the seventh century. And over the years the name became shortened to the Murren. Very unattractive name, isn't it? I think we should go back to the original – Saint Muranus. What do you think? The original's Saint Muranus. Don't you think we should go back to that?

(*No response.* OWEN *begins writing the name into the Name-Book.* MANUS *is now rooting about among the forgotten implements for a piece of rope. He finds a piece. He begins to tie the mouth of the flimsy, overloaded bag – and it bursts, the contents spilling out on the floor.*)

MANUS: Bloody, bloody, bloody hell!

(*His voice breaks in exasperation: he is about to cry.* OWEN *leaps to his feet.*)

OWEN: Hold on. I've a bag upstairs.

(*He runs upstairs.* SARAH *waits until* OWEN *is off. Then:* –)

SARAH: Manus . . . Manus, I . . .

(MANUS *hears* SARAH *but makes no acknowledgement. He gathers up his belongings.* OWEN *reappears with the bag he had on his arrival.*)

OWEN: Take this one – I'm finished with it anyway. And it's supposed to keep out the rain.

(MANUS *transfers his few belongings.* OWEN *drifts back to his task. The packing is now complete.*)

MANUS: You'll be here for a while? For a week or two anyhow?

OWEN: Yes.

MANUS: You're not leaving with the army?

OWEN: I haven't made up my mind. Why?

MANUS: Those Inis Meadhon men will be back to see why I haven't turned up. Tell them – tell them I'll write to them as soon as I can. Tell them I still want the job but that it might be three or four months before I'm free to go.

OWEN: You're being damned stupid, Manus.

MANUS: Will you do that for me?

431

OWEN: Clear out now and Lancey'll think you're involved
somehow.

MANUS: Will you do that for me?

OWEN: Wait a couple of days even. You know George – he's a
bloody romantic – maybe he's gone out to one of the islands
and he'll suddenly reappear tomorrow morning. Or maybe
the search party'll find him this evening lying drunk
somewhere in the sandhills. You've seen him drinking that
poteen – doesn't know how to handle it. Had he drink on
him last night at the dance?

MANUS: I had a stone in my hand when I went out looking for
him – I was going to fell him. The lame scholar turned
violent.

OWEN: Did anybody see you?

MANUS: (*Again close to tears*) But when I saw him standing there
at the side of the road – smiling – and her face buried in his
shoulder – I couldn't even go close to them. I just shouted
something stupid – something like, 'You're a bastard,
Yolland.' If I'd even said it in English . . . 'cos he kept
saying 'Sorry-sorry?' The wrong gesture in the wrong
language.

OWEN: And you didn't see him again?

MANUS: 'Sorry?'

OWEN: Before you leave tell Lancey that – just to clear yourself.

MANUS: What have I to say to Lancey? You'll give that message
to the islandmen?

OWEN: I'm warning you: run away now and you're bound to be–

MANUS: (*To* SARAH) Will you give that message to the Inis
Meadhon men?

SARAH: I will.

(MANUS *picks up an old sack and throws it across his
shoulders.*)

OWEN: Have you any idea where you're going?

MANUS: Mayo, maybe. I remember Mother saying she had
cousins somewhere away out in the Erris Peninsula. (*He
picks up his bag.*) Tell Father I took only the Virgil and the
Caesar and the Aeschylus because they're mine anyway – I
bought them with the money I got for that pet lamb I

432

reared – do you remember that pet lamb? And tell him that
Nora Dan never returned the dictionary and that she still
owes him two-and-six for last quarter's reading – he always
forgets those things.

OWEN: Yes.

MANUS: And his good shirt's ironed and hanging up in the press
and his clean socks are in the butter-box under the bed.

OWEN: All right.

MANUS: And tell him I'll write.

OWEN: If Maire asks where you've gone. . . ?

MANUS: He'll need only half the amount of milk now, won't he?
Even less than half – he usually takes his tea black. (*Pause.*)
And when he comes in at night – you'll hear him; he makes
a lot of noise – I usually come down and give him a hand
up. Those stairs are dangerous without a banister. Maybe
before you leave you'd get Big Ned Frank to put up some
sort of a handrail. (*Pause.*) And if you can bake, he's very
fond of soda bread.

OWEN: I can give you money. I'm wealthy. Do you know what
they pay me? Two shillings a day for this – this – this –
(MANUS *rejects the offer by holding out his hand.*)
Goodbye, Manus.
(MANUS *and* OWEN *shake hands. Then* MANUS *picks up his
bag briskly and goes towards the door. He stops a few paces
beyond* SARAH, *turns, comes back to her. He addresses her as he
did in Act One but now without warmth or concern for her.*)

MANUS: What is your name? (*Pause.*) Come on. What is your
name?

SARAH: My name is Sarah.

MANUS: Just Sarah? Sarah what? (*Pause.*) Well?

SARAH: Sarah Johnny Sally.

MANUS: And where do you live? Come on.

SARAH: I live in Bun na hAbhann.
(*She is now crying quietly.*)

MANUS: Very good, Sarah Johnny Sally. There's nothing to stop
you now – nothing in the wide world. (*Pause. He looks down
at her.*) It's all right – it's all right – you did no harm – you
did no harm at all.

433

(*He stoops over her and kisses the top of her head – as if in absolution. Then briskly to the door and off.*)

OWEN: Good luck, Manus!

SARAH: (*Quietly*) I'm sorry . . . I'm sorry . . . I'm so sorry, Manus . . .

(*OWEN tries to work but cannot concentrate. He begins folding up the map. As he does:–*)

OWEN: Is there a class this evening?

(*SARAH nods: yes.*)

I suppose Father knows. Where is he anyhow?

(*SARAH points.*)

Where?

(*SARAH mimes rocking a baby.*)

I don't understand – where?

(*SARAH repeats the mime and wipes away tears. OWEN is still puzzled.*)

It doesn't matter. He'll probably turn up.

(*BRIDGET and DOALTY enter, sacks over their heads against the rain. They are self-consciously noisier, more ebullient, more garrulous than ever – brimming over with excitement and gossip and brio.*)

DOALTY: You're missing the crack, boys! Cripes, you're missing the crack! Fifty more soldiers arrived an hour ago!

BRIDGET: And they're spread out in a big line from Sean Neal's over to Lag and they're moving straight across the fields towards Cnoc na nGabhar!

DOALTY: Prodding every inch of the ground in front of them with their bayonets and scattering animals and hens in all directions!

BRIDGET: And tumbling everything before them – fences, ditches, haystacks, turf-stacks!

DOALTY: They came to Barney Petey's field of corn – straight through it be God as if it was heather!

BRIDGET: Not a blade of it left standing!

DOALTY: And Barney Petey just out of his bed and running after them in his drawers: 'You hoors you! Get out of my corn, you hoors you!'

BRIDGET: First time he ever ran in his life.

434

DOALTY: Too lazy, the wee get, to cut it when the weather was good.

(SARAH *begins putting out the seats.*)

BRIDGET: Tell them about Big Hughie.

DOALTY: Cripes, if you'd seen your aul fella, Owen.

BRIDGET: They were all inside in Anna na mBreag's pub – all the crowd from the wake –

DOALTY: And they hear the commotion and they all come out to the street –

BRIDGET: Your father in front; the Infant Prodigy footless behind him!

DOALTY: And your aul fella, he sees the army stretched across the countryside –

BRIDGET: O my God!

DOALTY: And Cripes he starts roaring at them!

BRIDGET: 'Visigoths! Huns! Vandals!'

DOALTY: *'Ignari! Stulti! Rustici!'*

BRIDGET: And wee Jimmy Jack jumping up and down and shouting, 'Thermopylae! Thermopylae!'

DOALTY: You never saw crack like it in your life, boys. Come away on out with me, Sarah, and you'll see it all.

BRIDGET: Big Hughie's fit to take no class. Is Manus about?

OWEN: Manus is gone.

BRIDGET: Gone where?

OWEN: He's left – gone away.

DOALTY: Where to?

OWEN: He doesn't know. Mayo, maybe.

DOALTY: What's on in Mayo?

OWEN: (*To* BRIDGET) Did you see George and Maire Chatach leave the dance last night?

BRIDGET: We did. Didn't we, Doalty?

OWEN: Did you see Manus following them out?

BRIDGET: I didn't see him going out but I saw him coming in by himself later.

OWEN: Did George and Maire come back to the dance?

BRIDGET: No.

OWEN: Did you see them again?

BRIDGET: He left her home. We passed them going up the back

435

road – didn't we, Doalty?

OWEN: And Manus stayed till the end of the dance?

DOALTY: We know nothing. What are you asking us for?

OWEN: Because Lancey'll question me when he hears Manus's gone. (*Back to* BRIDGET.) That's the way George went home? By the back road? That's where you saw him?

BRIDGET: Leave me alone, Owen. I know nothing about Yolland. If you want to know about Yolland, ask the Donnelly twins.

(*Silence.* DOALTY *moves over to the window.*)

(*To* SARAH) He's a powerful fiddler, O'Shea, isn't he? He told our Seamus he'll come back for a night at Hallowe'en.

(OWEN *goes to* DOALTY *who looks resolutely out the window.*)

OWEN: What's this about the Donnellys? (*Pause.*) Were they about last night?

DOALTY: Didn't see them if they were.

(*Begins whistling through his teeth.*)

OWEN: George is a friend of mine.

DOALTY: So.

OWEN: I want to know what's happened to him.

DOALTY: Couldn't tell you.

OWEN: What have the Donnelly twins to do with it? (*Pause.*) Doalty!

DOALTY: I know nothing, Owen – nothing at all – I swear to God. All I know is this: on my way to the dance I saw their boat beached at Port. It wasn't there on my way home, after I left Bridget. And that's all I know. As God's my judge. The half-dozen times I met him I didn't know a word he said to me; but he seemed a right enough sort . . . (*With sudden excessive interest in the scene outside.*) Cripes, they're crawling all over the place! Cripes, there's millions of them! Cripes, they're levelling the whole land!

(OWEN *moves away.* MAIRE *enters. She is bareheaded and wet from the rain; her hair in disarray. She attempts to appear normal but she is in acute distress, on the verge of being distraught. She is carrying the milk-can.*)

MAIRE: Honest to God, I must be going off my head. I'm half-way here and I think to myself, 'Isn't this can very light?' and I look into it and isn't it empty.

436

OWEN: It doesn't matter.

MAIRE: How will you manage for tonight?

OWEN: We have enough.

MAIRE: Are you sure?

OWEN: Plenty, thanks.

MAIRE: It'll take me no time at all to go back up for some.

OWEN: Honestly, Maire.

MAIRE: Sure it's better you have it than that black calf that's . . . that . . . (*She looks around*.) Have you heard anything?

OWEN: Nothing.

MAIRE: What does Lancey say?

OWEN: I haven't seen him since this morning.

MAIRE: What does he *think*?

OWEN: We really didn't talk. He was here for only a few seconds.

MAIRE: He left me home, Owen. And the last thing he said to me – he tried to speak in Irish – he said, 'I'll see you yesterday' – he meant to say 'I'll see you tomorrow.' And I laughed that much he pretended to get cross and he said 'Maypoll! Maypoll!' because I said that word wrong. And off he went, laughing – laughing, Owen! Do you think he's all right? What do *you* think?

OWEN: I'm sure he'll turn up. Maire.

MAIRE: He comes from a tiny wee place called Winfarthing. (*She suddenly drops on her hands and knees on the floor – where* OWEN *had his map a few minutes ago – and with her finger traces out an outline map*.) Come here till you see. Look. There's Winfarthing. And there's two other wee villages right beside it; one of them's called Barton Bendish – it's there; and the other's called Saxingham Nethergate – it's about there. And there's Little Walsingham – that's his mother's townland. Aren't they odd names? Sure they make no sense to me at all. And Winfarthing's near a big town called Norwich. And Norwich is in a county called Norfolk. And Norfolk is in the east of England. He drew a map for me on the wet strand and wrote the names on it. I have it all in my head now: Winfarthing – Barton Bendish – Saxingham Nethergate – Little Walsingham – Norwich –

Norfolk. Strange sounds, aren't they? But nice sounds; like Jimmy Jack reciting his Homer. (*She gets to her feet and looks around; she is almost serene now. To* SARAH) You were looking lovely last night, Sarah. Is that the dress you got from Boston? Green suits you. (*To* OWEN) Something very bad's happened to him, Owen. I know. He wouldn't go away without telling me. Where is he, Owen? You're his friend – where is he? (*Again she looks around the room; then sits on a stool.*) I didn't get a chance to do my geography last night. The master'll be angry with me. (*She rises again.*) I think I'll go home now. The wee ones have to be washed and put to bed and that black calf has to be fed . . . My hands are that rough; they're still blistered from the hay. I'm ashamed of them. I hope to God there's no hay to be saved in Brooklyn. (*She stops at the door.*) Did you hear? Nellie Ruadh's baby died in the middle of the night. I must go up to the wake. It didn't last long, did it?

(MAIRE *leaves. Silence. Then.*)

OWEN: I don't think there'll be any class. Maybe you should . . .

(OWEN *begins picking up his texts.* DOALTY *goes to him.*)

DOALTY: Is he long gone? – Manus.

OWEN: Half an hour.

DOALTY: Stupid bloody fool.

OWEN: I told him that.

DOALTY: Do they know he's gone?

OWEN: Who?

DOALTY: The army.

OWEN: Not yet.

DOALTY: They'll be after him like bloody beagles. Bloody, bloody fool, limping along the coast. They'll overtake him before night for Christ's sake.

(DOALTY *returns to the window.* LANCEY *enters – now the commanding officer.*)

OWEN: Any news? Any word?

(LANCEY *moves into the centre of the room, looking around as he does.*)

LANCEY: I understood there was a class. Where are the others?

438

OWEN: There was to be a class but my father –

LANCEY: This will suffice. I will address them and it will be their responsibility to pass on what I have to say to every family in this section.

(LANCEY *indicates to* OWEN *to translate.* OWEN *hesitates, trying to assess the change in* LANCEY'*s manner and attitude.*)

I'm in a hurry, O'Donnell.

OWEN: The captain has an announcement to make.

LANCEY: Lieutenant Yolland is missing. We are searching for him. If we don't find him, or if we receive no information as to where he is to be found, I will pursue the following course of action. (*He indicates to* OWEN *to translate.*)

OWEN: They are searching for George. If they don't find him –

LANCEY: Commencing twenty-four hours from now we will shoot all livestock in Ballybeg.

(OWEN *stares at* LANCEY.)

At once.

OWEN: Beginning this time tomorrow they'll kill every animal in Baile Beag – unless they're told where George is.

LANCEY: If that doesn't bear results, commencing forty-eight hours from now we will embark on a series of evictions and levelling of every abode in the following selected areas –

OWEN: You're not –!

LANCEY: Do your job. Translate.

OWEN: If they still haven't found him in two days time they'll begin evicting and levelling every house starting with these townlands.

(LANCEY *reads from his list.*)

LANCEY: Swinefort.

OWEN: Lis na Muc.

LANCEY: Burnfoot.

OWEN: Bun na hAbhann.

LANCEY: Dromduff.

OWEN: Druim Dubh.

LANCEY: Whiteplains.

OWEN: Machaire Ban.

LANCEY: Kings Head.

OWEN: Cnoc na Ri.

LANCEY: If by then the lieutenant hasn't been found, we will proceed until a complete clearance is made of this entire section.

OWEN: If Yolland hasn't been got by then, they will ravish the whole parish.

LANCEY: I trust they know exactly what they've got to do.
(*Pointing to* BRIDGET.) I know you. I know where you live.
(*Pointing to* SARAH.) Who are you? Name!
(SARAH's *mouth opens and shuts, opens and shuts. Her face becomes contorted.*)
What's your name?
(*Again* SARAH *tries frantically.*)

OWEN: Go on, Sarah. You can tell him.
(*But* SARAH *cannot. And she knows she cannot. She closes her mouth. Her head goes down.*)

OWEN: Her name is Sarah Johnny Sally.

LANCEY: Where does she live?

OWEN: Bun na hAbhann.

LANCEY: Where?

OWEN: Burnfoot.

LANCEY: I want to talk to your brother — is he here?

OWEN: Not at the moment.

LANCEY: Where is he?

OWEN: He's at a wake.

LANCEY: What wake?
(DOALTY, *who has been looking out the window all through* LANCEY's *announcements, now speaks — calmly, almost casually.*)

DOALTY: Tell him his whole camp's on fire.

LANCEY: What's your name? (*To* OWEN) Who's that lout?

OWEN: Doalty Dan Doalty.

LANCEY: Where does he live?

OWEN: Tulach Alainn.

LANCEY: What do we call it?

OWEN: Fair Hill. He says your whole camp is on fire.
(LANCEY *rushes to the window and looks out. Then he wheels on* DOALTY.)

LANCEY: I'll remember you, Mr Doalty. (*To* OWEN) You carry

440

a big responsibility in all this.

(*He goes off.*)

BRIDGET: Mother of God, does he mean it, Owen?

OWEN: Yes, he does.

BRIDGET: We'll have to hide the beasts somewhere – our Seamus'll know where. Maybe at the back of Lis na nGradh – or in the caves at the far end of the Tra Bhan. Come on, Doalty! Come on! Don't be standing about there!

(DOALTY *does not move.* BRIDGET *runs to the door and stops suddenly. She sniffs the air. Panic.*)

The sweet smell! Smell it! It's the sweet smell! Jesus, it's the potato blight!

DOALTY: It's the army tents burning, Bridget.

BRIDGET: Is it? Are you sure? Is that what it is? God, I thought we were destroyed altogether. Come on! Come on!

(*She runs off.* OWEN *goes to* SARAH *who is preparing to leave.*)

OWEN: How are you? Are you all right?

(SARAH *nods: Yes.*)

OWEN: Don't worry. It will come back to you again.

(SARAH *shakes her head.*)

OWEN: It will. You're upset now. He frightened you. That's all's wrong.

(*Again* SARAH *shakes her head, slowly, emphatically, and smiles at* OWEN. *Then she leaves.* OWEN *busies himself gathering his belongings.* DOALTY *leaves the window and goes to him.*)

DOALTY: He'll do it, too.

OWEN: Unless Yolland's found.

DOALTY: Hah!

OWEN: Then he'll certainly do it.

DOALTY: When my grandfather was a boy they did the same thing.

(*Simply, altogether without irony*) And after all the trouble you went to, mapping the place and thinking up new names for it.

(OWEN *busies himself. Pause.* DOALTY *almost dreamily.*) I've damned little to defend but he'll not put me out without a fight. And there'll be others who think the same as me.

OWEN: That's a matter for you.

DOALTY: If we'd all stick together. If we knew how to defend ourselves.

OWEN: Against a trained army.

DOALTY: The Donnelly twins know how.

OWEN: If they could be found.

DOALTY: If they could be found. (*He goes to the door.*) Give me a shout after you've finished with Lancey. I might know something then.

(*He leaves.*)

(OWEN *picks up the Name-Book. He looks at it momentarily, then puts it on top of the pile he is carrying. It falls to the floor. He stoops to pick it up – hesitates – leaves it. He goes upstairs. As* OWEN *ascends,* HUGH *and* JIMMY JACK *enter. Both wet and drunk.* JIMMY *is very unsteady. He is trotting behind* HUGH, *trying to break in on* HUGH's *declamation.* HUGH *is equally drunk but more experienced in drunkenness: there is a portion of his mind which retains its clarity.*)

HUGH: There I was, appropriately dispositioned to proffer my condolences to the bereaved mother . . .

JIMMY: Hugh –

HUGH: . . . and about to enter the *domus lugubris* – Maire Chatach?

JIMMY: The wake house.

HUGH: Indeed – when I experience a plucking at my elbow: Mister George Alexander, Justice of the Peace. 'My tidings are infelicitous,' said he – Bridget? Too slow. Doalty?

JIMMY: *Infelix* – unhappy.

HUGH: Unhappy indeed. 'Master Bartley Timlin has been appointed to the new national school.' 'Timlin? Who is Timlin?' 'A schoolmaster from Cork. And he will be a major asset to the community: he is also a very skilled bacon-curer!'

JIMMY: Hugh –

HUGH: Ha-ha-ha-ha-ha! The Cork bacon-curer! *Barbarus hic ego sum quia non intelligor ulli* – James?

JIMMY: Ovid.

HUGH: *Procede.*

442

JIMMY: 'I am a barbarian in this place because I am not understood by anyone.'

HUGH: Indeed – (*Shouts*) Manus! Tea! I will compose a satire on Master Bartley Timlin, schoolmaster and bacon-curer. But it will be too easy, won't it? (*Shouts*) Strong tea! Black! (*The only way* JIMMY *can get* HUGH's *attention is by standing in front of him and holding his arms.*)

JIMMY: Will you listen to me, Hugh!

HUGH: James. (*Shouts*) And a slice of soda bread.

JIMMY: I'm going to get married.

HUGH: Well!

JIMMY: At Christmas.

HUGH: Splendid.

JIMMY: To Athene.

HUGH: Who?

JIMMY: Pallas Athene.

HUGH: *Glaukopis Athene?*

JIMMY: Flashing-eyed, Hugh, flashing-eyed! (*He attempts the gesture he has made before: standing to attention, the momentary spasm, the salute, the face raised in pained ecstasy – but the body does not respond efficiently this time. The gesture is grotesque.*)

HUGH: The lady has assented?

JIMMY: She asked *me* – *I* assented.

HUGH: Ah. When was this?

JIMMY: Last night.

HUGH: What does her mother say?

JIMMY: Metis from Hellespont? Decent people – good stock.

HUGH: And her father?

JIMMY: I'm meeting Zeus tomorrow. Hugh, will you be my best man?

HUGH: Honoured, James; profoundly honoured.

JIMMY: You know what I'm looking for, Hugh, don't you? I mean to say – you know – I – I – I joke like the rest of them – you know? – (*Again he attempts the pathetic routine but abandons it instantly.*) You know yourself, Hugh – don't you? – you know all that. But what I'm really looking for, Hugh – what I really want – companionship, Hugh – at my

443

time of life, companionship, company, someone to talk to. Away up in Beann na Gaoithe – you've no idea how lonely it is. Companionship – correct, Hugh? Correct?

HUGH: Correct.

JIMMY: And I always liked her, Hugh. Correct?

HUGH: Correct, James.

JIMMY: Someone to talk to.

HUGH: Indeed.

JIMMY: That's all, Hugh. The whole story. You know it all now, Hugh. You know it all.

(*As* JIMMY *says those last lines he is crying, shaking his head, trying to keep his balance, and holding a finger up to his lips in absurd gestures of secrecy and intimacy. Now he staggers away, tries to sit on a stool, misses it, slides to the floor, his feet in front of him, his back against the broken cart. Almost at once he is asleep.* HUGH *watches all of this. Then he produces his flask and is about to pour a drink when he sees the Name-Book on the floor. He picks it up and leafs through it, pronouncing the strange names as he does. Just as he begins,* OWEN *emerges and descends with two bowls of tea.*)

HUGH: Ballybeg. Burnfoot. King's Head. Whiteplains. Fair Hill. Dunboy. Green Bank.

(OWEN *snatches the book from* HUGH.)

OWEN: I'll take that. (*In apology.*) It's only a catalogue of names.

HUGH: I know what it is.

OWEN: A mistake – my mistake – nothing to do with us. I hope that's strong enough (*tea*). (*He throws the book on the table and crosses over to* JIMMY.)

Jimmy. Wake up, Jimmy. Wake up, man.

JIMMY: What – what-what?

OWEN: Here. Drink this. Then go on away home. There may be trouble. Do you hear me, Jimmy? There may be trouble.

HUGH: (*Indicating Name-Book*) We must learn those new names.

OWEN: (*Searching around*) Did you see a sack lying about?

HUGH: We must learn where we live. We must learn to make them our own. We must make them our new home.

(OWEN *finds a sack and throws it across his shoulders.*)

OWEN: I know where I live.

HUGH: James thinks he knows, too. I look at James and three thoughts occur to me: A – that it is not the literal past, the 'facts' of history, that shape us, but images of the past embodied in language. James has ceased to make that discrimination.

OWEN: Don't lecture me, Father.

HUGH: B – we must never cease renewing those images; because once we do, we fossilize. Is there no soda bread?

OWEN: And C, Father – one single, unalterable 'fact': if Yolland is not found, we are all going to be evicted. Lancey has issued the order.

HUGH: Ah. *Edictum imperatoris.*

OWEN: You should change out of those wet clothes. I've got to go. I've got to see Doalty Dan Doalty.

HUGH: What about?

OWEN: I'll be back soon.

(*As* OWEN *exits.*)

HUGH: Take care, Owen. To remember everything is a form of madness.

(*He looks around the room, carefully, as if he were about to leave it forever. Then he looks at Jimmy, asleep again.*) The road to Sligo. A spring morning. 1798. Going into battle. Do you remember, James? Two young gallants with pikes across their shoulders and the *Aeneid* in their pockets. Everything seemed to find definition that spring – a congruence, a miraculous matching of hope and past and present and possibility. Striding across the fresh, green land. The rhythms of perception heightened. The whole enterprise of consciousness accelerated. We were gods that morning, James; and I had recently married *my* goddess, Caitlin Dubh Nic Reactainn, may she rest in peace. And to leave her and my infant son in his cradle – that was heroic, too. By God, sir, we were magnificent. We marched as far as – where was it? – Glenties! All of twenty-three miles in one day. And it was there, in Phelan's pub, that we got homesick for Athens, just like Ulysses. The *desiderium nostrorum* – the need for our own. Our *pietas*, James, was for

445

older, quieter things. And that was the longest twenty-three miles back I ever made. (*Toasts* JIMMY.) My friend, confusion is not an ignoble condition.

(MAIRE *enters*.)

MAIRE: I'm back again. I set out for somewhere but I couldn't remember where. So I came back here.

HUGH: Yes, I will teach you English, Maire Chatach.

MAIRE: Will you, Master? I must learn it. I need to learn it.

HUGH: Indeed you may well be my only pupil.

(*He goes towards the steps and begins to ascend*.)

MAIRE: When can we start?

HUGH: Not today. Tomorrow, perhaps. After the funeral. We'll begin tomorrow. (*Ascending*) But don't expect too much. I will provide you with the available words and the available grammar. But will that help you to interpret between privacies? I have no idea. But it's all we have. I have no idea at all.

(*He is now at the top*.)

MAIRE: Master, what does the English word 'always' mean?

HUGH: *Semper – per omnia saecula*. The Greeks called it '*aei*'. It's not a word I'd start with. It's a silly word, girl.

(*He sits*. JIMMY *is awake. He gets to his feet*. MAIRE *sees the Name-Book, picks it up, and sits with it on her knee*.)

MAIRE: When he comes back, this is where he'll come to. He told me this is where he was happiest.

(JIMMY *sits beside* MAIRE.)

JIMMY: Do you know the Greek word *endogamein*? It means to marry within the tribe. And the word *exogamein* means to marry outside the tribe. And you don't cross those borders casually – both sides get very angry. Now, the problem is this: Is Athene sufficiently mortal or am I sufficiently godlike for the marriage to be acceptable to her people and to my people? You think about that.

HUGH: *Urbs antiqua fuit* – there was an ancient city which, 'tis said, Juno loved above all the lands. And it was the goddess's aim and cherished hope that here should be the capital of all nations – should the fates perchance allow that. Yet in truth she discovered that a race was springing from

446

Trojan blood to overthrow some day these Tyrian towers – a people *late regem belloque superbum* – kings of broad realms and proud in war who would come forth for Lybia's downfall – such was – such was the course – such was the course ordained – ordained by fate . . . What the hell's wrong with me? Sure I know it backwards. I'll begin again. *Urbs antiqua fuit* – there was an ancient city which, 'tis said, Juno loved above all the lands.

(*Begin to bring down the lights.*)

And it was the goddess's aim and cherished hope that here should be the capital of all nations – should the fates perchance allow that. Yet in truth she discovered that a race was springing from Trojan blood to overthrow some day these Tyrian towers – a people kings of broad realms and proud in war who would come forth for Lybia's downfall . . .

Black

GREEK AND LATIN USED IN THE TEXT

page 384 Τὸν δ' ἠμείβετ' ἔπειτα θεὰ γλαυκῶπις Ἀθήνη·
$\qquad$ (Homer, *Odyssey*, XIII, 420):
(*Lit.*) 'But the grey-eyed goddess Athene then replied to him'
ἀλλὰ ἕκηλος ἧσται ἐν Ἀτρείδαο δόμοις
$\qquad$ (Homer, *Odyssey*, XIII, 423–4):
(*Lit.*) '. . . but he sits at ease in the halls of the Sons of Athens . . .'

385 ῍Ως ἄρα μιν φαμένη ῥάβδῳ ἐπεμάσσατ' Ἀθήνη
$\qquad$ (Homer, *Odyssey*, XIII, 429):
(*Lit.*) 'As she spoke Athene touched him with her wand'
κνύζωσεν δέ οἱ ὄσσε (Homer, *Odyssey*, XIII, 433):
(*Lit.*) 'She dimmed his eyes'

386 Γλαυκῶπις Ἀθήνη: (*Lit.*) flashing-eyed Athene

387 Αὐτὰρ ὁ ἐκ λιμένος πρσσέβη (Homer, *Odyssey*, XIV, 1):
(*Lit.*) 'But he went forth from the harbour . . .'
ὅ οἱ βιότοιο μάλιστα (Homer, *Odyssey*, XIV, 3–4):
(*Lit.*) '. . . he cared very much for his substance . . .'

388 *Esne fatigata?*: Are you tired?
Sum fatigatissima: I am very tired
Bene! Optime!: Good! Excellent!

390 *Ignari, stulti, rustici*: Ignoramuses, fools, peasants
Responde – responde!: Answer – answer!
θέος: a god
θέα: a goddess

392 *Nigra fere et presso pinguis sub vomere terra*
Land that is black and rich beneath the pressure of the plough
cui putre: crumbly soil

397 *adsum*: I am present
sobrietate perfecta: with complete sobriety
sobrius: sober
ave: hail

caerimonia nominationis: ceremony of naming

βαπτίζειν: to dip or immerse

baptisterium: a cold bath, swimming-pool

398 *Gratias tibi ago*: I thank you

    studia: studies

    perambulare: to walk through

399 *verecundus*: shame-faced, modest

    conjugo: I join together

    acquiesco, acquiescere: to rest, to find comfort in

    procede:proceed

400 *Silentium!*: Silence!

    diverto, divertere: to turn away

    ἄπληστος πίθος: unfillable cask

401 *Jacobe, quid agis?*: James, how are you?

404 *Festinate!*: Hurry!

405 *Gaudeo vos hic adesse*: Welcome

    Nonne Latine loquitur?: Does he not speak Latin?

407 *opus honestum*: an honourable task

417 *Quantumvis cursum longum fessumque moratur*

    Sol, sacro tandem carmine vesper adest:

    No matter how long the sun delays on his long weary course

    At length evening comes with its sacred song

    expeditio: an expedition

427 *Tu es centurio in exercitu Britannico*: You are a centurion in the British Army

    Et es in castris quae sunt in agro: And you are in the camp in the field

435 *Ignari! Stulti! Rustici!*: Ignoramuses! Fools! Peasants!

442 *domus lugubris*: house of mourning

    infelix: unlucky, unhappy

    Bararus hic ego sum quia non intelligor ulli: I am a barbarian here because I am not understood by anyone

    procede: proceed

445 *edictum imperatoris*: the decree of the commander

445 *desiderium nostrorum*: longing/need for our things/people.

    pietas: piety

Semper – per omnia saecula: Always – for all time.

ἀεί: always

446 ἐνδογαμεῖν: to marry within the tribe

ἐξογαμεῖν: to marry outside the tribe

446 *Urbs antiqua fuit*: There was an ancient city

447 *late regem belloque superbum*: kings of broad realms and proud in war

SELECT CHECKLIST OF WORKS

Compiled by Frances-Jane French

STAGE PLAYS (published)

Philadelphia, Here I Come!, London, Faber & Faber, 1965; New York, Farrar, Straus & Giroux, 1966

The Loves of Cass McGuire, London, Samuel French, 1966; London, Faber & Faber, 1967; New York, Farrar, Straus & Giroux, 1967

Lovers, New York, Farrar, Straus & Giroux, 1968; London, Faber & Faber, 1969

Crystal and Fox, London, Faber & Faber, 1970; New York, Farrar, Straus & Giroux, 1970 (in *Two Plays*)

The Mundy Scheme, London, Samuel French, 1970; New York, Farrar, Straus & Giroux, 1970 (in *Two Plays*)

The Gentle Island, London, Davis Poynter, 1973

The Freedom of the City, London, Faber & Faber, 1974; New York, Samuel French, 1974

The Enemy Within, Newark, Delaware, Proscenium Press, 1975; Dublin, Gallery Press, 1979

Living Quarters, London, Faber & Faber, 1978

Volunteers, London, Faber & Faber, 1979

Faith Healer, London, Faber & Faber, 1980; New York, Samuel French, 1980

Aristocrats, Dublin, Gallery Press, 1980; London, Faber & Faber, 1984

Translations, Faber & Faber, 1981; New York, Samuel French, 1981

The Three Sisters (translated from Chekhov), Dublin, Gallery Press, 1981

The Communication Cord, London, Faber & Faber, 1983

453

STAGE PLAYS (unpublished)

A Doubtful Paradise (The Francophile), performed Belfast, 1959
The Blind Mice, performed Dublin, 1963

RADIO PLAYS

A Sort of Freedom, BBC Northern Ireland Home Service, 1958
To This Hard House, BBC Northern Ireland Home Service, 1958
The Founder Members, BBC Light Programme, 1964

RADIO ADAPTATIONS

The Loves of Cass McGuire, BBC Third Programme, 1961
The Enemy Within, BBC Third Programme, 1963
The Blind Mice, BBC Northern Ireland Home Service, 1963
Philadelphia, Here I Come!, BBC Third Programme, 1965
Winners (version of first part of *Lovers*), BBC Third Programme, 1968

TELEVISION ADAPTATION

The Enemy Within, BBC, 1965

FILM ADAPTATION

Philadelphia, Here I Come!, 1970

SHORT-STORY COLLECTIONS

The Saucer of Larks, London, Gollancz, 1962; Garden City, NY, Doubleday, 1962
The Gold in the Sea, London, Gollancz, 1966; Garden City, NY, Doubleday, 1966
Selected Stories, Dublin, Gallery Press, 1979; published as *The Diviner: The Best Stories of Brian Friel*, Dublin, O'Brien Press, 1982; London, Allison & Busby, 1982

CONTRIBUTIONS TO PERIODICALS

'A Visit to Spain', *Irish Monthly* (Dublin and London), vol. 53, November 1952
'The Theatre of Hope and Despair' (text of lecture), *Everyman* (Benburb, Co. Tyrone), no. 1, 1968

TEXT OF INTERVIEW

'An Ulster Writer: Brian Friel', conducted by Graham Morison, *Acorn* (Londonderry), no. 8, Spring 1965

BIOGRAPHY

Brian Friel, Desmond E. S. Maxwell, Lewisburg, Pa, Bucknell University Press, 1973